ESSENTIAL SKILLS for COLLEGE TEACHING

An Instructional Systems Approach
third edition

Practical suggestions on how to design more effective and exciting lectures and engage your students in their own learning. Reduce student note copying with appropriate study guides.

Thomas E. Cyrs

New Mexico State University
Box 30001 Dept. 3CED
Las Cruces NM 88003
505/646-2204

© copyright 1994
Thomas E. Cyrs
All rights reserved
Published by the Center for Educational Development, New Mexico State University
Printed in the U.S.A.

You cannot teach a man anything; you can only teach him to find it within himself.

Galileo

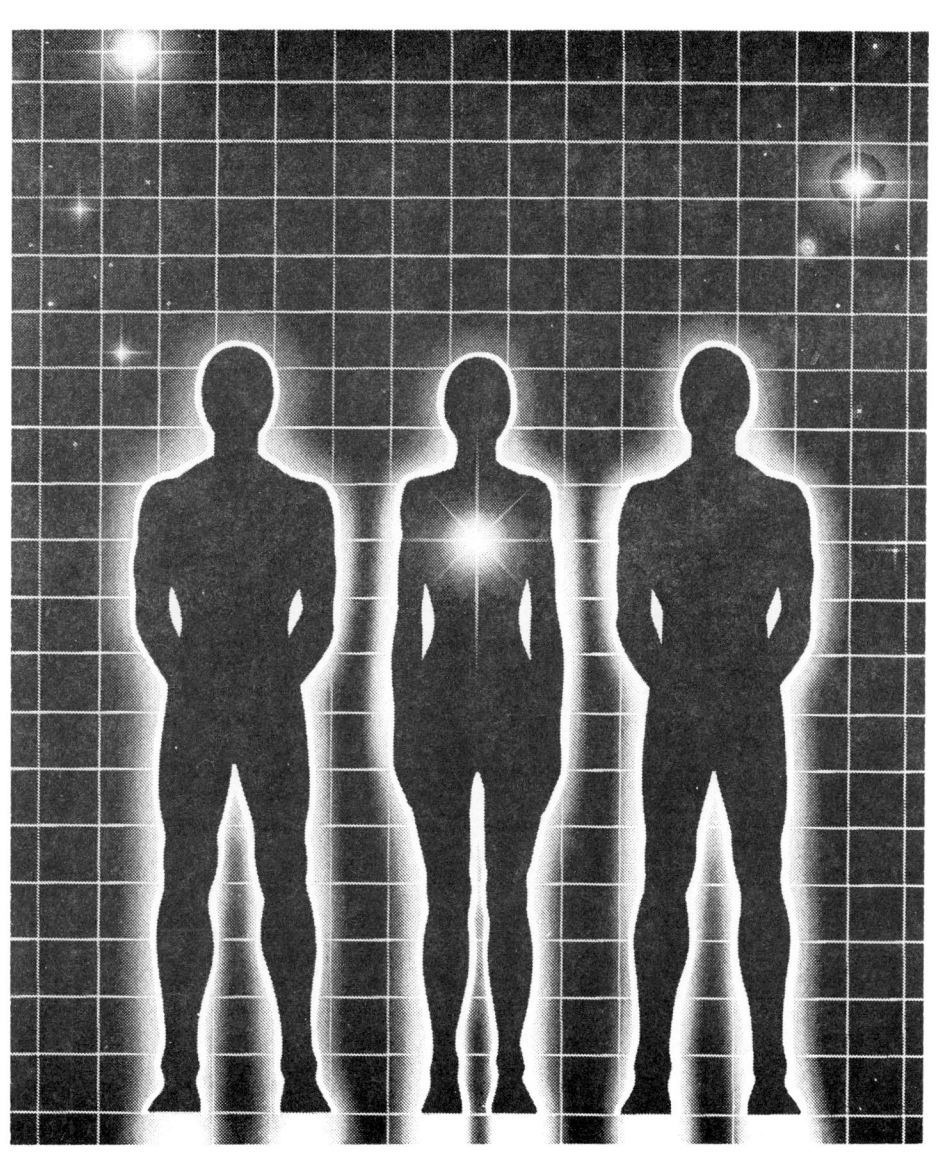

> **I do not *do* teaching.**
> **I AM TEACHING.**

Brad Blake

TABLE OF CONTENTS

Dedication v
Acknowledgments vi
Introduction vii

SECTION I. ACTIVITIES PRIOR TO CLASS: Plan and Organize

CHAPTER 1.	The Systems Approach to Teaching (S.A.T.) Model	1.3
CHAPTER 2.	Analyzing Your Teaching Assumptions	2.3
CHAPTER 3.	What the Research Says About Teachers and Teaching	3.3
CHAPTER 4.	Exploring Your Teaching Style with the Myers-Briggs Type Inventory	4.3
CHAPTER 5.	The Architecture of a Well-Planned and Organized College Course	5.3
CHAPTER 6.	The Course Syllabus: A Legal Covenant with Your Students	6.3
CHAPTER 7.	Writing Worthwhile Learning Performance Objectives	7.3
CHAPTER 8.	Sequencing Instruction to Address Higher Order Thinking Skills	8.3
CHAPTER 9.	Teaching for Critical Thinking	9.3
CHAPTER 10.	Adapting Instruction for the Adult Student: The Need for Participation	10.3
CHAPTER 11.	Creating an Active College Classroom	11.3
CHAPTER 12.	Student Involvement Activities	12.3
CHAPTER 13.	Alternatives to the Traditional Lecture	13.3
	a. Cooperative Learning	13.3
	b. Contract Learning	13.5
	c. Problem-Centered Learning	13.7

SECTION II. ACTIVITIES AND EVENTS DURING CLASS

CHAPTER 14.	The Art and Craft of Constructing an Exciting Lecture	14.3
CHAPTER 15.	Lecture Presentation Skills	15.3
CHAPTER 16.	Creating a Stimulating Classroom Environment	16.3
CHAPTER 17.	Classroom Questioning Strategies Above Recall	17.3
CHAPTER 18.	Alternative Student Handout Formats	18.3

SECTION III. ACTIVITIES AFTER CLASS: When Everything Must Be Assessed

CHAPTER 19.	Constructing Valid Tests to Match Your Learning Objectives	19.3
CHAPTER 20.	Classroom Formative Feedback Techniques	20.3
CHAPTER 21.	Self-Assessment of Your Teaching Effectiveness	21.3
CHAPTER 22.	Creating a Professional Teaching Portfolio	22.3
INDEX		23.1

Acknowledgements

William Conroy, Executive Vice President of New Mexico State University, for his interest in quality teaching and his encouragement by providing time to complete this text through a sabbatical.

Virginia Higbie, Dean of the College of Health and Community Services, for her on-going support, knowledge, and dedication to quality teaching.

Frank Smith, Assistant Director of the Center for Educational Development, for the many practical suggestions, examples, generous commentary, in-depth reviews, and especially for keeping me on track.

Jean Conway, Coordinator of Graphics in the Center for Educational Development, for the cover design, suggestions for word pictures, layout, proofreading the text, and especially for the many suggested text revisions and for her tolerance in the face of difficult deadlines.

Susan Jones, graduate student in Educational Management and Development and research assistant, for the constructive conversation about relevant topics and for proofreading.

Michael Glidewell, for his suggestions on the use of the Systems Approach to Teaching model at the beginning of each chapter as a way to introduce the relationship of each chapter topic.

Donald Roush, Executive Vice President Emeritus, New Mexico State University, for his permission to use his essay, "What Makes a Good Teacher," presented in Chapter Three.

Alvin Kent, former Director of Media Services at Iowa State University, colleague and constant creative critic who helped solidify my thinking abouth instructional systems design, for his help with the ideas presented in Chapter 19, "Constructing Valid Tests to Match Your Learning Objectives."

Irina Perkovina, graduate student in technical writing, for her editorial assistance in many difficult chapters.

INTRODUCTION

Why another book on college teaching? Simply because most books on college teaching talk about everything except what will help the instructor and student in the classroom. The intent of this book is to provide you with a synthesis of the most current research available in the fields of teaching and training. This synthesis of the literature has been drawn from the fields of education, corporate training, health professions practice, military training, and government training. When specific research is unavailable, heuristics have been proposed by the author based on many years of teaching and working with faculty and trainers in all aspects of teaching and training.

This text has been prepared specifically for a graduate class entitled, "Essential Skills for College Teaching," conducted at New Mexico State University by the author. The chapters deal with specific questions about classroom teaching at the postsecondary levels, namely:
1. What do we need to know to be a successful college instructor?
2. Why do we need to know it?
3. How do we learn it?
4. What are the most effective resources available?
5. When will we know if we have learned it?
6. How can we improve it once we have used it?
7. How do we go about developing an effective and dynamic lecture?

A major portion of the chapters deal with the design of an effective lecture on the assumption that the lecture as we currently know and use it will continue to be used as the primary instructional delivery system in higher education and training for many years to come (at least 25 more years). There are few texts that deal specifically with the design and construction of an effective and exciting lecture and the different components that could be incorporated into it such as verbal and visual analogies and metaphors; definitions; generation of examples and non-examples; techniques to engage students; questioning strategies to address critical thinking skills; and many others.

A review of the <u>Subject Guide to Books in Print</u> (Bowker, R.R., 1991-1992), identifies 35 books published under the title of "college teaching" and only four under the title of "lecture methods in teaching," and "lectures and lecturing." Three of these books were published in England and one in the United States. The details of developing and delivering a traditional lecture is addressed throughout this text.
The best single source about books on college teaching is found in a chapter by James R. Davies (1976) entitled, "A Bibliographic Essay: Books About College

Teaching," in his book entitled, <u>Teaching Strategies for the College Classroom</u>. Davies concludes that,

> Ironically, most of the books about college teaching are not about college teaching at all. They are about almost everything but college teaching. They discuss current issues in higher education, the history of higher education, and the aims of education. They exhort their readers to better teaching. They describe in detail the context in which teaching is carried on, how teachers are educated, and how good teaching is regarded or neglected. They tell what it is like to be a college teacher, how to evaluate college teaching, and what research on teaching has been done. But only rarely, if at all, is there any discussion of the <u>actual teaching-learning process itself</u>. It is as if there is a systematic avoidance of the subject... .

This text deals explicitly with the essential skills of traditional lecturing and alternatives to it within the traditional college classroom. It provides specific guidelines for the novice as well as possibly unexplored techniques for the experienced instructor.

Practical application is the hallmark of these chapters. They are readable and carefully organized. When applicable, relevant exercises have been included to assist the instructor with applications of the ideas.

This text is organized around three time periods in the life of the college instructor and the associated events that they have to address when preparing their courses. Each time period is treated in a different section. Section I treats what must be done to plan and organize a class. Section II encompasses those events that take place during a class when instructors are teaching and interacting with students. Section III treats those events that take place after class when everything must be assessed to determine how well the teaching and learning performance objectives were accomplished. Each of these three time sections and their events are based on the instructional systems approach to teaching (I.S.A.T.) model, which is explained in detail in Chapter One.

The I.S.A.T. model addresses all aspects of a course as it is designed as well as all aspects of a single class. The purpose of this model is to provide a structure or framework for the instructor so that rational decisions can be made about the effectiveness of what is done in the classroom through systematic feedback. This is accomplished through assessment of teaching and learning outcomes at the course level. This model is based on the premise that the teaching and learning taking place within the four walls of a college classroom does not exist in isolation from influences external to the classroom. If teaching was viewed as an independent activity with no input from external constituencies, it would be a closed looped system with change left to the independent judgment and chance of individual instructors, subject only to their values, prior experiences, and ideas. On the contrary, college courses must be designed as <u>open systems</u> with continuous inputs from a variety of external sources. This concept does not violate "academic freedom" since "how" the instructor teaches is left to his or her professional discretion. It is "what" is taught that is strongly influenced by these external sources. The external constituencies consist of the academic department, college, university, and society that financially supports the institution. Data from the review of the teaching and learning outcomes are provided to the course instructor and each of the constituencies that "need to know" these data. The individual course assessment data should support first the academic department goals and objectives, and then the college and university goals and objectives. This model supports the notion of outcomes assessment since it shows the direct relationship between individual course learning performance objectives and the departmental goals and objectives.

During the institutional outcomes assessment process, data from a variety of sources are provided by the academic departments to administration. These data can include such things as results from normative tests as well as data as to how well the department is achieving their goals and objectives. Faculty are a rich source of data. They can demonstrate how their individual courses support each departmental goal and objective. This is accomplished by linking each end of course learning performance objective to each of the departmental goals and objectives.

The instructional systems approach to teaching (I.S.A.T.) model addresses the individual college class and the whole course (a collection of 45-50-minute classes, or, 30 75-minute classes, or 16-150-minute graduate classes). There are five (5) major components of the I.S.A.T. model:

1. Specification of the end of course or terminal learning performance objectives and intermediate learning performance objectives. The latter constitutes the signposts within the course that the students must master.
2. The range of assessment techniques that will validly determine the degree to which the learning performance objectives have been mastered.
3. The different instructional strategies chosen by the instructor to deliver the subject matter.
4. The interactive student learning activities that engage the students with their own learning through individual and small group activities.
5. Feedback channels to students and instructors that provide data about student mastery of the teaching-learning objectives to those who "need-to-know."

Each chapter addresses the appropriate teaching time period and those components within the I.S.A.T. model for that period. A reduced graphic of the I.S.A.T. model has been reproduced for each chapter with the appropriate component addressed in the particular chapter highlighted so that the reader knows exactly which section of the model is addressed within that particular chapter.

SECTION 1: Activities Prior to Class-Plan and Organize, deals with all of the I.S.A.T. components. Chapter 1 explains the instructional systems approach to teaching model and how and why the notion of system is used to improve teaching in the college classroom. Chapter 2 explores those assumptions held by the individual instructor that strongly influences what is done and why it is done in the classroom. Often instructors use teaching techniques and procedures that influenced and worked for them as students, but may not have an empirical base. Chapter 3 reviews the research on teaching and summarizes the results. It closes with a delightful essay on what constitutes good teaching by Donald Roush, Executive Vice President Emeritus at New Mexico State University. Instructors are then invited to compare their assumptions against empirical evidence. Specific teaching styles characteristic of teachers can be identified by use of the Myers-Briggs Type Inventory, which is reviewed and explained in Chapter 4.

Chapter 5 explains the level of detail needed in planning and organizing a new undergraduate or graduate course. Most of the individual components are further described in full chapters, each of which contains an extensive up-to-date bibliography. How relevant course content can be identified and selected for the many conflicting options is described in this chapter. The components of a course syllabus as a legal covenant with students are explained in Chapter 6. Various levels of detail are suggested.

Translating the course content into learning performance objectives is presented in Chapter 7. This chapter explains not only what we want our students to know, but also what we want them to do with the specific knowledge. This is the first master step in the instructional systems approach to teaching model.

Chapter 8 explores how to sequence the learning performance objectives from lowest to highest levels of cognitive thinking skills often referred to as critical thinking. This technique is based on a modified format of Bloom's Taxonomy which has been reduced from six to four levels. Chapter 9 expands on the concept of critical thinking and explains in detail what researchers have found.

The adult learner as a student and the special requirements that they will demand is explored in Chapter 10. How to assist them to integrate their life experiences into the college classroom is explained.

Student passivity in the classroom has long been a hallmark of classrooms in colleges and universities. How to develop an active classroom in which students are involved and engaged in their own learning is presented in Chapter 11. More than 100 different student involvement techniques are described in Chapter 12 with references for further study.

Chapter 13 outlines three major alternatives to the traditional lecture as the organizing principle for a course. These techniques of cooperative learning, the student contract, and problem-based learning create an environment for the development of critical thinking skills.

SECTION II: Activities and Events During Class, describes those events that take place during actual teaching and interaction with students within the classroom.

How to construct an exciting lecture and all of the possible variations of the lecture are highlighted in Chapter 14. This is one of the major chapters around which this book is based. Some of the components of a lecture that are described include such things as: the use of icebreakers and grabbers; how to develop definitions and examples; the use of analogy; and many other possibilities.

Chapter 15 outlines the mechanics of lecture presentation skills and deals with such things as how you look, sound, and move. A technique of how to obtain maximum feedback through practice is presented as part of the concept of a lecture laboratory.

Chapter 16 explores a variety of inexpensive techniques to create a stimulating classroom environment for students. Described are such things as posters, poster hang-ups, flip charts, cartoons, overhead transparencies, and many other techniques to help the instructor communicate visually. How to ask a variety of questions that range from recall of factual data through critical thinking and values exploration is presented in Chapter 17.

Chapter 18 describes and provides examples of 17 different types of handout formats that can be used to assist students with notetaking. A review of the research on the use of handouts is included.

SECTION III: Activities After Class When Everything Must be Assessed, describes all of those things available to the classroom instructor to assess student learning and the effectiveness of the teaching and instructional strategies used during the class.

Assessing student learning is one of the most important tasks of teaching. It is one of the areas that instructors, new and experienced alike, have a great deal of difficulty because of minimal or no training. This results in many invalid tests that never measure actual learning. At best, many of these instructor-developed tests measure the lowest level of learning–recall of factual data. Specific strategies to develop a variety of testing types are explained in Chapter 19.

Formative assessment during a course is a procedure to make mid-course corrections and adjustments. Several techniques are described in Chapter 20. A self-assessment instrument that will help instructors to document their teaching effectiveness is reviewed in Chapter 21. This instrument can be used several times a year to document professional growth over a short period of time. It can also be used as a component of the Professional Teaching Portfolio, Chapter 22.

The Professional Teaching Portfolio, one of the newest techniques for faculty self-assessment, is outlined and detailed in Chapter 22. This dossier-approach to self-assessment allows the instructor to identify strengths and areas of needed improvement in teaching. It also provides a forum for the instructor to reflect on his or her perceptions of teaching strengths and professional growth in teaching.

Section I

Activities prior to class: Planning and organizing

Chapter 1
The Instructional Systems Approach to Teaching (S.A.T.) Model

Chapter 2
Analyzing Your Teaching Assumptions

Chapter 3
What the Research Says About Teachers and Teaching

Chapter 4
Exploring Your Teaching Style With the Myers-Briggs Type Inventory

Chapter 5
The Architecture of a Well-Planned and Organized College Course

Chapter 6
The Course Syllabus: A Legal Covenant With Your Students

Chapter 7
Writing Worthwhile Learning Performance Objectives

Chapter 8
Sequencing Instruction to Address Higher Order Thinking Skills

Chapter 9
Teaching for Critical Thinking

Chapter 10
Adapting Instruction for the Adult Student: The Need for Participation

Chapter 11
Creating an Active College Classroom

Chapter 12
Student Involvement Activities

Chapter 13
Alternatives to the Traditional Lecture

Chapter 1

The Instructional Systems Approach to Teaching (ISAT) Model

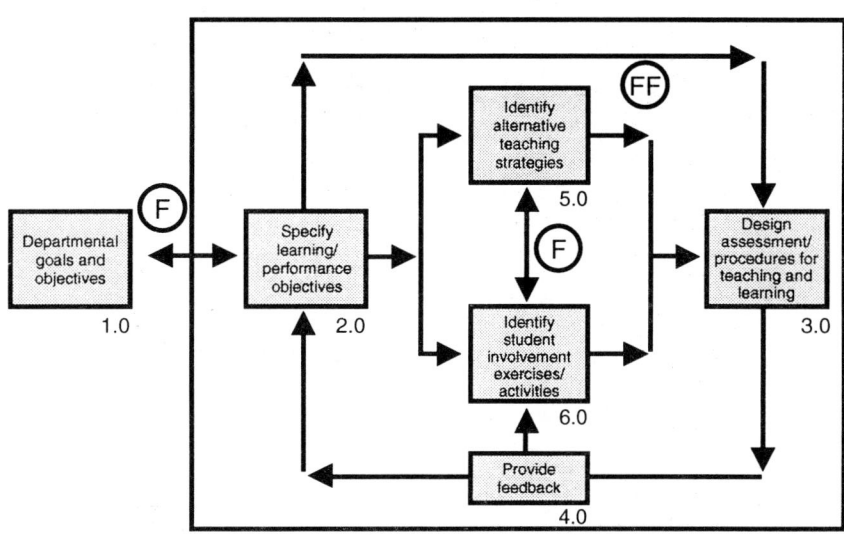

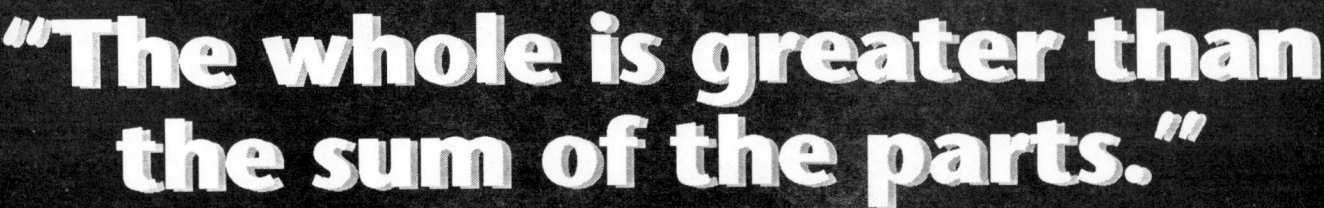

"The whole is greater than the sum of the parts."

AN INSTRUCTIONAL SYSTEMS APPROACH TO TEACHING MODEL

LEARNING PERFORMANCE OBJECTIVES
Design a course utilizing all components of the Instructional Systems Approach to Teaching model. (Level 4).

Construct lesson plans which incorporate all components of the instructional systems approach to teaching model. Explain how each lesson plan adheres to the I.S.A.T. principles. (Level 4).

KEY IDEAS FOR CHAPTER 1
1. A college classroom can be treated as an instructional system.
2. The instructional systems approach to teaching is an open system influenced by external constituencies.
3. Learning performance objectives are the foundation for the I.S.A.T. model.
4. Valid assessment will determine the level of mastery of the learning performance objectives.

NEW VOCABULARY
- system
- instructional system
- learning performance objective
- teaching strategy
- student involvement
- open and closed system
- goal and objective
- assessment
- feedback

The use of the concept "system" allows us to look at the forest as well as the individual trees when we observe something. It looks at the purpose of the "thing" under study, all of the parts, and the relationships among the parts. Kaufman (1988) defines a system as the "... sum total of parts working independently and working together to achieve required results based on needs." Greive (1989) defines a system as an "...organized whole composed of parts which interrelate and interact in order to accomplish some predetermined purposes." Cyrs and Lowenthal (1970) extended the notion of "system" to a procedure from which curriculum could be developed. "A systems approach to curriculum development is a rational problem-solving method of analyzing the educational process and making it more effective. The system is this process taken as a whole, incorporating all of its parts and aspects, including the students, the teachers, the curriculum content, the instructional materials, the instructional strategy, the physical environment, and the evaluation of instructional objectives."

Viewing teaching as a system can provide some insights into the process that can help instructors make decisions of how to design instruction. This book is based on the notion that college and university teaching can be viewed as an instructional system. An instructional system specifies WHAT a student should learn and do at the completion of a course and each lesson period; the MEANS available to the student to master the learning performance objectives; HOW the students will be taught; and the performance criteria to determine WHEN the student has mastered the stated learning performance objectives satisfactorily. The effectiveness of an instructional system can be measured by determining the degree to which it provides for the learner a system of learning. Banthy (1968) observes that an "...instructional system serves its purpose to the extent to which it brings about in the environment of the learner all of the possible interactions that result in the attainment of the desired performance."

The concept of an instructional system is derived from the field of systems research, which has been widely used and adapted in the fields of education and training (Branson, 1975; Buckley, 1968; Carter, 1969; Churchman, 1975; Cleveland, 1968; Corrigan, 1975; Corrigan and Corrigan, 1985; Corrigan and Kaufman, 1966, 1967; Dick and Carey, 1985; Cyrs and Lowenthal, 1970; Kaufman, 1968, 1971, 1972, 1982, 1983; Means,1967; Rappaport, 1986; Silvern, 1968, 1975; Banthy, 1968; O'Neil, 1979; Grieve, 1989; Zalatimo and Sleeman, 1975).

WHY the student should master the learning performance objectives defined in the instructional system goes beyond the individual classroom. Course learning performance objectives should be consistent with and validly reflect the goals and objectives of the academic department in which the course resides. These departmental goals and objectives have been developed through the collective expertise of the whole departmental faculty to provide guidance to the individual faculty planning a course. Departmental goals and objectives, in turn, should be consistent with and validly reflect the more general goals and objectives of the college in which it is located. The individual college goals and objectives should be consistent with and validly reflect the mission, goals, and objectives of the total university. Furthermore, public universities are accountable to the immediate society that supports them financially. The collective values of this supporting society, as reflected in needs assessment statements, should direct the missions and goals of the university. Private universities are not bound by the same societal directives but reflect the collective values of special interest groups within society.

What happens and WHAT is taught in the classroom of a public university is strongly influenced by and accountable to these hierarchical constituencies—department, college, university, and society. It is the responsibility of these groups to determine WHY something should be taught. HOW a subject is taught can be influenced by these constituencies, but is usually left to the judgment of the individual instructor.

Note in Figure 1 that the broad goals specified by the society are refined and made more specific as they move toward the individual classroom. Goals are broad general statements. Objectives are more specific statements that refine and clarify the meaning of the goals. As the goals and objectives move toward the individual classroom, they become more and more specific until they are defined as learning performance objectives at the end-of-course level and at the end-of-class level.

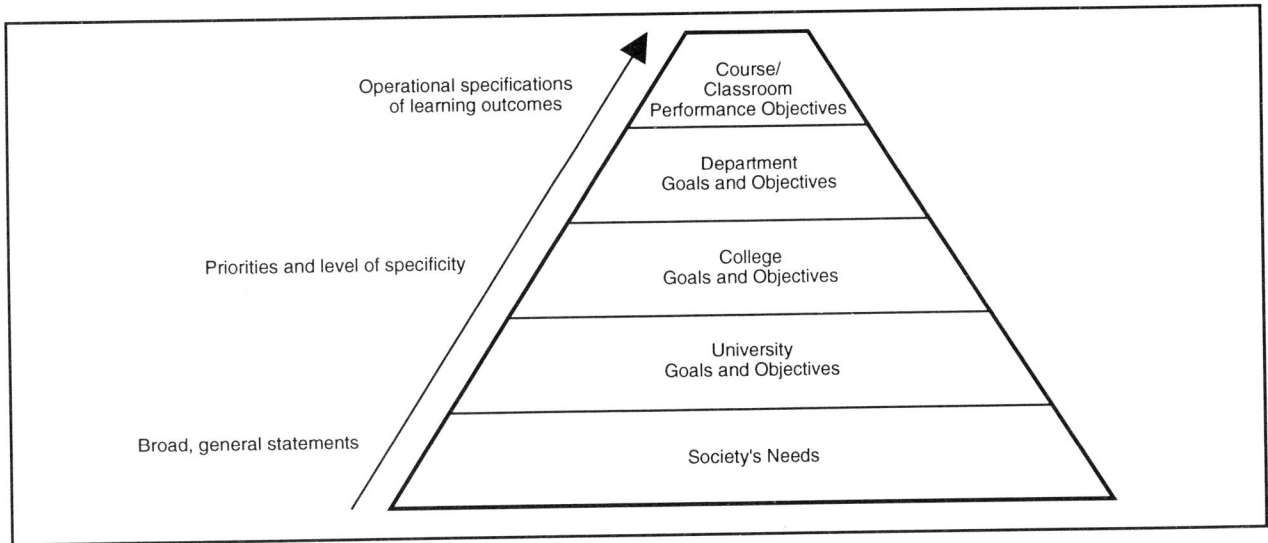

Figure 1

This text will deal only within the classroom context. It assumes that the instructor has reviewed the departmental goals and objectives and will develop course objectives consistent with them.

There are six major components to the instructional systems approach to teaching model. These are the review of the departmental goals; specification of the learning performance objectives; determination of means to assess these stated learning objectives and the effectiveness of the teaching; the identification of different teaching strategies, including the means by which the instructor communicates with the students and how the instruction is delivered; identification of different exercises and activities to involve the students in their own learning; and identification of feedback channels to those people who need the information such as students, instructors, and administrators.

The whole is greater than the sum of its parts.

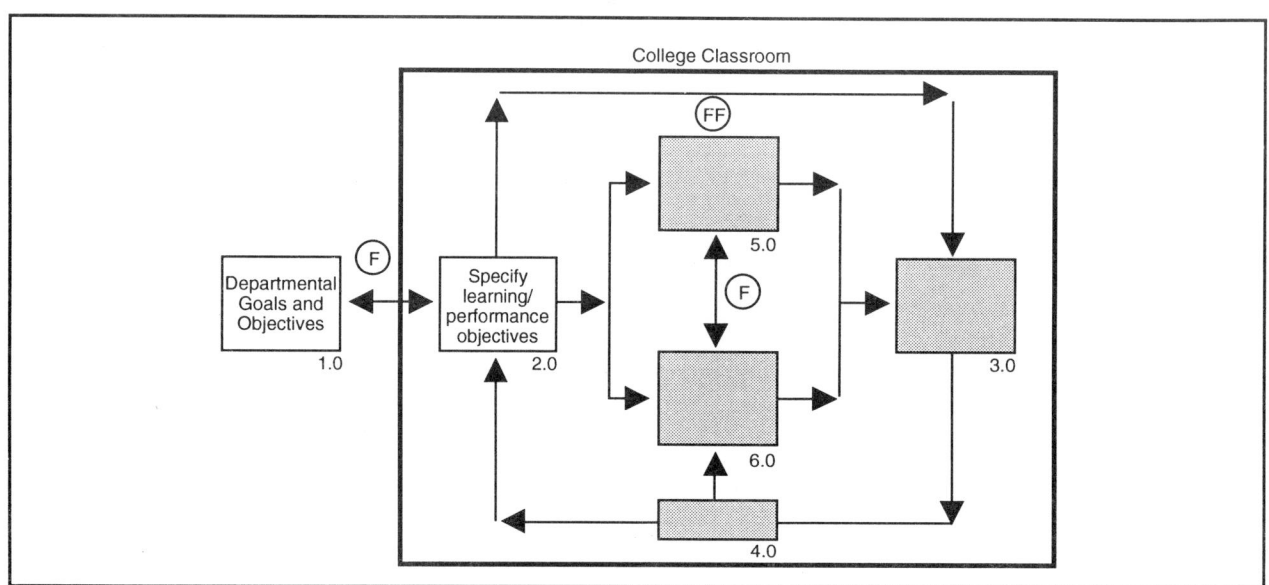

Figure 2

The college classroom is viewed as an open instructional system in Figure 2.* The major communication with the world external to the individual classroom is seen in Box 1.0, the departmental goals and objectives, that each course is purported to support. These goals and objectives should be the singular major influence on what the instructor specifies as the course learning performance objectives, Box 2.0. As the departmental goals and objectives (Box 1.0) change, so too do the learning performance objectives reflect these changes.

STEP 1: <u>Review departmental goals and objectives</u> that have been developed and approved by department faculty (Fig. 2, Box 1.0).

STEP 2: <u>Specify the learning performance objectives</u> (Fig. 2, Box 2.0). Learning performance objectives include a statement of end-of-course objectives, which are called terminal learning objectives. These answer the question, "**What** is it that I want the student to know and do at the completion of this course?" The instructor must answer this question in terms of cognitive or intellectual skills, affective or attitudinal and values skills, and psychomotor or manipulative skills. The end-of-course objectives are usually summarized in three to five statements. Some instructors specify only cognitive skills and avoid statements of attitudes and values. The course learning performance objectives must support the departmental goals and objectives and be consciously linked to them.

In Figure 2 the large interior box symbolizes the individual college classroom. Note the arrow entering Box 2.0 from outside the classroom. This represents the external constituencies, departmental goals and objectives, which direct and influence the selection of learning performance objectives.

---

* In this figure and those that follow, each box is numbered 1.0 through 6.0 and represents a specific step in the design of a course.

The double arrow indicates that there is an interchange of information or feedback.

In addition to the specification of the course and lesson learning performance objectives, the instructor must also identify the intended intellectual skill required of all learning performance objectives in order to properly sequence the instruction. These intellectual levels, from the lowest to the highest, are described as knowledge (factual recall); comprehension (understanding)–the ability to describe and explain concepts and compare and contrast ideas; application–the ability to apply principles and procedures to unfamiliar problems; and critical thinking–the ability to select which rules to apply to solve a problem. This highest level of intellectual skill, critical thinking, is composed of analysis, synthesis, and evaluation.

This first step in this instructional systems approach to teaching model involves the planning and organization of the entire course.

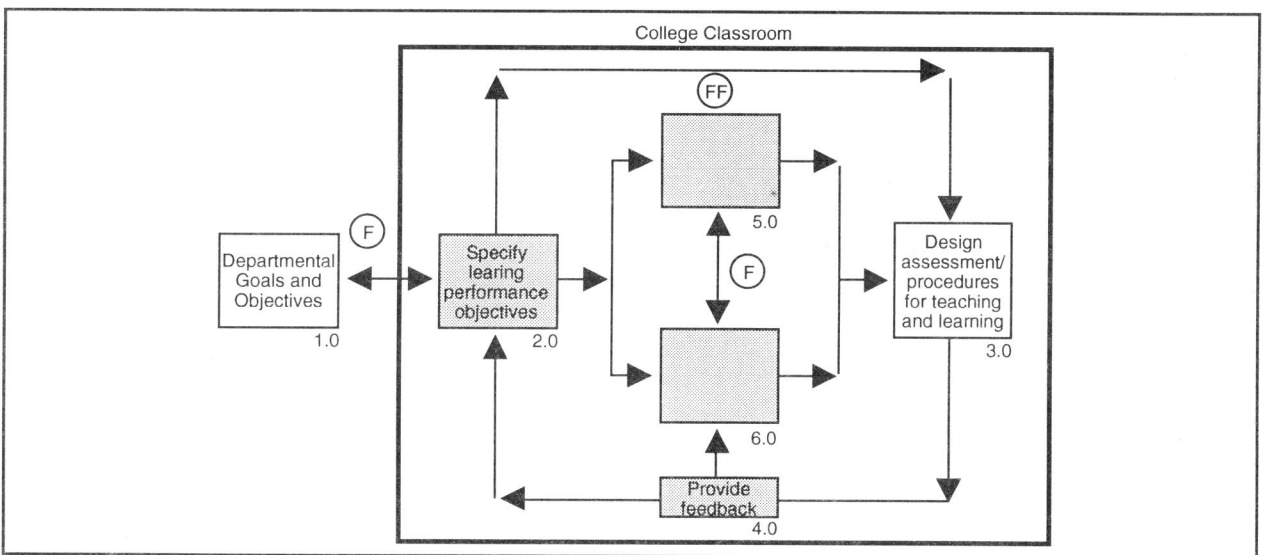

Figure 3

STEP 3: <u>Design assessment procedures for teaching and learning</u> (Fig. 3, Box 3.0). Assessment of teaching and learning is the second major step in the instructional systems approach to teaching model. The feedback arrows between Box 2.0 and Box 3.0 are crucial for the validity of the assessment procedures identified. In the area of learning, the feedback arrows mean that the assessment procedures, in whatever form, must be at the same intellectual level as the stated learning performance objectives. If the learning objective is at the application or rule-using level, then the measurement procedure must be at the same intellectual level. This may be one of the most serious errors made by classroom instructors in their teaching. Often an instructor will teach at the comprehension level, yet ask the student to apply a rule or procedure to an unfamiliar problem. This is invalid because the instructor taught at one level (comprehension) and tested at a higher level (application).

Assessment of teaching effectiveness involves self-assessment, student assessment, peer assessment, and possibly administrative assessment, depending on the purpose of the assessment. These data are meant to provide feedback to the instructor so that the course can be improved in the future.

Assessment should also include teaching methods, student activit es, and exercises.

The FF, feed forward loop, at the top of the model between Boxes 2.0 and 3.0 means that Box 3.0, design assessment procedures for teaching and learning, is the next logical step after the specification of the learning performance objectives, Box 2.0. The instructor moves back and forth between 2.0 and 3.0 until valid assessment procedures have been determined.

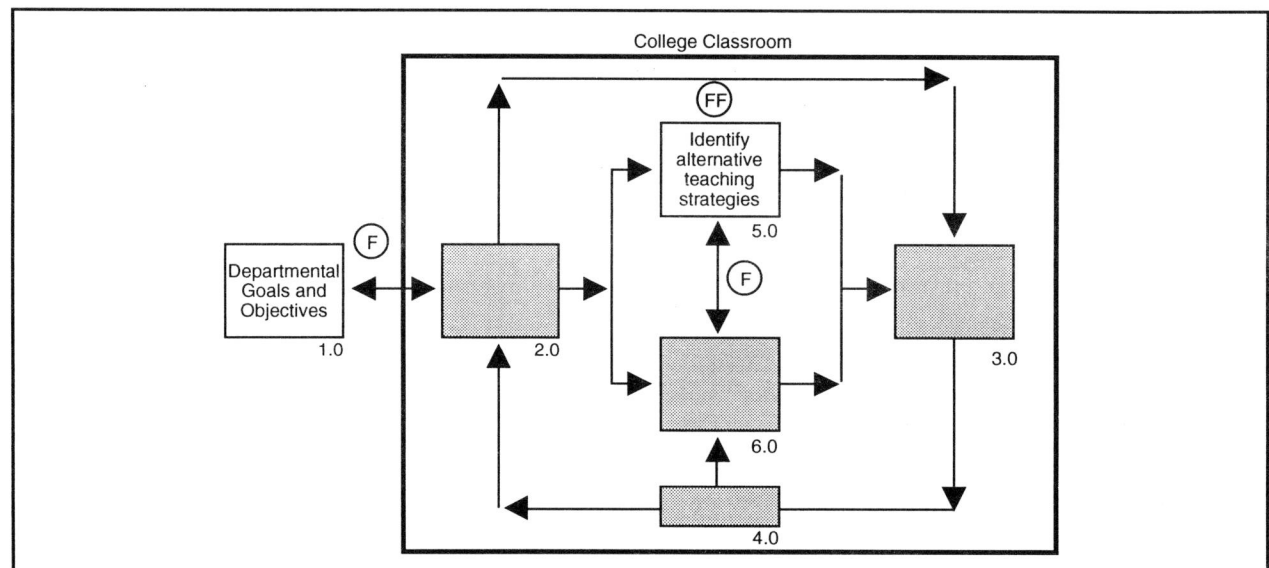

Figure 4

STEP 4: <u>Identify alternative teaching strategies</u> (Fig. 4, Box 5.0). Teaching strategies define what the teacher will do. Teaching strategies include methods of communication with students such as a monologue by the instructor, two-way interaction, high-level questions, student-to-student dialogue, peer teaching, etc. Strategies also include the means by which we deliver the instruction such as live one- or two-way television, computer assisted instruction, live tutorials, or tradtional lectures. Teaching strategies answer the questions of HOW the instructor will teach.

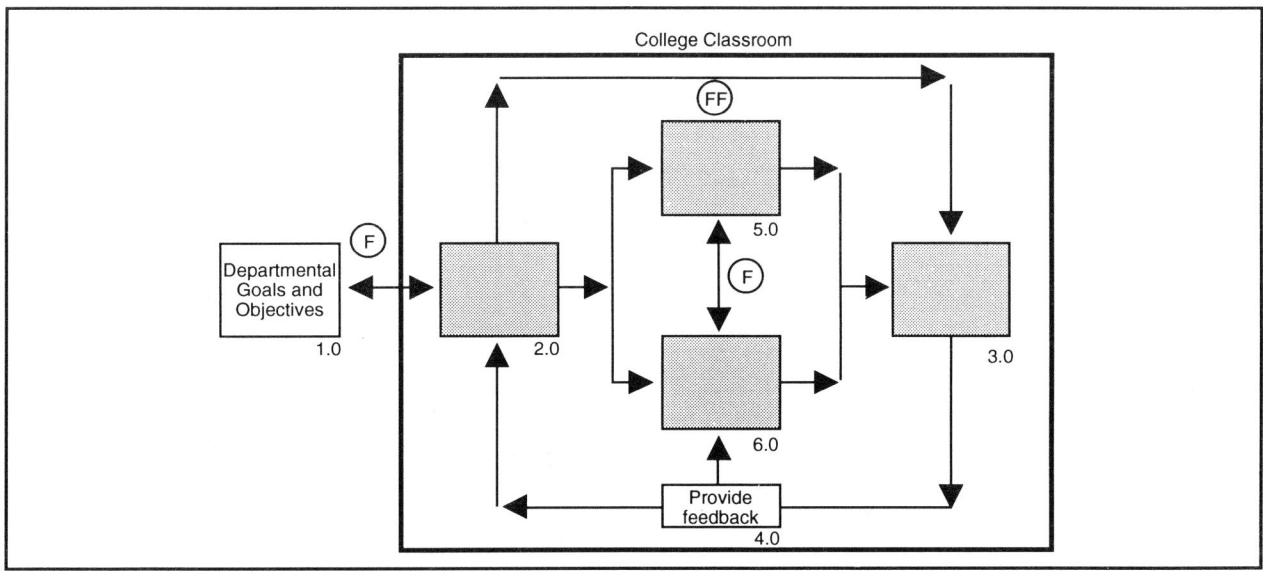

Figure 5

STEP 5: <u>Provide feedback</u> (Fig 5, Box 4.0). There are two types of information fed back to the instructor–formative and summative. Formative feedback provides data to the students and instructor during the conduct of the course for the purpose of letting the students know how well they are mastering the learning objectives. Formative feedback is also provided to the instructor so that he/she knows how well the students are learning and how to make mid-course corrections if warranted.

    Summative evaluation is conducted at the end of a course and provides feedback to students in the form of a final grade or some other symbol to indicate the degree of learning. For teaching it could take the form of student evaluations and the development of a teaching portfolio.

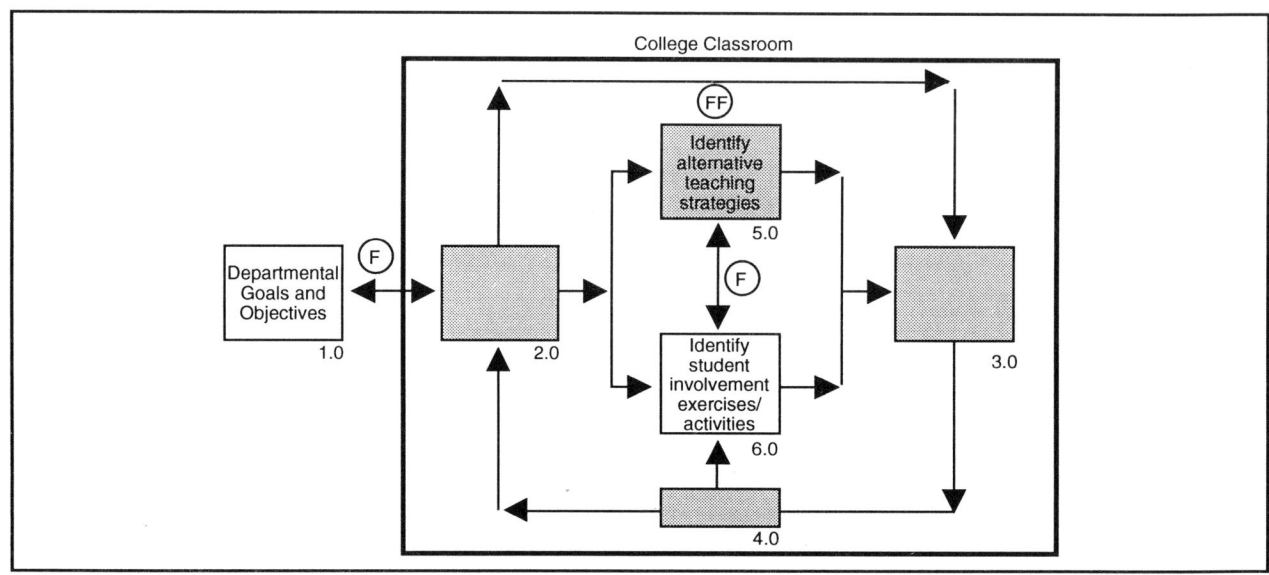

Figure 6

STEP 6: <u>Identify student involvement exercises and activities</u> (Fig 6, Box 6.0). The research has indicated that the more students are involved in their learning the more permanent the learning will be. Learning at this level takes place in small groups of two to five students interacting and solving problems of varying levels of complexity. The feedback loop between Box 5.0 and Box 6.0 indicates that the instructor selects and monitors as well as evaluates these exercises and activities. The responsibility for learning rests with the students.

Quality teaching does not
JUST HAPPEN.

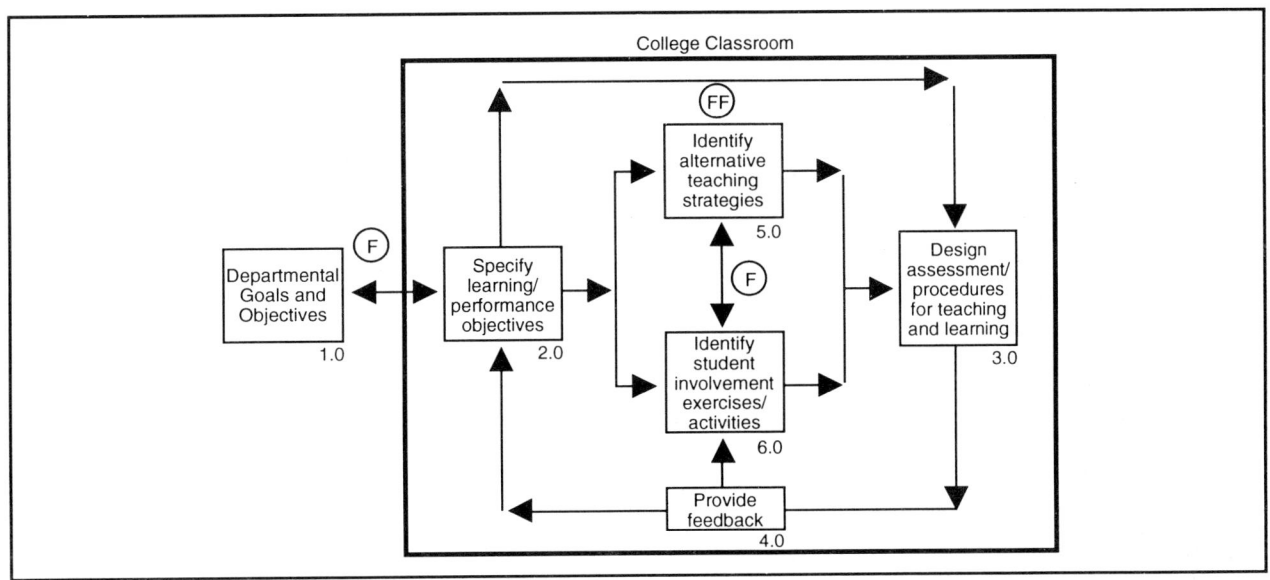

Figure 7

The total instructional systems approach to teaching model is shown in Figure 7. The instructional systems approach to teaching model presented in this chapter provides an exciting and viable model for college teaching that is flexible and responsive to the departmental goals and objectives. The latter provide inputs and influences in the selection of course learning performance objectives, since teaching faculty were instrumental in their definiton and specification. Instructors should note with each of their terminal learning objectives which departmental goal(s) and objective(s) it supports. Other constituencies besides the academic department include the college in which the academic department exists, the university in which the college resides, and the society within which the public university exists and is supported.

This model allows for the systematic selection of learning outcomes that reflect and make operational the missions, goals, and objectives of the other constituencies. It provides positive direction for the teaching faculty and makes public the expectations of individual courses in unambiguous language for students and other instructors and administrators.

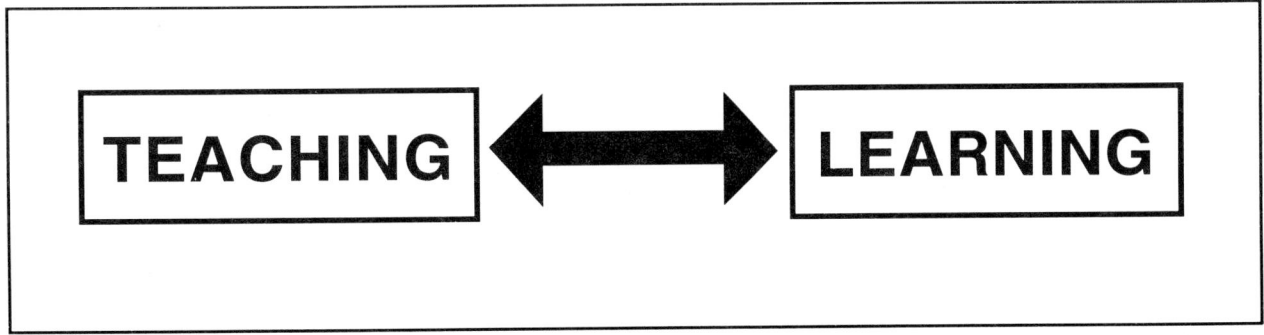

BIBLIOGRAPHY

Banthy, Bela H. (1992). <u>A systems view of education</u>. Englewood Cliffs, NJ: Educational Technology Publications.

_____. (1991). <u>Systems design of education: A journey to create the future</u>. Englewood Cliffs, NJ: Educational Technology Publications.

_____. (June 1988). Systems inquiry in education. <u>Systems Practice</u>.

_____. (1987). Instructional systems design, in Robert M. Gagne (Ed.), <u>Instructional technology: foundations</u>. Hillsdale, NJ: Lawrence Erlbaum Associates, Publishers.

_____. (1973). <u>Developing a systems view of education</u>. Salinas, CA: Intersystems Publications.

_____. (1968). <u>Instructional systems</u>. Belmont, CA: Fearon.

Branson, R.K., et al. (August 1975). <u>Interservice procedures for instructional systems development</u>. Phases I, II, III, IV, V, and Executive Summary. U.S. Army Training and Doctrine Command (Pamphlet 350). Ft. Monroe, VA.

Buckley, W. (Ed.). (1968). <u>Modern systems research for the behavioral scientist</u>. Chicago, IL: Aldine Publishing sompany.

Carter, L.F. (1969). <u>The systems approach to education—The mystique and the reality</u>. System Development Corporation, Report SP-3921.

Checkland, Peter. (1981). <u>Systems thinking, systems practice</u>. NY: John Wiley and Sons.

Churchman, C.W. (1969, 1975). <u>The systems approach</u>. (1st and 2nd eds.). NY: Dell Publishing Company.

Cleland, D.I., & King, W.R. (1968). <u>Systems analysis and project management</u>. NY: McGraw-Hill Company.

Corrigan, R.E., & Corrigan, Betty O. (1985). <u>SAFE: System approach for effectiveness</u>. Anaheim, CA: R.E. Corrigan Associates.

Corrigan, R.E., et al. (1975). <u>A system approach for education (SAFE)</u>. Garden Grove, CA: R.E. Corrigan Associates.

Corrigan, R.E., Kaufman, R.A., & Corrigan, Betty O., et al. (1967). <u>PEP: Preparing educational planners</u>. A series of instructional and training modules prepared under ESEA Title III Funds in cooperation with the California State Department of Education, Chapman College and Litton Industries.

Corrigan, R.E. & Kaufman, R. (1966). <u>Why system engineering</u>? Palo Alto, CA: Fearon Publishers.

Cyrs, Thomas E., & Lowenthal, Rita. (May 1970). A model for curriculum design using a systems approach. <u>Audiovisual Instruction</u>.

Dick, W., & Carey, L. (1985). <u>The systematic design of instruction</u> (2nd ed.). Glenview, IL: Scott Foresman & Co.

Doney, Lloyd D. (1975). A systems approach to curriculum development. In Zalatimo, Suleiman D. and Sleeman, Phillip J. (Eds.) (1975), <u>A systems approach to learning environments</u>. Roselle, NJ: MEDED Projects, Inc.

Grieve, Donald. (Ed.). (1989). <u>Teaching in college: A resource for college teachers</u>. Cleveland, OH: Info-Tec, Inc.

Kaufman, Roger. (1988). <u>Planning educational systems</u>. PA: Technomic Publishing Co., Inc.

_____. (1983). A holistic planning model: A system approach for improving organizational effectiveness and impact. <u>Performance & Instruction Journal</u>, 22(8), 3-12.

_____. (1982). <u>Identifying and solving problems: A system approach</u> (3rd ed.). San Diego, CA: University Associates Publishers.

_____. (1972). <u>Educational system planning</u>. Englewood Cliffs, NJ: Prentice-Hall, Inc.

_____. (1968). A system approach to education—derivation and definition. <u>AV Communication Review</u>, 16, 415-525.

Meals, D. (January 1967). Heuristic models for systems planning. <u>Phi Delta Kappan</u>, Bloomington, IN.

O'Neil, Harold F., Jr. (1979). <u>Issues in instructional systems development</u>. NY: Academic Press, Inc.

Rappaport, A. (1986). <u>General system theory</u>. Cambridge, MA: Abacus Press.

Silvern, L.C. (1972). <u>Systems engineering applied to training</u>. Houston, TX: Gulf Publishing Company, Book Division.

_____. (March, 1968). Cybernetics and education K-12. <u>Audiovisual Instruction</u>.

U.S. Army Training & Doctrine Command. (1975). <u>Inservice procedures for instructional systems development</u> (TRADOC Pamphlet 350-30). Ft. Berry, GA: Author.

Zalatimo, Suleiman D. and Sleeman, Phillip J. (1975). <u>A systems approach to learning environments</u>. Roselle, NJ: MEDED Projects, Inc.

Chapter 2
Analyzing Your Teaching Assumptions

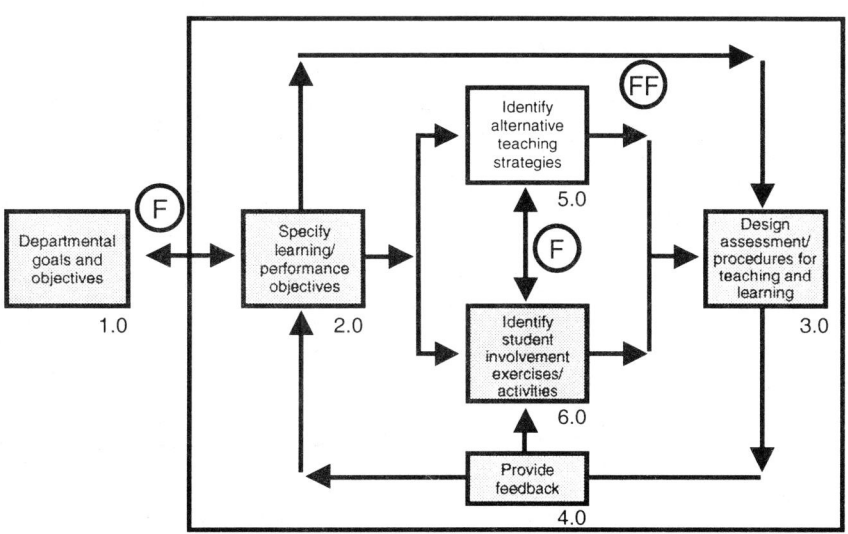

FACULTY PERCEPTIONS OF THE "GOOD" TEACHER THROUGH ANALYSIS OF THEIR ASSUMPTIONS ABOUT GOOD TEACHING

LEARNING PERFORMANCE OBJECTIVES
Conduct an analysis of the assumptions that drive and strongly influence your classroom techniques by selecting from the list provided. Analyze the relationships among your teaching assumptions, outcome measures, and sources of information.

KEY IDEAS FOR THIS CHAPTER
1. An assumption is something taken for granted without necessary proof to back it up. Many assumptions have no factual support.
2. Assumptions are prerequisites that drive action.
3. Assumptions influence the myths we create about teaching.
4. Assumptions will strongly influence how we define "good teaching" and the criteria used to make these judgments.
5. An analysis of teaching assumptions will assist instructors to make informed judgments about what they do in the classroom that will have an impact on students.

NEW VOCABULARY
- assumption
- myth
- informed judgment
- belief

Regardless of what the research has to say about the attributes of "good" teachers and as helpful and interesting as these may be, it is what instructors believe to be these attributes that will influence what they do in the classroom and help them to establish professional priorities. Good teachers develop a philosophy of practice, a well thought out and critical rationale for what they do, and why they do it. They identify and reflect on those habitual assumptions that underlie and influence their actions and ideas that permeate their teaching. One technique suggested by Fuhrman and Grasher (1983) proposes that by identifying the underlying assumptions that faculty have about teaching, they can begin to make rationale decisions about what and what not to do in the classroom to improve their teaching.

    An assumption is something that we take for granted without the necessary proof to back it up. In most cases they are hidden or unstated and are potentially deceptive (Brown & Keeley, 1981). An assumption is a postulate which we hold that claims the existence of a truth as the basis for our reasoning. Our assumptions are prerequisites to our actions; those beliefs that we hold about the causes of behavior regardless of their validity. They consist of facts, half-truths, myths and personal theories about teaching and learning, biases and prejudices, and theories and opinions about why students do what they do. Most of us are the product of our own experiences and environment. We form strong opinions on what we like and believe and these strong opinions become our assumptions. Assumptions guide and direct our actions as instructors. If instructors assume something about what works best in teaching because it has benefitted them in some way, in the past, then they will probably incorporate it into their teaching. Opinions may be so strong that they will inhibit instructors from objectively examining alternative points of view. This is consistent with the statement, "Don't bother me with the facts, my mind is already made up."

When basic assumptions are faulty and inaccurate, everything that is predicated on those faulty assumptions is inaccurate and probably in error. Since people behave in terms of their beliefs, any action that they take or conclusions that they reach can only result in false or inaccurate outcomes. For example, if an instructor believes that a person is dishonest (an unsubstantiated assumption), they will not trust him or her. On the other hand, if an instructor believes that this person is honest, they will trust him or her. Light (1990) noted several surprises that resulted, about myths and teaching, during the Harvard Assessment Seminars,

> A third surprise is that concrete data—often simple data—can do more than improve teaching and learning. They can debunk myths or widely held perceptions that are simply wrong. As a member of the Harvard Community for twenty-five years, I assumed, together with my colleagues, that certain things are true. After all, when repeated often enough, many myths gradually become part of a 'common wisdom' (pp. 4-5).

Assumptions will affect how "good teaching" is defined. In order to develop a defensible idea of what instructors constitutes as "good teaching," they need to systematically examine the assumptions that drive their beliefs and actions. This will reduce the arbitrariness of what they do in the classroom and provide them with a sound rationale for their actions. Svinicki (Spring 1991) notes that "Most currently used instructional methods were not developed out of research and theory. They arose out of tradition, familiarity, or administrative necessity."

Beliefs or assumptions help to create myths about teaching. Today, in teaching, instructors are just as much a victim of our myths as our ancestors were the victims of their myths. A myth is a "...widely held belief that is not true. ... Myths are the major factors behind the inefficiency of institutions and breakdown in communications" (Combs 1979).

There are five characteristics of myths that cause them to be especially treacherous in human affairs.

1. <u>Myths are generally held.</u> They are so widely believed that they are protected from careful analysis. They appear to be self-evident and, therefore, no one stops to question them. These myths are often proceeded by the comment, "It is clear that...;" "As everyone knows...;" "It's true... ."
2. <u>Myths are often expressed as dichotomies.</u> For example, examine the statements: either/or; for/against; black/white; naughty/nice, etc.
3. <u>Myths sometimes contain a germ of truth</u>. As a result, they encourage continued thinking in the same direction.
4. <u>Myths are used to justify behavior.</u> They frequently support preferred behavior.
5. <u>Myths often become institutionalized</u>. They provide a kind of sanctity by

custom (Combs 1979).

Eble (1976) identified and systematically examined ten common assumptions that help create a mythology of teaching:
1. Teaching is not doing.
2. Teaching is not a performing art.
3. Teaching should exclude the personality.
4. Students' "worst" teachers now will become their "best" teachers later.
5. The popular teacher is a bad teacher.
6. Teachers are born and not made.
7. Good and bad teaching cannot be identified.
8. Research is complementary to teaching.
9. Teaching a subject matter requires only that we know it.
10. College teaching is not a profession.

An instructor needs a clear definition of what he/she believes to be "good teaching" since their actions will follow and build upon their definition of "good teaching." This definition should be based upon an analysis of the assumptions (the myths of teaching) that mirror clearly and unambiguously the personal and professional educational goals and values of the instructor after they have carefully reflected upon them and after they have reviewed the literature on teaching and learning. This process will provide the data for informed judgment rather than vacuous assumptions. The instructional strategies and delivery systems that are selected and used in classrooms should be related to and be consistent with these <u>informed judgments</u>. Lastly, an instructor should be able to describe how effective their teaching practices are and what evidence they have used to make this determination. Each generation of college teachers is a victim of their own myths.

This analysis will provide the instructor with the kinds of data needed to effectively describe what they are doing in the classroom. This will be useful in promotion and tenure decisions, salary considerations, and the development of a professional portfolio for future teaching positions. These data will indicate that the instructor has taken the time to thoughtfully and systematically analyze what they are doing in the classroom and how they have established their priorities.

EXERCISE: Analyzing Your Teaching Assumptions

This exercise will consist of five steps:
1. Review the list of possible teaching assumptions and check those assumptions that you believe to be true. Select the five (5) assumptions that have had the greatest impact on the way that you currently teach. Answer the following questions for each of the five assumptions that you have identified.
   a. Have you examined any alternative points of view?
   b. Is the assumption consistent with your university, college and departmental policies and beliefs?
   c. Can this assumption be supported in the research on teaching and learning?
2. Determine if you want to change, delete or modify any of your assumptions.
3. Make a list of things that you currently do in your classroom to support each

assumption in terms of content, assignments, evaluation procedures, and your own classroom behavior.
4. Which outcomes of effective teaching are most appropriate for your assumptions?
5. What kinds of evidence can you provide to support each outcome?

POSSIBLE TEACHING ASSUMPTIONS

_____ 1. The instructor should assist students to become independent thinkers.
_____ 2. Most classroom learning is the direct result of effective lecturing.
_____ 3. Learning is facilitated when students compete with each other rather than work cooperatively.
_____ 4. Students should not be too assertive in class.
_____ 5. Textbook facts are generally accurate.
_____ 6. The primary purpose of a course is to transmit a body of substantiated knowledge.
_____ 7. Values exploration takes up too much time and diverts attention away from cognitive skills.
_____ 8. Textbooks should be the primary source of information in undergraduate classes.
_____ 9. Adult students should be taught with the same classroom methods as non-adult students.
_____ 10. Increased classroom interactions benefit learning.
_____ 11. Students should be encouraged to question the instructor.
_____ 12. The responsibility for learning rests with the student.
_____ 13. Most students learn independently.
_____ 14. Teaching is an acquired skill.
_____ 15. Students will learn as they are tested.
_____ 16. The lecture is the most efficient method to transmit information in a college classroom.
_____ 17. A course syllabus is a contractual agreement with students.
_____ 18. Teaching and research use a different set of skills that are not necessarily complimentary.
_____ 19. Critical thinking is a more important goal than content acquisition.
_____ 20. Learning to work in collaboration with other students is a very important part of college life.
_____ 21. Students can learn higher order thinking skills during a lecture.
_____ 22. Grades are inappropriate measures of real learning.
_____ 23. Students are ineffective note-takers.
_____ 24. Students prefer to work in small groups than listen to a lecture.
_____ 25. Students want to know what the instructor's expectations are so that they can prepare more effectively for tests.
_____ 26. Today's students are inferior to those of the last generation.
_____ 27. Instructors teach the truth.
_____ 28. An educated person is more worthwhile than an uneducated person.
_____ 29. The young are naturally opposed to learning.
_____ 30. Students learn best from repetition.

POSSIBLE OUTCOME MEASURES (Results of our teaching)

_____ 1. Factual knowledge.
_____ 2. Attitudes and values.
_____ 3. Skill development.
_____ 4. Critical thinking skills (analysis, synthesis and evaluation).
_____ 5. Application of ideas.
_____ 6. Creative thinking.
_____ 7. Improved self-concept.
_____ 8. Improved student questioning skills.
_____ 9. Social skill development.
_____ 10. Student interest in pursuing a career in this discipline.
_____ 11. Satisfactory learning achievement at the completion of class.
_____ 12. Satisfactory use of new instructional strategies.
_____ 13. Improved instructor knowledge of teaching issues.
_____ 14. Student satisfaction with the class.
_____ 15. Increased requests by students for further information.

SOURCES OF INFORMATION (About Learning)

_____ 1. Tests and exams.
_____ 2. Self-tests–ungraded.
_____ 3. Student self-reports.
_____ 4. Interviews with students by instructor and third parties.
_____ 5. Student questionnaires.
_____ 6. Student performance in simulations and case studies.
_____ 7. Peer assessment and reviews.
_____ 8. Course evaluations by students, peers, and administrators.
_____ 9. Self-assessment of teaching effectiveness.
_____ 10. Field exercises and evaluations by field supervisors.
_____ 11. Alumni interviews and evaluations.
_____ 12. Employer evaluations.
_____ 13. Criterion rating sheets for products such as art, plans, music, and so forth.
_____ 14. Learning objectives analysis by students.
_____ 15. Student evaluation of new instructional strategies.
_____ 16. Student portfolios.
_____ 17. Journals.

YOUR CURRENT TEACHING ASSUMPTIONS:

1.

2.

3.

4.

5.

WHAT CLASSROOM METHODS, PROCEDURES, OR PROCESSES DO YOU USE TO SUPPORT EACH ASSUMPTION?

1.

2.

3.

4.

5.

WHAT OUTCOMES OF EFFECTIVE TEACHING ARE MOST APPROPRIATE FOR EACH ASSUMPTION AND CLASSROOM ACTIVITY?

1.

2.

3.

4.

5.

WHAT TYPES OF EVIDENCE CAN YOU PROVIDE FOR EACH OUTCOME MEASURE?

1.

2.

3.

4.

5.

SUMMARY
Repeat this exercise for other assumptions that you have identified. As you gather more information about teaching effectiveness and alternative instructional strategies, you will want to review your assumptions periodically.
 The product of this exercise will be a collection of defensible teaching strategies based on current research.

BIBLIOGRAPHY

Brown, M. Neil, & Keeley, Stuart M. (1981). <u>Asking the right questions</u>. NJ: Prentice-Hall, Inc.

Combs, Arthur W. (1979). <u>Myths in education</u>. Boston: Allyn and Bacon, Inc.

Covey, Stephen R. (1989). <u>The seven habits of highly effective people</u>. NY: Simon and Schuster.

Eble, Kenneth E. (1976). The mythology of teaching. In Eble, Kenneth E. (1976). <u>The craft of teaching</u>. San Francisco: Jossey-Bass.

Fuhrman, Barbara S., & Grasha, Anthony F. (1983). <u>A practical handbook for college teachers</u>. Boston: Little, Brown and Co.

Rando, William C., & Menges, Robert J. (1991). How practice is shaped by personal theories. In Robert J. Menges & Marilla D. Svinicki, (Eds.), <u>College teaching: From theory to practice</u>. San Francisco: Jossey-Bass Publishers.

Svinicki, Marilla D. (1991). Theories and metaphors we teach by. In Robert J. Menges & Marilla D. Svinicki, (Eds.), <u>College teaching: From theory to practice</u>. San Francisco: Jossey-Bass Publishers.

Chapter 3
What the Research Says About Teachers and Teaching

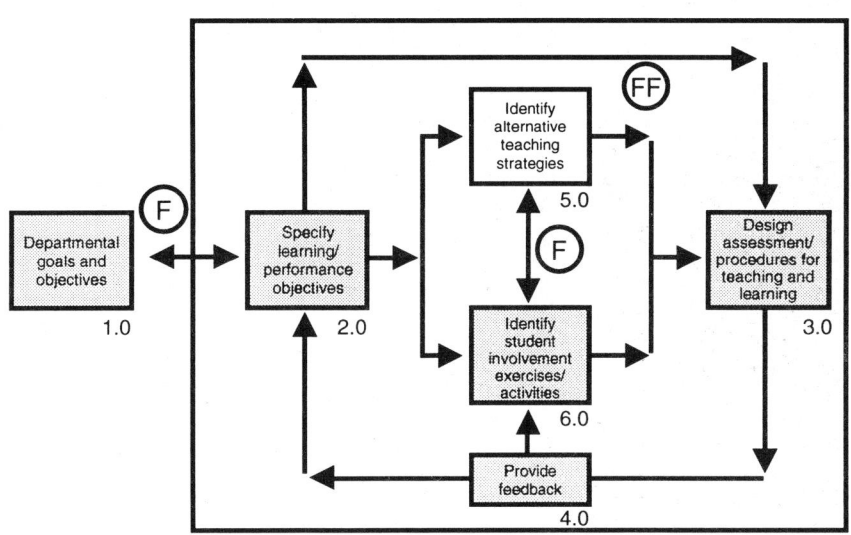

"The more you know about teaching, the more doors you can help students to open."

RESEARCH ON TEACHING: WHAT DO WE KNOW?

LEARNING PERFORMANCE OBJECTIVES
Describe the common characteristics of effective teachers as identified from a synthesis of research on teaching. Explain a variety of general findings of useful teaching research that can be applied immediately in the classroom.

KEY IDEAS
1. Process product research, the dominant methodology underlying teaching research in higher education, can and has produced reliable information about the nature of effective teaching.
2. Research synthesis will provide usable research results that will help to put teaching on a more sound scientific basis.
3. The three key predictors of teaching effectiveness are lecture clarity, course organization and planning, and student-instructor interactions.

NEW VOCABULARY
- process-product
- research synthesis
- meta-analysis

The effects of teaching in higher education are most commonly researched in terms of academic achievement of students, usually measured by teacher-made final examinations (McKeachie and others, 1986). Comparative studies of different teaching methods are the best examples of achievement criteria being used in research on teaching in higher education. Other criteria of effectiveness are often employed and include student evaluations or ratings; time to complete courses; withdrawal or completion rates; and student attitudes towards a course.

The dominant methodology underlying teaching research in higher education has been the process-product paradigm (Dunkin, 1986), which views teaching effectiveness as the systematic observation of teaching behaviors in the classroom that leads to student learning.

Today, in addition to measures of teaching effectiveness based on student learning, researchers are also examining measures of teacher behavior derived from a systematic observation of classroom interactions and information about teachers' intentions or purposes as stated in performance objectives. Process-product research can produce and has produced reliable information about the nature of effective teaching (Peterson and Walberg, 1979).

The 1980s have been a productive time in the history of teaching and the 1990s will be even more productive with the use of research synthesis techniques. The latter will help to put teaching on a more sound scientific basis. Research synthesis "...explicitly applies scientific techniques and standards to the evaluation and summary of research; it not only statistically summarizes effects across studies but also provides detailed descriptions of replicable sources of literature, selection of studies, and so forth..." (Walberg, 1986).

Characteristics of effective instructors
Based on the research of Benton (1982), there are three predictors of teaching effectiveness, namely: (1) the skills of the instructor in terms of lecture clarity in presentations; (2) course organization and planning; and (3) student-instructor interactions. These three predictors, in addition to enthusiasm, have been found in numerous other studies (Eble, 1972; Pace 1973; Ellner and Barnes, 1983; Bridges, Ware, Brown, and Greenwood, 1971; Feldman, 1976; Rovecher, 1986).

Other characteristics of effective college teachers include such things as: honesty, generality of actions, variety of presentations, use of examples, energy (Eble, 1972; Pace, 1973; Ellner and Barnes, (1983); interest in students, availability, approachability, personal appearance, class discussions, evaluation of students, fair and constructive criticism (Bridges, Ware, Brown, and Greenwood, 1971); knowledge of subject matter, stimulation of interest (Feldman, 1976); explanations, outlines and summaries, instructor-group interaction and instructor-individual student interactions, humor, an analytic-synthetic approach that emphasizes contrasting theories and implications (Hildebrand, 1971); and group instructional skills (Seldin, 1980).

According to Rosenshine and Stevens (1986), effective instructors do certain things when they teach well-structured subjects. They begin a class with a short review of previous learning that is prerequisite to the current class. The lesson is begun with a short statement of goals and objectives. The subject under study is presented in small steps with student practice after each step. Instructions and explanations are crystal clear and detailed. A high level of active practice is provided for all students. These instructors ask a large number of questions and check for student understanding through student responses. Systematic feedback and correction are provided during class and for all homework assignments.

In addition to these observations, Guskey (1988) notes that these effective instructors plan detailed course outlines within the context of an overall course description. A syllabus is provided with a topical outline and associated readings from the text and outside sources. There is an overall class structure in terms of review, preview, presentation, and summary. These instructors involve students and have a high regard for their abilities. They move about the class rather than fix themselves at a podium or desk. Individual help is made available to students when they request it. Student progress is rewarded through verbal praise during class and comments on papers.

Given these data, the characteristics that are predominate for the most effective college instructors are enthusiasm for the subject taught and for the act of teaching; course organization and planning; clarity of presentations; and instructor-student interactions during and after class.

OTHER GENERAL FINDINGS OF USEFUL RESEARCH FOR COLLEGE INSTRUCTORS
The state of the art on research in all aspects of education including college classroom instruction has improved significantly in the past decade. Researchers have reviewed hundreds of studies in "reviews of research" using the technique of research synthesis or meta-analysis. Although not as exact as the approaches used in the physical sciences, these findings offer direction and confidence in these procedures, strategies, and techniques. The behavioral sciences cannot control for external variables as

easily as the physical sciences and therefore must develop techniques that control for experimental contamination. This results from the fact that behavioral scientists deal with people in real world environments. In spite of these difficulties, behavioral scientists have made great strides in an effort to provide useful results for the instructional practitioner.

The findings presented throughout this section are not complete nor presented in great detail. It is the conclusions of the extensive research rather than the details of procedure that are presented for consideration. References for each conclusion are provided for further study. The conclusions are not presented in any order or priority.

Audio-tutorial teaching, in which students work at their own pace, has shown to be significantly more effective than conventional college teaching. This is based on 42 studies that showed 69% improvement in achievement on a final examination; 53% positive results in 22 studies in terms of course completion; and positive course ratings by students of 50% in 6 studies (Durkin, 1986).

Personalized Systems of Instruction (PSI), known also as the Keller Plan, has the largest systematic body of research to prove its value. The research has shown it to be clearly superior to all other instructional methods. There was a significant improvement in learning (93.2%) in 103 independent studies (Durkin, 1986). Mastery learning showed a 96.7% positive result in 30 studies.

Discussion methods of teaching are more effective than the lecture when the instructor wanted to teach higher order learning skills such as critical thinking or problem-solving skills (Durkin, 1986). Discussion methods were also favored when the instructor wanted students to explore and change attitudes (McKeachie, 1970). Erbb (1967) found that student led discussions were favored over instructor led discussions for cognitive achievement. This teaching method was found to be no more effective than the traditional lecture if the objective was learning factual information (Peterson and Walberg, 1979).

College grades have no more than a modest correlation with success in later life, no matter how success is defined (Hoyt, 1965).

College classroom tests influence to a marked extent how students study and what they learn (Milton and Eison, 1983). Students learn as they are tested. They concentrate study efforts on what they think will be on the test or examination (McKeachie and others, 1986). Scores on final exams are almost invariably better in courses with frequent quizzes. The latter leads to improved performance in college classes. This finding is consistent with findings from the effects of mastery learning (Kulick, J.A. and Kulick, C.C., 1984; Dustin, D., 1971; Fitch, M.L., 1951; Keys, N., 1934).

Dubin and Taveggia (1968) found that students learn as much from unsupervised independent study as they did from conventional college teaching.

There are three features of individualized college teaching, in which the student progresses at his or her own pace, that appear to have clear effects on student study. These are: (1) the number of times students are examined on their proficiency of the subject matter; (2) the timing of the feedback from the instructor of scores after each examination or test; (3) and the degree to which students are required to correct learning deficiencies in testing and retake the test as soon as possible (Kulick and Kulick, 1979).

The time students spend engaged in learning is the best single predictor of their actual achievement (Brandt, 1984). Student participation, student-to-student interaction and instructor encouragement correlated positively and quite strongly with student growth in critical thinking ability and higher level study processes (Dunkin, 1986).

There have been hundreds of studies completed on the traditional lecture in terms of its effectiveness in comparison with other teaching strategies. The available research consistently concludes that lectures are one of the least effective methods of conveying information (Lowman, 1985). It has been found that it is best used for those learning objectives at the lower end of Bloom's taxonomy, namely, recall of factual data (University of London Teaching Methods Unit, 1978). When instructors lecture, students are not attending to what is being said 40% of the time (Pollio, 1984). During the first 10 minutes of a lecture, students retain approximately 70% of the information while in the last 10 minutes, they retain only 20% of the information (McKeachie, 1986). Verner and Dickinson (1967) found that students lose their initial interest in a lecture and their attention levels continue to drop as a lecture proceeds. Nonverbal cues used during a lecture are recognized as very important in the instructor-student communication process. These include: eye contact; body gestures; overall mannerisms; movement toward a student; touch; facial expressions; posture; energy level; and use of space, time, and silence (Bailey, G.D., 1981; Knalp, L., 1978; Morris, D., 1977).

Research on student note-taking finds support for the value of some note-taking. The latter was found to be ineffective when the notes were inadequate, incomplete, and disorganized. Verbatim notes provided by the instructor were not helpful. If the subject or topic was very complex, difficult concepts overload the cognitive capacity of the student so that they miss much of the lecture (Hartley and Davies, 1978; Hartley, 1986). This results from too many points being covered in a short period of time. Research on what students can remember following classes indicates that most college students can absorb only three or four points during a 50-minute class period and four or five points in a 75-minute class, regardless of the subject being taught (Lowman, J., 1985; Eble, K.E., 1976; McKeachie, W.J., 1978).

There is a wealth of evidence that peer teaching is extremely effective for a wide range of goals, content, and students of different levels and personalities (McKeachie, and Others, 1986; Johnson, D.W. and Others, 1981).

Students who change the most intellectually, politically, and creatively have had the most frequent interactions with the instructor outside of the formal class (Gaff, J.G., 1975; Wilson, R., 1975). High ability students benefitted most when the contact involved clarification of learning points (Siegel and Siegel, 1964).

There are generally no significant differences between remote (students physically separated from the instructor–television, telephone, and audiographic), and on-campus students in academic performance (Wergin, J.F. and Haas, T.W., 1986; Whittington, N., 1987; Chu, G. and Schramm, W., 1967; Kulick, J.A. and Jaksa, P.M., 1977). The research clearly indicates that students achieve as well in videotaped courses as in traditional courses (Dutton, J.C., 1988).

These conclusions only begin to scratch the surface of usable research for the college instructor. Throughout this book, conclusions of the author have been based on documented evidence. Please review the bibliographies for the evidence that supports these conclusions.

Regardless of what the research says, there are certain ways that effective college instructors act that make them distinctive. Dr. Donald Roush, Executive Vice-President Emeritus at New Mexico State University, was formerly the Dean of the College of Education and has had a special sensitivity to teaching at all levels. Several years ago he was asked to write a chapter in a book entitled, In Celebration of Teaching. The chapter was titled, "What Makes A Good Teacher?" It is a result of many years of dealing with teachers, a knowledge of their needs, their strengths and their weaknesses. As a master teacher who possesses all of the characteristics identified in the research, he has been able to convey this love of teaching and teachers. If I could choose one teacher whose ideals and skills I would like to emulate, it would be this great teacher, Donald Roush. The chapter is reproduced here with his permission.

What Makes A Good Teacher?

Donald C. Roush
Executive Vice President Emeritus
New Mexico State University

Good teachers convey to students a sense of excitement about learning and involve them in a skillful mix of intense hard work and fun. An atmosphere of caring about each other is quickly established through countless displays of high expectancies and helpfulness. For example, good teachers are accessible to their students nearly any time, conduct extra sessions for students who need them, meet with students informally out of class, instill self-confidence in their students; in short, they share generously of themselves.

Good teachers are proud to teach. They command respect of their students and the community. Their enthusiasm is contagious. Their students develop an inherent desire and inspiration to learn. Good teachers know and believe that there is something special about every human being, especially those they teach, and have as their purpose to make a difference in the lives of others.

Good teachers have met face to face the sometimes difficult decision to devote their lives to the service of mankind by choosing a career in the profession of teaching. Perhaps the struggle is best described by John Lester Buford in his address "Proud to Teach" before the 1956 representative assembly of the National Education Association when he quoted a former president of the association, Mr. Sutton, as to why he chose teaching:

> I shall never forget the difficult time I had in deciding what I was going to do in life. My father was the type of man who thought everybody ought to know his plans for life when he was 15 years old. When I saw him picking the lovely blades of corn, I would say: 'I must be a farmer.' When I rode to town and saw the bridges, I would say: 'I had to be an architect, or builder.' My uncle was a preacher, and when I saw how much his congregation liked him, I said: 'I have just got to be a preacher!' I had another uncle for who I was named who was a country doctor. When I would ride around with him, and see how he was adored, I would say: 'I just must be a doctor!'
>
> Then I wanted above everything else to write a book. Oh, I had a thousand things I wanted to do. I couldn't decide. Before my graduation in June, Father wrote me a long letter. I have it yet. Then I took all the arguments from the seven things he said he thought I might be, and wrote them down on a piece of cardboard, and I tried to put them in parallel columns.

> Then being religious, I knelt down, with the shades drawn, and I tried to decide what I was going to be. I wanted to be a lawyer; I wanted to be a doctor; I wanted to be a preacher; I wanted to be a farmer; I wanted to be an architect; I wanted to write a book.
> About that time, the shade fluttered and the light came in, and there seemed to be a voice that said, 'Would you like to do them all?' I said I would. "I can tell you how to do every one of them." I said, 'How?' And the answer came, 'Just be a teacher. Some boy will write your book. It will be better than any book you ever thought of. Some girl will paint your picture, and another will give it veracity, somebody else will be the doctor, and somebody else will be the lawyer. Just be the teacher!'

Good teachers are filled with heavy doses of passion and compassion—a passion for teaching and compassion for those they teach.

Finally, good teachers are driven by a powerful force, one which makes all teaching worthwhile—that is to witness learning in others, the satisfaction of seeing students become wiser, more knowledgeable, and more sure of themselves.

Now the second question: What do good teachers know about teaching? All good teachers possess a thorough knowledge of the subjects they teach. Good teachers cannot know too much about their subjects. A comprehensive knowledge of the subject matter is a "given."

A similar understanding of the substantive body of knowledge about teaching processes also helps good teachers reach their maximum effectiveness. In their quest for excellence, good teachers know how to (1) organize for teaching, (2) motivate learners, and (3) select and implement teaching strategies.

Organizing for teaching begins with the planning teachers do *before* the first class meeting. Included in these deliberations are crisp goals, selected with great care, which form the basis for all teaching decisions. Such preplanning ensures consistency, avoids classroom management problems, and makes learning easier.

A major impact on planning and organizing is the 10 to 20 minute attention span of most students. Moreover, Hartley and Davies found in their studies of student attention during lectures that,

> Typically, attention increases from the beginning of the lecture to 10 minutes and decreases after that point. Evidence collected shows that after the lecture, students recalled 70 percent of the material covered in the first 10 minutes and only 20 percent of the material covered in the last 10 minutes. (Hartley and Davies, p. 207)*

Lectures which continue without interruption beyond 15 or 20 minutes are an inefficient use of student and faculty time. Thus, good teachers take advantage of the opportunity during a class to see that students learn as much as they possibly can. The reorganizational implications are enormous.

Good teachers know that students learn more when they are exposed to a number of teaching methods. The lecture is the least efficient teaching and learning mode. Lecturing is an effective way to present information, but an optimal combination of teaching methods is required to meet all student learning styles. Alternate ways for students to learn are selected for 26 teaching and learning modes. The inclusion of these alternatives requires astute planning.

High scholarly standards are clearly stated in both the rigor and currency of course content and the level of expected student performance with respect to those standards. The currency of a teacher's information about a given course is and should be the primary responsibility for the teacher, but at the same time discussions with colleagues are needed to update course syllabi, to keep up with the changes in the class level and subjects, and to avoid duplication of information. Otherwise, organizing and planning takes place in a vacuum.

In every course, the major ideas or concepts are clearly identified with specific facts taught in relationship to those concepts. Good teachers know that unstructured instruction is rapidly forgotten.

The nature of the subject, anticipated maturity level of the students to be taught, and the adoption of teaching strategies that fit the skills of the instructor are crucial considerations. In most classes of 25 to 30, five to seven students, or perhaps more, will be "lost" from time to time as the course proceeds. Good teachers anticipate this fact and include alternative ways for students to "catch up" without unduly occupying precious teacher time.

Good teachers know that testing and grading of students greatly influence student performance. When the first test is given, the "moment of truth" has arrived. Students take their cues from the manner in which they are evaluated and graded. When students are tested for facts, they learn to memorize; when students are tested for understanding, they learn to think. A test that is fair, impartial, reasonable, and consistent with everything the teacher has said gives students the best opportunity to succeed.

Motivating students is the principal task of the teacher. The good teacher realizes the high correlation between the amount of motivation and the amount of learning. Motivation is the cornerstone of any serious quest for quality in teaching.

Motivating learners is simultaneously challenging, complicated, traumatic, climactic, exciting, and wonderful--all of which is confirmed as good teachers follow these assumptions:

> Learning is of itself a great motivator. A teacher of mathematics is one of my seminars said, "I have no problem with motivation. Mathematics is beautiful." When we help students reach that gestalt, commonly referred to as the "Aha, I understand," they are unusually motivated. Learner participation, response, and experience contribute significantly to motivation.

> Experiences related to the subject are crucial to motivation and learning. For example, Mark Twain said, "I never let my schooling interfere with my education." He recognized the critical need for the integration of student experiences with education and the extensive implications to motivation.

> To motivate, teaching strategies are designed to enhance learner security, acceptance, self-esteem, and self-actualization; that is, the satisfaction of knowing something or achieving one's potential.

> Raising the sights of students motivates them. When students ask the perennial question, "How long does this paper have to be?" the good teacher answers with another question, "How good do you want to be?," the effective teacher makes "have to" become "want to" and helps students discover that academic excellence is clearly within their reach.

> Perhaps the most important factor in motivation is that learners can receive major motivations from the classroom climate or atmosphere. The climate in which learners find themselves can be a major deterrent or a major contributor to motivation. Classrooms that motivate are "user friendly."

> Teachers also receive major motivations from the institutional climate or atmosphere. Motivated teachers motivate students. Motivated students drive teachers to do their best. Therefore, the conditions where teaching takes place should be ideal, not just adequate.

Finally--good teachers in their quest for quality know there is something special in everyone and that helping students discover and enhance that specialty is a most powerful motivator.

Good teachers know how to select and implement teaching strategies--they are clever strategists. These strategies include, but are not limited to, teaching and learning modes, student response and experience, student confidence, and values related to the discipline.

For example, discussion in teaching is much more than the elicitation of questions and answers. Good teachers are interested in the quality of student response and employ strategies to evoke *meaningful* responses that clarify the lesson and present additional information.

Strategies of a teacher's quest for quality are designed to involve students in their own education--help them apply ideas and facts in their lives and gain insights into current problems. The central purposes of these strategies are the comprehension and retention of information, helping students develop confidence in their ability to learn, and providing continuous student motivation.

But the most effective and least used teaching strategy is the inculcation of values related to the discipline in the teaching and learning plan. Why is student discussion of these values so powerful?

    a. Perceptions are constantly infiltrated with values.
    b. Values serve as the authorities in the name of which choices are made and actions are taken. (Morrill, p. 62).
    c. What students do and believe depends upon their attitudes, philosophies, and value judgements.

Susan Gardner, honor student at New Mexico State University, stated in one of her papers:

> The idea of value-free education is hard to contemplate. I cannot think of a subject that could be considered completely objective, uninfluenced by human ideas and prejudices. . .Most of the students I talked with said that the most drastic changes in their values have come from their social interactions. But whether they realize it or not, I think their classes are often responsible for planting the seeds that lead to continued thoughts. These are the thoughts that the students then discuss with their friends... A free discussion about values can raise ten questions for every question answered...Value discussion, with guidance, is one of the most interesting aspects of education I have encountered...What students need is the opportunity to think about their values, so they can also live by them.

Faculty in my teaching seminars always devote considerable time and discussion to these statements on values. The same will happen in the classrooms of good teachers, and their students will 1) gain a deeper understanding of the subject, 2) display a greater interest in the subject, and 3) retain more information about the subject. Good teachers help students learn how to make a living and how to lead a life.

In summary, it is through these critical components--organizing, motivating, and postulating teaching strategies that our classrooms are more apt to serve as places where the zeal of the student to learn and the zeal for scholarship of the professor meet head-on. Good teaching incorporates and integrates the processes of planning, organizing, motivating, evaluating, and strategically employing selected strategies.

In the descriptions contained in Part II of this book of teachers most remembered by their successful students, it will be most interesting indeed to compare the responses with the content of what makes a good teacher and what good teachers know about teaching. My guess is that a large number of reflections will be value-laden.*

*Reprinted with permission of the author.

Roush, Donald C. (1987). What makes a good teacher? In Gerald Thomas and Donald Ferguson (1987). In celebration of the teacher. Las Cruces, N.M.: New Mexico State University Foundation, 11-16.

BIBLIOGRAPHY

Bailey, G.D. (1981). <u>Teaching self-assessment: A means for improving classroom instruction</u>. Washington, DC: NEA. Bass, Publishers.

Benton, Sidney E. (1982). <u>Rating college teaching: Criterion validity studies of student evaluation-of-instructor instruments</u>. AAHE-ERIC/Higher Education Research Report Number One. Washington, DC: American Association of Higher Education.

Bess, James L. (1990, May/June). Miscast professionals. <u>Change</u>, 19-22.

Brandt, Ronald. (1971). On mastering learning: An interview with James H. Block. <u>Educational Leadership</u>, ASCS, <u>33</u>(8).

Ware, Charles, M. & Others. Characteristics of best and worst teachers. <u>Science Education</u>. <u>55</u>(4).

Browne, M. Neil, & Keeley, Stuart M. Achieving excellence: Adult to new teachers. <u>College Teaching</u>. <u>33</u>(2), 78-83.

Characteristics of best and worst teachers. <u>Science Education</u>, <u>55</u>(4), 545-553.

Chu, Godwin C., & Schramm, Wilbur. (1967). <u>Learning from television: What the research says</u>. Washington, D.C.: National Association of Educational Broadcasting.

Combes, A.W. (1965). <u>The professional education teachers</u>. Boston: Allyn and Bacon.

Common, Dianne L. (Summer 1989). Master teachers in higher education: A matter of settings. <u>Review of Higher Education</u>, <u>12</u>(4), 375-87.

Donald, J.G. The state of research on university teaching effectiveness. In J.G. Donald & A.M. Sullivan (Eds.). Using research to improve teaching. <u>New directions for teaching and learning</u>. (23).

Donald, Janet G. (1985). The state of research on university teaching effectiveness. In J.G. Donald & A.M. Sullivan, (Eds.). <u>Using research to improve teaching</u>. San Francisco: Jossey-Bass Publishers. Also in <u>New Directions for Teaching and Learning</u>, (23).

Donk, M.M.J. (1986). Research on teaching in higher education. In Merlin C. Wittrock (Ed.). <u>Handbook of research on teaching</u>. NY: Macmillan Publishing Co..

Dubin, Robert, & Taveggia, Thomas C. (1968). <u>The teaching-learning paradox</u>. Eugene, OR: Center for the Advanced Study of Educational Administration, University of Oregon.

Dunkin, Michael J. (1986). Research on teaching in higher education. In Merlin C. Wittrock (Ed.). <u>Handbook of research on teaching</u> (3rd ed.). NY: Macmillian Publishing Company.

Dustin, David. (1971). Some effects of exam frequency. <u>Psychological Report</u>, <u>21</u>, 409-414.

Dutton, J.C. (1988). A comparison of live and videotaped presentations of a graduate mechanical engineering course. <u>Engineering Education</u>, 243-246.

Eble, Kenneth E. (1984). The mythology of teaching. In <u>The craft of teaching</u>, 9-22.

____. (1972). <u>Professors as teachers</u>. San Francisco: Jossey-Bass Publishers.

____. <u>The craft of teaching: A guide to mastering the professor's art</u>. San Francisco.

Eison, James. Confidence in the classroom: Ten maxims for new teachers. <u>College Teaching</u>, <u>38</u>(1), 21-24.

Ellner, C.L., & Barnes, C.P. (1983). <u>Studies of college teaching</u>. Lexington, MA: Lexington Books.

Feldman, Kenneth A. (1976). The superior college teacher from the students' view. Review of Research in Higher Education, 5, 243-288.

Fitch, Mildred L., & Others. (1951). Frequent testing as a motivation factor in large lecture classes. Journal of Educational Psychology, 42, 1-20.

Gaff, Jerry G. (1975). Making a difference: The impacts of faculty. The Journal of Higher Education.

Gage, N.L. Reviewing what we know: The results of recent research in the scientific basis of affecting instruction in higher education. In A force for change in higher education, 91-101.

Goldschmid. M.L. (1971). The learning cell: An instructional innovation. Learning and Development, 2, 1-6.

Greenwood, Gordon. (1971). Characteristics of best and worst teachers. Science Education, 55(4), 545-553.

Guskey, Thomas R. (1988). Improving student learning in college classrooms. Springfield, IL: Charles C. Thomas, Publisher.

Hahn, Robert. (1990, Sept./Oct.). What we talk about when we talk about teaching. Change, 45-49.

Hartley, J. (1986). Improving study skills. British Educational Reseach Journal, 12(2), 111-123.

Hartley, J., & Davies, K. (1978). Notetaking: A critical review. Programed Learning and Educational Technology, 15, 207-225.

Hauser, Jerald A. (Winter 1990). Teaching on the cheap. The Journal of Professional Studies, 33-40.

Highet, G. (1950). The art of teaching. NY: Alfred A. Knoff.

Hildebrand, M., Wilson, R.C., & Dienst, E.R. (1971). Evaluating university teaching. Berkeley: Center for Research & Development in Higher Education, University of California.

Holbrook, Steven M., Mathis, B. Claude, & Holbrook, Steven T. Major factors.

Hoyt, D.P. (1965). The relationship between college grades and adult achievement—A review of the literature. Research Report No. 7. Iowa City, IA: American College Testing Program.

Jersild, A.T. (1955). When teachers face themselves. NY: Columbia University.

Johnson, R.T., & Others. (1973). Cooperation and competition in the classroom: Perceptions and preferences as related to students' feelings of personal control. Elementary School Journal, 73, 306-313.

Johnson, D.W., & Others. (1981). The effects of cooperative, competitive and individualistic goal structures and achievement: A meta-analysis. Psychological Bulletin, 89, 47-62.

Keys, Noel. (1934). The influence on learning and retention of weekly as opposed to monthly tests. Journal of Educational Psychology, 25, 427-436.

Knapp, L. (1978). Nonverbal communication in human interaction. NY: Holt, Rinehart, and Winston.

Kulik, James A., & Jaksa, Peter. (1977). A Review of research on PSI and other educational technologies in college teaching. Educational Technology, 17, 12-19.

Kulik, James A., & Kulik, Chen-Lin C. (1979). College teaching. In Penelope Peterson & Herbert Walberg, (Eds.). Research on teaching: Concepts, findings and implications. CA: McCutchin Publishing Corporation.

Kulik, James A., & Kulik, Chen-Lin C. (1978). College teaching. In Penelope Peterson & Herbert Walberg, (Eds.). <u>Research on teaching: Concepts, findings and implications.</u> CA: McCutchin Publishing Corporation.

Lowman, Joseph. (1985). The art, craft, and techniqes of masterful teaching. In <u>Mastering the technique of teaching</u>, 210-229.

____. (1985). <u>Mastering the techniques of teaching</u>. San Francisco: Jossey-Bass Publishers.

____. (1978). <u>Mastering the techniques of teaching</u>. San Francisco: Jossey-Bass Publishers.

McKeachie, Wilbert. J. (1978). <u>Teaching tips: A guidebook for the beginning college teacher</u> (7th ed.). Lexington, MA: Heath.

____. (1970). <u>Research on college teaching: A review</u>. ERIC Clearinghouse on Higher Education. Report No. 6. Washington, DC: George Washington University.

____. (1965). <u>Teaching tips</u>. Ann Arbor, MI: The George Wahr Publishing Co.

McKeachie, W.J., Lin, Y.G., & Mann, W. (1971). Student ratings of teacher effectiveness: Validity studies. <u>American Educational Research Journal</u>, 8, 435.

McKeachie, Wilbert, & Others. (1986). <u>Teaching and learning in the college classroom: A review of the research literature</u>. Ann Arbor, MI: University of Michigan.

Melton, Reginald F. <u>Instructional models for course design and development</u>.

Milton, Ohmen, & Eison, James A. (1983) <u>Textbook tests: Guidelines for item writing</u>. NY: Harper and Row Publishers.

Miron, Mordechai. (1983). The good professor as perceived by university instructors. In <u>Improving University Teaching–Ninth International Conference–contributed papers III</u>, 14-41.

Morris, D. (1977). <u>Manwatching: A field guide to human behavior</u>. NY: Harry A. Abrams.

Neff, Rose, & Weimer, Maryellen (Eds.). (1990). <u>Teaching college–collected readings for the new instructor</u>. Madison, Wisconson: Magna Publications, Inc.

Ornstein, Allan C. (April 1976). Can we define a good teacher? <u>Peabody Journal of Education</u>, 201-207.

Pace, R.C. (Ed.) (1973). <u>Evaluating learning and teaching</u>. San Francisco: Jossey-Bass Publishers.

Peterson, Penelope, & Walberg, Herbert (Eds.). (1979). <u>Research on teaching: Concepts, findings and implications</u>. CA: McCutchan Publishing Corporation.

Pinsker, Sanford. (1989). Teaching in a litigious time. <u>Change</u>. 50-54.

Pullras, Earl V., Lockhard, A., Bond, Marjorie H., & Clifton, Marguirite. (1963). The roots of excellence. In <u>Toward excellence in college teaching</u>, 5-33.

Rippey, Robert M. (1981). <u>The evaluation of teaching in medical schools</u>. NY: Springer Publishing Co.

Rose-Levinson, Judith, & Menges, Robert J. (1981, Fall). Improving college teaching: A critical review of research. In <u>Review of Educational Research</u>, 51(3).

Rosenshine, B., & Furst N.F. (1971). Research on teacher performance criteria. In B.O. Smith, (Ed). <u>Research in teacher education: A symposium</u>. Englewood Cliffs, NJ: Prentice-Hall.

Rosenshine, Barak, & Stevens, Robert. Teaching functions. In Merlin C. Wittrock.

Handbook of research on teaching, (3rd ed.). NY: Macmillan Publishing Company.

Rovecher, John, & Blake, George A. III. (1986). Profiling excellence in America's schools. Current Issues in Higher Education. 102-107.

Schwarts, L.L. (1980). Criteria for effective university teaching. Improving College and University Teaching, 28,(3), 120-123.

Seldin, P. (1980). Successful faculty evaluation. NY: Coventry Press.

Siegel, L., & Siegel, Lila. (1964). The instructional gestalt: A conceptual framework and design for educational research. AV Communications Review, 12.

Skinner, B.F. (1965) The technology of teaching. Proceedings of the Royal Society, B., 162, 427-443.

Solas, John. (1992, Spring/Summer). Effective teaching as constructed by social work students. Journal of Social Work Education, 2, 145-154.

Thomas, Gerald W., & Ferguson, Donald G. (1987). In celebration of the teacher. NM: The New Mexico State University Foundation.

Trues, Harold. (1975). Factors critical to college teaching success or failure. Improving College and University Teaching, 14(4).

Turney, C., & Others. (1973). Microteaching: research, theory, and practice. Sydney, Australia: Sydney University Press.

University of London Teaching Methods Unit. Improving teaching in higher education. London: The Cavendish Press, Ltd.

Webb, N.J., & Grib, T.F. (1967). Teaching process as a learning experience: The experimental use of student-led groups. (Final Report HE00-882). Washington, DC: Department of Health, Education and Welfare.

Webster, David S. (Winter, 1990). Research: The dragon of good teaching. The Journal of Professional Studies. 22.

Weimer, Maryellen. (1990, Winter). The scholarship of teaching. The Journal of Professional Studies. 5-20.

Wergin, Jon F., & Haas, Thomas W. (1986, Nov.) Televising graduate engineering courses: Results of an instructional experiment. Engineering Education. 111.

Whittington, N. (1987). Is instructional television educationally effective? A research review. The American Journal of Distance Education, 1, 47-57.

Wilson, Robert, et al. (1975). College professors and their impact on students. John Wiley and Sons. (Chapter 10).

Wlodkowski, Raymond J. (1985). Enhancing adult motivation to learn. San Francisco: Jossey-Bass Publishers.

Wood, Lynn, & Wilson, Robert C. (1972). Teachers with impact. The Research Reporter, VII.

Chapter 4
Exploring Your Teaching Style With the Myers-Briggs Type Inventory

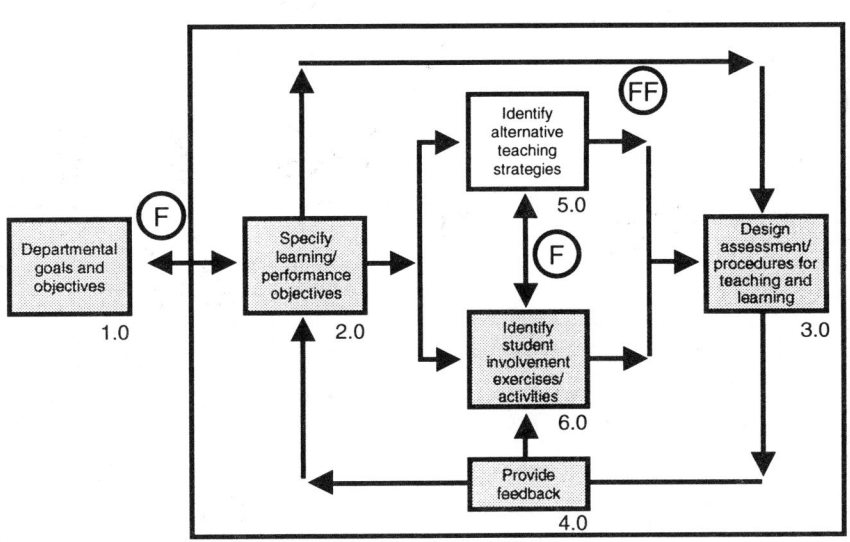

"Teaching is like fishing.

You use different lures for different fish.

You use different instructional strategies for different students."

Exploring Your Teaching Style With the Myers-Briggs Type Inventory

LEARNING PERFORMANCE OBJECTIVES
Identify your teaching style by taking, analyzing, and reflecting on the data provided. Relate each action and decision of your teaching by reflecting on your teaching style. (Level 4).

KEY IDEAS
1. Instructors knowledge of their teaching style will help them to become more effective instructors.
2. The Myers-Briggs Type Inventory is an instrument that will help instructors to identify their teaching style. It is highly respected and well-established in the research literature.
3. Knowledge of teaching styles will strongly influence instructional strategies selected by instructors.

NEW VOCABULARY
- teaching style
- sensory perception
- introvert
- extrovert
- MBTI perception
- intuition perception and thinking judgment
- feeling perception and feeling judgment

We can become more effective instructors by becoming more aware of our own teaching styles, the sum total of what we do in a college classroom (Eble 1980). Teaching style includes not only the technical skills of teaching–the ability to specify learning performance objectives, select learning activities, construct valid tests, etc.–but the total personality and character of the instructor that influences students. There are a variety of different teaching styles (Sheffield, 1974). These can be nurtured and developed with practice, feedback, and reflection.

The Myers-Briggs Type Indicator (MBTI) is an instrument to help instructors identify their teaching style. The primary purpose of the MBTI is to identify, from a self-report of easily recognized reactions, basic preferences of people in regard to perception and judgment. It is based on the theory of psychological types described by Jung. This theory is based on the idea that behavior that seems to be random is, in reality, quite orderly and consistent. This is true because of the basic differences in how people use their perception and judgment. Myers-Briggs (1985) notes that

> Perception involves all of the ways of becoming aware of things, people, happenings, or ideas. Judgment involves all of the ways of coming to conclusions about what has been perceived. If people differ systematically in what they perceive and in how they reach conclusions, then it is only reasonable for them to differ correspondingly in their reactions, interests, values, motivations, skills, and interests.

According to Jung every person has four basic mental processes: sensing, intuition, thinking, and feeling. He classified all activities that required perception into the two broad categories of sensing and intuition.

Sensing perception describes all of those things observable through the senses. It establishes what exists. People who are inclined toward sensing perception focus on immediate experiences. These people develop characteristics associated with such awareness as enjoyment of the present moment, realism, acute powers of observation, memory for details, and practicality.

Intuitive perception refers to perception of possibilities, meanings, and relationships. Intuition comes on a person in a rush as a "feeling" or as a hunch. We have a flash of some new possibilities or as a new way of viewing a problem. We begin to see the big picture. We see beyond the immediate sensual experience. People in this category are imaginative, theoretical, abstract, future-oriented, or creative.

Jung described two kinds of judgment as thinking and feeling. Thinking judgment links or connects ideas so that new relationships can be detected. It uses the principles of cause-and-effect and tends to be impersonal. Those people characterized as thinking have a well-developed analytical ability, objectivity, concern with principles of justice and fairness, and good critical judgment.

Feeling judgment means the ability to weigh the relative values and merits of issues. This relies on an understanding of personal and group values. Feeling people tend toward an understanding of people, a concern for the human as opposed to the technical side of a problem. It is associated with a need for affiliation, a capacity for warmth, a desire for harmony, and an orientation that seeks to preserve the values of the past (Stice, 1987).

The MBTI has been well-established in the research literature. It is basically non-judgmental and used primarily with "well" people.

There are four basic preferences according to Jung which direct the use of perception and judgment:
1. Extroversion/introversion (EI)
2. Sensory perception/intuitive perception (SN)
3. Thinking judgment/feeling judgment (TF)
4. Judgment/perception (JP) (Myers-Briggs, 1985)

Extroverts develop student-centered classrooms. These instructors are very active and like to talk, assign group projects, and promote experiential learning. Students in these classes will have more choices about what they will study and how they will go about studying it.

Students who are extroverted learn best in active classrooms where there is movement, talk, and group projects. They prefer to learn theories or facts that connect with their past experience. They tend to jump into assignments and use trial-and-error rather than problem-solving methods.

Introverts tend to develop teacher-centered classes where the lecture is preferred to class discussions. The textbook and other instructional materials are used to structure the learning tasks.

Students are more quiet and less active during class time. They do not take part actively in discussions unless they have had time to prepare and reflect on what they are going to talk about. If pressured to participate, these students tend to withdraw.

Sensory perception instructors emphasize factual and concrete questions where there is a right and wrong response. They keep instruction focused on a narrow range of choices.

Students learn best when they move from the concrete to the abstract in a step-by-step progression. These students are exceptional at memorizing facts. Precision and accuracy are highly valued.

Intuitive instructors allow for a wide range of choices of student assignments. They focus on questions that involve conjecture and extrapolation—"What if...?"

Students value flashes of insight but are careless about details. They leap to a conceptual understanding of material and may daydream or act out during drill work or predominately factual lectures. These students tend to do well at imaginative tasks and theoretical topics.

Thinking judgment instructors do well at challenging students. They tend to offer little feedback and can be overly critical. At times they intimidate rather than motivate. This group of instructors is more likely to treat a class as a collective rather than individuals.

Students need a logical rationale for each project for maximum motivation. These students need acknowledgement of their competence from the instructor. They prefer topics that help thematically to understand systems or cause-and-effect relationships. Their thought is syllogistic and analytic.

Feeling judgment instructors treat a class as individuals and attempt to attend to individual student needs. They are more likely to motivate their students with praise and empathy.

Students are most motivated when given personal encouragement and when shown the human side of a topic. These students think to clarify their values and to establish their own network of values. Although their logic appears to be syllogistic, they usually evolve from some personally held belief or value.

Judgment types of instructors develop very orderly classrooms with schedules and deadlines. These instructors want to get things settled and wrapped up. They may decide things too quickly and may not notice new things that need to get done. They are satisfied when they reach a judgment on a thing, situation, or person.

Students gauge their learning by the completion of specific tasks and assignments. They prefer more structured learning environments that establish specific goals for them to meet.

Perceptive instructors develop more spontaneous classrooms in which there is more movement and open-ended discussion. They use flexible schedules and are good at adapting to changing situations. They are open to alternative approaches to doing things. This group of instructors has trouble making decisions. They often start too many projects and have difficulty realizing closure on them.

Students view learning as a free-wheeling, flexible quest. Deadlines are unimportant to them. Preference is for open and spontaneous learning environments rather than a structured classroom.

SENSING TYPES

	ANALYTICAL	AMIABLE
INTROVERTS – JUDGING	**ISTJ** Serious, quiet, earn success by concentration and thoroughness. Practical, orderly, matter-of-fact, logical, realistic, and dependable. See to it that everything is well-organized. Take responsibility. Make up their own minds as to what should be accomplished and work toward it steadily, regardless of protests or distractions. Live their outer life more with thinking, inner more with sensing.	**ISFJ** Quiet, friendly, responsible, and conscientious. Work devotedly to meet their obligations and serve their friends. Thorough, painstaking, accurate. May need time to master technical subjects, as their interests are not often technical. Patient with detail and routine. Loyal, considerate, concerned with how other people feel. Live their outer life more with feeling, inner more with sensing.
INTROVERTS – PERCEPTIVE	**ISTP** Cool onlookers, quiet, reserved, observing and analyzing life with detached curiosity and unexpected flashes of original humor. Usually interested in impersonal principles, cause and effect, or how and why mechanical things work. Exert themselves no more than they think necessary, because any waste of energy would be inefficient. Live their outer life more with sensing, inner more with thinking.	**ISFP** Retiring, quietly friendly, sensitive, modest about their abilities. Shun disagreements, do not force their opinions or values on others. Usually do not care to lead but are often loyal followers. May be rather relaxed about assignments or getting things done, because they enjoy the present moment and do not want to spoil it by undue haste or exertion. Live their outer life more with sensing, inner more with feeling.
EXTROVERTS – PERCEPTIVE	**ESTP** Matter-of-fact, do not worry or hurry, enjoy whatever comes along. Tend to like mechanical things and sports, with friends on the side. May be a bit blunt or insensitive. Can do math or science when they see the need. Dislike long explanations. Are best with real things that can be worked, handled, taken apart, or put back together. Live their outer life more with sensing, inner more with thinking.	**ESFP** Outgoing, easygoing, accepting, friendly, fond of a good time. Like sports and making things. Know what's going on and join in eagerly. Find remembering facts easier than mastering theories. Are best in situations that need sound common sense and practical ability with people as well as with things. Live their outer life more with sensing, inner more with feeling.
EXTROVERTS – JUDGING	**ESTJ** Practical realists, matter-of-fact, with a natural head for business or mechanics. Not interested in subjects they see no use for, but can apply themselves when necessary. Like to organize and run activities. Tend to run things well, especially if they remember to consider other people's feelings and points of view when making their decisions. Live their outer lives more with thinking, inner more with sensing.	**ESFJ** Warm-hearted, talkative, popular, conscientious, born cooperators, active committee members. Always doing something nice for someone. Work best with plenty of encouragement and praise. Little interest in abstract thinking or technical subjects. Main interest is in things that directly and visibly affect people's lives. Live their outer life more with feeling, inner more with sensing.

PERSUASIVE INTUITIVES ASSERTIVE

INFJ Succeed by perseverance, originality, and desire to do whatever is needed or wanted. Put their best efforts into their work. Quietly forceful, conscientious, concerned for others. Respected for their firm principles. Likely to be honored and followed for their clear convictions as to how best to service the common good. Live their outer life more with feeling, inner more with intuition.	**INTJ** Have original minds and great drive which they use only for their own purposes. In fields that appeal to them they have a fine power to organize a job and carry it through with or without help. Skeptical, critical, independent, determined, often stubborn. Must learn to yield less important points in order to win the most important. Live their outer life more with thinking, inner more with intuition.
INFP Full of enthusiasms and loyalties, but seldom talk of these until they know you well. Care about learning, ideas, language, and independent projects of their own. Tend to undertake too much, then somehow get it done. Friendly, but often too absorbed in what they are doing to be sociable or notice much. Live their outer life more with intuition, inner more with feeling.	**INTP** Quiet, reserved, brilliant in exams, especially in theoretical or scientific subjects. Logical to the point of hairsplitting. Interested mainly in ideas, with little liking for parties or small talk. Tend to have very sharply defined interests. Need to choose careers where some strong interest of theirs can be used and useful. Live their outer life more with intuition, inner more with thinking.
ENFP Warmly enthusiastic, high-spirited, ingenious, imaginative. Able to do almost anything that interests them. Quick with a solution for any difficulty and ready to help anyone with a problem. Often rely on their ability to improvise instead of preparing in advance. Can always find compelling reasons for whatever they want. Live their outer life more with intuition, inner more with feeling.	**ENTP** Quick, ingenious, good at many things. Stimulating company, alert and outspoken, argue for fun on either side of a question. Resourceful in solving new and challenging problems, but may neglect routine assignments. Turn to one new interest after another. Can always find logical reasons for whatever they want. Live their outer life more with intuition, inner more with thinking.
ENFJ Responsive and responsible. Feel real concern for what others think and want, and try to handle things with due regard for other people's feelings. Can present a proposal or lead a group discussion with ease and tact. Sociable, popular, active. Live their outer lives more with feeling, inner more with intuition.	**ENTJ** Hearty, frank, able leaders in activities. Usually good in anything that requires reasoning and intelligent talk, such as public speaking. Are well-informed and keep adding to their fund of knowledge. May sometimes be more positive and confident than their experience in an area warrants. Live their outer life more with thinking, inner more with intuition.

Left margin labels: INTROVERTS (JUDGING, PERCEPTIVE), EXTROVERTS (PERCEPTIVE, JUDGING)

BIBLIOGRAPHY

Eble, Kenneth E. (Ed.), (1980). <u>Improving teaching styles</u>. San Francisco: Jossey-Bass Publishers.

Grindler, Martha C., & Stratton, Beverly D. (1990, Spring). Type indicator and its relationship to teaching and learning styles. <u>Action in Teacher Education, VXII</u>(1), 31-34.

Jung, C. (1971). Psychological types (H.G. Baynes, trans. revised by R.F.C. Hull). Volume 6. <u>The Collected Works of C.G. Jung</u>. Princeton, NJ: Princeton University Press (original work published in 1921).

Myers, I.B., & McCaulley, M.H. (1985). <u>A guide to the development and use of the Myers-Briggs type indicator</u>. Palo Alto, CA: Consulting Psychology Press.

Stice, J.E. (Ed.), (1987, Summer). Developing critical thinking and problem-solving abilities. <u>New Directions for Teaching and Learning</u>. San Francisco: Jossey-Bass Publishers, 30.

Provost, Judith A., & Anchors, Scott (Eds.). (1988). <u>Applications of the Myers-Briggs type indicator in higher education</u>. Palo Alto, CA: Consulting Psychologists Press.

Chapter 5

The Architecture of a Well-Planned and Organized College Course

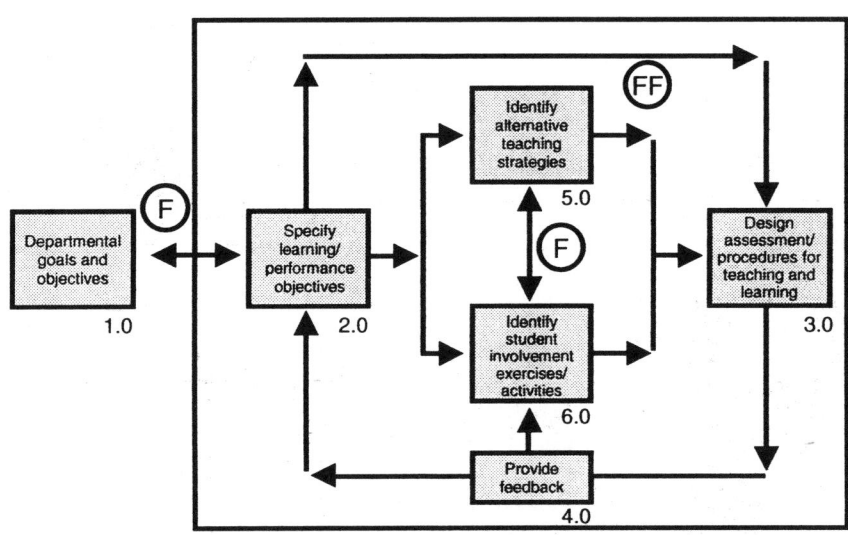

PLANNING AND ORGANIZING A COURSE

Learning performance objective
Design a new course, or redesign an existing course using the Instructional Systems Approach to Teaching (I.S.A.T.) model. Include in your course plan all items necessary for preplanning, delivery, administration, and evaluation. (Level 4)

Key ideas
1. The major areas of course organization include: preplanning, delivery, evaluation, and administration.
2. The selection of key subject matter topics will be influenced by the history of the course; prior instructors, the training and research interests of the instructor.
3. Every class should be articulated in a lesson plan, which is the class blueprint. It specifies what the instructor will do and what the students are expected to do.

New vocabulary
- plan and organize
- course structure
- prerequisite skills
- biographical sketch
- lesson plan
- preplanning
- teaching philosophy
- instructional strategy
- course delivery

Course planning and organization involves: (a) identifying all the elements and components needed to make up a course of instruction; (b) identifying the connections among these components; and (c) putting them together systematically to increase the probability of student learning. Course planning is enhanced by using the instructional development process which is part of the Instructional Systems Approach to Teaching (I.S.A.T.) model. The key elements of the instructional development process are
- goal specification
- learner analysis
- learning performance objectives
- criterion tests and other valid assessment procedures
- student activities and teaching strategies
- revision of instruction based on feedback about how well the students are learning.

Many of these elements individually have been found in teaching practices but not systematically applied (Earle, 1992).

Good course planning and organizing will result in improved classroom communication, which is the essence of good teaching. Planning and organizing are valued most when they simplify, clarify, and show relationships to a meaningful purpose. The course plan or blueprint encompasses every detail that the instructor incorporates into the course. The overall plan includes the course syllabus, a detailed outline of the course, that is provided to the students. This is covered in Chapter 6.

The purpose of this chapter is to provide the instructor with a broad outline of the four major areas that make up a course. These areas are not presented in any order since some can take place simultaneously. The most important course components include:
- A. Preplanning
- B. Course delivery
- C. Course administration
- D. Course evaluation

A. Preplanning

Preplanning includes all of the things that must be completed prior to actually teaching a class. It is done on a semester, unit (one to four weeks), and daily class basis. This phase ranges from topic and textbook selection to reviewing alternative instructional strategies and producing the audiovisual materials that will be used during class presentations. Most instructors will be producing these instructional materials several days before each class or even the day of the class if it is the first time the class has been taught.

This preplanning phase of course development provides the structure and threads that hold the course together. Students need to perceive and understand this structure if they are to be successful. It will be revealed in the statement of the end-of-course and the end-of-class learning performance objectives.

1. Selecting the Subject Matter Topics

One of the first and most important things the instructor will have to do in designing a new course is to determine which subject topics to include and which to exclude. This will be influenced by three major factors:

a. Prior instructors. Has the instructor inherited a course taught in the department for some time by senior faculty members? If so, can topics be deleted or added or are these topics locked in by tradition and politics or both? Have powerful senior faculty always done it a certain way? If the instructor is a new faculty member, how political would it be to attempt to make any major changes? Will the instructor be stepping on any "toes" by suggesting new changes? How big are the "toes" and how amenable are the senior faculty to these kinds of suggested changes? Will the instructor have some latitude in modifying the emphasis and time allocations for specific topics.

b. The history of the course. If the instructor is developing a brand new course, some general guidelines will be found in the departmental goals and objectives that will influence what is actually done in courses. Most of these goals and objectives will be very general statements of expected student learning outcomes for the department. For example, the instructor might find statements such as, "Instill a sense of justice and moral reasoning," or "Develop an ability to use critical thinking skills." General statements such as these will allow the instructor a great deal of latitude as to what and how to teach since each of these broad statements can be interpreted different ways. One technique is to list each departmental goal and objective. Then under it list each of the subject topics and course learning performance objectives to demonstrate how the departmental goals or objectives have been interpreted and how the course supports them.

c. <u>Professional values and research interests of the instructor</u>. Review the final topic selections with respected colleagues. Incorporate their ideas and suggestions when reasonable, political and practical. Keep notes of their suggestions and which suggestions were incorporated. Keep colleagues informed. Send them a memo and tell them of any action taken. This is important information that will be useful in a professional teaching portfolio.

2. Gathering Course Information

The selection of topics will involve many professional value judgments. Choices must be consistent with the goals and objectives of the academic department, which in turn must be consistent with the goals and objectives of the college and university. The choice of topics must also match the needs and interests of the intended student audience, otherwise the course will not attract students.

Begin by free thinking about the subject area. List at random in the upper left-hand corner of a 5" x 8" index card all the topics that come to mind—one topic per card. This larger card is recommended because it will be used to outline each topic. Write the learning performance objectives on one side at the top and the rationale for inclusion in the course on the back side. Speculate and dream. Don't question any choices. Don't worry about time or priorities. Just write the topics down. Put the cards away for a day or two. Add topics as they come to mind. Group the cards into logical units of instruction that appear to be related in some way around the same topic.

Given this initial and inclusive topic list, review all of the major textbooks available in the library, through colleagues, or on approval from textbook companies. Identify which of the selected topics are in the tables of content of these texts. Which topics were left out? Add, modify, and delete topics as needed. Copy the textbook tables of content for future reference since they are probably state-of-the-art in the subject discipline. If there are past course syllabi on file in the departmental office, review them for other topics.

Ask any colleagues who may have taught in related areas if they would review the proposed topic list. Also ask them if they know of any faculty at other institutions that may be teaching a similar course. Write to them and offer to exchange syllabi. Revise the topic list as data are gathered. Review any computer data bases available in the discipline such as PsychLit, ERIC, Agricola, or INFORM. Review what has been published in this area. Some additional topics will probably be identified that were not included in the original topic list. If there isn't enough information on a topic, decide whether to eliminate or include it. If the course is in a professional discipline such as engineering, nursing, teaching, or social work, ask potential employers to suggest relevant topics.

Write a one- or two-paragraph rationale for each of the topics on the back of the 5" x 8" card explaining why this topic is important within the context of the course. This may influence the decision to eliminate a topic or re-examine the emphasis placed on it. This rationale can be used later as part of the course syllabus. Prioritize the final topic list at this point.

If a graduate-level class is taught, there will be 15 150-minute classes. If an undergraduate class is taught, there will be 45 50-minute classes. The number of classes will influence the final number of topics selected and the depth in which they will be presented. Although some topics can be covered in a single class, others may require several classes. Make the final list of course topics, and sequence them within the course. Assign a temporary time limit for each topic and unit.

Enough data have been gathered at this point to write the course description. Avoid sweeping generalities. Use operational language, if possible, to describe the knowledge, skills, attitudes, and values that students will master at the completion of this new course. If a specific instructional strategy, such as lecture-discussion or case study, has been identified for use, describe it briefly. Take the final course description, topical outline, and sequence, and seek the advice of several senior faculty. Listen to them. They may have constructive suggestions based on years of experience. If they suggest changes, don't become defensive. Ask them to elaborate on their suggestions. Listen, and then listen some more. The final choice is that of the instructor of record.

3. Articulating a Teaching Philosophy

Review the teaching and learning assumptions identified earlier in Chapter 2. Define a philosophy of teaching that will describe how teaching will be approached. Actions in the classroom will be based upon this definition. If teaching is defined as lecturing, then the lecture will dominate most of the time, and the classroom will be passive. On the other hand, if teaching is defined as assisting students to become involved in their own learning, then the classroom will be active rather than passive and will require different instructional strategies. A teaching philosophy documented from the research literature will strengthen an instructor's credibility when a course is reviewed. A teaching philosophy should be included in the course syllabus and in a professional teaching portfolio.

4. *Alternative Instructional Strategies*

The philosophy of education will greatly influence the choices of instructional strategies. An instructional strategy consists of two parts. First, it is the way in which the instructor will communicate with students. For example, will the instructor lecture at students with minimal interactions, or will the instructor preplan many higher level questions that require application and critical thinking? Will the instructor create exercises and activities that involve students in problem solving and critical thinking such as simulations, case studies, role playing, peer teaching, contract teaching, or the use of situational analysis?

Second, an instructional strategy specifies how the instruction will be delivered physically. For example, will the instructor teach in a live classroom with students physically present or through instructional television? Will there be any use of audiographic teaching or telephone conferencing? Will programmed texts or computer-assisted instruction be incorporated in any way? Each of these strategies will require a different set of teaching skills as well as classroom planning procedures.

5. *Prerequisite Course Skills*

Describe in specific language the prerequisite knowledge, skills, and attitudes that students were expected to have learned prior to this new class in order to succeed. Review them with the instructors who taught these prerequisite courses. Also, consider the expectations of this new course against what the students, in fact, have covered in their classes. Include in the new course skills, knowledge, and attitudes that have not been covered in the prior classes. If students cannot meet the prerequisite expectations, and they have no means to master them, the probability of a high failure rate is significantly increased. Who will have failed?

6. *Student Audience*

Who are the students that will probably take this course? What is the age range? Are they mostly young students, adults, or a mixture? What kinds of real-world experiences will they bring to class? Why are they taking this course? Is this course required or elective? Will these students be highly motivated or somewhat indifferent? What are their previous education and training?

7. Preparation of Instructional Materials

If the instructor intends to use overhead transparencies, 35mm slides, videotapes, posters, handouts, or other media, advanced planning is paramount in order to prevent a last-minute rush. The use of well-developed instructional materials will enhance instructor presentations and improve communication skills with students. Investigate what kind of teaching support services are available and what the associated costs are. Determine what is realistic to prepare and what departmental funds are available for preparation by media specialists.

If handouts are anticipated for use, who will type them, proofread them, and make arrangements to have them reproduced, collated, and assembled? This is an enormous task. The instructor must be realistic as to how much he or she is physically capable of doing. Materials may have to be planned over several courses.

8. Selection of a Classroom

If a lot of projected instructional media or television materials will be used throughout the course, the instructor should look around the campus for the best classroom facilities. Many classrooms will have permanent screens and overhead projectors as well as television sets. Schedule these rooms well in advance of the course–several semesters if possible. If television will be used frequently, will it be shown without interruption on videotape, or will the videotape be stopped and replayed? Is there a videotape playback unit permanently installed in classrooms or will the instructor have to bring one to class each time it is needed?

9. Biographical Sketch (sample on following page)

The biographical sketch is a brief, one-page narrative outline that provides information for students about the instructor's professional background and possibly some personal information. Information that could be included covers such things as: instructors name; place of birth; schools attended; work experiences and special training; any special honors; kinds of publications; research interests; teaching philosophy; activities in regional and national organizations. On the personal side, mention might be made of interests and hobbies; leisure time interests and activities; and special vacation interests.

The biographical sketch can be used in a course; for professional introductions; newspaper releases; background information for consultancies and special seminars; or whenever someone needs background information. A brief biographical sketch is an interesting technique to gather data on students. It will provide the instructor with some interesting background information that could be used in class to personalize a course.

BIOGRAPHICAL SKETCH

THOMAS E. CYRS, ED.D.

As the Director of the Center for Educational Development and Professor of Educational Management and Development at New Mexico State University in Las Cruces, New Mexico, Thomas E. Cyrs is responsible for assisting faculty in the development of distance education courses, training faculty for television teaching, consulting with faculty in all aspects of traditional teaching, and a broad range of media services.

Prior to his current position, he was Director of Curriculum and Associate Professor of Pharmaceutical Education at the University of Minnesota (1975-1978). In this position he specialized in competency-based health education. During this time he was the 1978 recipient of the Rufus A. Lyman Award for outstanding research in pharmaceutical education.

From 1970-1975 he was the Director of the Division of Instructional Systems Development at Northeastern University in Boston. Responsibilities included identifying, developing, and evaluating innovative alternatives to traditional course development via television and other media. During this period of time two of the first major interactive television courses were designed in the areas of psychology and history.

Advanced degrees include a Master (1963) and Doctor of Education (1970) in Instructional Systems Design and Administration from Boston University.

Major published texts are in the areas of health education, competency-based pharmaceutical education, teleclassroom teaching, and traditional college teaching. Other publications have been aimed primarily at practical approaches to course design in all aspects of traditional and non-traditional teaching and training. His most recent text, used in a graduate class on college teaching, is entitled, <u>Essential Strategies for College Teaching</u>.

As a national and international consultant and seminar leader to faculty and staff from numerous post-secondary institutions, the National Dairy Council, the U.S. Military, business and industry, government groups, community colleges, and research universities, he has provided services in all aspects of teaching, training, program, and course design. He is president of his own consulting firm, Educational Development Associates. He has been active in numerous professional organizations including the Association for Educational Communications and Technology; American Educational Research Association; and the American Association of Higher Education.

Hobbies include birding, fishing, and hunting as well as bird sculpting and carving.

B. Course Delivery

Delivery involves the presentation of the themes, concepts, and topics (either live or mediated) to large or small groups of students. This includes the actual oral presentation with or without the use of audiovisuals, or presentation through media such as videotape, film, or computer-based instruction. The most important guide will be the lesson plans that have been developed. In reality, time may not be available to develop all of the lesson plans before the start of class. They may have to be developed as the course is taught. Try to plan these as far in advance as possible.

C. Course Evaluation

The purpose of evaluation is to provide feedback to determine the degree to which learning is taking place as well as the effectiveness of the teaching methods. Evaluation should take place during the class (formative) and at the completion of a class (summative). It can be done by the students, instructor (self-evaluation), peers, and administration. Some evaluation data should be used solely for the purpose of teaching improvement while other evaluation data can be used for the purpose of tenure, promotion, and salary advancement. The more data there are to support an instructor's teaching competence, the stronger the case will be for promotion and tenure.

D. Course Administration

The administration of a course includes all those things that must be done to make the course run smoothly including the use of the course syllabus; arranging for the use of audiovisual equipment; scheduling a television cable system; typing and proofreading lectures and handouts; the use of library resources; arranging for field trips; computer center utilization; and classroom scheduling.

In addition to these important items, consideration must be given to such things as absences and make-ups for quizzes and tests; policies for consistent tardiness to class; ways of handling unanticipated discipline problems; after-class office hours; instructor availability by telephone; and out-of-class activities.

Other important areas will require the outline of the responsibilities of any teaching assistants assigned to the course. What does the instructor expect them to do? How much latitude do they have to determine course content and teaching methods? How much time will the instructor spend with them to improve their teaching skills? How will they be evaluated?

What policies are needed in case the instructor is sick and misses one or more classes? Do arrangements have to be made in advance with another instructor to cover classes in return for covering their classes for the same reasons? This is where lesson plans would be very helpful to provide continuity for a class.

Is class attendance required or optional? Who will take attendance? How should this be done?

THE LESSON PLAN

Instructors walk into the classroom the first day of each semester for each assigned course. What do they do and say? What do they teach and how do they go about teaching it? What guides their actions? The lesson plan is the master blueprint designed by instructors to guide and document their teaching. It spells out for each class period exactly what to teach, why the topics are important to teach, and how to teach them. Good planning results in instructor positive self-confidence that generates enthusiasm in knowing that he or she is well prepared.

The lesson plan will allow the instructor to reflect on what worked and what did not work within the lesson and why; what the students liked and what they did not; what would be done differently the next time and why. These reflections can be used later and can be incorporated into a professional teaching portfolio.

A lesson plan can be used to cover one class period or an entire unit of instruction made up of two or more class periods. If multiple lesson plans are used within a unit, it should be noted on the plan.

How much detail should be used in a lesson plan depends upon the instructor. For future planning, it is better to have too much information than not enough. The following items should be incorporated into a lesson plan regardless of its physical format.

1. Course title and number.
2. Lesson title and the date. The number of each lesson for later reference.
3. Unit title if there are multiple lessons.
4. Instructional strategies for the lesson.
5. Audiovisual and/or television equipment needed.
6. Student questions and the intended intellectual level (knowledge, understanding, application, critical thinking).
7. Presentation outline–key points and sequence. The level of detail in an outline depends on the familiarity of the instructor with the subject matter to be taught. Each presentation outline should begin with a brief review of the previous lesson; a review of the learning performance objectives of the current lesson; key presentation points; and a brief summary of the lesson.
8. Exercises and activities used to involve the students.
9. References for students' outside readings.
10. Homework assignments.

11. Personal reflections of teaching.
12. End-of-lesson terminal learning performance objective(s).
13. Intermediate learning performance objectives.
14. Identification of all overhead transparencies, 35mm slides, flipcharts, videoclips, hang-ups, posters, artifacts etc., and their place in the presentation. If relevant, outline the content of each.
15. Names of any guest speakers and what they will speak about.
16. Handouts.
17. List of books, articles, or any other reference materials needed for class.
18. A time guesstimate for each intermediate learning performance objective.

A physical layout of the lesson plan is suggested on the following page along with a sample lesson plan from GS590, "Essential Skills for College Teaching."

**If you don't know where you are going with your teaching and what you want your students to learn,
any path will get you there.**

Lesson Plan

Instructor

Course Title

Lesson Title	Time ☐50 ☐75 ☐150

Date

Learning Performance Objectives	Level

Assessment Procedures

Outline/Strategies	Visuals

Handouts	Learning Activities	References

Lesson Plan

Instructor

Course Title

Lesson Title No. 3 Good News as Storytelling; trigger videos; Teaching Portfolios

Time ☐ 50 ☐ 75 ☐ 150

Date Sept 20, 1993

Learning Performance Objectives	Skill Level
• Describe the components of a story & how it can be used in teaching	2
• Describe a trigger video & video scenario & how it can be used in teaching.	2
• Explain the elements of a Teaching Portfolio & how it can be used to promote teaching faculty.	2

Assessment Procedures

5-16

Outline/Strategies	Visuals
1. Explain "Good News" as storytelling- 10 points grade	
2. TC tell story - McDuff - FS tell story - Mark Twain	Dog Puppet
3. Pass out sign up sheet for "Good News"	

4. Pass out & explain Good News Presentation Assessment Criteria & review
   a. Each instructor will rate/comment - average
   b. Each student will rate/comment - average of class
   c. Class average & instructor average = total points (10)	

5. Explain trigger videos & video scenarios Tell story: Lesson Plan	Show triggers - Susan's Keys & Nick Nolte- decision

6. Explain "The Professional Teaching Portfolio"
   Mandatory if you are now teaching. May write paper or grant on teaching subject
   Recommend Peter Seldin
	Trumpet & horns
	Trumpet music in

7. Assignment: Chapters 14, 15, 16	

Handouts	Learning Activities	References
4. Wrap it in a story Good News Presentation Assessment Criteria		
5. Trigger videos & Video scenarios		
6. Nancy Baptiste Sample Portfolio Peter - Biology		

BIBLIOGRAPHY

Bass, R.K., & Dills, C.R. (1984). <u>Instructional development: The state of the art</u>. IA: Kendall/Hunt.

Briggs, L., & Gagne, R.M. (1974). <u>Principles of instructional design</u>. San Francisco: Holt, Rinehart and Winston.

Briggs, L.J., et al (Eds.). (1981). <u>Handbook of procedures for the design of instruction</u>, (2nd ed.). NJ: Educational Technology Publications.

Carey, L., & Dick, W. (1978). <u>The systematic design of instruction</u>. Dallas: Scott, Foresman.

Eble, K.E. (1989). <u>The craft of teaching</u>. San Francisco: Jossey-Bass.

Earle. (1992)

G.P. Courseware. (1983). <u>Designing and managing instructional programs</u>. MD: General Physics.

Grasha, A.F. (1975). A planning sequence to assist faculty in selecting course designs. <u>Educational Technology</u>, 9-16.

Kozma, R.B., Belle, Lawrence W., & Williams, G.W. (1978). <u>Instructional techniques in higher education</u>. NJ: Educational Technology Publications.

Melton, R. F. (1982). <u>Instructional models for course design and development</u>. NJ: Educational Technology Publications.

Milton, O., & Associates. (1985). <u>On college teaching</u>. San Francisco: Jossey-Bass.

Reigeluth, C. (1983). <u>Instructional design theories and models: An overview of their current status</u>. NJ: Lawrence Eribaum Associates.

Segall, A.J., et al. (1975). <u>Systematic course design for the health fields</u>. NY: John Wiley.

Taba, H. (1962). <u>Curriculum development: Theory and practice</u>. Chicago: Harcourt, Brace and World.

Chapter 6

The Course Syllabus: A Legal Covenant With Your Students

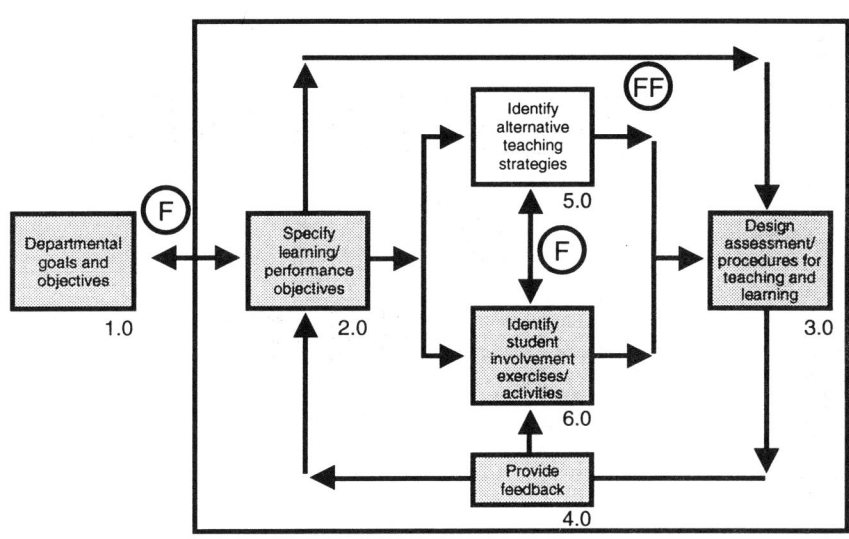

THE COURSE SYLLABUS: A COVENANT WITH YOUR STUDENTS

LEARNING PERFORMANCE OBJECTIVE
Construct a course syllabus which includes all data relevant to the course administration, general course information, class information and special information. (Level 4).

KEY IDEAS
1. A course syllabus is a legal covenant with students. It is the most important communication device that an instructor can use to provide critical course information.
2. Information in a syllabus is organized as administrative, general course, class and special information.
3. It is preferable to provide too much detail than not enough.
4. If it isn't in writing in the syllabus, it doesn't exist.

NEW VOCABULARY
- syllabus
- target audience
- class policies
- grading
- special options information

The course syllabus is one of the most important communication devices that can be used with students. It is a permanent, written document that provides all of the critical information that a student will need to complete a course. The syllabus is a "legally written covenant" between the student and instructor. It is a publicly binding agreement as to what the instructor expects, how the student should proceed, and how the student will be evaluated. Any changes in the syllabus must be communicated in writing to the students (Neff and Weimer, 1990). When all directions and expectations are in writing, little room is left for doubt and confusion as so often exists in the college classroom.

The primary purpose of the course syllabus is to bring the instructor and the student together on the same communication track with enough detail to provide unambiguous direction.

There are many variations of a course syllabus ranging from an abbreviated single page listing of topics, dates, and textbook chapters to very comprehensive outlines which deal with almost every detail of a course. Many faculty feel that too much detail detracts from course flexibility and use the abbreviated format. This instructor/author feels that the syllabus should provide as much detail as is reasonable in a comprehensive format. The latter demonstrates how much planning and thought an instructor has put into a course.

SPECIAL SYLLABUS COMPONENTS
When constructing a course syllabus, information is organized under the following four areas:

A. Administrative information
B. General course information
C. Class information
D. Special course options information

A sample course syllabus used by this author has been included at the end of this chapter.

Administrative information
Administrative information contains all of the details and procedures to make a course run smoothly. Included are the course title; catalogue number and section as it appears in official university records; meeting time, day, and location; name and highest degree of the instructor of record; textbook(s) title; mention of books and articles on reserve in the library.

Other data to be provided in a syllabus include official and unofficial office hours; office and home address; telephone numbers including a personal home number if the instructor is willing to talk to students on his or her free time; and fax and E-mail numbers. How much of these data is provided to students is a matter of personal choice. Some data such as office hours will be mandated by the academic department. If the instructor posts office hours, keep them without exception. If the instructor cannot be available for some reason, students should be told in advance during class. There is nothing more frustrating for students than to go to an office during posted hours and consistently find that the instructor is unavailable. The syllabus will have a general course description and a rationale as to why the course is important.

General course information
The general course description is usually taken from the course catalogue. This description in the catalogue and in the syllabus should avoid sweeping generalizations. The instructor should provide very specific information detailing what the course is all about and what the students can learn.

The instructor should include a description of the course target audience(s). For example, is the course primarily for history majors, students with a broad background of technical experience, or possibly students with a low math ability? If there are any prerequisite courses, knowledge bases, or skills, that the students are expected to possess when they begin a course, list them in order to prevent any confusion and probable failure.

Also included in this section is a biographical sketch of the instructor of record. It is important for students to see where the instructor has worked and what type of educational and special training experiences he or she has had. The biographical sketch should not exceed a single page. If there are teaching or graduate assistants working with the instructor, a one- or two-paragraph background sketch on each student would be helpful and should be included in the syllabus.

Some instructors have requested that each student in their classes also write a brief one-page background information sheet about themselves. This will provide personal information about your students and their special interests. Information can be requested about their education, work experience, special interests, skills, and hobbies. Each class can start by directing questions to several students about information contained in their information sheet. It adds a little personal touch to your class. If the instructor wants to be more formal with the student biographical sketch, a special handout form has been included on the next page.

What are the general course goals and specific learning performance objectives of the course? Goals are broad umbrella statements such as, " I want my students to develop an understanding and real appreciation of... in my course." Learning performance objectives are specific observable statements of learning outcomes. Course learning performance objectives define in specific operational language what it is that the students are expected to know, feel, and do at the end of a course. Intermediate learning performance objectives define what it is that all students should know, feel, and do at the end of each class period.

How was the course developed? Is there a specific format or instructional strategy that has been selected? Will the primary source of information be in the lectures? Will students be allowed to ask questions–when? Will handouts and/or study guides be used–what kind? What are the responsibilities of the students? Will the instructor use a variety of instructional media such as films, videotapes, overhead transparencies, 35mm slides, etc? What are the specific class policies? Is attendance required or optional? Will class attendance have any impact on the final grade of the student? Will excused absences be allowed–how many? If a student calls the instructor in advance of class with a legitimate excuse, will it be accepted verbally or will a written note be required? What are the times and dates of a drop/add in the course and what is the university policy? Repeat this in your syllabus.

Will the instructor give an incomplete grade if it is justified? What are the conditions under which the university will allow an incomplete grade? If a student has reading and writing problems (dyslexia), what are the conditions to provide more time and give an incomplete grade? What about disabled students, are there any provisions for them to provide more time? What are the condition under which tardy students are accepted or rejected? Is there a number of tardy classes that will be allowed? What are the consequences? Will daily attendance be taken–by whom? If the student feels that there is an error, how can they appeal this to the instructor? Under what conditions will a student be allowed to make up a test or exam if they have a reasonable excuse? Are there any restrictions? Is there a departmental policy or college policy within which the instructor must work? How will the instructor handle a student who constantly disrupts a class presentation or needs to leave because of illness?

Does the instructor have a policy for accepting late homework? How much makeup time will be allowed? Will homework tardiness have any effect on the final grade?

If a student has an unprepared project or presentation, is there a policy that requires a written excuse, verbal explanation only, or both? How much time will be allowed for make up? Will this have any impact on the final grade–how?

Explain grading procedures in detail. How will the instructor compute the final grade? What goes into the final grade? How much is each part worth? Will special papers or projects be allowed to boost the final grade? What kinds and when are they due? Can a test or exam be re-taken if the student does poorly? How much and under

Student Biographical Sketch
GS 590

1. Name_____

2. Home Address_____ Home Telephone_____

3. Place of Business_____ Business Telephone_____

4. Status: Senior Undergraduate_____ Master's _____ Doctoral _____

5. Department_____ Major _____

6. Married (response is optional): Yes _____ Spouse's Name _____ No _____

7. Do you have experience teaching?   Yes _____ No _____
   Level of teaching and number of years: Elementary _____ Secondary _____
   University _____ Vocational _____ Military _____
   Business _____ Health Professions _____

8. What do you expect to learn in this course? What objectives and/or skills do you hope to learn. Please be as specific as possible.

   _____

   _____

   _____

   _____

9. Are you taking this course for: S/U   Grade   Audit   (Circle One)

10. Hobbies or special interests:

    _____

    _____

    _____

    _____

what conditions will class participation count on the final grade? How will the instructor make this determination? How important are papers and projects in the computation of the final grade? Exactly how many points or other criteria?

Class information

The class information begins with a course calendar by class, day, and/or week. It includes the class number and the date on which it will meet. If the instructor will be attending a convention or it is known in advance that the instructor will miss a class, this is noted on the calendar. It should be noted on the instructor's calendar if another instructor will teach the class, or if the instructor will give a presentation on instructional television, or if the class will be canceled. Holidays are also listed. Indicate all due dates for special projects and term papers as well as other types of student activities. Under this section, which usually comes at the front end of the syllabus, the instructor might establish a condition for any changes to the course syllabus.

This author puts the following condition on the FIRST PAGE of the syllabus:

> **This syllabus is comprehensive and covers a lot of detail. Read it carefully and ask questions about anything that you do not understand. Because of any extenuating circumstances, this syllabus is <u>subject to change</u>. I will provide all changes to you <u>in writing</u> as far in advance as possible.**

Special course options information

In addition to the types of information suggested to this point, there is one other section, called the special course options, which would include things that are not commonly found in a course syllabus. Here the instructor would explain his or her particular approach to teaching and why it was chosen. For example, the instructor could address the following questions:

1. Do you believe that teaching is primarily instructor-centered–all primary course information will be provided within the lectures and textbook?
2. Do you believe that the role of the instructor is that of a facilitator–the students must accept primary responsibility for their own learning?
3. Do you subscribe to the idea of cooperative learning–the students will work in small groups on common projects and share a common grade?
4. Will you provide a series of learning contracts with individual students and allow them to work independently with optional class attendance?
5. What is the level and quality of thinking you expect of your students that goes beyond the level of factual recall such as understanding, application, and critical thinking and problem-solving?
6. Do you expect your students to apply ideas, principles, and rules?
7. Do you expect your students to analyze data, produce original papers or products, and evaluate the fruits of their efforts by generating criteria to make judgments? A sample test or exam question could be included to demonstrate exactly what is meant.
8. Do you intend to use Interactive Study Guides or other types of handouts

that are closely correlated to your presentations? If so, explain what they are and why you are using them. Explain how to use the learning performance objectives to study for a test. Set up special help sessions and explain how they will be conducted.
9. To what degree do you want your students to freely express their opinions and explore their personal and professional values and attitudes? Explain why this is important and any ground rules that you feel are important to this type of discussion.

The syllabus, or student reference manual, is an important document that is intended to communicate to the students all of the important information within a course. Enough detail should be included so that the student will know exactly what the course is all about; what topics will be covered and at what times; how they will be graded; and what intellectual and attitudinal skills they will be required to master.

A sample course syllabus has been included on the following pages from a course taught by this author entitled, "GS 590: Essential Skills for College Teaching." The syllabus from a course taught by the instructor is included for your review. It is based on the philosophy <u>that more is better</u>.

GS 590: ESSENTIAL SKILLS for COLLEGE TEACHING

Syllabus

Course Instructor **Thomas E. Cyrs, Ed.D.**
Director, Center for Educational Development
Professor, Educational Management and Development

assisted by

Frank A. Smith, M.A.
Assistant Director, Center for Educational Development

Fall 1993

Essential Skills for College Teaching
GS 590

Please Follow Directions

**Bring this syllabus as well
as the text with you
to each class.**

**In case of extenuating circumstances
this syllabus is subject to change.
I will provide all changes to you
in writing as far in advance
as possible.**
      T. Cyrs

Course Title: Essential Skills for College Teaching

Catalogue Number: GS 590

Graduate Catalogue Description: 3 credits. Provides a broad overview of teaching skills that have been shown to be effective and are founded in current research in a college classroom and/or training environment. A lecture laboratory provides a diagnostic instrument to improve presentation and planning skills.

Meeting Date, Time and Location: Monday, 4:30-7:00 p.m., Milton Hall Room 84

Course Instructor: Thomas E. Cyrs, Ed.D.
                     Director, Center for Educational Development
                     Professor, Educational Management and Development

                     Assisted by: Frank A. Smith, M.A.
                                    Assistant Director, Center for Educational Development

Office Hours: The instructor is available by appointment in the Center for Educational Development
                     Located in Milton Hall Room 50
                     Office telephone: 646-2204
                     Home telephone: 523-9565
                     Office FAX: 646-5010

Textbook: Cyrs, Thomas E. (1993). <u>Essential Skills for College Teaching: A Systems Approach</u>. Las Cruces, NM: Center for Educational Development, New Mexico State University. (Available in the Center for Educational Development, Milton Hall Room 50).

Reserve Articles: Copies of all required articles will be made available on reserve in the New Library.

TERMINAL LEARNING PERFORMANCE OBJECTIVES

COURSE OBJECTIVES:
Upon completion of GS 590, Essential Skills for College Teaching,
each student will critically analyze and personally reflect upon their current strengths and areas in need of improvement in their teaching practices and skills by:
1. Identifying their professional teaching style.
2. Reflect upon the impact of a past teacher on their professional development and present this to the class as "Good News."
3. Identify areas of professional growth in teaching by developing a professional teaching portfolio.
4. Observe three other college instructors teaching and analyze their teaching strengths that they would incorporate into their teaching.
5. Working with a small group of students (4-6), identify a common topic of interest in college teaching, conduct a literature review, and present the conclusions to the class, modeling the teaching strategies presented during class.

INTRODUCTION

As director of a Center charged with assisting faculty to improve their teaching, I am asked many questions in a variety of contexts in many different places on campus. All questions are serious concerns of teaching faculty which are often asked tangentially: "Suppose an instructor...; A teacher whom I once knew...; This friend of mine who teaches at another university had a problem with teaching that concerned...; What if an instructor had a problem with...; I heard that... ." All queries are important to the instructor and need attention at that moment. Let's visit with one very concerned and sensitive instructor who was seriously searching for priorities among conflicting values.

A second-year faculty member came to visit me a number of years ago. This instructor was an assistant professor in arts and sciences and was confused about professional priorities. The instructor really liked to teach but knew that promotion and tenure would be based more on publishing and a good research record. The first year of teaching was described as a first year of learning about teaching since the instructor had never had any training on how to teach. The department head, in one of their rare meetings, advised this instructor that a Ph.D. in a specialty area qualified one to teach. In other words, if an instructor knew the subject area well, it could be taught. This sensitive and concerned instructor felt badly about the students taught in the first year. It was felt that they had been cheated by having a less than adequate teacher.

When I met this instructor the first time, the informal dialogue led to a plea for help to improve teaching. "I don't know what I should know," was the conclusion. "I'm not sure that I'm teaching the right things in the right way." Looking at me with a seriousness that I hadn't seen in a long time, the instructor asked, "What do I need to know about college teaching?" "Can you help me?" I knew that I could work with this instructor. What an opportunity to work with a professional who really cared and wanted to improve teaching skills.

During some initial informal conversation I asked this instructor to help me by being specific about what was perceived to be problem areas. The instructor pulled out a note pad and almost outlined this course. These were the perceived needs:
1. How do I organize a course?
2. How can I be sure that I am covering the right "stuff?"
3. My questions during my class seem to cluster around recall of factual data. How can I improve my questioning skills?
4. Speaking in front of groups of students petrifies me. How can I improve my delivery skills?
5. Students in most of my classes complain that my tests are unfair. They say that I teach one thing and then test for another. What is my problem?
6. Too many of my students seem bored with my lectures. How can I turn them on to my discipline?
7. I seem to talk too much during my class. How can I get my students involved?
8. I would like to use different kinds of audiovisual techniques but have no idea of how to do it. What do I need to know?
9. I'm going to a conference to present a poster session. How do I develop a good one?
10. I really like to teach but have a lot of trouble organizing my lectures. How can I improve my skills?
11. I attended a series of lectures at my old alma mater in which the instructor used great handouts. How can I develop them?
12. Can you recommend some good teachers on our campus that I can observe? And, by the way, what is it in their teaching that they do or say that makes you recommend them?

These questions are fundamental to college teaching. They are honest, incisive, basic, fundamental, and essential to the process of college teaching.
I receive many of these questions every semester. For me, they are challenging and exciting because I know that every one can be addressed. Teaching is an acquired skill that can be developed and improved with training, practice, caring, and reflection.

This course is designed to address these questions in a highly participative environment.

Punctuality: Class begins promptly at 4:30 p.m. Please be on time. The instructors are as busy and committed as the students. We respect your time commitments. Please respect ours.

Class Attendance: Class attendance is <u>required</u> and will reflect on the final grade unless there is an <u>excused</u> absence. Each unexcused absence will result in the deduction of two (2) points from your final point total. There may be no more than three (3) excused absences. After the fourth absence, you will be dropped from the course. Call 646-1019 to request an excused absence.

Homework: All classes have assigned readings which you are expected to complete <u>before</u> class. Late assignments will not be accepted without <u>prior</u> approval.

Course Overview

This course has been developed to provide basic and advanced skills for the entry level and experienced college instructor and professional trainer. A major portion of the course will deal with student involvement strategies; handout alternatives; lesson plans; the teaching portfolio; critical thinking; and the active classroom. Current research on what is known about effective teachers and teaching will be reviewed.

Course Audiences

This course has been designed to address teaching and training skills needed by instructors in community colleges; research universities; industry; military; health professions; and government trainers.

Course Preface: No one cares unless they share.

We appreciate that you have valued teaching enough to take this course from 4:30 to 7:00 p.m. after a long and hard day. We realize that you are tired (we are, too) and hungry. We appreciate that you are extremely busy during the week and are always pressed for time (we are, too). We would appreciate it if you realized that we have spent a great deal of time and effort developing this course and have tried to be sensitive to your needs. Each topic has been thoroughly researched and readings have been carefully selected. We are sensitive to the fact that you are less interested in theory and are more concerned with what you can use <u>now</u> in your teaching. We will begin class <u>on time</u> so that we can best use the time available. Please respect those colleagues that do arrive on time. If you are late for any reason, you will miss some of the material presented. At times you will have conflicts or other priorities. You will be held responsible for all material covered. We care and hope that you do also. If you know that you will be absent, please call us to make whatever arrangements are necessary to help you.

Your feedback and constructive criticism are valued. Let us know what you like and dislike. We encourage your questions and frequent comments. Often they really make us think and reflect on what we are teaching. At times you will stump us–great–we will learn together. If we can't respond on the spot, we will find the answer and respond to all of you in writing. We hope that you will do the same.

Please share your ideas and teaching treasures with us. <u>Help us</u> to make this a rewarding course.

Biographical Sketch
Frank A. Smith

Frank A. Smith is the Assistant Director of the Center for Educational Development at New Mexico State University. His responsibilities include coordination of instructional development, faculty development, and media services, teaching improvement and evaluation, consulting with faculty, and the design of telecourses and training seminars for television instructors.

Prior to his current position he was the Director of the Learning Resource Center in the College of Education at NMSU; Head of Media Services and Research Associate at the Southwest Regional Laboratory for Educational Research and Development in Los Alamitos, California; instructor and research assistant at Arizona State University and public school teacher.

Academic credentials include the Bachelor of Arts Degree and the Master of Arts Degree in Instructional Technology from Arizona State University. Also completed were two years of post-Master's level study and teaching in the area of Educational Psychology (55 credit hours) at Arizona State University.

Publications are in the areas of instructional development, training for television teachers, distance education networks, promoting students' involvement in instruction, designing interactive study guides with word pictures, presenting a positive image on television. The most recent book, Teleclass Teaching: A Resource Guide, Second Edition, was co-authored with Thomas E. Cyrs.

By consulting and leading more than 50 seminars, he has provided leadership in the areas of course development and teacher training to community colleges, universities, businesses, and the military.

Professional associations have included the Association for Educational Communications and Technology, the American Educational Research Association, the National Society for the Study of Education, Phi Delta Kappa, the Rural Education Association, and the Professional and Organizational Development Network.

(A biographical sketch for Thomas E. Cyrs can be found on page 5-9 of this text.)

Class Information - GS 590

Assignment and Grade

Those students taking this course for a grade can opt for an S/U or a letter grade and must complete each assignment as specified unless approved by the instructor. If you are auditing this course, you have no obligation to complete any assignment. Most faculty and staff who have audited this course have opted to participate in all assigned activities in order to derive the maximum benefit. The decision is yours. You will be asked to make your choice by the end of the second class.

Maximum Points	Points Earned	Assignment	Due Date
10	_____	The Good News	_____
25	_____	Group Project (average of class ratings and instructor ratings)	_____
15	_____	Individual Contributions to Group Project (average of team member ratings)	_____
15	_____	Three (3) Teaching Observations (5 pts. per observation)	12-6-93
20	_____	Professional Teaching Portfolio OR Research Paper/Proposal/Article	12-13-93
12	_____	Progress Quizzes (4 @ 3 pts. each)	Unannounced
3	_____	Teaching Analogy (either hat or artifact)	_____
100*			

Translation of points earned to letter grade:

90 - 100   A
80 - 89   B
70 - 79   C
60 - 69   D
0 - 59   F

* Each unexcused absence will result in a deduction of two points from the final points earned. If absences exceed three classes, the student will be dropped.

Course Outline - GS 590

Session	Date	Topics	Text Chapters
1	8-30	Instructor & student introduction; class format; take MBTI	
	9-6	No Class	
2	9-13	MBTI interpretation-guest; group assignments; teaching observations	4, 22
3	9-20	"Good News" as storytelling; trigger videos & video scenarios; Teaching Portfolio (due 12-13-93); group meet #1	14, 15, 16
4	9-27	Presentation skills; sample trigger; group meet #2 (topic approval)	5, 6, 19
5	10-4	Good news #1 & #2; sample trigger; developing the lesson plan; group meet #3	1
6	10-11	Good news #3 & #4; sample trigger; systems approach to teaching; group meet #4	7
7	10-18	Good news #5 & #6; constructing learning performance objectives; group meet #5	8, 9
8	10-25	Good news #7 & #8; sequencing instruction; critical thinking; group meet #6	11, 12
9	11-1	Good news #9 & #10; mid-course evaluation; active classrooms; student involvement activities; group meet #7	17
10	11-8	Good news #11 & #12; Questioning skills for higher levels of learning; group meet #8	2, 3
11	11-15	Good news #13 & #14; sample trigger; what does the research say about effective college teachers; project presentation #1	19, 20, 21
12	11-22	Good news #15 & #16; alternatives to traditional testing & grading; project presentation #2	10
13	11-29	Good news #17 & #18; sample trigger; gender issues in the college classroom; project presentation #3	17, 18, 20
14	12-6	Good news #19 & #20; sample trigger; teaching observations; project presentation #4	
15	12-13	Self-esteem & the college instructor; final course evaluation; video: "Classroom of the Heart"	

Your Responsibility as a Student in This Class

This is a special class developed for a very special group of students–current and future college teachers. This is a very mixed audience: New faculty; experienced faculty; administrators; teaching assistants who may have never taught a class before.

You will receive the greatest benefit by reading the assigned text chapters and outside readings <u>before</u> class. These assignments will provide you with background material and the research basis for many of the conclusions and suggestions. It has been our experience that without this informational foundation, you will not be able to actively participate beyond simple clarification of basic vocabulary. Yes, we do have a specialized vocabulary in teaching just as you do in your discipline. When you hear classmates comment, "What does that mean? I never heard of that," you can be sure that they have not done their "homework." Just like your own students, you, too, must understand the basic concepts of teaching which are founded in research. This understanding will provide a sound basis for your important decisions about the teaching methods that you will select.

Throughout this course, the instructors will give a series of five or six "Quick Quizzes" which will be graded. All grades will be posted by Social Security Number. We hope that this will provide an external incentive to complete the background readings. These Quick Quizzes will consist of recall, comprehension, and application questions. Some will be multiple choice, true-false, or fill-ins. Others will consist of short exercises in which you will have to apply key ideas and principles.

Those students <u>auditing</u> this course will not be graded. However, unless you understand the basic vocabulary, concepts, and principles of teaching, you will find it difficult to function adequately in the group projects, which is the essence of your ability to synthesize ideas to improve your teaching.

Since the group projects are based on cooperative learning principles, you will have to decide immediately on your intentions to participate. If your decision is not to participate, you will not be assigned to an active group since the group is totally interdependent. Their grade will be based on both the group project grade (everyone gets the same grade earned), plus an individual grade based on the group's peer assessment of your individual contribution to the project.

As an auditor, your have the following choices:
1. Full participation in a group project and acceptance of all group responsibilities.
2. Assignment to an auditor's group in which the group decides what they want to do.
3. Circulate and observe groups at work without any type of comment or participation.

Please indicate your level of participation below–(check one):

☐ Full participation
☐ Assignment to an auditor's group
☐ Circulate and observe only

Approach To Teaching

This course has evolved over the past two years into the present format. The evolution has resulted from feedback from students, interviews with faculty around the United States who are teaching similar courses (only five identified), and what we have derived from an extensive review of the research. Of the texts written in the area of college teaching, few have dealt with the problems of college instructors in the college classroom and how to overcome them—in other words, the act of teaching with college students.

A special text has been prepared entitled <u>Essential Skills for College Teaching</u>.

Our approach is practical, hands-on, and based on known synthesis of many years of research on teaching.

Our approach to teaching is cooperative. We provide new information with 15- to 20-minute lecturettes. Students, working in cooperative groups, deal with problems of classroom teaching. Our philosophy is expressed in an old saying, "Nobody is smarter than all of us." Our job as instructors is to function as facilitators, which is consistent with this previous statement. We will present what we know and then turn to you to enhance, refute, and expand.

Class Format

After the first several classes during which you examine your personal teaching style using the Myers-Briggs Teaching Inventory and your personal teaching assumptions, you will be intimately involved in all aspects of the class. Each ch class will begin with "Good News."

This will be followed with a "trigger video" and explanation (starting the fourth week).

The instructors will then introduce the evening's topics with one or more 15- to 20-minute lecturettes followed by class discussion.

Many classes will involve a variety of participative techniques drawing on the experiences of the participants.

The instructors have prepared detailed lesson plans for each class. These will be available upon request to all students as "living" models.

Each assignment is highly reflective and usable immediately by each student.

Because of the potential diversity of the students and their needs, adjustments can be made in specific assignments with prior approval of the instructor.

Classes have been carefully prepared as models of what can be done in a college classroom. Note what is happening around you when you arrive in your class. Read, listen, observe. Why have the instructors developed the class the way you observe? Every cartoon, hang-up, build-up, poster, or whatever has a purpose. If you like it, say so. If you object or can suggest a way to improve them, say so.

Share, evaluate, criticize, share, speak up, and share some more.

The instructors really believe in what they are doing and know that you can help to improve the class. Your ideas will be shared with future classes.

BIBLIOGRAPHY

Caden, Brian W. (Fall 1985). Utilization of course syllabi and behavioral objectives. Journal of Optometric Education, 11(2), 26-28.

Cyrs, Thomas E., & Smith, Frank A. (1990). Teleclass teaching: A resource guide, second edition. NM: Center for Educational Development, New Mexico State University.

Dressel, P., & Marcus, D. (1982). Teaching and learning in college. San Francisco: Jossey-Bass Publishers.

Eisener, E.W., & Valance, E.C. (Eds.). (1974). Conflicting concepts in curriculum. Berkeley, CA: McCutchan Press.

Elliott, Linda C. (Summer 1983). The legal ramifications of proper instruction: Some considerations for division heads in community colleges. Community College Review, 1, 3-12.

Fisher, Michele (Ed.). (1985). Teaching at Stanford. Stanford, CA: Center for Teaching and Learning.

Grosz, Karen (Ed.). (1986). A bridge to excellence: Faculty handbook. Santa Monica, CA: Santa Monica College.

Lowther, Malcom A., & Others. (1989). Preparing course syllabi for improved communication. Ann Arbor, MI: Office of Educational Research and Improvement.

Miller, Allen H. (1987). Course design for university lecturers. NY: Nichols Publishing Co.

Neff, Rose Ann, & Weimer, Maryellen. (1990). Teaching college. Madison, WI: Magma Publications.

Ryan, Michael P., & Martens, Gretchor. (1989). Planning a college course: A guidebook for the graduate teaching assistant. Ann Arbor, MI: The National Center for Research to Improve Post-Secondary Teaching and Learning.

Segall, Ascher J., & Others. (1975). Systematic course design for the health fields. NY: John Wiley and Sons, Inc.

Chapter 7

Writing Worthwhile Learning Performance Objectives

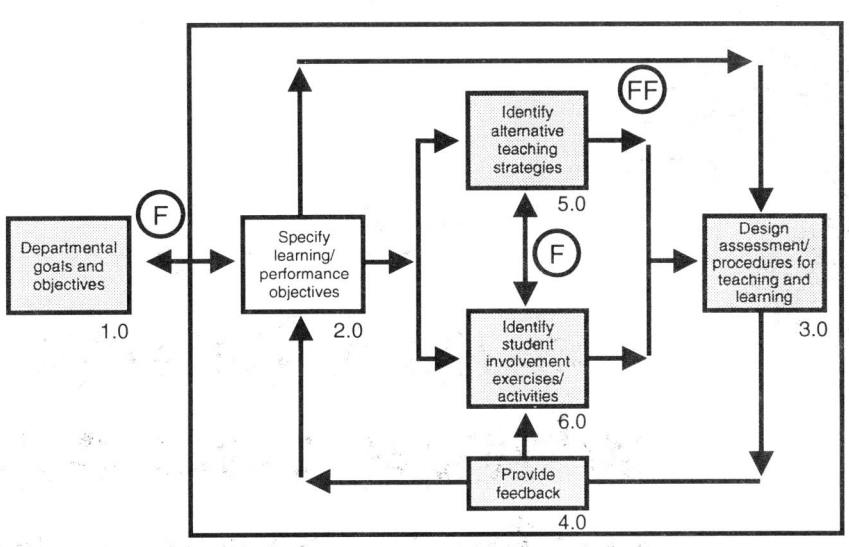

LEARNING PERFORMANCE OBJECTIVES

Learning performance objective
Construct examples of performance objectives including the performance; behavior; task; general content; the circumstances of learning and assessment; and the performance proficiency. These performance objectives must deal with a class or domain of learning behavior. (Level 4)

Key ideas
1. Learning performance objectives describe in operational language what the students are to learn; how they are to learn it; and the level of mastery required.
2. Learning performance objectives that are ultraspecific deal with recall of data and look just like the test items. These are not worthwhile.
3. Worthwhile learning performance objectives deal with a whole range of learning possibilities and usually deal with application and critical thinking skills.
4. Learning performance objectives are made up of the following components: a performer (student); the behavioral task; specific or general content; the circumstances of assessment; performance proficiency; and referent situation.
5. Learning performance objectives are the foundation for teaching strategies and learning activities as well as all assessment procedures.

New vocabulary
- means-ends
- inferred capability
- behavioral task
- circumstances of assessment
- proficiency variables
- directly observable behavior
- class of learning outcomes
- specific/general content
- performance proficiency
- expert consensus

Organization and planning are the cornerstones of good instruction and include the sequencing of the subject matter as well as arranging the conditions under which students will learn. Procedures that aid in the organization and planning of the subject matter will facilitate learning. Providing the students with a preview of what to expect helps them to put their efforts into a useful perspective and structure. It also serves as a framework for the later application of knowledge to other units and to professional practice. Objectives, which describe the desired learning result or outcome, provide the student with information about what to anticipate and how to organize and focus their current efforts toward these desirable ends.

Learning performance objectives are distinct from teaching performance objectives. The latter describe what the teacher will do to help the students master the learning objectives. Learning performance objectives define what students will know, how they will apply the knowledge and describe valuable attitudes that are related to the knowledge and skills.

The differences between teaching and learning objectives are best told in the story about Dr. Erma Padilla. Dr. Padilla taught an undergraduate course in training management in the College of Business and Economics. Her students thought that she was a very good teacher, as shown in her student evaluations. She started her fourth class by telling her students, "Today, I am going to teach you how to write training performance objectives and how important they are in a training situation." A bright looking young lady put her hand up and asked, "Dr. Padilla, I understand what you are going to teach us today, but what am I supposed to learn?" Dr. Padilla hesitated for a moment and replied, "At the end of this class I want each of you to construct five examples of performance objectives that deal with application and critical thinking skills. Each objective is to contain the actor, the behavioral task, the circumstances of performance, the performance proficiency, and consequences of non-mastery. I also want you to describe how the objectives relate to training strategies and assessment procedures. Given a choice, you will elect to use training performance objectives." The young student replied, "Oh, is that all?"

Definition of Learning Performance Objectives

Learning performance objectives provide an organizational and planning method for clearly distinguishing between the means of instruction, and the planned ends that the instruction is meant to accomplish, namely, learning.

Historically, during the 1960s and 1970s, these objectives were referred to as behavioral objectives, which implied a behaviorist philosophy. Many instructors who do not espouse behaviorism prefer the term performance objectives, since performance can be equated with behavior. Other synonymous terms to describe behavioral objectives have included: learning objectives; instructional objectives; student outcomes; results; expectations; operational definitions; intents; testable objectives; training outcomes; terminal performance objectives; and intermediate performance objectives. Today, they are referred to primarily as learning performance objectives.

Two definitions of learning performance objectives are offered. The first, an abbreviated definition, provides a quick reference. A learning performance objective is a description of an anticipated change in the behavior of a student after exposure to instruction. It is the outcome or result of instruction–learning–that is measurable rather than the process of instruction itself. The primary purpose of a learning performance objective is to communicate precise information to those people who need to know it, namely, students, instructors, and administrators.

The second definition of learning performance objective is much more inclusive. A learning performance objective is a descriptive statement of a class or range of learning outcomes that leads to a prescribed level of achievement. The performance is defined as any visible activity displayed by students and includes attitudinal as well as intellectual and manual skills. It must be stated in a measurable, action-oriented form. The desired outcome will be an observable change in the behavior of students as demonstrated in newly acquired skills and attitudes as well as expansion of their informational data base. This outcome will result from some type of academic, laboratory, or clinical instructional efforts.

<u>Directly Observable Behavior</u>

- Write
- Palpate
- Measure
- Describe a Procedure
- Explain a Concept
- Construct an Example in Writing

Inferred Capabilities from Observed Behavior
- Personal Warmth
- Computational Skill
- Problem-solving
- Ethical Behavior
- Body Language
- Intonation

Performance Objectives with General Content

Worthwhile learning performance objectives deal with a class or range of learning outcomes rather than specific instances of behavior or content. Each of the following nine examples of learning performance objectives is content-general. This means that a variety of content possibilities within the objective statement could be provided for the student. Specific content has not been included in any of the examples.

1. Given descriptions of incidents of job related conflicts and the actions of the participants, identify each instance of sexual discrimination or harassment according to the institutional standards of impartiality, conduct, honesty, and integrity.
    (Any description could be provided.)

2. Given brief video scenarios of types of power, label each as charismatic, expert, legal, implied, or reward.
    (Many different varieties of video scenarios could be provided.)

3. Working in a small group of five participants, apply the principles of group problem-solving or interaction according to the criteria provided during class.
    (The student could be observed in a variety of small groups.)

4. Given a diagram of an electrical circuit in the starting mechanism of a machine, write a short report stating your evaluation of the capacity of the given circuit to start the given machine. Be as specific as possible in your evaluation and provide as much evidence or support for your evaluation as possible. Keep your report to a maximum of two pages (double-spaced type).
    (Many different diagrams could be provided.)

5. Given 20 prescriptions containing a variety of errors, identify 100% of the errors and suggest corrections.
    (Any combination of prescriptions could be provided.)

6. Using a PA chart radiograph of an ambulatory patient, explain why the radiograph is acceptable, using the criteria provided in class.
    (Any type of PA chart radiograph could be provided.)

7. Without using any notes, speak extemporaneously for three minutes on a topic assigned by the instructor. (According to the presentation criteria discussed in class, each student will be rated by the instructor and other students. A minimum rating of 50 points is required.)

(Any topic could be assigned.)

8. Given five unknown blood samples, determine with 100% accuracy the ABO grouping and the Rh typing. Both slide and test type methods can be used. (A variety of blood samples could be provided.)

9. Given patient data in a case study form, identify and classify any of the four listed possible factors that can elevate or decrease the BUN present in the case. (Any number of case studies could be provided.)

If the instructor called for a specific instance of content, then that specific instance would have to be used as a test item or assessment procedure. For example, the following statements call for a specific response and do not deal with a class or range of behavior.
- List the general rules given during the lecture for role playing episodes.
- Define simulation game and explain the components of a simulation as discussed in class.
- Describe how a neuron is now viewed as the basic unit of the nervous system.

Each of these statements calls for an ultraspecific response and is satisfied with a specific bit of subject matter. These objectives are really test items. If the content is that important, then provide those test items to your students before the class begins.

Learning performance objectives are frequently confused with teaching methodology, learning activities, and Instructional media.

Statements of Teaching Methods. Teaching methodology deals with the delivery system or the process by which the student will be exposed to the subject matter, for example: prepare a lecture; demonstrate an experiment; write performance objectives; select a video for class. The boundaries of this delivery system are determined by instructor performance objectives. Teaching methods are chosen on the basis of the student behavior which, in its turn, is prescribed in the learning objectives.

Learning Activities. Learning activities such as viewing films, attending lectures, discussing critical issues, simulations, and case studies, describe the conditions or circumstances under which the student will be expected to master the objectives. These activities are the means that will be used by the student to accomplish the learning performance objectives. They are prescribed by the instructor or selected by the student. For example, discussing critical issues is a method to learn critical thinking skills. If the instructor is teaching discussion skills, then "discuss" becomes the main behavior. Discussion is usually a method to achieve another behavior.

Instructional Media. Instructional media such as audio tapes, filmstrips, 35mm slides, or video tapes describe the physical means for presenting the subject matter. Students never learn from technology per se. They learn from competent instructors teaching through the technology using specific types of presentation formats such as higher order questions, interactive activities, and other types of active learning techniques.

Exercise: Ten statements are listed below. Label each as primarily a learning performance objective (LPO) or learning activity (LA).

1. _____ Circle all words which are participles.
1. _____ Describe the advantages of essay tests.
3. _____ View the film entitled "Teachers."
4. _____ Explain how hydrogen is converted into usable energy.
5. _____ Attend the museum lecture on Neolithic archeological artifacts.
6. _____ Listen to the song entitled "Tradition" from the movie "Fiddler on the Roof."
7. _____ Underline the point in the plot where circumstances begin to turn against the antagonist.
8. _____ Identify the cognitive level of each test item.
9. _____ Justify the need for tighter gun controls. Cite several authorities on each side of the issue.
10. _____ Discuss the possible consequences of the impeachment of Boris Yeltsin.

Uses of Learning Performance Objectives

Learning performance objectives are used primarily to (a) design instruction, (b) guide classroom questions, and (c) assess students. They communicate to the students exactly what is expected of them in terms of knowledge, skill, and attitudes; under what circumstances they are expected to learn; and the standards under which they will be assessed. Learning performance objectives are intended to make learning outcomes more evident and understandable to students and instructors, thus improving communications among professional staff and students. The use of performance objectives provides the basis for instructional decision-making prior to, during, and after instruction. They provide for planned change toward individualized and personalized curriculum development. They also help to determine if students are making sufficient progress.

For the purpose of student assessment, learning performance objectives provide a basis for increased clinical and didactic accountability in a professional setting. They help in designing test item pools that provide a measure of student performance as required in the performance objectives. Valid test data can then be used as a means to redesign instruction. They can also be used to determine whether assessment should be based on paper and pencil or performance measures.

Misconceptions about Specific Learning Performance Objectives

Time Consuming. Learning performance objectives take time to generate. Only those objectives that are important and critical to learning should be worthy of specification. Specificity of intent does not automatically mean that the objective is useable and worthwhile. It is more important to specify a few critical objectives than dozens having questionable scope, worth, and relevance.

Need for Improvement. Learning objectives can always be improved. As the instructor gains more experience and confidence, many objectives may have to be changed to specify more clearly the intent of the learning to be mastered by the student. Since lower-level knowledge and comprehension objectives are the easiest to write, there will probably be a preponderance of these in the beginning. Application and critical thinking learning performance objectives are difficult and time-consuming to write. These will evolve as instructors gain more experience and confidence.

Test Item Specificity. Too many existing learning performance objectives are specific test items in which the objective and the test item read exactly the same. This is particularly true at the knowledge and comprehension levels of learning and will result in hundreds of objectives for each course or unit, and in instructor frustration. Learning objectives should deal with general content, which can be assessed with a range of possible test items.

Test Item Validity. Test items or performance situations that have been selected to assess student performance must meet the intellectual requirements of the learning performance objectives. Too frequently, the objective calls for the understanding of a specific skill, and the test requires the student to analyze or evaluate a specific situation. The intellectual level of individual learning performance objectives must be assessed at the same intellectual level as the test item. If the learning performance objective calls for the student to apply a principle, the test must require the student to apply the same principle.

Prerequisites to Objective Writing

Instructors have often used one form of objective writing throughout most of their careers. They define what and how they will teach rather than describe what they want their students to learn. The concept of objective writing was first mentioned by Franklin Bobbit in *How to Make a Curriculum*, published in 1924. The more formal and precise manner of objective writing in terms of student outcomes is a recent development.

There are several techniques that be can used to more formally describe instructor's intended learning performance objectives:
- ask the big questions
- review past tests and exams
- analyze the table of contents in current texts
- perform a job analysis for professional fields.

Ask the Big Questions. Ask yourself what it is that the students are expected to accomplish at the end of a course, unit, or lecture. What are the big questions students must answer? These questions can be easily translated into objective form to guide the development of instruction.

Review Past Tests and Exams. These test items will identify the most critical aspects of a course. It is possible to "back up" from these questions and identify the class of behavior the test item was designed to assess. If the objective and the test item read exactly the same (or would with slight modifications), it should be determined if the point is really worth your time testing. Here are several examples of test items and the learning performance objectives inferred from them.

> *Test Item*: Which of the following phenothiazine structures are likely to have anti-emetic activity?
> *Inferred Objective*: The student will predict the pharmacologic activity when given the chemical structure of a compound.
>
> *Test Item*: From the data listed below, which of these two salts is more completely absorbed?
> *Inferred Objective*: The student will determine the bioavailability of a drug when given blood level-time course data.

Examine the learning performance objective closely. Observe that the test item may not exhaust the range of subject matter possibilities for testing. Alternative test items with different subject matter could be constructed. They would assess the student's capability just as well as the chosen test situation. Since the purpose of teaching and testing is to determine student ability to generalize or transfer skills to an unknown situation, this type of objective would be of more value than those objectives that are nothing more than specific test items. Collections of parallel test items from which individual items could be randomly selected would be of more value than test items for ultraspecific objectives. Decide the number of "correct" instances in a test to judge student's competence.

Conduct a Content Analysis. Given a professional competency area, skill, or area of information to be studied, analyze the supporting content and outline the important concepts, skills, principles, and procedures necessary for the student to master. These data can then be analyzed and translated into learning performance objectives. The final outline should be reviewed by peers, practitioners, and students to ensure that it is complete and appropriate.

Perform a Job Analysis. A job analysis entails "on-site" observations of professionals in a variety of settings in order to record all professional activity. Different observers work at different times. These data are then translated into learning performance objectives. However, this technique is almost impossible for a single instructor to accomplish without some assistance. The next best alternative would be to bring groups of professionals together and have them describe their professional activities as they relate to specific areas of professional competence. In the absence of either of these procedures, expert consensus among qualified faculty would guard against personal bias.

Components of Learning Performance Objectives

Learning performance objectives are distinct from competency and goal statements. Regardless of form, the primary purpose of objective specification is to state clearly what the instructor expects the students to know and how to apply the knowledge. Exactly how specific an objective should be is still a matter of concern for researchers.

The form advocated in this chapter avoids the superspecificity advocated by some groups, but still requires enough specificity for adequate communication to other instructors and especially to students who will be expected to master the learning performance objectives.

The proper form of objectives is one of the most misunderstood concepts in contemporary postsecondary education. Abuses abound as witnessed by the prolific shopping lists of objectives found in schools. The result has been frustration and, in many instances, rejection of the logic by instructors. Objective writing for the planning of learning and student assessment is a difficult task that cannot be accomplished overnight or during a two-day retreat. All too often objectives are written to satisfy an administrative directive, only to be discarded when instruction is designed and tests constructed. Worthwhile and valued learning objectives are difficult to generate.

All learning performance objectives have both *substance* and *form*. The *substance* of an objective is the content or subject matter that is used or acted upon by the student and instructor. This content describes the stimuli to which the student will be expected to respond during instruction and assessment. The *form* of the objective emphasizes the behaviors that the student will have to demonstrate as a result of having acquired the content. A balance must exist in the objective between the substance (content) and form (specificity) of the action or behavior. The proposed use of the objective will often determine the form that it will take. It must be emphasized that specificity of the objective does not mean usability or value. An example of substance or subject matter could be the concepts of: phenytoin; pharmacokinetic dosing gentamicin; the constitution; or the laws of thermodynamics. Examples of form or action could include: evaluate; apply an idea to...; describe a process...; analyze an outcome of...; or compare and contrast an idea.

Each major end-of-course, end-of-unit, or end-of-lesson learning performance objective contains the following elements:

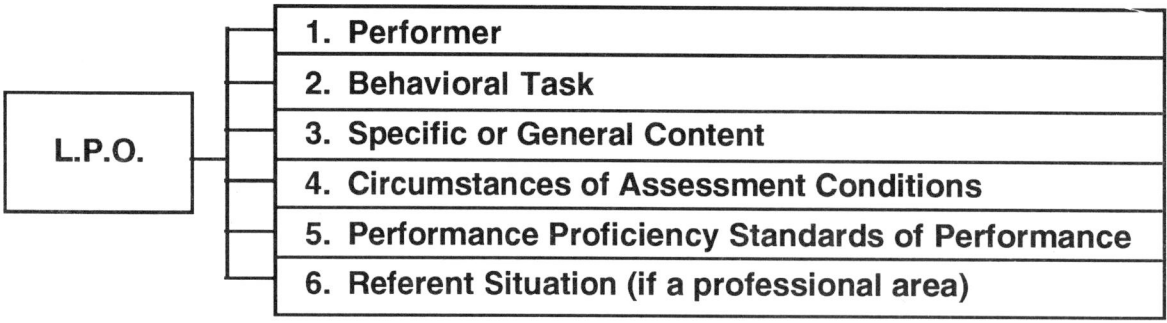

Should all components be present in every learning performance objective statement? End-of-course learning performance objectives should contain all six components. End-of-unit (multiple classes) and end-of-unit learning performance objectives should contain only those components necessary to communicate clearly, otherwise the information may become too verbose.

Component 1: A Performer
A performer is the person, student, participant, enrollee, or other individual who will be expected to demonstrate the accomplishment of the learning performance objective. It may not be necessary to name the performer for every objective if the reference is self-evident. The only purpose for naming the performer is to establish specific responsibility for an individual or class of students.

Component 2: The Behavioral Task
The behavioral task is the most important component of the learning performance objective and specifies WHAT the student will be expected to know and do, or what type of attitude to develop. This task can require either an observable (overt) action such as compounding, counting, counseling, or a nonobservable action from which the capability can be inferred, such as analyzing, calculating, evaluating.

Example of an observable action:
The student will use nonverbal cues to encourage a client during a counseling session.
   (Nonverbal cues such as a head nod or smiling are directly observable behaviors.)

Example of inferred capability:
The student will calculate the proper amounts and volumes of diluents to prepare accurately various strengths and solutions.
   (The act of calculation is a mental skill which cannot be directly observed. The student can be observed writing down or stating the amounts to be calculated. This capability is inferred from the product of the observed behavior.)

Exercise: Label each of the following statement as "O" for observable behavior or "N" for nonobservable behavior.

1. ___ The student will comprehend thoroughly the ways in which our constitution permeates our everyday life.
2. ___ When presented with a list of nouns and pronouns, the student will label each correctly.
3. ___ The student will recite the names of six chemical compounds containing three or more elements.
4. ___ The student will be able to see the value of reading the "classics" in his or her leisure time.
5. ___ The student will construct an essay in writing and will use one of the three logical organizations given in class.

In seemingly well-conceived statements of learning performance objectives are often found nonessential performance statements. Care must be taken not to incorporate nonessential and trivial parts of an objective. For example, "The student will circle each word that suggests a directly observable behavior." The task of circling is secondary to the identification of the behavior to be observed. Circling is a motor skill and at best an activity. A better way to state this learning performance objective would be, "Identify each directly observable behavior by circling the term."

The behavioral task should identify only the principal performance or *primary capability* that the student will be expected to demonstrate. This will be the basis for the design of instruction and assessment of the student. How specifically the task must be described is still the subject of debate. The primary use of the objective should determine the level of specificity or generality. If the instructor intends that the objectives are to be test item specific (the test item and objective read almost exactly alike), use action terms such as these:

ACTION TERMS		*NONACTION TERMS*
construct		learn
name		understand
label		appreciate
describe	NOT	know
count		value
insert		think critically
stain		
bandage		
list		

Component 3: Specific or General Content

If a learning performance objective specifies one segment of limited subject matter as a requirement for testing, then it is test item equivalent. These learning objectives have use for test construction if the instructor wants students to develop baseline information only. However, it must be understood that students will neither generalize from this type of learning nor will be able to transfer their learning to a broader range of similar learning situations.

Test item specific objective
The student will list the features of a properly written prescription.
Test item
List the features of a properly written prescription.

Test item specific objective
The student will cite five ways in which laboratory tests are useful in drug therapy.
Test item
Cite five ways in which laboratory tests are useful in drug therapy.

Worthwhile learning performance objectives should address a *range* of possible content choices, all of which have the same characteristics, but none of which exhaust the objective's content possibilities for either practice or assessment. This range (class, domain, or universe) of possible content provides parallel examples that have been judged equally difficult. A specific example of content drawn from this domain of possibilities provides for a specific practice or assessment situation.

Content specific
Identify and describe the major theme in Hemingway's *Old Man and the Sea*.

Content general
Given any short story by Hemingway, identify and describe the major theme.
or
Given any short story by a 20th-century author, identify and describe the main theme.

Objectives that refer to specific content are test item specific and allow for no substitution of parallel subject matter. General content describes a range of possible subject matter substitutions and allows more latitude of subject matter selection among instructors. Transfer of learning from one subject area to another is possible with these skills.

Component 4: Circumstances of Assessment
The circumstances of assessment prescribe the range of possible situations or instances under which the student will be assessed. They specify the constraints and latitude for assessment and directly influence performance. It may be unnecessary to specify the circumstances for every objective since the same circumstances may address several objectives in a learning sequence. The circumstance explain HOW the behavioral task is to be accomplished by the student and describe the important aspects of the performance environment. These are the learning variables (stimulus attributes) that the instructor can manipulate and which include any selection of media, teaching methodology, learning environment, special equipment or instruments. The circumstances should be based on the nature of the behavior to be performed.

If the instructor is working in a professional field that requires some type of certification, these circumstances should approximate the real professional setting in which the student will be expected to work. They should be critical to the expected outcomes and should not address insignificant or trivial elements.

Under certain circumstances the instructor might want to provide the student with resources, which could include such things as:
- scientific instruments
- equipment
- profiles
- journal articles
- general information
- special instructions
- professional references
- problem situations
- special environments
- patients (real and role-played)

Depending on the level of specificity desired, the circumstances could also identify where or with whom the student would be observed performing the behavioral task:
- alone
- in the presence of a preceptor

- in a group
- a member of a HMO
- in the clinic
- on the telephone
- using a programmed textbook
- in the laboratory
- in an urban setting
- under simulated conditions
- in an emergency situation
- viewing
- reading
- listing

Under special circumstances the instructor might require the student to present the information or solution in a certain manner:

- in writing
- in an oral report
- in the style prescribed
- in outline form
- with all references
- according to journal style
- working in a sterile environment
- given actual clinical records
- after reading a case history
- using the encyclopedia
- without the use of notes
- from memory
- working under simulated conditions
- working without the use of compendia

Delimiting and clarifying statements such as these depend on the writing style of the instructor and could be found any place within an objective statement.

Component 5: Performance Proficiency

Performance proficiency defines what will be accepted as the evidence that the student has achieved the prescribed behavioral task. This component of the objective usually specifies some numerical evidence of performance or delineates specific criteria for judgment and is very important for licensure in professional practice.

It will not always be necessary to specify the performance proficiency for every objective as a part of the objective statement. This should be included only if it has not been previously stated or if a question should arise as to the desired outcome. In many instances the level of proficiency is arbitrary and negotiable, particularly if you are dealing with informational level objectives. If there are consequences as a result of nonmastery of the objective, it may be necessary to establish minimum or safe performance proficiency levels, especially in professional fields. A grade of B- in a history test would not be comparable to a grade of B- in a surgical procedure.

Proficiency Levels. Different objectives or sequences of objectives will require different performance standards or proficiency levels. These may be dictated by professional practice or result in the arbitrary judgment of the instructor. Some of the factors to consider should include:

- **time to complete**
Time should only be considered if it is critical to the performance of the behavioral task. Time as a proficiency measure should not be applied arbitrarily.
    e.g. Dose of epinephrine in a case of cardiac arrest.
    Request for IV compatibility of drugs while on the phone.

- **manual speed**
Some tasks must be performed as soon as their need is recognized.
    e.g. First aid application would be required in case of an accident such as arterial bleeding, artificial respiration, dispensing an emergency drug.

- **degree of accuracy or level of precision**
    e.g. Prescriptions must be dispensed with absolute accuracy.

- **latitude for error**
How much error in judgement can be tolerated?
    e.g. "Cracked" emulsions are expensive.

- **probable consequence of error**
What effect will an error have on the consumer? If a drug is given too rapidly, death will result. This could mean loss of life, injury, or damage. Is the consequence intolerable or negligible? A missing auxiliary label may contribute to improper storage and consequent product deterioration.

- **stability of the performance**
Must the degree of accuracy be constant over long periods of time? How often will the student be expected to perform over time? Will the student be expected to maintain proficiency? How will this be reinforced?

- **maintenance of skill level**
If there will be a delay before the skill is used, will relearning or additional practice be required? How will the skill level be maintained?
    e.g. After reviewing a balance sheet, the pharmacist selects a drug brand based on bioavailability studies.

- **safety requirements**
What are the risks involved?
    e.g. Sterility in IV and lab environments must be maintained.
    Volatile gases must be contained in a safe environment.

- **probability of demonstrating the skill**
    e.g. Does the preparation of one example of a frequently dispensed dosage form provide evidence of mastery?

Does one demonstration of the addition of an additive to an I.V. solution give evidence of mastery?

Expressing Proficiency Levels. Proficiency levels indicate the desired mastery of a learning performance objective. Mastery learning means that a student has demonstrated proficiency in a professional competency. There are two types of mastery that should be considered: *absolute* and *variable*. *Absolute* mastery indicates an absolute level of performance with no latitude for achievement variance and is represented by proficiency levels such as 100%. This is an all or nothing mastery level. The student must either meet or exceed the standard. *Variable* mastery establishes a range or continuum of acceptable performance between minimum and maximum levels.

Proficiency levels can be expressed in a number of ways:
- 80% correct
- all must be correct
- four out of five
- without any errors
- accurate to four decimal places–your response must be in accordance with XYZ requirements
- your description of the process must include the following...
- neat, clean, and free of spelling errors
- within 300 calories

Establishing Proficiency Levels. Too often these levels are arbitrarily derived by instructors, based on the "feeling" that the student should achieve at the prescribed level. However, it must be justified in terms of factors. There are four possible choices for arriving at proficiency levels:

1. *Subjective*–70%; 80%; 90%. This is often difficult to justify, but professional judgment may sometimes be the only criteria available.
2. *Expert consensus*–Still arbitrary but less susceptible to error. Judgments such as 90% proficiency would be based on pooled estimates.
3. *Current state of proficiency in practice*–This involves the administration of a test to a criterion group of practitioners who had been judged competent by faculty and other practitioners. The scores obtained could represent the requirements for practice. The lower limits of this group performance would constitute the lower limits of knowledge of existing practice.
4. *Tradition*–The institution arbitrarily establishes proficiency levels as reflected in grades, although it has been firmly established that there is little correlation between grades and success in the real world.

Component 6: Referent Situation

The referent situation relates the learning performance objective to some criterion of relevance that is usually external to the course or unit of instruction. This referent helps the student to answer the question, "Where will I be able to use or apply what I have learned–at some future time, in another unit of instruction, another course, or in professional practice?" It will be found most frequently in professional fields.

The six components of performance objectives have been described in detail. It must be kept in mind that not all six elements are present explicitly in all learning performance objectives at all times. If the student can understand the expectations of the instructor, that is all that is necessary.

It has been suggested that ultraprecision in objective specification may not be necessary or desirable. The purpose for which the objectives will be used should determine the level of specificity or generality necessary. The most significant criterion for learning performance objective specification is:

Is this performance objective *really* worth the time and effort to teach and assess?

REVIEW FORM

WRITING PERFORMANCE OBJECTIVES

A. What is the behavioral task?
  1. What do you want the student to do?
     a. Does the task deal with a specific instance of behavior (ultraspecific) or does it encompass a more generalizable task which can be transferred to other learning situations?
        e.g. ultraspecific: The student will add 10 + 1
        expanded: The student will add any two digit numbers from 10 to 99.
     b. Does the behavioral task communicate exactly what is expected of the student?
     c. Is this an intermediate or terminal performance task?

B. What are the circumstances of assessment?
  1. Are these circumstances really important or do they deal with trivial matters?
  2. Are the circumstances explicit or implied?

C. How will the student be evaluated?
   Paper and pencil _____ Simulation _____ Practice _____

D. What is the expected proficiency level for competent performance?
  1. Is this proficiency level an absolute minimum or is there a continuum of proficiency?
  2. How was this proficiency level derived?

E. How does this task relate to another course, unit, or professional practice?

F. How will the objectives be used?
  1. To design instruction
  2. To generate paper and pencil tests
  3. To design observational rating scales

G. Estimated time for the student to achieve the learning performance objective (if important).

Chapter 8
Sequencing Instruction to Address Higher Order Thinking Skills

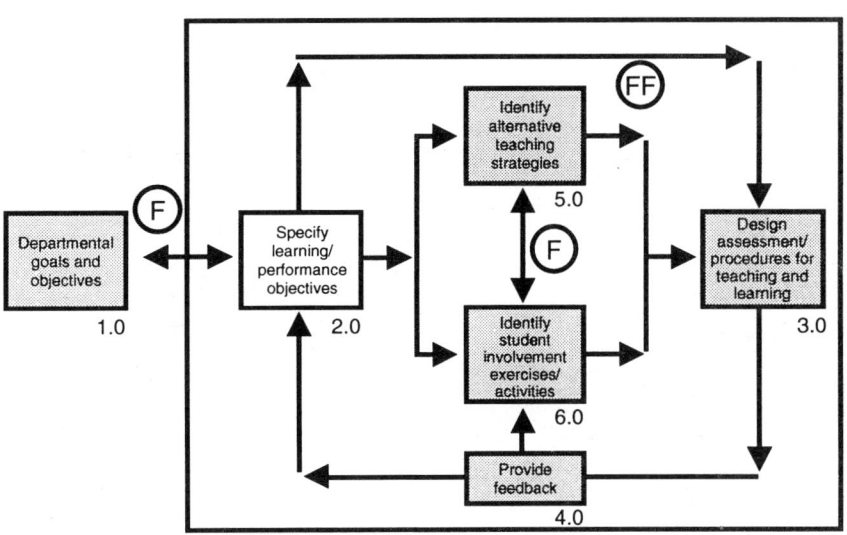

"If you don't know where you are going, any path will get you there."

DESIGNING A LEARNING SEQUENCE

LEARNING PERFORMANCE OBJECTIVE
Design a learning sequence with a terminal performance objective at the critical thinking level. Working backward, identify all intermediate performance learning objectives including application, comprehension and recall. (Level 4).

KEY IDEAS
1. Designing a learning sequence requires the instructor to decide not only what the student is to learn but also in what order it is to be learned.
2. A learning sequence is developed by rating the terminal learning performance objective(s) on the four-level taxonomy (Bloom level modified) and then working backward to include intermediate learning performance objectives at each prior level.
3. The four-level learning taxonomy is used to rate the cognitive levels of objectives, classroom questions, learning activities, and assessment procedures.
4. A learning sequence progresses from lowest (recall) level learning through understanding, application, to critical thinking/problem solving.

NEW VOCABULARY
- terminal learning performance objective
- flat horizontal structure
- vertical hierarchical structure
- learning activity
- knowledge, comprehension, application, analysis, synthesis, evaluation
- taxonomy
- rule using
- intermediate learning performance objective(s)
- entry level
- critical thinking
- translation
- rule selection
- affective objectives
- receiving, responding, valuing, characterization

INTRODUCTION
The previous chapter dealt with writing worthwhile learning performance objectives in the correct format. This chapter will cover how to sequence these objectives from the lowest level of learning to the higher levels of learning such as critical thinking. A learning sequence should be developed prior to the preparation of a lesson, unit, or module of instruction. This assures that all of the important and critical knowledge and skill components have been included and are arranged in a logical order. Designing a learning sequence requires the following decisions:
- *what* the student will learn.
- in *what order* it is to be learned.
- *how* it is to be learned.
- *how to assess* when it has been learned.
- the best method to *teach* it.

Sequencing addresses the question of how to decide in *what order* the content and skills should be presented to the student. A presentation sequence should be designed to govern the order of group-paced lecture presentations. New topics are presented from simple concepts to complex principles. When students have not attained the level of achievement desired, the presentation sequence should be reviewed and the students questioned to determine if they had the necessary prerequisite skills and understood the concepts as developed during the presentation. It may be that a wider variety of examples is necessary.

The sequencing of topics and objectives provides the overall structure of the course which becomes the learning blueprint for the student to follow.

ELEMENTS OF A LEARNING SEQUENCE

Designing a learning sequence requires the analysis of two important components. These include the subject matter or content and the specific student behavior. The analysis of content addresses what the instructor wants the students to know about the topic and any associated attitudes that should be expressed. The analysis of behavior addresses what it is that the instructor wants the student to do with the knowledge.

The *content analysis* identifies all of the important information, concepts, principles, rules, and procedures that the student will have to know and understand in order to perform a skill or apply a principle. This analysis traditionally deals with cognitive or intellectual skills but should also address attitudinal behavior associated with the content.

The *behavioral analysis* requires that the instructor translate the content into learning performance objectives that describe exactly what the students will do once they possess the content and in what logical order they will be expected to perform.

CRITERIA FOR JUDGING ADEQUATE LEARNING SEQUENCES

Learning sequences must identify the *logical steps* that will lead the student to achievement of the learning performance objectives. The approach recommended should be based on your experience and a great deal of common sense. To be usable, a learning sequence should be based on a practical and logical approach. The student should be able to achieve the learning sequence within a reasonable amount of time, which is established by the instructor or negotiated with the student. This sequence is based on sound learning theory. A usable sequence also should discriminate between intellectual and attitudinal components and the actual tasks to be performed by the student. It assists and leads the students to the desired proficiency level. To be totally effective, the instructor should consider the prerequisite knowledge and skills the students need. The complexity of the subject matter will influence many decisions on how much detail to include. An adequate amount of appropriate practice is required by the student. The optimal conditions under which the learning should take place is also a major consideration.

STRUCTURE AND HIERARCHY

All academic disciplines have a structure that implies a relationship among the critical components. This structure shows both cumulative knowledge and skill development and prerequisite relationships as the concepts develop from simple to complex. These structures can be described as:

Flat Horizontal Structure: The sequence of teaching units is somewhat arbitrary since the teaching units are independent of each other. In some disciplines the content and learning performance objectives could be presented in almost any order, since they are not interdependent.

Vertical or Hierarchical Structure: Sequencing is extremely important since the units and topics are totally interdependent. There is a logical cumulative relationship among the content components and learning performance objectives. This type of hierarchical or vertical structure provides the building blocks for student achievement. However, the procedures are relative. Experience with students and adequate feedback from them will provide the data for optimal sequencing.

TERMINAL AND INTERMEDIATE PERFORMANCE OBJECTIVES

The highest level of student performance is called the terminal performance objective (TPO). This TPO usually prescribes the most complex intellectual, attitudinal, or motor skill. The student will be expected to master these at the end of a lecture, unit, module or course at a prescribed level of proficiency. Mastery of these TPOs indicate when the student has reached closure for the skill or knowledge base.

The prerequisite supporting components or steps which lead to the terminal learning performance objectives are called the intermediate learning performance objectives (IPOs). These could be linear or branched in some fashion. The point is that the IPOs must always precede the TPOs and lead the student to mastery of them. For example, if you want the students to apply a principle, they must understand each concept contained within the principle and know the facts implicit in each concept.

Sequencing of the subject matter requires that you identify all of the facts, information, concepts, and principles that, in your judgment, the student requires to learn the skill. Given the terminal learning performance objective(s), you will constantly work backward asking what the prior information or skill is that will be needed by the student to achieve the desired outcomes.

ENTRY LEVEL

Continue your analysis until you reach the point where you feel that the student should already know the data or skill. This is called the entry level of knowledge or skill. This entry level knowledge could be covered in a prior lecture, unit, or course. Assumptions are usually made about the prior entry level skills of students unless some type of entry level assessment is conducted. This could be accomplished through the use of a handout with a check list of entry level skills required for the course. This is true particularly when other instructors have not provided the terminal learning performance objectives for their courses. If these objectives are available then the entry level skills for one unit are the terminal learning performance objectives from a prior unit or course. In the absence of these previously mastered objectives you will have to make some adjustments in your course. These "assumptions" about entry skills may be one of the greatest causes of student failure.

LEARNING ACTIVITIES

Learning objectives, whether terminal or intermediate, describe what the student is to know and do with the knowledge and under what circumstances. How the student is expected to achieve the objective is referred to as the learning activity. As discussed in the last chapter, activities are the means by which the objectives or ends are learned. Learning activities, or means, lead to the achievement of learning performance objectives.

Activities and learning performance objectives are often confused by instructors. For example, discussing an issue is not an objective unless the intent is to improve discussion skills _per se_. Discussion is a means to achieve an objective. An example of a learning performance objective that includes discussion is:

After reading the background materials and discussing the abortion issue, the student will identify logical inconsistencies on each side of the issue.

Discussion in this case helps the student to clarify points, probe values, and identify the problems with the arguments. Discussion is not an end in itself.

A learning activity could address several intermediate learning performance objectives simultaneously. Single activities usually do not address single intermediate learning performance objectives. The selection of the learning activities must be based on the nature of the behavior called for in these objectives. The design of a complete learning sequence attempts to answer the question, "Will students, as a result of participating in these activities, be able to achieve the intermediate and terminal learning performance objectives?"

Each activity is based on or directed toward achievement of an objective. It is usually possible to identify different activities that are suitable for achievement of an individual or a cluster of IPOs:

EXAMPLE: Given the following intermediate learning performance objectives the student could receive the same information by:
- attending a lecture,
- listening to the lecture on audio tape,
- reading a transcription of the lecture,
- viewing a videotape of the lecture,
- reviewing the notes of the lecture taken by a friend,
- reading six chapters of the text.

The most important consideration is the fact that the student demonstrated satisfactorily the achievement of the learning performance objectives as a result of participation in one or more of these activities.

DETERMINING THE COMPONENTS OF A LEARNING UNIT

Designing a learning sequence requires that all of the necessary components of a terminal learning performance objective be identified in terms of what the student has to know and do. This sequence will identify either a flat or horizontal structure (no logical sequence) or a vertical or hierarchical structure (cumulative learning) in which there is an apparent logical sequence.

There are three categories or domains of learning performance objectives which can be used in developing a learning sequence. These include the cognitive or intellectual domain; the affective or attitudinal domain; and the psychomotor or physical domain. Although treated separately in this chapter, the domains are intimately related and overlap.

One tool that has aided instructors for many years is *The Taxonomy of Educational Objectives: Cognitive Domain* developed by Benjamin Bloom and his colleagues (1956). This classification scheme describes the logical and cumulative development of learning outcomes from the lowest level of remembering information to the highest level of evaluation. The original taxonomy described six levels of learning:

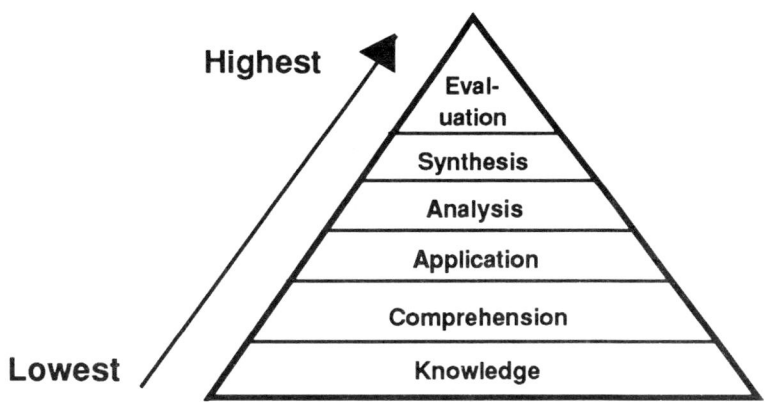

The purpose of the taxonomy is to determine the level of the intended intellectual skill required in a learning performance objective, a classroom question, and a test item.

For ease of use and training, the entire taxonomy can be reduced to four general levels. Because of the complexity of the upper three levels of analysis, synthesis, and evaluation, the upper three levels of the classification scheme can be reduced to the heading "critical thinking" or "rule selection." Application has been subtitled "rule using," and knowledge has been changed to "memory" with the subtitle of "recall."

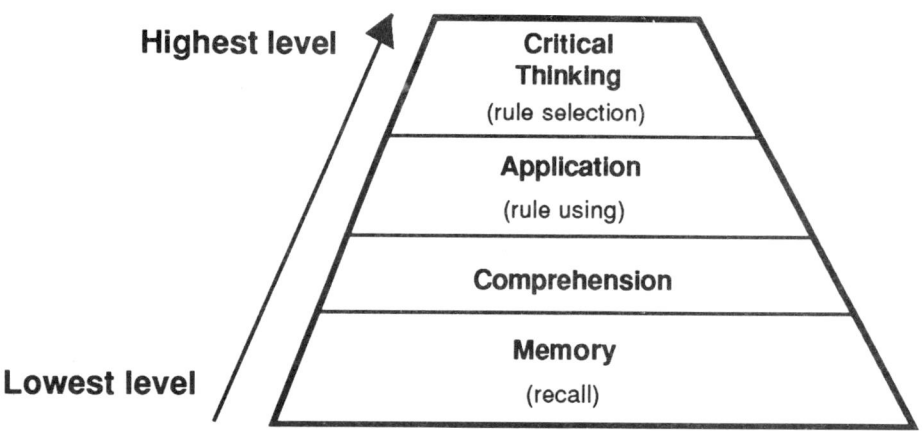

Since the four-level intellectual classification scheme is also hierarchical (progressing from the lowest to the highest level of learning), it provides a logical means for development of a learning sequence. A learning performance objective rated at the application or rule-using level incorporates the skills of comprehension and memory and would therefore have components of comprehension objectives as well as memory objectives.

HOW TO USE THE TAXONOMY

Rating Learning Performance Objectives

When a learning performance objective is rated at one of the four levels of the taxonomy, only the intended cognitive outcome of the stated objective is described. It is possible that the actual outcome resulting from instruction could be different. For example, in the judgment of the instructor, the student may be learning at a higher level than that called for in an objective. If you had rated the learning outcome at critical thinking-analysis, the student may be operating at the comprehension level.

When rating learning performance objectives, it is always prudent to work in small groups of instructors (interrator reliability is quite high) or at least have the ratings reviewed by a colleague. The first hint of the complexity of the required skill will be found in the behavioral task; however, it is the context of the *total* objective that will dictate the required cognitive level. While reviewing the cognitive level with colleagues, talk, argue and revise thinking until there is agreement.

The Terminal Learning Performance Objective as the Highest Cognitive Level

The terminal learning performance objectives, end of course or lesson objectives, should always be rated at the highest level of the taxonomy since they will incorporate all prior learning performance objectives. Objectives written at the application or critical thinking levels constitute the highest levels of cognitive intellectual activity and are usually generalizable or transferable to a broad array of learning situations. This is not to imply that there could not be terminal learning performance objectives at the memory or comprehension levels. It may be that a unit of instruction is prerequisite to higher levels of intellectual activity. An example at this lower level would be the memorization of prefixes and suffixes in medical terminology, specific anatomical terminology, vocabulary in language training, or the recognition by name of an insect in entomology.

The taxonomy has a number of different uses when designing a learning sequence. It is used to determine the cognitive intellectual level of learning performance objectives, test items and other assessment techniques, classroom questions, learning activities, and exercises.

QUICK REFERENCE GUIDE TO COGNITIVE LEARNING CLASSIFICATION

DIRECTIONS: Review each learning performance objective, classroom question, test item or other assessment technique, exercise, or activity, and determine what the intended intellectual level is. Review this with other instructors and resolve any differences. Remember that a learning performance objective rated at the application level will incorporate objectives at the comprehension and memory levels. Objectives rated at the application level will demand tests, questions, and exercises at the same level for validity.

CATEGORY	QUESTIONS TO ASK
1.0 MEMORY (Recall) Memorize information without understanding it. This includes recognition and recall.	Will the student have to name, list, or state from memory: • terms • procedures • facts • definitions • criteria • principles
2.0 COMPREHENSION The student will be able to identify relationships among ideas.	Will the student have to: • describe or explain a procedure? • compare and contrast ideas? • summarize or paraphrase data?
3.0 APPLICATION (Rule Using) The student will apply a principle, rule, procedure, or skill, and given a rule, use it.	Will the student have to apply the given concepts, information, rules, skills, or procedures to new and unfamiliar learning situations?

4.0 CRITICAL Thinking (Rule Selection)

    4.1 ANALYSIS
    The student will break a communication down into its constituent parts and identify the real and implied relationships among the parts.

Will the student have to:
- make inferences?
- identify logical inconsistencies?
- identify organizational principles?

    4.2 SYNTHESIS
    The student will have to apply knowledge and skill to produce a unique (to the student) and original product.

Will the student have to:
- produce an original communication?
- produce an original plan of operation such as a nursing care plan, laboratory technique, or specialized diet?
- produce an original set of criteria?
- design a new piece of equipment?

    4.3 EVALUATION
    The student will judge the worth of a product based on specific criteria, given or generated.

Will the student have to:
- evaluate the effectiveness of a new procedure using some external criteria?
- evaluate the internal consistency and logic of a point of view?

LEVEL 1.0: MEMORY–(recall)

Memory or recall, is usually associated with the acquisition of verbal information, rules, principles, numbers, formulas, facts, words and names without necessarily understanding the concepts. There are two types of memory. The first is recall of verbal data in the <u>absence</u> of any cues or prompts: for example, "Write the definition of the following terms… ." The second is recognition of verbal data in the <u>presence</u> of cues and prompts. These data have been previously encountered and are familiar to the student: for example, "Which of the following is the correct definition for electron?"

    Mnemonic skills or memory aids can be extremely helpful at this level of learning. An example would be the skill of verbal association of relating a new piece of data with something already known. The first letters of the known piece of data are arranged into a statement that is remembered for later recall. For example:

- The lines of the treble clef = E, G, B, D, F, - "Every Good Boy Does Fine."
- The names of the Great Lakes = HOMES - Huron, Ontario, Michigan, Erie, Superior
- The members of a quartet = STAB - Soprano, Tenor, Alto, Bass

Learning performance objectives at this level are really test items. In most cases the objective and test item read almost exactly alike.

Sequencing at the memory level may not be as important as the higher levels of the taxonomy, but the data must be presented in a meaningful context. If long term retention is important then two conditions must be met. The student must understand the relevance of the memory activity and appropriate practice and review must be provided for the student over a period of time in order for the student to maintain the memory sequence.

Knowledge is the foundation for higher order intellectual skill development. Whether the student can recall mass amounts of data or know where to locate it is an important question to consider. Too many test items, class questions, and statements of learning performance objectives are found at this cognitive level.

Examples of Learning Performance Objectives at the Memory Level:
- Name twelve prefabricated drugs.
- The student will name the date when women were first permitted to vote.
- Define "central processing unit."
- List five sources of literature for bioequivalence of drugs.
- State three references on drug nomenclature.
- List dosage strengths.

Possible Behavioral Action Terms at the Memory Level:
These action terms appear frequently at the memory level as the primary behavior. Before deciding that a learning performance objective, test item, classroom question, or activity requires memory, examine the total context and intent of the learning performance objective. The presence of one of these action terms usually means that the objective will require memory only.

- press
- say
- copy
- list
- quote
- recall
- locate
- place

- imitate
- match
- select
- tell
- define
- recite
- state

LEVEL 2.0: COMPREHENSION

Comprehension skills are made up of three main categories: translation, interpretation, and extrapolation of data. Comprehension skills build on memory. At the comprehension level students are expected to explain the concepts learned by rote memory or usage. Concepts such as "hard", "atom," or "love" are abstract ideas that have been generalized from specific instances. Concepts, once comprehended, aid us in organizing and classifying our experience. A building is a building (a concept) whether it is one or ten stories, round or square. A comprehension or understanding of the concept of a building will allow us to classify a broad range of structures, regardless of shape, construction, or color as a "building."

Translation

Translation, the lowest level of comprehension, requires the student to change information accurately from one form to another. The original form of the communication must be preserved without altering the meaning in any way. This is the skill of paraphrasing.

Examples of Learning Performance Objectives at the Translation Level

- Translate the following graph into a narrative description and tell what the graphic symbols mean.
- Using this map, explain how you would travel from point A to point B.
- Define in your own words each of the following terms.
- The pharmacy intern will explain what the following terms mean: T.I.D., B.I.D., O.T.C.

Interpretation

Interpretation requires the student to summarize or explain a communication in a *new* way by reordering or rearranging the sequence of events. *Relationships* among major ideas must be clearly seen and understood. It is the explicit content that the student deals with, not the form or structure in which the content is presented as in analysis.

Examples of Learning Performance Objectives at the Interpretation Level

- The student will explain drug stability and usage.
- Describe six common research designs.
- Explain the PSRO monitoring standards according to the assigned chapter and modifications given during class.

Extrapolation

Extrapolation is the extension of data in time in order to make predictions of possible outcomes or consequences of the action. Extrapolation often involves IF-THEN types of questions, which are answered by informed opinion.

Examples of Learning Performance Objectives at the Extrapolation Level
- The nutrition student will predict personal health problems that might develop because of particular eating habits and will describe how the community in general might be affected.
- The instructor will explain the implications if there were a paradigm shift from "teaching as transmitting information" to "teaching as dialogue."

Possible Behavioral Action Terms at the Comprehension Level
The following action terms have been found frequently at the comprehension level:
- Distinguish
- Extrapolate
- Rearrange
- Rephrase
- Give an example of
- Illustrate
- Discriminate (between good and poor examples of...)
- Select (from given selections, those which...)
- Organize (the following data...)
- Pick out (the best specimen...)
- Reorganize (the data dealing with...)
- Choose (those characteristics that exemplify...)
- Describe (the process by which...)
- Explain (how the cells...)
- Compare and contrast (these two positions on...)
- State (in your own words...)

LEVEL 3: APPLICATION
The process of application involves the student's ability to combine the concepts of known principles and rules into meaningful relationships and apply them to *unfamiliar* and previously unencountered learning situations. The rules (abstractions) are applied in concrete situations that require some type of fixed solution or product. The students must have a clear understanding of the data and procedures before they can apply them. Application always transfers training to new learning situations. Learning performance objectives at this level are *never* test item specific since there are many different test situations that could be used to assess the ability of the student. Extreme testing situations should be avoided since they will frustrate the student.. Once the student is able to deal with a broad range of new situations, less common applications can be introduced. The student is almost always informed as to which rules to apply in a given situation. Rule using is prerequisite to and forms the basis for critical thinking strategies. It is at this latter level of thinking that the student will have to make decisions as to which rules to use to solve problems.

Examples of Learning Performance Objectives at the Application Level
- Construct six examples of performance objectives, each containing the essential elements as previously described.
- Using any person as a hypothetical subject, the student nurse will apply a figure eight bandage.
- Given a table of incidents of heart attacks among men of varying ages and weights, the student *will compute* the change in risk of heart attack in a 40-year-old male effected by a 20% weight loss.
- Weigh and measure a given pharmaceutical substances.

Possible Behavioral Action Terms at the Application Level
These action terms have been found frequently at the application level:
- Test
- Construct
- Solve
- Choose
- Calculate (the perimeter of this room...)
- Apply (the principle of... to...)
- Estimate (the value of...)
- Figure (the area of...)
- Convert the following to the metric system...
- Construct an example of a performance objective...
- Perform the following test...
- Demonstrate the use of...
- Set up and operate...
- Classify each specimen as...

LEVEL 4.0: CRITICAL THINKING or PROBLEM SOLVING

The application of principles and concepts in a rule-using situation is fairly obvious. We apply X type of rule in a Y type of situation. Someone else provides directions for the student as to which rules to apply. Critical thinking requires that the students select the most appropriate rule or rules and then apply them. In many instances these concepts and rules will have been learned in other contexts. Problem solving requires the students to integrate previously learned solutions to new and novel situations and thus expand their problem solving ability. This type of learning has been referred to as discovery learning. It requires divergent thinking when fixed and obvious solutions are the exception. Critical thinking requires the student to develop cognitive strategies and involves the mental gymnastics of analysis, synthesis and evaluation. These are explained separately as subclasses of critical thinking, but are treated collectively for the purposes of classifying objectives, test items, and questions.

Problem-solving, or metacognitive strategies, are usually developed independently of specific content and can be used in any subject area. Unless individual rules have been previously mastered, problem solving skills will be difficult and almost impossible, since these strategies involve novel combinations of individual rules as proposed hypotheses. The process is repeated until a satisfactory solution is derived. This process results in new learning for the student that can be applied in other learning situations.

LEVEL 4.1: ANALYSIS

Analysis involves breaking a communication or product down into the essential components and relating the parts to each other to discover new relationships and connections. This process deals with the form or structure in which the data is presented as well as the explicit content. A student could be required to analyze the various elements or parts of a communication, such as a problem being investigated or conclusions reached in an investigation by a researcher. Another type of analysis deals with the relationships among the various elements of a communication , as between the hypothesis and conclusion of a study. The highest form of analysis deals with the principles by which a communication is organized. The students must have a formal knowledge of analytical principles such as induction, deduction, or formal logic before they can analyze.

Examples of Learning Performance Objectives at the Analysis Level
- The student nurse will distinguish facts from fallacies on a given list of statements about food.
- Given an article dealing with current historical research, the student will determine in a written paper if the conclusions reached by the author support the hypothesis.
- Given a speech by Martin Luther King, the student will identify the assumptions of the speaker that influenced his remarks.

Possible Behavioral Action Terms at the Analysis Level
- Categorize
- Support
- What assumptions are made by the author in...
- Analyze (the relationship between… and…)
- Diagnose (the problem with…)
- Identify (the true intent of…)
- Discover (the cause-effect relationship…)
- Resolve (the differences between…)
- Detect (the techniques used to…)

LEVEL 4.2: SYNTHESIS

Synthesis, also referred to as creative behavior, involves combining elements of a communication in such a way as to make it unique and original for the student at a certain period of time. The new structure of the product or idea must be clearly distinguishable from the prior structure. The act of synthesis could be expressed as a unique communication for the purpose of describing, persuading, or entertaining.

Synthesis could also be expressed by producing a new plan of operation or set of procedures to do something. The ability of a student to develop a set of abstract relations in the form of a theory or hypothesis is also involved.

Examples of Learning Performance Objectives at the Synthesis Level
- Given a set of data, the student will propose an original hypothesis and test it. Based on the test results the student will verify or modify the hypothesis.

- Each nutrition student will write an original paper concerning reasons why vitamin supplements should not be taken indiscriminately. Three reasons given by the A.M.A. should be included plus specific documentary evidence for your own reasons.

- Given a case study of a child with infantile eczema, each student will write a nursing care plan identifying two problems in each of the following areas: medical, psychological, growth and development; and plan two interventions applicable in a hospital setting for each of these problems.

- Each college instructor will develop a lesson plan that includes the learning performance objectives for the lesson; a presentation outline; all exercises and activities; and valid assessment procedures.

Possible Action Terms for the Synthesis Level
- Create
- Makeup
- Formulate a solution
- Synthesize
- Put together
- Compose (an original...)
- Develop (a theory that...)
- Devise (an original solution...)
- Invent (a way that...)
- Produce (a story that...)
- Tell (an original tale...)
- Plan (a meal that...)
- Design (a set for the plan...)

LEVEL 4.3: EVALUATION
Evaluation is the highest category of intellectual skill in which the results of analysis and synthesis are judged according to some internal or external criteria. The judgments may be either quantitative or qualitative and may be generated by the students or given to them in some form. Evaluation might involve some value judgments.

Examples of Learning Performance Objectives at the Evaluation Level
- Given opposing arguments dealing with the use of marijuana, the student will evaluate them according to the following criteria:

- Given a patient diagnosed with an upper extremity problem, the student will assess the extent of the abnormality according to the criteria:
  - atrophy
  - loss of mobility
  - obvious patterns of compensation

After observing an instructor in a classroom teaching situation, the teaching consultant will evaluate the quality of teaching based on the following criteria:
- level of questions
- pacing
- lecture format

Possible Action Terms at the Evaluation Level
- Choose
- Evaluate
- Decide
- Defend
- Assess (the accuracy of...)
- Judge (the efficiency of this method...)
- Estimate (the real worth of...)
- Argue (the value of...)

EXERCISE: Rating the Intended Cognitive Level of Learning Performance Objectives

Directions: Listed below is a series of learning performance objectives. Rate each one as to the intended intellectual levels of knowledge, comprehension, application, or critical thinking.

1. _____ Given a brief description of needs, label each according to Maslow's hierarchy.
2. _____ Describe the components of a learning performance objective as given in this seminar.
3. _____ Define "central processing unit" and identify three locations where they can be found.
4. _____ Given descriptions of incidents of job-related conflicts and the actions of the participants, identify each instance of sexual discrimination or harassment according to the institutional standards of impartiality, conduct, honesty, and integrity.
5. _____ Without using any notes, the student will speak extemporaneously for three minutes on a topic assigned by the instructor.

SUMMARY

Most learning performance objectives fall within the cognitive domain. The classification scheme has been used for many years and has a great deal of validity. The upper three levels of analysis, synthesis, and evaluation were grouped under the category of critical analysis for the ease of use.

AFFECTIVE LEARNING PERFORMANCE OBJECTIVES

Up to this point, we have discussed mainly learning performance objectives that fall into the cognitive category. Evidence of achievement is relatively concrete to measure, particularly at the lowest three levels of the taxonomy—knowledge, comprehension, and application. When affective behaviors are discussed, concrete evidence of objective achievement is more difficult to measure. We can only make inferences from observed behavior that the objectives have been achieved.

Affective behavior is an internal state and cannot be measured until the student exhibits behavior from which we infer certain attitudes and values. These internal states are influenced by cognitive learning both formally in school and informally in other environments.

All instructors want their students to like their subjects and be interested in school. Measurement of such lofty goals can only be accomplished by observing behaviors that appear to indicate that the student is achieving the objectives. Such "indicator behaviors" might include smiles, frowns, expressions of excitement, eagerness, boredom, restlessness, or commitment. All of these indicators reflect some change in attitude that could be affected by environment, background, abilities, and interests, and even the personality of the instructor. Although most attitudes are learned incidentally, it is possible to structure certain elements in a learning situation that are designed to influence student attitudes.

Cognitive learning performance objectives imply a capability to do something. Observation indicates that a student *can* perform an intellectual skill at some level of proficiency. Why the student does it and whether the student will choose to do it at some future time is a matter of value and attitude. Affective learning performance objectives imply a preference that students will do something even though they know how to do it.

An attempt to develop a hierarchy of objectives in the affective domain was made by Krathwohl, Bloom, and Masia (1966). There are five categories of affect. The hierarchical relationships among these categories are logical. There is no empirical evidence to suggest any cumulative development. These categories include from lowest (receiving) to highest order of affect (characterization by a value).

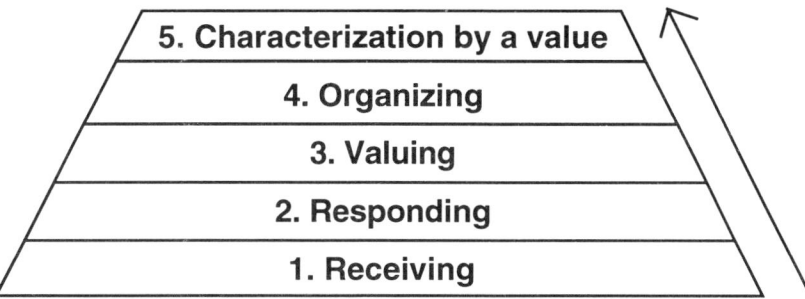

LEVEL 1.0: RECEIVING

When students are receiving or attending to something they are demonstrating an awareness of its existence through some type of stimulus in the environment. Once aware of the stimulus (color, sound, music, and so forth), the student must then give it some measure of attention by accepting it.

Examples of Learning Performance Objectives at the Receiving Level
- The student listens attentively to a speech by a noted author.
- The student notices the furnishings in the museum.
- The student appreciates the native costumes worn by the foreign students.

Possible Action Terms at the Receiving Level
- Select
- Accumulate
- Share
- Accept

LEVEL 2.0: RESPONDING

The students not only receive the stimuli from their environment, they actively respond in some way to it without knowing in detail or depth why they are doing it. It is possible that the students are acting out of fear of punishment or reprisal rather than respect, concern, or love. Responding consists of voluntary actions and personal satisfaction.

Examples of Learning Performance Objectives at the Responding Level
- The student willingly obeys the "No Smoking" signs in designated areas.
- The technologist obeys the laboratory regulations for safety.

2.1: Voluntary Actions
The next level of responding is characterized by the student's voluntary actions. They actually desire to perform the act.

Examples of Learning Performance Objectives at the Voluntary Action Level
- The student volunteers to discuss the topic of therapeutic abortion.
- The student volunteers to look the reference up in the library.

2.2: Personal Satisfaction
Once the student responds willingly without fear of reprisal, some type of personal satisfaction usually follows, accompanied by joy and pleasure.

Examples of Learning Performance Objectives at the Personal Satisfaction Level
- The student vigorously applauded the noted speaker on laser optics.
- The student seeks out other students interested in abortion rights to discuss the topic.

Possible Action Terms at the Responding Level
- Comply
- Approve
- Discuss
- Volunteer
- Follow

LEVEL 3.0: VALUING
When students value something, they place a certain worth on it. Things or ideas that are valued become part of an individual's belief and are consistently reflected in the actions of the individual. These actions are consistently applied in most situations The value exerts a great influence over the student's behavior and constantly motivates. There are degrees of valuing that range from acceptance of a value (lowest level of certainty), to preference for a value (student seeks it out and wants it), to commitment to a value (highest degree of certainty).

Criteria for Valuing
According to Raths & Simon (1966), the process of valuing must meet the following criteria:

Choosing:
1. freely
2. from alternatives
3. after thoughtful consideration of the consequences of each alternative

Prizing:
4. cherishing, being happy with the choice
5. willing to affirm the choice publicly
6. doing something with the choice
7. repeatedly, in some pattern of life

Examples of Learning Performance Objectives at the Valuing Level
- The student contributes money to help support the local Audubon Society.
- The student constantly argues in favor of condom distribution.

Possible Action Terms at the Valuing Level
- Assist
- Help
- Support
- Argue
- Protest

LEVEL 4.0: ORGANIZATION

As students begin to value different ideas and things, it becomes necessary for them to organize and synthesize their value structure into some type of hierarchy and to identify relationships among different values. The student also conceptualizes or abstracts the values so that new values can be related and compared. This begins to form the basis for a personal philosophy of life.

Examples of Learning Performance Objectives at the Organization Level
- The students formulate criteria by which they will conduct their moral behavior.
- The students form judgments as to the responsibility of individuals for actively participating in movements against all forms of abortion.

Possible Action Terms at the Organization Level
- Form judgments
- Seek evidence
- Prioritize values
- Organize a value system
- Select
- Judge
- Identify with

LEVEL 5.0: CHARACTERIZATION BY A VALUE OR VALUE COMPLEX

Students at this level of internalization are characterized as being guided by certain beliefs that affect their total behavior. Given certain situations, you can almost predict behavior because the value system is so much a part of the individual. They act consistently and at times almost unconsciously. This level is actually the guiding philosophy of life that controls a student's every action.

Examples of Learning Performance Objectives at the Characterization Level
- The student refuses to accept answers offered by another student on an anatomy final exam, even though he or she knows the test will end in failure.
- The student revises personal judgments in the presence of alternative evidence.
- When eating in the cafeteria, the student will consistently choose a balanced meal that contains foods from each of the four basic food groups.

Possible Action Terms at the Characterization Level
- Seek evidence
- Develop a lifestyle
- Practice
- Believe in
- Carry out
- Continue to

SUMMARY

These five levels of affective outcomes should be reviewed as a guide and not as an absolute hierarchy. The examples provided should be refined in some instances and expanded in others. When reviewing each, try to identify as many indicator behaviors as possible that would provide evidence that the student has achieved the objectives.

PSYCHOMOTOR LEARNING PERFORMANCE OBJECTIVES

Psychomotor skills involve fine and gross muscular functions for the purpose of manipulating objects and materials. Different types of classification schemes have been developed by educators (Kibler, Barker, and Miles, 1970; Goldberger and Moyer, 1982; Simpson, 1966). The most comprehensive system was developed by Simpson (1966). She identified seven levels of skill development in the psychomotor domain. These included from lowest to highest: perception, set, guided response, mechanism, adaptation, and origination. Each level is described in some detail.

LEVEL 1.0: PERCEPTION

This is the first essential step in performing a motor act. It is the process of becoming aware of objects, qualities, or relations by way of the sense organs. It is a necessary, but not sufficient, condition for motor activity. It is basic in the situation–interpretation–action chain leading to motor activity. The category of perception has been divided into three subcategories indicating three different levels of the perception process. This level is a parallel of the first category, receiving or attending, in the affective domain.

> **1.1 Sensory stimulation**-• Impingement of a stimulus upon one or more of the sense organs.
> **1.1.1 Auditory** -• Hearing or the sense of hearing organs.
> **1.1.2 Visual** - Concerned with the mental pictures or images obtained through the eyes.
> **1.1.3 Tactile** -• Pertaining to the sense of touch.
> **1.1.4 Taste** -• Determine the relish or flavor of by taking a portion of food into the mouth.
> **1.1.5 Smell** - To perceive by excitation of the olfactory nerves.

1.1.6 Kinesthetic - The muscle sense, pertaining to sensitivity from activation of receptors in muscles, tendons, and joints.

Example of a Learning Performance Objective at the Perception Level
- Sensitivity to auditory cues in playing a musical instrument as a member of a group.
- Awareness of difference in "hand" of various fabrics.

1.2 Cue selection • Deciding to what cues one must respond in order to satisfy the particular requirements of task performance. This involves identification of the cue or cues and associating them with the task to be performed. It may involve grouping of cues in terms of past experience and knowledge. Cues relevant to the situation are selected as a guide to action, irrelevant cues are ignored or discarded.

Example of a Learning Performance Objective at the Cue Selection Level
- Recognition of operating difficulties with machinery from the sound of the machine in operation.

1.3 Translation • Relating of perception to action in performing a motor act. This is the mental process of determining the meaning of the cues received for action. It involves symbolic translation, that is, having an image or being reminded of something, "having an idea," as a result of cues received. It may involve insight which is essential in solving a problem through perceiving the relationships essential to solution. Sensory translation is an aspect of this level. It involves "feedback," that is, knowledge of the effects of the act being performed.

Examples of Learning Performance Objectives at the Translation Level
- Ability to relate music to dance form.
- Ability to follow a recipe preparing food.
- Knowledge of the "feel" of operating a sewing machine successfully and use of this knowledge as a guide in stitching.

LEVEL 2.0: SET
Set is a preparatory adjustment or readiness for a particular kind of action or experience. Three aspects of set have been identified: mental, physical, and emotional.

2.1 Mental set • Readiness, in the mental sense, to perform a certain motor act. This involves, as prerequisite, the level of perception and its subcategories. Discrimination, that is, using judgment in making distinctions, is an aspect of mental set.

Examples of Learning Performance Objectives at the Mental Set Level
- Knowledge of steps in setting the table.
- Knowledge of tools appropriate to performance of various operations.

2.2 Physical set • Readiness in the sense of having made the anatomical adjustments necessary for a motor act to be performed. Readiness, in the physical sense, involves receptor set, that is, sensory attending, or focusing the attention of the needed sensory organs and postural set, or positioning of the body.

Examples of Learning Performance Objectives at the Physical Set Level
- Achievement of bodily stance preparatory to bowling.
- Positioning of hands preparatory to typing.

2.3 Emotional set • Readiness in terms of attitudes favorable to the motor acts taking place. Willingness to respond is implied.

Examples Learning Performance Objectives at the Emotional Set Level
- Disposition to perform sewing machine operations to the best of one's ability.
- Desire to operate a production drill press with skill.

LEVEL 3.0: GUIDED RESPONSE
This is an early step in the development of skill. Emphasis here is upon the abilities that are components of the more complex skill. Guided response is the overt behavioral act of an individual under the guidance of the instructor or in response to self-evaluation in which the students have a model or criteria against which they can judge their performance. Prerequisites to performance of the act are readiness to respond, in terms of set to produce the overt behavioral act and selection of the appropriate response. Selection of response may be defined as deciding what response must be made in order to satisfy the requirements of task performance. There appear to be two major subcategories: imitation and trial and error.

3.1 Imitation • Imitation is the execution of an act as a direct response to the perception of another person performing the act.

Examples of Learning Performance Objectives at the Imitation Level
- Imitation of the process of stay-stitching the curved neck edge of a bodice.
- Performing a dance step as demonstrated.
- Debeaking a chick in the manner demonstrated.

3.2 Trial and error • Trying various responses, usually with some rationale for each response, until an appropriate response is achieved. The appropriate response is one that meets the requirements of task performance, that is, "gets the job done" or does it more efficiently. This level may be defined as multiple-response learning in which the proper response is selected out of varied behavior, possibly through the influence of reward and punishment.

Examples of Learning Performance Objectives at the Trial and Error Levels
- Discovering the most efficient method of ironing a blouse through trial of various procedures.
- Determining the sequence for cleaning a room through trial of several patterns.

LEVEL 4.0: MECHANISM
Learned response has become habitual. At this level, the learner has achieved a certain confidence and degree of proficiency in the performance of the act. The act is a part of his or her repertoire of possible responses to stimuli and demands of situations in which the response is an appropriate one. The response may be more complex than at the preceding level; it may involve some patterning in carrying out the task.

Examples of Learning Performance Objectives at the Mechanism Level
- Ability to perform a hand-hemming operation.
- Ability to mix ingredients for butter cake.
- Ability to pollinate an oat flower.

LEVEL 5.0 COMPLEX OVERT RESPONSE
At this level, the individual can perform a motor act that is considered complex because of the movement pattern required. At this level, skill has been attained. The act can be carried out smoothly and efficiently, that is, with minimum expenditure of time and energy. There are two subcategories: resolution of uncertainty and automatic performance.

> **5.1 Resolution of uncertainty** • The act is performed without hesitation of the individual to get a mental picture of the task sequence. That is, the required sequence is known and so the student proceeds with confidence. The act is here defined as complex in nature.

Examples of Learning Performance Objectives at the Resolution of Uncertainty Level
- Skill in operating a milling machine.
- Skill in setting up and operating a production band saw.

> **5.2 Automatic performance** • At this level, the individual can perform a finely coordinated motor skill with a great deal of ease and muscle control.

Examples of Learning Performance Objectives at the Automatic Performance Level
- Skill in performing basic steps of national folk dances.

- Skill in tailoring a suit.
- Skill in playing the violin.

LEVEL 6.0: ADAPTATION
Altering motor activities to meet the demands of new problematic situations requiring a physical response.

Example of a Learning Performance Objective at the Adaptation Level
- Developing a modern dance composition through adapting known abilities and skills in dance.

LEVEL 7.0: ORIGINATION
Creating new motor acts or ways of manipulating materials out of understandings, abilities, and skills developed in the psychomotor area.

Examples of Learning Performance Objectives at the Origination Level
- Creation of a modern dance.
- Creation of a new game requiring a psychomotor response.

EXERCISE: Primary Domains of Learning Performance Objectives

Directions: Listed below is a series of learning performance objectives. Classify each as primarily:
(C) Cognitive   (A) Affective   (P) Psychomotor

_____ 1. Choose the best of two solutions to a geometry problem using the standards given by the teacher.

_____ 2. A student displays interest in higher mathematics by voluntarily attending lectures sponsored by the math club.

_____ 3. A student plays table tennis according to the rules well enough to beat three inexperienced players 100% of the time.

_____ 4. Exhibits tolerance for others by displaying good manners toward those of minority groups.

_____ 5. The intern will tie the proper suture knot.

_____ 6. The instructor will develop lesson plans using all proper instructional development procedures.

_____ 7. Recite the Gettysburg Address from memory with proper inflection and varied pace.

SUMMARY

The three taxonomies—cognitive, affective, and psychomotor—form the basis for developing a learning sequence. They are logical and in the case of the cognitive domain, hierarchical. The taxonomies can be used to rate learning performance objectives; classroom questions; learning activities; student assessment procedures; and team activities.

BIBLIOGRAPHY

Bloom, B.S. (1953). Thought-processes in lectures. Journal of General Education, 7, 160-169.

Bloom, B., & Others (1956). Taxonomy of educational objectives, Handbook I: Cognitive domain. NY: McKay.

Calder, J.R. (1983). In the cells of the 'Bloom taxonomy.' Journal of Curriculum Studies, 15(3), 291-302.

Clary, Joan, & Mahaffy, John. (1985). The cognitive domain: The last frontier. Portland, OR: Northwest Regional Education Lab. (ERIC Document Reproduction Service No. ED 265 496)

Clegg, Ambrose A., Jr., Farley, George T., & Curran, Robert U. (1967). Training teachers to analyze the cognitive level of classroom questioning. University of Massachusetts: Research Report No. 1, Applied Research Training Program.

Clevenstine, Richard F. (1987). A classification of the ISIS program using Bloom's cognitive taxonomy. Journal of Research in Science Teaching, 24(8), 699-712.

Covington, Helen C., & Tiballi, Terry. (1982). Using Bloom's taxonomy for precision planning and creative teaching in the developmental math classroom. San Diego, CA: Western College Reading Association Convention. (ERIC Document Reproduction Service No. ED 221 253)

Cryer, Patricia. (1985). A model for structuring training activities: A personal view. PLET, 22(3), 262-266.

Drumheller, Sidney J. A model for applying the Bloom taxonomy of educational objectives in curriculum design. NSPI Journal, 6(5), 10-17.

Ennis, Robert H. (1982). Identifying implicit assumptions. Synthese, 51, 61-86.

Farley, George T., & Clegg, Ambrose A., Jr. (1969). Increasing the cognitive level of classroom questions in social studies: An application of Bloom's taxonomy. Los Angeles, CA: Paper presented as part of a symposium on "Research in Social Studies Education."

Furst, Edward J. (1983). Communicability of the taxonomy of educational objectives for the cognitive domain. (ERIC Document Reproduction Service No. ED 235 194)

____. (1981). Bloom's taxonomy ef educational objectives for the cognitive domain: Philosophical and educational issues. Review of Educational Research, 51(4), 441-453.

Gentry, Darrell L. (1989). Teacher-made test construction. Little Rock, AR: Annual Meeting of the Mid-South Educational Research Association. (ERIC Document Reproduction Service No. ED 313 444)

Goldberger, Michael, & Moyer, Steve (1982). A schema for classifying educational objectives in the psychomotor domain. Quest, 34(2), 134-142.

Holleman, Wes. (1985). The fourth domain of educational objectives: Induction. Instructional Science, 14, 169-178.

Hoste, Roland. (1982). What do examination items test? An investigation of construct validity in a biology examination. Journal of Biological Education, 16(1), 51-58.

Irby, David M., Lippert, Frederick G., & Schaad, Douglas C. (1991). Psychomotor skills for the general professional education of the physician. Teaching and Learning in Medicine, 3(1), 2-5.

Jarolimek, John. (1962). The taxonomy: Guide to differentiated instruction. Social Education, 445-447.

Kibler, R.J., Barker, L.L., & Miles, D.T. (1970). Behavioral objectives and instruction. Boston: Allyn and Bacon.

Kottke, Janet L., & Schuster, Donald H. (1990). Developing tests for measuring Bloom's learning outcomes. Psychological Reports, 66, 27-32.

Krathwohl, D.R., Bloom, B.S., & Masia, B.B. (1964). Taxonomy of educational objectives, Handbook II: Affective Domain. NY: McKay.

Krendl, Kathy A., Agostino, Don E., & Brancolini, Eugene. (1986). Assessing new instructional technologies: Interactive video learning tools. ERS Spectrum, 4(3), 3-7.

Kropp, R.P., Stopker, H.W., & Bashaw, W.L. (1966). The validation of the taxonomy of educational objectives. The Journal of Experimental Education, 34(3), 69-76.

Kunen, Seth, Cohen, Ronald, & Solman, Robert. (1981). A levels-of-processing analysis of Bloom's taxonomy. Journal of Educational Psychology, 73(2), 202-211.

Lipscomb, John Wilson, Jr. (1965). Is Bloom's taxonomy better than intuitive judgment for classifying test questions? Education, 106(1), 102-107.

Madaus, George F., Woods, Elinor M., & Nuttall, Ronald L. (1973). A causal model analysis of Bloom's taxonomy. American Educational Research Journal, 10(4), 253-262.

Martin, David S. (1989). Restructuring teacher education programs for higher-order thinking skills. Journal of Teacher Education, 2-8.

Michael, William B. (1978). Book reviews. Educational and Psychological Measurement, 631-634.

Moore, David S. (1982). Reconsidering Bloom's taxonomy of educational objectives, cognitive domain. Educational Theory, 32(1), 29-34.

Neumann, Lily, & Mahler, Sophia. (1985). A non-metric method for assessing the class size effect upon medical instruction. Journal of Instructional Psychology, 12(3), 159-172.

Ormell, C.P. (1974). Bloom's taxonomy and the objectives of education. Educational Research, 17(1), 3-17.

Paul, Richard W. (1985). Bloom's taxonomy and critical thinking instruction. Educational Leadership, 36-39.

Pollio, H.R. (1984). What students think about and do in college lecture classes. University of Tennessee, Knoxville: Learning Research Center.

Poole Richard L. (1972). Characteristics of the taxonomy of educational objectives: Cognitive domain—A replication. Psychology in the Schools, 9, 83-88.

____. (1971). Characteristics of the taxonomy of educational objectives: Cognitive domain. Psychology in the Schools, 8, 379-385.

Popham, W. James. (1987). Two-plus decades of educational objectives. International Journal of Educational Research, 11(1), 31-41.

Pring, Richard. (1971). Bloom's taxonomy: A philosophical critique (2). Cambridge Journal of Education, 1, 83-91.

Raths, Louis E., Harmin, Merrill, & Simon, Sidney B. (1966). Values and teaching. Columbus, OH: Charles E. Merrill Books, Inc., 30.

Romiszowski, Alexander J. (1989). Attitudes and affect in learning and instruction. Educational-Media-International, 26(2), 85-100.

Schrag, Francis. (1989). Are there levels of thinking? Teachers College Record, 90(4), 529-533.

Scribner, Duane C. (1967). Learning hierarchies and literary sequence. English Journal, 56(3), 385-401.

Seddon, G.M. (1978). The properties of Bloom's taxonomy of educational objectives for the cognitive domain. Review of Educational Research, 48(2), 303-323.

Smith, Richard B. (1968). An empirical examination of the assumptions underlying the taxonomy of educational objectives: Cognitive domain. Journal of Educational Measurement, 5(2), 125-128.

Solman, Robert, & Rosen, Gaye. (1986). Bloom's six cognitive levels represent two levels of performance. Educational Psychology, 6(3), 243-263.

Stedman, Carlton H. (1973). An analysis of the assumptions underlying the taxonomy of educational objectives: Cognitive domain. Journal of Research in Science Teaching, 10(3), 235-241.

Strom, Robert, & Ray, William. (1971). Communication in the affective domain. Theory into Practice, 10(4), 268-275.

Tittle, Carol Kehr, & Others. (1989). From taxonomy to constructing meaning in context: Revisiting the taxonomy of educational objectives: II, affective domain. San Francisco, CA: Paper presented at the Annual Meeting of the National Council on Measurement in Education. (ERIC Document Reproduction Service No. ED 306 272)

Chapter 9
Teaching for Critical Thinking

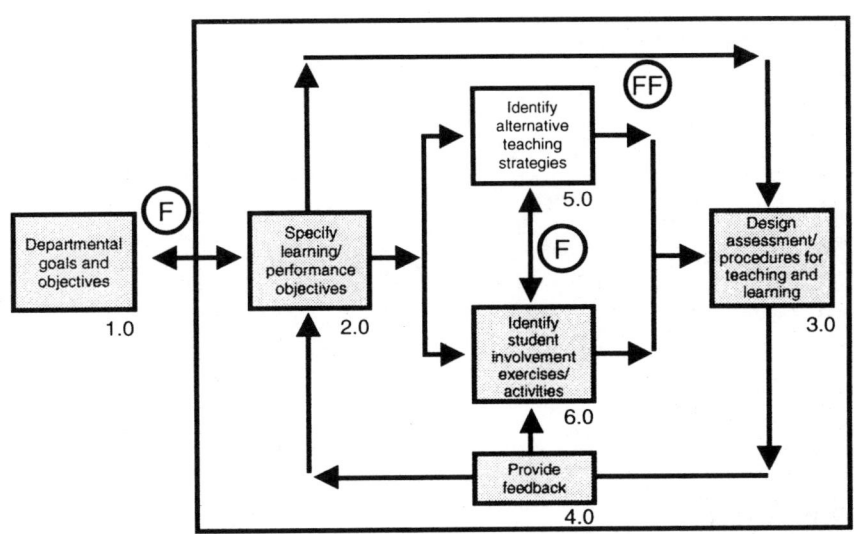

"What we hope begins when education ends."

TEACHING FOR CRITICAL THINKING

LEARNING PERFORMANCE OBJECTIVE
Design a lesson plan using the format provided that will assist students to develop critical thinking skills. The lesson plan must include all intermediate learning performance objectives; student exercises and activities; teaching strategies; and assessment procedures. The lesson plan should be accompanied with a rationale explaining why it will create an environment for critical thinking. (Level 4).

KEY IDEAS
1. Critical thinking combines the upper three levels of Bloom's cognitive taxonomy.
2. Students think critically when they are taught to use critical thinking skills formally and with practice.
3. Critical thinking cannot be taught through lecture. There must be active student involvement.
4. Trigger videos—short and dramatic visual scenarios—can stimulate critical thinking.

NEW VOCABULARY
- critical thinking
- metacognition
- trigger video

In the previous chapter the upper three levels of Bloom's cognitive taxonomy (analysis, synthesis, and evaluation) were grouped together and titled, "critical thinking." This was done for convenience and to reduce the training time necessary to develop a learning sequence. This chapter will probe the concept of critical thinking in more detail because of its importance to teaching and learning.

We have always <u>assumed</u> that college students learned how to think critically during their school years and could apply these "thinking skills" to solve problems and analyze communications. Professors say they teach "it." Textbooks state that they promote "it." Many instructor-designed assignments intended for students to learn "it." But look at mid-term and final examinations. Do they assess "it?" The research indicates that there is a preponderance of classroom questions that require recall of factual information (Barnes, 1983; Boyer, 1987; Hamblen, 1984). It has been reported that medical schools overemphasize memory skills in the subject matter to the extent that 80% of information is forgotten by the day of graduation. (Russell, 1984). Michalak (1986) observes that,

> ... no stronger myth reigns on our campuses than the belief that when professors lecture and assign papers, students learn to think. It is a myth that reigns impervious to a growing body of scholarly literature that casts overwhelming doubt upon its validity.

During the past 10 years there have been numerous major reports on American education calling for the development of critical thinking in our schools as a national priority for civic and economic reasons (National Institute of Education, 1984; National

Commission on Excellence in Education, 1983; Newman, 1985; Boyer; 1987, Bok, 1986). Why so much emphasis on memory in lieu of critical thinking skills? One reason is that recall or memory test items are quick and easy to write and score. Yet, when asked what type of intellectual skills they are teaching and testing, most instructors honestly believe they are addressing "critical thinking" and "problem-solving skills." How often have you heard it said, "Don't teach economics. Teach how economists think." We cannot teach "thinking skills" when students are conditioned to memorize facts which is the way they are questioned and tested in the college classroom.

Competence in critical thinking is not an incidental outcome of instruction. Instructors must employ direct, systematic instruction to develop the metacognitive skills necessary to foster critical thinking across academic disciplines.

Metacognition is the

> ...use of strategies to monitor and control attention and memory and to make decisions about how to proceed on a task... . Metacognition is distinct from procedural knowledge in that procedural knowledge is domain specific, while metacognitive strategies support problem-solving in any domain. (Kurfiss, 1988)

Meyers (1986) observes that "Critical thinking abilities do not develop unaided during a course of study, nor will they arise solely from students listening to lectures, reading texts, and taking exams." The students must know and understand the skills of critical thinking; be aware of the existence of a problem; understand the nature and context of the problem; reflect on what would be the most appropriate approach to solve a problem; and then consciously apply these skills. After application of the specific solution skills, the students then determine the validity of the outcomes or solutions and the consequences of these outcomes. Teachers need to know explicitly what they mean by critical thinking within the context of their disciplines and then provide opportunities for their students to practice critical thinking skills and develop critical thinking values and attitudes. Lockhart (1963) reinforces this notion of critical thinking not only as an attitude but also involves the use of a,

> ...system of values (a search for the verifiable truth) by which we determine choices, and a system of searching for these values. ... If critical thinking is to be contagious, the student must be surrounded by it. The student yearns to be shown by example.

Students cannot learn critical thinking skills from or during a lecture. At best, they can observe a talented instructor working through a problem in a quantitative or qualitative context as they apply different solution techniques and reflect out loud as they go through the steps. This type of modeling example has a great deal of benefit especially if the student is allowed to intercede and ask questions as to why the instructor is doing what he or she is doing. In the final analysis students must participate in the solution process, and not just as an observer. They must be given time to work with other students and practice the skill of critical thinking with guidance and feedback from the instructor.

Presseisen (1986) has identified some of the key features of higher-order cognitive processes. These skills are non-algorithmic. The path of action is not fully specified and known in advance. Higher-order thinking is complex. The action path is not totally seen by the student from any one point of view. There is no "one" action path or "one" solution. There may be many options available to approach the problem, each with different resource needs. Higher-order thinking involves "advanced" judgment and interpretation as well as the application of different sets of criteria. There may be certain levels of uncertainty since all data may not be known. This type of thinking will require a level of independence and self-paced working with other students in small group situations so that they can find meaning and structure in apparent disorder through their discussion and investigations.

There are different definitions and interpretations of critical thinking, many of which are usable in one way or another. One of the earliest definitions was proposed by Glaser (1941). He notes that the ability to think critically involves three interrelated things:

> (1)... an attitude of being disposed to consider in a thoughtful way the problems and subjects that come within the range of one's experiences; (2) knowledge of the methods of logical inquiry and reasoning; and (3) some skill in applying those methods. Critical thinking calls for a persistent effort to examine any belief or supposed form of knowledge in the light of the evidence that supports it and the further conclusions to which it tends.

Beyer (April, 1985) defines critical thinking as "...the assessing of the authenticity, accuracy, and or worth of knowledge claims and arguments." He views critical thinking skills as consisting of three essential kinds of attributes:
1. A set of procedures, steps, or operations you would employ in executing the skills.
2. Distinguishing criteria are idealized standards, clues, or evidence that distinguishes what the particular skill seeks to identify such as bias, reluctancy, logical necessities, or assumptions.
3. Set of rules which are those guidelines that tell users when to employ the skill and what to do next.

Every critical thinking skill has a set of procedures, criteria and rules that make it what it is.

Scriven (1976) described the following steps in the procedures by which one executes the critical thinking skill of judging: (1) clarify the meaning of all major words; (2) Identify the stated and implied conclusions and the structure of the argument as well as any unstated assumptions; (3) the student should then identify and critique any premises and inferences that need to be made; (4) seek other relevant arguments; (5) evaluate the quality of the argument in light of the preceding steps.

Feeley (1956) views critical thinking as a, "collection of discrete skills or operations which combines analysis and evaluation." The core of these operations is that the student is able to distinguish between verifiable facts and value claims; determine the source reliability; determine the factual accuracy of a statement; distinguish relevant from irrelevant information, claims, or reasons; determine bias in an argument or position; identify unstated assumptions; identify ambiguous or equivocal claims or arguments; recognize logical inconsistencies of fallacious reasoning; distinguish between warranted and unwarranted claims; and determine the strength of an argument. In later writings Feeley (August, 1976) expanded his idea of critical thinking as "...the judging of statements based on acceptable standards."

Ennis (1962) reporting in the <u>Harvard Educational Review</u> defined critical thinking, "...to be the correct assessing of statements." He then identified 12 aspects of critical thinking in his research in which the student:
1. Grasps the meaning of a statement.
2. Judges the ambiguity of a line of reasoning.
3. Judges the contradictions among statements.
4. Judges that a conclusion follows necessarily from the data provided.
5. Judges the specificity of a statement.
6. Judges that a statement is actually the application of a certain principle.
7. Judges the reliability of an observation.
8. Judges if an inductive conclusion is warranted.
9. Judges if a problem has been identified.
10. Judges if something is an assumption.
11. Judges the accuracy of a definition.
12. Judges whether an authoritative statement is acceptable as presented.

Furedy and Furedy (1985) reported that critical thinking involved the students' ability to do some or all of the following: identify the central issues and assumptions in an argument; recognize important relationships; make correct inferences from data; deduce conclusions from information or data provided; interpret whether conclusions are warranted on the basis of the data given; and evaluate evidence or authority.

One of the most current definitions of critical thinking is proposed by Kurfiss (1988) in a review of the theory, research, practice, and possibilities of teaching critical thinking skills. She viewed critical thinking "...as an investigation whose purpose is to explore a situation, phenomenon, question, or problem to arrive at a hypothesis or conclusion about it that integrates all available information and that can therefore be convincingly justified." This researcher goes on to note that,

> In critical thinking, all assumptions are open to question, divergent views are aggressively sought, and the inquiry is not biased in favor of a particular outcome. The outcomes of a critical inquiry are twofold: a *conclusion* or hypothesis and the *justification* offered in support of it.

In her conclusion to the current research on critical thinking, Kurfiss identified several broad implications for instructors who would like to do more work with their students in critical thinking:
1. Use problems as organizing principles for instruction. Link new data to the experiential backgrounds of the students. She suggests that instructors use inquiry methods and familiar examples to enhance understanding and accessibility of declarative knowledge.

2. Use modeling, coaching, practice, review, and feedback. Teach students when and how to use what they are learning.
3. Create situations in which students can discuss their beliefs and values about what they are learning and create learning experiences in which students can examine and modify their beliefs.
4. Explain a variety of metacognitive processes and demonstrate them frequently in class. Build activities and exercises that allow the instructor to prompt students to use these metacognitive skills.
5. Motivate students by using social and cognitive instructional strategies.

Translating all of this theory into practice presents wonderful challenges for creative instructors. Teaching and creating a classroom environment for the development of critical thinking skills may be the greatest challenge for college instructors. Creating instructional strategies that allow students to become involved in critical thinking activities is time-consuming and difficult to create and manage because students need time and freedom to explore alternative solutions.

Using Trigger Videos to Develop Critical Thinking Skills
Frequently used instructional strategies for critical thinking include such techniques as case studies, simulations, role-playing, scenarios, and games. One technique that combines many of the features of these strategies, and that is relatively inexpensive to develop, is the trigger film or trigger video. The latter is a one- to five-minute (longer if necessary) visual scenario of a problem, opportunity, or event that raises questions or concerns and requires some type of solution or action. The trigger is used to stimulate discussion around the topic. The emphasis of the scenario is the subject matter rather than the production. Other than a reasonably good picture and audio, production quality is de-emphasized. There is minimal or no editing. This can be precluded with good preplanning. Since the clip is very short, reshooting is easy in case of error. Produced with a small video camcorder and using students and colleagues as talent, the instructor outlines a role-play situation with varying levels of detail. The level of detail can be used to allow the viewing students more or less latitude to make assumptions about antecedent events not shown in the video clip. The more assumptions that the students are allowed to make, the more they can affect the final solution or recommendations. In some instances you may not want to allow the students to make any assumptions and therefore you must provide all necessary data. The students will deal with the information provided within the video clip only.

A powerful source of trigger videos can be found in the wide range of commercial movies available at video rental stores. Scenes can be identified that provide a dramatic incident or social dilemma dealing with specific concepts, principles, and ideas covered in class.

Trigger videos are used to open a class discussion. A three- or four-minute trigger is presented and the students are asked to describe what they see and what the implications are for some topic under study. This could be a dramatic scenario that will require a conclusion or a recommendation. Triggers can present a partial scenario that requires a recommendation and then the second half of the trigger is shown with a professional acting out what should be done. Triggers can be shown at the beginning of class to create a basis for discussion. Brief documentaries such as a medical emergency, bridge collapsing, or natural disaster could be used to begin an analysis of a problem. The use of historical propaganda films are an excellent source of triggers. Another technique is a simple dialogue between two or more people. As the dialogue unfolds there is a prejudice, bias, or use of faulty information. Non-repeatable events such as time motion, costly or dangerous experiments can be used to build observational skills. Another very interesting technique is to have the <u>students</u> create a trigger video to be used by other groups of students for analysis.

Most trigger videos use dramatic scenes to present a problem. After viewing the original or commercial trigger, students, working in small groups during and/or after class, are asked to describe exactly what they have seen and discuss the facts only. They then begin to make inferences and assumptions; describe the problem or opportunity; identify all legal, political, economic, ethical, and practical implications; explain all possible courses of action and the probable consequences of each course of action; and then make a recommendation based on the criteria provided by the instructor or generated by the students. The analysis can take one or more class periods. After the student group has made a recommendation, the instructor critiques the recommendation or turns the video back on for a resolution of the problem by the professional in the film.

Several examples of short case studies that could be translated into video scenarios or trigger videos include:

1. A new instructor meets his class for the first time. As he begins to introduce himself to the class, the classroom door opens, his distraught wife runs into the classroom, and screams, "You cannot treat me that way any more." In a hysterical and uncontrolled fit of anger, she throws a set of keys at him and declares that she is filing divorce papers that afternoon. She turns, runs out of the classroom, and slams the door. The shocked instructor, obviously embarrassed, looks at the class, picks up the thrown keys, excuses himself, and walks slowly out of the classroom. As he reaches the classroom door, he turns, walks quickly back to the podium, and states with enthusiasm, "Although this is your first class, write a story about what you have just witnessed."

2. A person dressed in a raincoat and standing in front of a drug store on a rainy evening walks quickly toward the store. Upon entering, this unknown person (you cannot tell if it is a man or woman) walks toward the counter. The pharmacist awaits with a smile as this nervous customer approaches. The customer hands the pharmacist a tightly folded piece of paper. The pharmacist smiles and opens the folded paper to find a fifty dollar bill and the printed words "One pint of paregoric (a prescription drug)". At this point the videotape is turned off and the students are asked to record exactly what they just observed and if they thought there was a problem.
After discussion and consideration of the possible alternative courses of action, the students collectively reach a consensus as to the problem and the correct course of action. The videotape is then turned back on and the students view how a professional pharmacist handled the situation.

3. During a lecture in social work two students (both adults) talk constantly during the presentation by the instructor to the point that several other adult students are visibly annoyed and complain to the instructor during the break. Students viewing the videotape scenario are asked to articulate the problem, identify several courses of action that the instructor could take, and then make a recommendation as to how to handle the problem. The videotape is turned back on and the students view how the instructor handled the problem.

4. Students are asked to watch three two-minute videoclips of different teaching styles presented in the videos entitled, "Flatliners," "Paper Chase," and "Dead Poets Society." After viewing these videoclips, students are asked to discuss what they have seen and how they thought each of the different teaching styles would impact on their students. These students were then asked to write a one page summary on their own perceived teaching styles and which of the three videotapes best represented their "teaching style."

5. An English instructor is sitting in her office one week after the semester has closed. Grades have been sent to the students. An irate student walks into her office unannounced. The student asks why she received a B in the course when all of her work except one paper (a B-) was A work. The instructor states that in her judgment the student deserved a B and no more. The student screams that she will appeal the grade. The instructor calmly states, "So be it."

Throughout this chapter we have reviewed a number of definitions and components of critical thinking and the need for purposeful and formal teaching of these skills. It was noted that critical thinking cannot be taught by the formal lecture. Students must work in small groups and be given the freedom to explore alternative solutions.

One effective instructional strategy is the use of trigger videos, one- to five-minute presentations of a problem or opportunity that require a solution or resolution. These brief and inexpensive video clips, produced by both the instructor and students, offer a wide range of possibilities to get students involved in critical thinking activities.

BIBLIOGRAPHY

Barnes, Carol P. (1983). Questioning in college classrooms. Studies of college teaching, Carolyn L. Elner and Carol P. Barnes (Eds.). Lexington, MA: Lexington Books.

Beyer, Barry K. (1985, April). Critical thinking what is it? In Social Education, 269-276.

Bok, D. (1986). Higher learning. Cambridge, MA: Harvard University Press.

Boyer, E. (1987). College: The undergraduate experience in America. NY: Harper and Row.

Brookfield, Stephen D. (1988). Developing critical thinkers. San Francisco: Jossey-Bass Publishers.

Brown, M. Neil, & Keeley, Stuart M. (1981). Asking the right questions. NJ: Prentice-Hall.

Ennis, R.H. (1962, Winter). A concept of critical thinking. In Harvard Educational Review, 32, 83-89.

Feeley, Ted J. (1976, August). Critical thinking: Toward a definition, paradigm, and research agenda. Theory and research in social education, IV(1).

Furedy, C., & Furedy, J. (1985). Critical thinking: Toward research and dialogue. In J. Donald and A. Sullivan, (Eds.), Using research to improve teaching. New Directions for teaching and learning no. 23. San Francisco: Jossey-Bass Publishers.

Glaser, Edward M. (1941). An experiment in the development of critical thinking. NY: Bureau of Publications, Teachers College, Columbia University.

Goodlad, John (1983, March). A study of schooling: Some findings and hypotheses. Phi Delta Kappan, 463-470.

Hamblen, Karen A. (1984). The application of questioning strategy research to art criticism instruction. Paper presented at the Annual Meeting of the American Educational Research Association, April, New Orleans, LA (ERIC Document Reproduction Service No. ED 243 787)

Kurfiss, Joanne G. (1988). Critical thinking: Theory, research, practice, and possibilities. ASHE-ERIC Higher Education Report No. 2. Washington, DC: Association for the Study of Higher Education.

Lockhart, Aileen. (1963). Toward critical thinking. In Earl V. Pullias and Others, Toward excellence in college teaching. Dubuque, IA: Wm. C. Brown Company Publishers.

Meyers, Chet (1986). Teaching students to think critically. San Francisco: Jossey-Bass Publishers.

Michalak, Stanley J. (1986). Enhancing critical-thinking skills in traditional liberal arts courses: Report on a faculty workshop. Association of American Colleges Liberal Education, 72,(3), 253-262

National Commission on Excellence in Education. (1983). A nation at risk: The imperatives for educational reform. Washington, DC: U.S.Department of Education.

National Institute of Education. (1984). Involvement in learning: Realizing the potential of higher education. Washington, DC: U.S. Department of Education.

Newman, F.(1985). Higher education and the American resurgence. Princeton, NJ: Carnegie Foundation for the Advancement of Teaching.

Nickerson, R.S., Perkins, D.N., & Smith, E.E. (1985). The teaching of thinking.

Peters, R. (1987). Practical intelligence. New York: Harper and Rowe.

Presseisen, Barbara Z. (1986). Thinking skills: Research and practice. Washington, DC: National Education Association.

Russell, I. Jon, Hendricson, William, & Herbert, Robert J. (1984). Effects of lecture information density on medical student achievement. Journal of Medical Education, 59, 881-889.

Rubinstein, Moshe. (1986). Tools for thinking and problem-solving. Prentice-Hall.

Ruggiero, Vincent R. (1984). The art of thinking. NY: Harper and Rowe.

____. (1988). Teaching thinking across the curriculum. NY: Harper and Row.

Scriven, Michael. (1976). Reasoning. NY: McGraw-Hill Book Co.

Stice, James E. (Ed.). Developing critical thinking and problem-solving abilities. San Francisco: Jossey-Bass, Publishers.

Whimbey, A., & Lockhead, J. (1980). Problem solving and comprehension. The Franklin Institute Press.

Young, Robert E. (Ed.). (1980). Fostering critical thinking. New Directions for Teaching and Learning No.3. San Francisco: Jossey-Bass Publishers.

Chapter 10

Adapting Instruction for the Adult Student: The Need for Participation

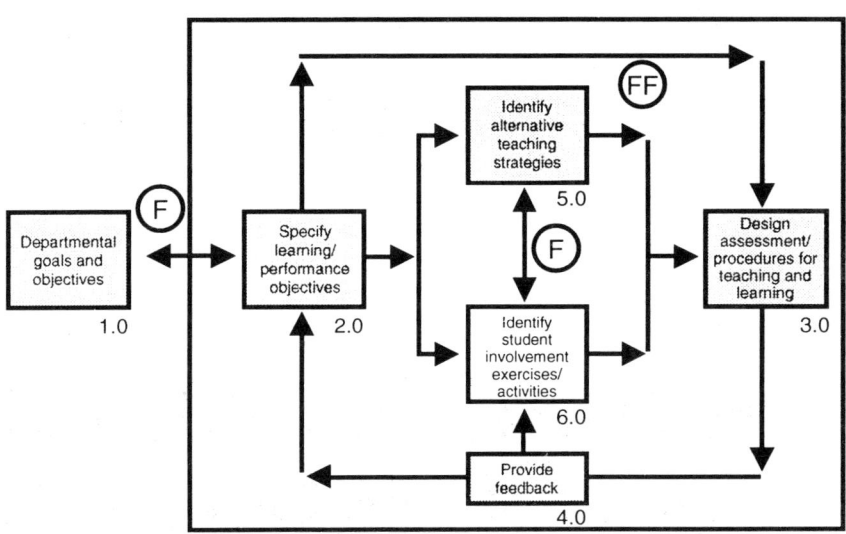

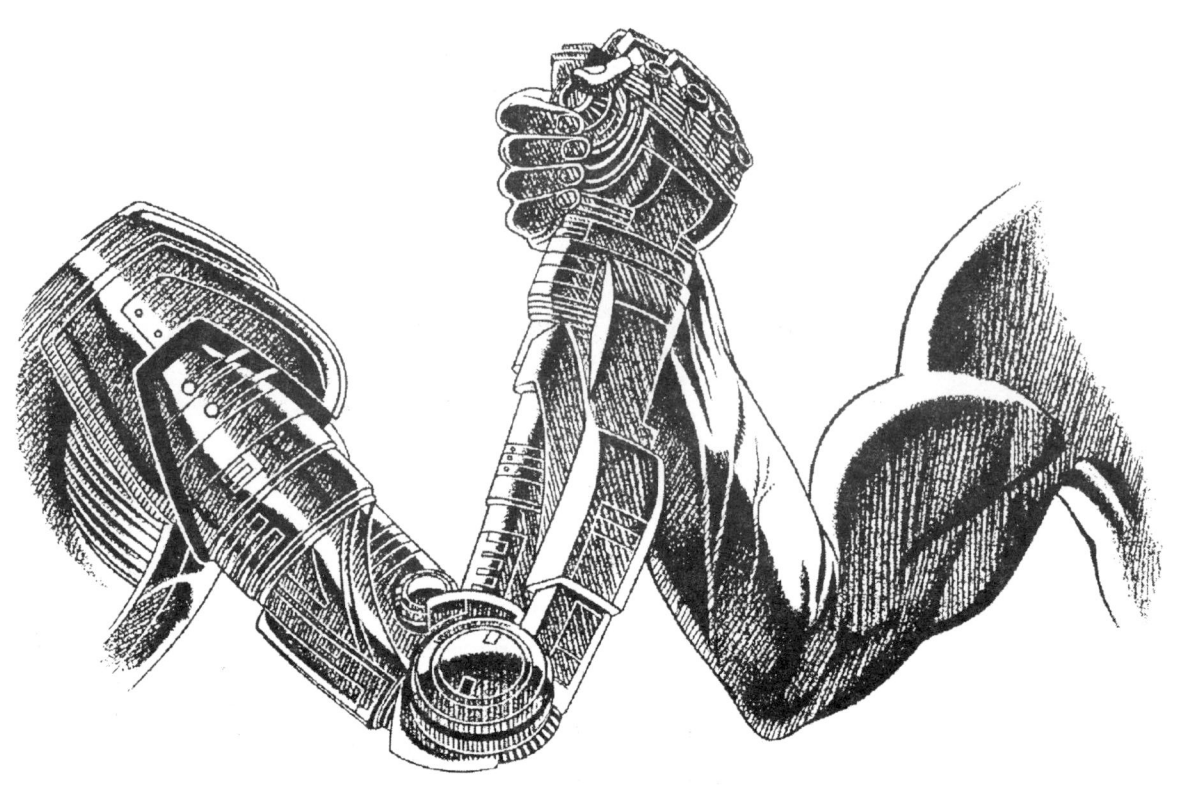

"Teaching is not talking at. It is talking with."

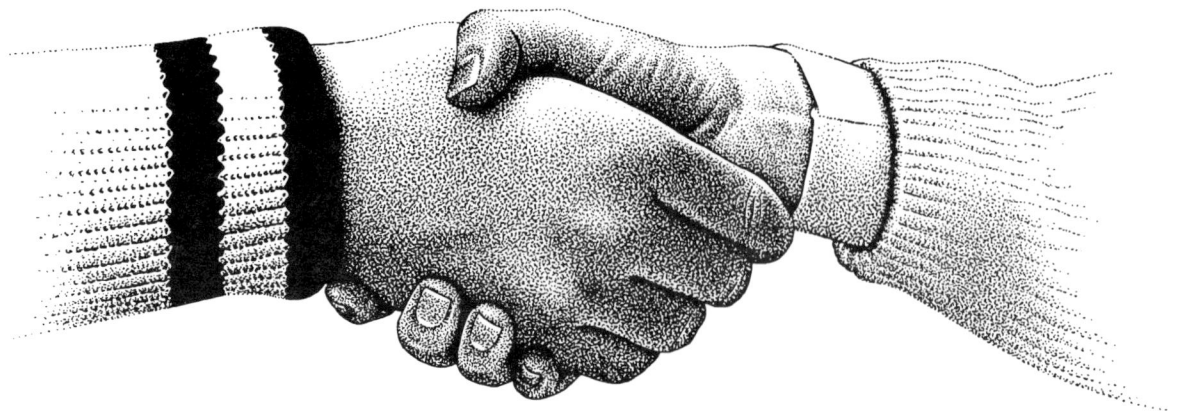

ADAPTING INSTRUCTION FOR THE ADULT STUDENT

LEARNING PERFORMANCE OBJECTIVE
Design learning activities and exercises that would appeal to adult students and explain the appeal. (Level 3).

KEY IDEAS
1. Adults should be taught differently than children. They demand an active involved learning environment.
2. Adults want to use, discuss and build on their life experience.
3. Learning contracts have been used successfully with adult learners.

NEW VOCABULARY
- adult learner
- andragogy and pedagogy
- learning contract

Betty Negere is 42 years old. She has been a medical secretary for 16 years and has received exceptional evaluations for every position that she has held. She has been active in the local Democratic party organization for many years.

Billy Gates is 19 years old. He was the president of his high school graduating class. His work experience has included three months at the local ice cream parlor and three months summer employment as a counselor at a local Boy's Club camp.

Juan Hernandez is 27 years old. He graduated at the top of his high school class but had to go to work immediately after graduation to help support his family. He has been working as an automotive mechanic and is well respected by his fellow workers. He has decided to return to college and get a degree in mechanical engineering.

Paula Womchock is a mother of three children. She came to the United States 20 years ago from Poland where she graduated from a vocational school. Now that her three children have graduated from a local community college, she has decided to go back to school for a degree in English. Paula has been very active in her church and in the local Girl Scout organization.

All four students are in the same class. Three are adults with a great deal of real-life work and social experience and one is a teenager with limited life and work experience. How does teaching life and work-experienced adults differ from teaching teenagers with limited life and work experience?

When asked the philosophic and psychological basis of their teaching, most instructors would describe it as pedagogy. Pedagogy translates as the study of children. Is this the same as the study of the adult learner? Children are not adults. The study of adults is called andragogy. It is important to make this distinction since a student audience is strongly influenced by their background and experience. This in turn will influence how you design and deliver your instruction in terms of learning performance objectives, pacing, vocabulary, use of examples, types of questions, and use of humor.

Adults are not children. Teaching adults will vary significantly since they will learn and study differently. They cannot be taught as a captive audience as we do with younger students. The greatest resource we have when teaching adults is the adults themselves with their vast life experiences and rich work experiences.

Some of the central elements common to models of adult learning include such things as their ability to direct their own learning and their need for autonomy; past personal and professional work experience; their ability to creatively reflect on their learning experiences; and their need for immediate action and application of what has been learned.

Some of the characteristics that make adults different from children are their broad and mature emotional experience dealing with the problems and opportunities of life in general. The physical differences and needs of adults differ from children in terms of physical stature, strength, and tolerance. Mental maturity has been conditioned with experience and feedback. The social needs of adults differ from children in the types of motivations that move them to action.

WHAT MOTIVATES ADULTS TO LEARN?

Adult learners are motivated to learn in a variety of ways. They can generally postpone immediate rewards for longer term payoffs. Some of the things that motivate adults include job advancement in the short run but especially the possibilities in the longer term. Job security is an immediate motivator but usually is viewed as years down the line. Salary increases, although a more immediate reward, are often viewed over a career. Power within a position is always a motivator. Advanced degrees lead to promotions which put people in positions of power. Recognition is a social payoff that is of extreme importance. It costs little but has great psychological benefit. Advanced education provides a basis for job mobility, which leads to advancement in salary and security. Adults tend to be very competitive when there are long term rewards. They are impatient with a lot of nice-to-know information that does not have immediate application. They will often ask why such-and-such is important to know. They expect and want need-to-know information and skill.

ASSUMPTIONS OF ANDRAGOGY AND THEIR IMPLICATIONS FOR INSTRUCTION

There are a number of assumptions that researchers have made about teaching adults that have very clear implications about the way we approach instruction.

The self-identity, the "who I am," of the adult learner is derived from a vast reservoir of personal and professional experience. Adults want and need to apply their experience to the immediate learning assignments since they are a product of their work and personal experience. Instructors must learn to accept this experience and need to talk about it. They should encourage meaningful discussion and other types of involving activities that allow adults to focus on their experience. However, this may mean that less information will be given by the instructor during the actual class time.

Older students have a strong need for self-esteem which is based on their feedback from past achievement. Self-esteem is built through a strong need for participation. Instructors need to respect the age and experience of their students. They must listen carefully and develop class activities and exercises that maximize student-to-student involvement.

Adults are ready to learn when they perceive that a real need exists in a social or professional setting. Therefore, they need to clearly distinguish between the need-to-know and the nice-to-know. They must be able to show the immediate application of what is taught.

The role of the instructor in an adult learning environment is that of a facilitator who provides the tools and resources rather than all of the information. This facilitator shows the students where to find the information and how to analyze it to solve the problems presented to them.

Self-direction is a hallmark of the adult learner. This is a result of professional growth, perceived need, and maturity. Older students always move emotionally and intellectually toward independence. A major implication for teaching is involvement of the students in the choice and priority of the learning performance objectives and the pace at which the instruction will be delivered. Self-assessment of student progress is essential for the adult student. Self-tests will be an important mechanism to provide feedback. These are not graded. They provide progress data to the learner only.

Adult students are performance-centered. They perceive learning as a means to solve practical and real problems. They do not want a lot of irrelevant theory that does not have immediate application. Emphasis in this type of active classroom is on learning critical thinking skills rather than teaching information. The latter will be tolerated within limits, but only as a means to apply it and solve problems. The intellectual level of learning will be very important.

Teaching strategies must reflect these important concerns. Adults demand active learning strategies rather than passive learning. These strategies, described in Chapter 12, must be used in these classes.

One of the most effective instructional strategies with adult learners is the learning contract, which allows maximum decision-making on the part of the student as to what is to be learned, how it will be learned, and how it will be assessed. This strategy is explained as one of the major alternatives to the traditional lecture in Chapter 18.

In his book, *How to Teach Adults,* Draves (1989), makes four suggestions for teaching adults. He uses the acronym *DIVE.*

1. *D:* Discover learners
2. *I:* Involve learners
3. *V:* Vary teaching techniques
4. *E:* Energize learning

Discover learners means that the instructor should know something about the adult students in terms of their backgrounds, interests, aspirations, and any other demographic information that would be helpful. He suggests that on the first day of class you could ask why they are taking the class; what they consider their greatest challenge or opportunity; and where they expect to be professionally three years from now.

Involve learners in their own learning by drawing on their personal and professional experience. Encourage questioning at any time. Look for the keys and handles to help the students to motivate themselves.

Vary techniques that you use to teach at least three times during any one class. Use games, simulations, videos, case studies, etc.

Energize learning by teaching enthusiastically. Prepare each class as if it was your last. Prepare yourself from within by believing in yourself.

BIBLIOGRAPHY

Check, John F. (1984). <u>Teaching-learning preferences of the adult learner</u>. Paper presented at the National Adult education conference at Louisville, Kentucky.

Cross, Patricia. (1981). <u>Adults as learners</u>, San Francisco: Jossey-Bass.

Gorham, Joan. (1985, Summer). Differences between adults and pre-adults: A closer look. <u>Adult Education Quarterly</u>, <u>3</u>(4), 194-209.

Hengstler, Dennis D., and others. (1984). <u>Andragogy in public universities: Understanding adult education needs in the 1980's.</u> (ERIC Documentation Reproduction Service No. ED 246 777)

Imel, Susan. (1988). <u>Guidelines for working with adult learners</u>. ERIC Digest No. 7. (ERIC Documentation Reproduction Service No. ED 299 456)

Kazmierski, Paul. (1989). The adult learner. In Greive, Donald. (Ed.). <u>Teaching in college: A resource for college teachers</u>.

Kelly, Diana. (1986). <u>Adult learners! Implications for faculty</u>. (ERIC Documentation Reproduction Service No. ED 277 442)

Kidd, J.R. (1973). <u>How adults learn</u>. New York: Associative Press.

Knowles, Malcolm. (1973). The emergence of a theory of adult learning. In <u>The adult learner: A neglected species</u>, second edition.

Knox, Alan B. (1977). <u>Adult development and learning</u>. San Francisco: Jossey-Bass.

Lam, Y.L. Yack. (1985). Exploring the principles of andragogy: Some comparison of university and community college learning experiences. <u>Canadian Journal of Higher Education</u>, <u>15</u>(1), 39-52.

Lovell, R.B. (1980). <u>Adult learning</u>. New York: Halstead.

Moore, Janet R. (1988). <u>Principles of andragogy in collegiate faculty development</u>. (ERIC Document Reproduction Service No. ED 301 095)

Sass, Edmund J. (1989, April). Motivation in the college classroom: What students tell us. <u>Teaching of Psychology</u>, <u>16</u>(2), 86-88.

See, Laurs A. (1987). <u>Student perceptions regarding use of andragological instructional techniques</u>. Paper presented at the National Conference on the Adult Learner. Columbia, South Carolina.

Skinner, B.F. (1968). The motivation of the student. In <u>The technology of teaching</u>.

Stern, Milton R.M. (1978). Working with older students. In Milton, Ohmar, & Associates. <u>On college teaching</u>, 340-355.

Warren, Virginia B. (ed.) (1964). <u>A treasury of techniques for teaching adults</u>. Washington, D.C.: National Association for Public School Adult Education.

Chapter 11

Creating an Active College Classroom

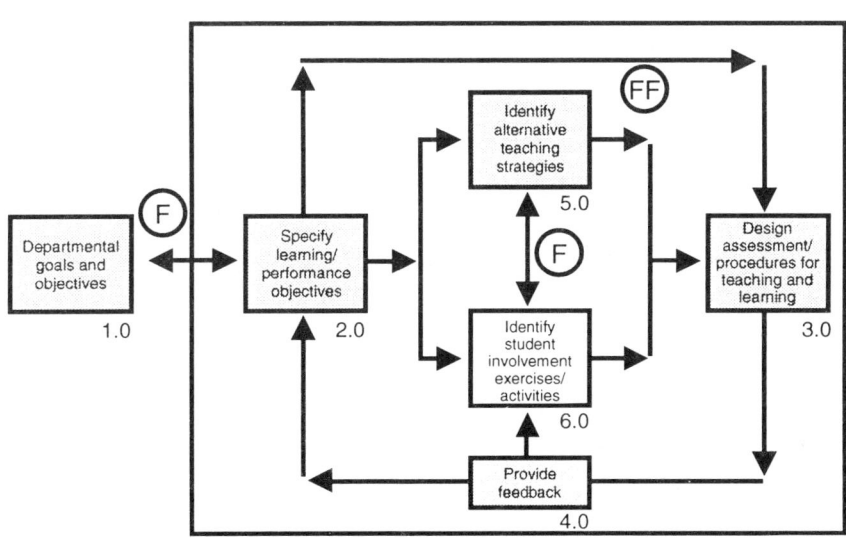

"Tell them and they will forget. Involve them and they will remember."

CREATING AN ACTIVE COLLEGE CLASSROOM

LEARNING PERFORMANCE OBJECTIVES
Using any of the suggested learning activities in this chapter, select one and design it for a class that you teach. (Level 4).

Compare and contrast active and passive learning relative to your discipline. (Level 2).

KEY IDEAS
1. Active learning involves students in their own learning, working in small groups and alone.
2. A teaching method involves the communication technique chosen by the instructor to teach students. These are passive and active.
3. An instructional strategy involves both teaching methods and the physical delivery system.
4. There are three broad categories of interactivity: instructor and individual student; small groups of students; and an individual student and media, such as a programmed text; video disc simulation, computer-based instruction.

NEW VOCABULARY
- active learning and passive learning
- physical media
- instructional strategy
- experiential
- interactivity and involvement
- teaching method
- instructional-centered individualized

Dean Smith is discussing the third principle of thermodynamics with two fellow students after listening to and taking notes during a 15-minute lecturette by the instructor. The group has identified two important questions that they need answers to before they can continue. They pose the questions to the instructor who in turn asks the class and guides their responses with other probing questions.

Pat Makers has just finished writing her reactions to a provocative presentation on the economics of providing health care to AIDS patients. She is about to share her ideas and opinions with her class.

Celestina Hernandez, working with four other students, has spent the past twenty minutes identifying several alternative's to Iven Illich's approaches to education as expressed in *Deschooling Society*. As the recorder for the group, Benny Schwartz will present the group's ideas to the whole class. Each of these ideas and their possible long term consequences will be debated during the next class.

Shelia Morrison and two of her fellow students are about to show a three-minute trigger video which they completed this past weekend. The title of this trigger video is "A Difficult Decision." The topic deals with the abortion issue. After viewing the trigger video, the class, working in groups of five, will discuss the issue and attempt to reach a consensus of opinion. They will report their consensus or non-consensus during class. This will serve as the basis for future research.

What do all of these brief descriptions have in common? Each classroom scenario described what the students were discussing, reflecting upon and judging. They did not describe what the instructor was doing. Yet, it was the instructor who designed the learning events and created the environment that allowed this kind of *active learning to take place.*

The term **active learning** describes the role of the student as they act on their own learning. Traditionally, students were passive recipients of the information dispensed by the instructor was frequently the results of their own narrow area of research. The role of the student was that of spectator who was to sit, listen, and write important notes for later review. The role of the instructor was to "tell" students through the traditional and time-honored lecture. As was noted in Chapter 13, the lecture does not promote problem solving or critical thinking skills

Current research has indicated that the maximum **attention span** of a student during a 50- to 75-minute lecture presentation is only 15 to 20 minutes. Research has also revealed that a maximum of three or four main points should be covered in a 50-minute lesson period. Given these research conclusions, how have college instructors responded? The "talking lecture" is still used as the preferred teaching method. Student passivity is still the best descriptor of college and university classrooms. Active learning is the exception rather than the rule.

Reasons for the predominance of the lecturer, or as some have come to call it, the sage on stage, are due to the lack of training of most college instructors in the basic skills of teaching. Most are not acquainted with viable alternatives to the traditional lecture or how to modify it to involve their students. Other reasons include the tradition of the lecture, the resistance of faculty to change, and the attitudes of department heads that equate the lecture with teaching. Many feel that if you are not talking (professing) then the students are not learning.

DEFINITION OF ACTIVE LEARNING

Active learning means that students are involved in what they are learning. They not only seek out and possess information, they do something with it. They apply the concepts, reflect on what they have done, and make judgments as to the worth or value of their conclusions. The research literature on active learning conducted by Chickering and Gamson (1987) suggests that students must do more than listen during a lecture. They must be moved beyond passive listening. Active learning implies that the students are using combinations of viewing, listening, writing, talking, feeling, touching, and tasting. They are not sitting, listening, viewing, and copying notes as in passive learning. As the students receive the information they act upon it and do something with it.

During active learning the students experience interactions with the instructor (usually through questioning), with other students, and with the media as in programmed instruction or computer-based instruction.

Bonwell and Eison (1991) suggest that active learning is anything that "...involves students in doing things and thinking about the things they are doing." They also note that active learning as a concept has not been adequately defined or described in the educational literature. Some general descriptors commonly associated with the use of instructional strategies that promote active learning in the college classroom have been identified by these researchers,

1. Students are involved in more than listening.
2. Less emphasis is placed on information transmission skills. It is placed on the development of applied skills.
3. Students are involved in the skills of analysis, synthesis, and evaluation.
4. Students are engaged in activities which use as many sensory inputs as possible such as reading, discussing/writing, and speaking.
5. Students are involved in the exploration of their own attitudes and values.

Schomberg, (1986), describes active learning as follows,

...it involves students both in acquiring information and in interpreting and transforming it. Students work with the subject first-hand: exploring ordinary materials in organizing data, making observations, solving problems, or conducting experiments. ... Students are required to produce some type of product by interpreting information through analysis, synthesis, evaluation or some other form of reflection. The product may be a paper, report, debate, role play, problem solution, or model.

This same researcher goes on to note the changing roles of instructors in an active learning environment,

Faculty... have to make changes in their role. Whereas they previously may have focused their attention on organizing and interpreting information through lectures, they now concentrate on designing assignments, exercises, and tasks through which students will learn from first-hand experiences with the subject. Faculty act as monitors; guiding students through the subject, instructing, responding to students questions, encouraging student investigation.

Active learning is called interactive learning by Jones (1988). He views it as,

Interactive learning can be described as a wide range of activities in which participants in an event interact with each other for the purposes of education and training. The events include discussions, exercises, role-plays, simulation and games. The teacher (trainer, instructor, tutor) either abandons or greatly reduces the amount of direct instruction.

He notes that "an event is what actually happens, not what is supposed to happen. An event is whatever the participants think, feel and do."
Simpson and Galbo (1986) propose that interaction in a classroom is "...central to the learning process."
They define interaction as

... all manner of behavior in which individuals and groups act upon each other. The essential characteristic is reciprocity in actions and responses in an infinite variety of relationships: verbal and nonverbal, conscious and nonconscious, enduring and casual. Interaction is seen as a continually emerging process, as communication, in its most inconclusive sense.

In the *Final Report of the Study Group on the Conditions of Excellence in American Higher Education* (1986), the editors state that student involvement is the most important element for the purpose of improving undergraduate education along with higher expectations of students as described in educational outcomes and assessment and feedback to students. Cross (1987) urges faculty to actively involve and engage students in the process of their own learning. She notes that "Learning is not so much an additive process, with new learning simply piling up on top of existing knowledge, as it is an active, dynamic process in which the connections are constantly changing and the structure reformatted."

INSTRUCTIONAL STRATEGIES THAT SUPPORT ACTIVE LEARNING

There are many types of instructional strategies that can be used to promote active learning. An **instructional strategy** describes both the teaching methods and the physical delivery system. A teaching method is a communication technique selected by the instructor in order to assist students to master the learning performance objectives. For example, the instructor might select the lecture method because in his or her opinion that it is the most efficient method to provide information. On the other hand, the instructor might use a highly interactive approach such as small group problem solving.

The **delivery system** consists of the physical resources used to deliver the subject matter through the instructor to the student. Physical resources includes such things as videotape, live interactive television, and computer-assisted instruction. Students never learn from the physical media. They learn from the different communication techniques selected by the instructor and delivered by these physical media.

Westin and Cranton (1986), have provided a framework to explore different types of teaching methods. These researchers have grouped teaching methods into four categories: instructor-centered, individualized, experiential, and interactive.

Instructor-centered teaching methods

These teaching methods place the instructor at center stage in the classroom. They are characterized as the "talk and chalk" approach to teaching in a traditional classroom. There is little, if any, interaction. Students are not encouraged to ask questions. Most of the talking is done by the instructor with minimal input from students. Handouts are used occasionally at best. Students must copy extensive notes and hope that they have identified the key points. The instructor is in complete control of the subject matter presented, pacing, how much is taught and when it is taught. They control the time and length of any type of student intervention. This is low risk teaching and is the most prevalent type in post-secondary education. Lecturing or "talking at" is equivocated with teaching. The source of knowledge, wisdom, and truth reside within the instructor stationed at the front of the classroom. Research has indicated that this is the least effective form of teaching and will hinder students from developing critical thinking skills.

Individualized teaching methods

Self-direction and self-pacing are the best descriptors for individualized teaching methods. Students work independently of an instructor to achieve the learning performance objectives provided for them or negotiated with them by the instructor. Activities and exercises are either given to the student or developed and selected in collaboration with the instructor. Time rather than performance is the major variable when this technique is used. A learning contract is frequently employed in which the student agrees in writing to complete certain activities for a pre-determined grade within a predetermined time period. In addition to self-direction and self-pacing, individualized teaching methods are self-correcting and self-contained.

The use of learning packages, computer-based instruction, programmed textbooks, multi-media packages, and other forms of instruction under the direct control and pace of the studentare used with this teaching approach.

Interactive teaching methods

This teaching method fosters maximum communication and involvement between the instructor and students and among students. Which interactive method is chosen and how it will be used will depend upon the learning performance objectives. Interaction is promoted with quality questions that require more than recall of factual data. This technique emphasizes a **cooperative** rather than a competitive student **learning** environment. There is minimal formal lecturing. This does not just happen. It is planned.

Experiential teaching methods

These teaching methods involve real-life experiences or simulations of those experiences. Experiential teaching methods involve aspects of all three previous teaching methods. They usually deal with application and critical thinking skills. Information gathering and comprehension take place outside regular classroom settings.

There are a variety of experiential teaching methods which include:

- **Field experiences**- include on-the-job tasks under the guidance of an expert. Field experiences could be preceded by lectures, demonstrations, and the use of simulations to prepare the student.
- **Clinical experiences**- take place within a clinical setting under the real-time tutelage of a clinical preceptor. Videotapes and simulations could be used to prepare the students for the skill they are to master. Demonstrations followed by practice with immediate feedback are common techniques.
- **Laboratory experiences**- take place in a laboratory environment under the direction of an instructor. Videotapes and demonstrations under ideal conditions could be used as a pre-lab experience.
- **Role playing**- The student is given a description of a situation and the characters in the situation. The student takes on the role of one of the characters and attempts to behave like the character in the situation. This method allows the student to try out attitudes and behaviors and to observe other people's reaction to them. This method requires a great deal of imagination and a willingness to get involved on a high emotional level.

Simulations- approximate real world situations in a simplified and well-controlled manner and under strict supervision. This method emphasizes the processes one uses as the real learning experience rather than the outcomes. Specific rules are used to guide actions independently of the instructor. This is one of the best techniques for developing planning and decision-making skills and has the strong potential to influence values and attitudes.

In summary, this chapter has dealt with a variety of instructional strategies that could be used to increase and improve student interactions within a classroom by getting them involved in viewing, observing, writing, speaking, reading, listening, and a combination of these. Increased involvement will improve learning outcomes.

BIBLIOGRAPHY

Bonwell, Charles C., & Eison, James (1991). <u>Active learning: Creating excitement in the classroom</u>. ASHE-Eric Higher Education Report No. 1. Washington, DC: The George Washington University, School of Education and Human Development.

Boyer, Ernest L. (1987). The undergraduate experience in America. NY: Harper & Row.

Brookfield, Stephen D. (1990). <u>The skillful teacher: On technique, trust, and responsiveness in the classroom</u>. San Francisco: Jossey-Bass Publishers.

Bruffee, K. (1987). The art of collaborative learning. <u>Change</u>. 42-47.

Chickering, Arthur W., & Gamson, Zelda F. (1987). Seven principles for good practice. <u>AAHE Bulletin</u>, <u>39</u>, 3-7.

Cowan, John. (1984, December). The responsive lecture: A means of supplementary resource-based instruction. <u>Educational Technology</u>, <u>24</u>, 18-21.

Cross, K.P. (Spring 1991). Every teachers a researcher, every classroom a laboratory. <u>Tribal College: A Journal of American Indian Higher Education</u>, <u>2</u>(4), 7-12.

Johnson, David W., Johnson, Roger T., & Smith, Karl A. (1991). <u>Active Learning: Cooperation in the college classroom</u>. Edna, MN: Interaction Book Company.

Jones, K. (1988). <u>Interactive learning events: A guide for facilitators</u>. London: Kogan Page.

Jones, Ken. (1988). <u>Interactive learning events</u>. NY: Nichols Publishing.

Katz, Joseph. (Ed.). (1985). <u>Teaching as though students mattered. New Directions for Teaching and Learning</u>, No. 21. San Francisco: Jossey-Bass Publishers.

MacGregor, Jean T. (1992). What is collaborative learning? In A. Goodsell, M. Maher, & V. Tinto, with B.L. Smith & J.T. MacGregor, <u>Collaborative learning: A sourcebook for higher education</u>. University Park, PA: National Center on Postsecondary Education, Learning & Assessment, 9-22.

Meyers, Chet, & Jones, Thomas B. (1993). <u>Promoting active learning: Strategies for the college classroom</u>. San Francisco: Jossey-Bass Publishers.

Schomberg, Steven F.E. (1986). <u>Strategies for active teaching and learning in university classrooms</u>. Minneapolis: University of Minnesota.

Simpson, Raymond J., & Galbo, Joseph J. (1986). Interaction and learning: Theorizing on the art of teaching. <u>Interchange</u>, <u>17</u>(4), 37-51.

<u>The final report of the study group on the conditions of excellence in American higher education</u>.

Tiberius, R.G. (1986). Metaphors underlying the improvement of teaching and learnng. <u>British Journal of Educational Technology</u>, <u>17</u>(2), 144-156.

Weimer, Maryellen. (1990). <u>Improving college teaching: Strategies for developing instructional effectiveness</u>. San Francisco: Jossey-Bass Publishers.

Weston, Cynthia, & Cranton, P.A. (1986). Selecting instructional strategies. <u>Journal of Higher Education</u>, <u>57</u>(3), 259-288.

Chapter 12

Student Involvement Activities

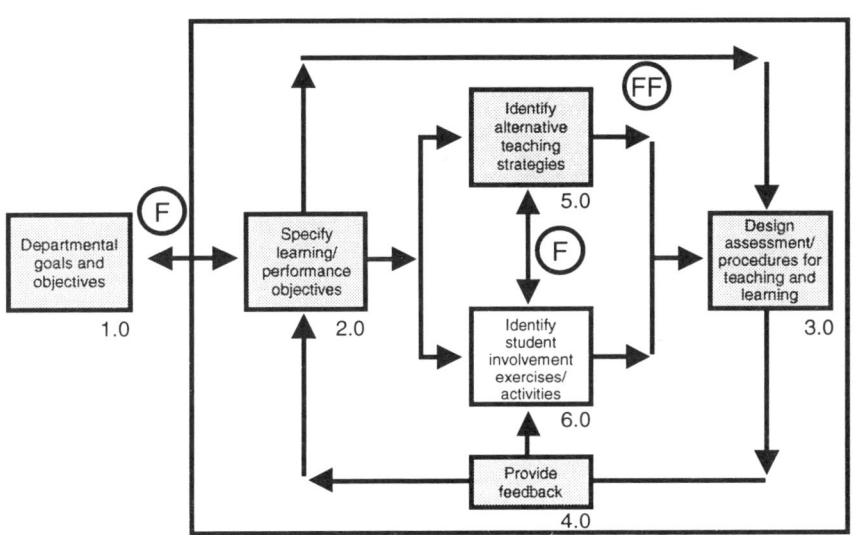

SELECTING INTERACTIVE LEARNING ACTIVITIES

LEARNING PERFORMANCE OBJECTIVE
Using any of the suggested learning activities in this chapter, select one and design it for a class that you teach. (Level 4).

KEY IDEAS
1. An interactive student activity usually involves application and critical thinking skills.
2. Interactive activities should be short (5 to 20 minutes), maximize involvement; to the point; intensive; well-planned; and results-oriented.
3. Learning activities must correspond to the intended cognitive level of the learning performance objective.

NEW VOCABULARY
Each learning activity introduces new vocabulary. The new terms are too numerous to elaborate.

The research on active learning was reviewed in the last chapter. Student involvement is so important in active learning that it is addressed as part of the S.A.T. instructional model (6.0 in the model). An instructional strategy was explained as composed of two parts: 1) the means by which the instructor communicates with students as exemplified in the interactive learning activities and 2) the means by which the communication is delivered (as in the different forms of media). Student involvement activities focus attention on learning rather than teaching. Lessons are designed to stress what the instructor wants the students to do as a result of the teaching. The use of these interactive strategies will require the instructor to give clear and concise directions to the students orally and in writing as to:
- What to do...
- How to do it...
- What the final product should look like...
- How much time to do it in...

Whatever type of interactive student activity the instructor chooses, it should be manageable within the total lesson time (50 minutes, 75 minutes, or other time allocations). These activities should be:
- Short
- Brief
- To the point
- Intensive
- Well-planned
- Results-oriented

A list of very brief descriptions of a variety of active learning activities that could be used in the traditional classroom to involve students is presented during the remainder of this chapter. They are meant to stimulate the instructor's imagination as to what could be done rather than stand as all-inclusive and definitive descriptions.

They are stepping stones to further creative activities. As the instructor reads each suggested activity, he or she should note the variety of sensory inputs involved. Read them and then adapt them to your needs.

INTERACTIVE LEARNING ACTIVITIES

1. **Lecture, Interactive.** This type of lecture is designed to involve students by focusing their attention on key words and phrases that they must fill in on a handout. It is designed to emphasize information transfer at the knowldge recall and compehension levels of learning. The major purpose is to provide a structure to assist the students with notetaking. The interactive lecture can use a general outline with blanks for fill-ins or to present word pictures.

2. **Lecturette.** A short (10- to 20-minute) presentation, or a number of three- to five-minute presentations followed by a variety of other involving learning activities interspersed between lecturettes. Like the interactive lecture, the lecturette can use a general outline or some type of word pictures or other graphics in a handout.

3. **Lecturette With Listening Team.** The instructor or guest lecturer gives a short (10- to 20-minute) lecturette. Students are assigned to small groups of three to five and given a listening assignment. During the lecturette, each group generates questions about one aspect of the presentation. They are given five minutes to organize and prioritize their questions. Each group presents their questions to the presenter.

4. **Interviews, Student**. Students form pairs and interview each other on a preselected topic. This is a good technique for exploring values and attitudes. Questions for the interview may be given to the students by the instructor, or students may generate their own questions. Results can be reported as a percentage of a group response, i.e., 60% of the group agrees.

5. **Buzz Sessions.** A small group of three to five students work within a determined time limit without a leader to answer a question or solve a problem and come to some kind of conclusion. The results/conclusions of the short discussion are reported to all students who may be asked to write a short paper of their discussion.

6. **Brainstorm Session.** This involves creative thinking through free association of ideas. Participants should be briefed on the strategies of good brainstorming. Working with a group leader on a given problem within a determined time period (5 to 30 minutes), students call out solutions in single words or short phrases without any commentary or discussion. All judgments are suspended until all ideas are out. One person records the ideas on a flipchart or blackboard. The group should not exceed 10 to 15 members in order to be effective. As the session progresses, one creative idea stimulates another. At the conclusion of the call-out, each list of ideas is edited and evaluated. This is

followed by questions from the participants for clarification and comment. The discussion is moderated by the instructor or another student.

7. **Discussion Panel.** A limited presentation (three to five minutes) by a group of experts (usually four to seven) is the mainstay of this technique. The panel is moderated by either the instructor or a student. A variety of points of view on a given topic are explored. A question and answer (Q/A) period follows from students not involved on the panel.

8. **Peer Teaching.** A student is selected to conduct a short class on an assigned or selected topic. Given the topic, the student draws from his/her personal experience. This requires careful planning and monitoring. The student presentation could use an interactive study guide and word pictures. The peer teacher could also use a peer review and self-assessment guide.

9. **Guest Speaker.** A presentation by a known expert followed by questions and answers from all students. The instructor of record should provide a specific topic and sub-topics to be covered by the speaker. The students should be provided with a biographical sketch of the speaker, topic and sub-topics to be covered, and any points they should pay special attention to. Some instructors note the intellectual quality of the questions asked by the participating students and review them during the next class. They note whether the questions were for clarification, probing, extensions, comprehension, application, or critical thinking.

10. **Scenario, Written.** A brief (one- or two-paragraph) description of a real or fabricated situation that is analyzed in stages by small groups of students one of whom functions as the recorder. Each group presents their project for a given amount of time. All data can be provided or only partial data. In the latter case students are asked to make assumptions that will affect the final outcome or recommendations.The same technique could be used with a visual scenario–still or motion.

11. **Case Studies, Full**. Real world descriptions of problems with all accompanying data are developed by the instructor. Students, working in small groups, are asked to resolve the problem within a given period of time. Each small group makes recommendations as to how to solve the problem. The instructor acts as a resource person and as moderator during the final presentations.

12. **Minicase Study.** Students are asked to construct their own cases given some guidelines that are related to the learning performance objective(s). The instructor selects one or more minicases and asks students to make recommendations.

13. **Exercises, Individual**. These provide an opportunity for the students to practice skills. These could include labeling, rank ordering, multiple choice, true/false. and completion. Exercises must be completed in a defined time period. After the

exercises are corrected, a discussion follows with the instructor moderating comments and asking questions.

14. **Quizzes, Progress**. Short self-tests that are not graded. Answers are provided to the students. The purpose is to provide a quick feedback mechanism to the student so that he or she can check progress toward mastering the learning performance objectives.

15. **Readings, Short Discussion**. Read a short (one- to three-page) explanation or description, break into small discussion groups, discuss the topic, and then complete a worksheet. Instructor asks questions of each group.

16. **Role Play**. The students are given a situation and a role to play of a character in the situation. Without practice, they act out the events of the situation as they think the character they are portraying would act. The situation could provide a broad outline or a detailed confrontational event. This technique provides feedback to the students about their own behavior. It is an excellent technique for developing communication skills.

17. **Simulation**. Presents cases, problems, or scenarios, in which the members must role play. A critical situation is discussed and analyzed and group decisions made about how to resolve the situation. This technique provides good team building skills. The in-basket is a one person simulation where the student must immediately respond to letters, memos, or telephone calls taken from real-life situations.

18. **Games**. Similar to a simulation, except that individuals are competitive and there are winners who are rewarded.

19. **Trigger Video**. Very short (one- to five-minute) visual scenarios. The students, working in small groups, are asked to view the situation, identify the problem, identify different potential courses of action, and then make a recommendation. The trigger video is turned off after the situation is presented. The group makes a recommendation. The video is turned back on and students view the course of action taken by a professional.

20. **Practice Activity**. Students practice a skill under the direction of the instructor. This includes fine motor skills (focus a microscope, soldering), interactions for interview, presentations for public speaking, or drills for rote learning such new vocabulary or object recognition.

21. **Values Clarification**. Students explore and express their values on given topics through the use of values exercises. Values are then discussed among themselves with the instructor acting as moderator.

22. **Demonstrations.** Correct "how to" techniques and skills taught by the instructor or expert in the field. It is either live or mediated. Students control the pace of the demonstration through their questioning and commentary.

23. **Demonstration With Practice.** The instructor conducts a demonstration. Students practice with corrective feedback from the instructor.

24. **Exampling.** Given a concept, problem, situation, or principle, the student is asked to provide examples and non-examples from their professional and personal experiences.

25. **Mnemonics.** Given data to be remembered, the students, working in small groups, are asked to create memory aids by making up words and rhymes from the first letters of ideas and concepts to be memorized. Some examples are:
MADD–Mothers Against Drunk Drivers
ROY G. BIV–(colors of the spectrum) Red, Orange, Yellow, Green, Blue, Indigo, and Violet.
This is formally taught as a memory device in a high content-memory course.

26. **Critical Incidents.** This is a variation of the case method. The students are given a short description of an incident that happened but with too little information to make a decision. Additional information is revealed by the instructor only if the students ask the right questions. The critical incident is printed on a handout and read by the instructor. Students work in a small group and ask questions for additional data as needed. Another critical incident technique is to give an explanation of a situation or a concept to the students and ask them to generate critical incidents. For example,
    What is a good supervisor?
Students would think of the best supervisor that they had known, and then write a two- to three-sentence description of an incident that led them to think of this supervisor as exemplary. They would then think of the worst supervisor that they had known and write a two- to three-sentence description describing an incident in which they were involved that explained why they chose this person as a non-exemplary supervisor. Names are never revealed.

27. **Incomplete Statements.** The instructor provides incomplete statements such as "My feelings about abortion are…" The student is asked to complete this statement on a handout (or display in an interactive study guide) and then share their thoughts with the class.

28. **Programmed Instruction.** Either in text or mediated form, this is a very good technique to build recall skills. It can be used as a preclass activity to build skills such as medical vocabulary, grammar, or spelling.

29. **Theatrics.** The use of theatrical devices such magic tricks, costuming, or other techniques to capture attention and reinforce a point. The technique must relate

to and reinforce the learning performance objectives and the specific teaching point to be effective. The students are led to ask questions about the theatric.

30. **Character Dialogue.** The instructor assumes the role of two or more characters and creates a dialogue with himself/herself. Another technique would have the instructor, playing one character, talk to a preselected student(s) who assumes the role of another character. Puppets are sometimes used with this technique with the instructor speaking to one puppet or two puppets speaking to each other. Both speak from a script outline.

31. **Field Trips.** These are taken before class and discussed during class. The instructor can use slides taken during the field trip to reinforce certain points. This may be difficult if the sites are too far. Students must know the exact learning purpose of the field trip and what is expected of them when they return.

32. **Play, View a.** Students view a segment of a taped play that reinforces an important point. Their attention is focused on certain critical characteristics, circumstances, or outcomes prior to viewing. These are discussed after viewing.

33. **Questioning Strategies, Student-Generated.** The instructor explains the intellectual levels of questioning (recall, understanding, application, and critical thinking) and then asks the students to write a series of questions about the topic under discussion which they will ask each other.

34. **Debate.** This is an organized and civil argument that requires a good moderator and a set of ground rules. After the debate students ask questions. The debate can be conducted by the instructor, an invited guest, several students, a student and instructor, an instructor and invited guest, or a student and an invited guest.

35. **Guest Interview.** The instructor (or preferably a single student or small group of students) interviews a guest expert on a previously chosen topic in the guest's field of expertise. Other students ask questions at the completion of the interview. In some instances the speaker is sent the questions in advance.

36. **Reaction Panels.** Any presentation method followed by reactions from a small group of students who have made a special study of the topic. There is a Q/A period from the students after the reaction panel. Either the instructor or a student would moderate.

37. **Modeling.** The student is shown an ideal product, situation, or person. Through questioning and discussion, they are able to explain why this is a "model" of what is, should, or could be.

38. **Puzzles.** The students are given a puzzle to solve in order to learn a skill.

39. **Skits.** A brief play or portrayal to make a specific point. It requires rehearsed dialogue from a script as opposed to a role play, which contains spontaneous dialogue. This could be used as a theatrical device to begin a lesson.

40. **Pantomime.** A non-verbal, more involving skit using non-verbal language only.

41. **In-Basket.** A form of simulation. Actual memos, letters, and reports are provided. The students write responses to each memo or letter. It is used for decision making and problem solving. Students work through packets of these materials identify problems, look for alternative solutions and consequences of the proposed solution, and then make a recommendation. The instructior moderates discussion of the exercises.

42. **Symposium.** Two or more five- to 10-minute presentations on different aspects of the same subject. These are then discussed briefly and followed by Q/A. Each student writes a short paper on their part of the topic. A copy of each paper is provided to each student.

43. **Personal Vignette.** Given a topic or learning objective by the instructor, the students are asked to relate it to their real personal experiences (personal or professional) by telling a brief story about it. The story must relate to a given objective. A story is made up to make a point or it is told about another person based on personal knowledge.

44. **Flip-Flop Lecturette.** Two instructors alternate while giving the presentation. One presents the topic while the other gives examples and non-examples or turns to the students and asks them for examples. One presentor can remind the other of significant points. This technique enhances the lecture but needs practice and good transition statements. It is followed by Q/A.

45. **Quizzicals.** After a presentation, students working in pairs ask questions of each other that focus on the presentations. These questions are based on the learning performance objectives that are given to the students at the beginning of the lecture.

46. **Videoclips.** A short video section (two to 15 minutes) made by the instructor or edited from commercial videos that focus on a single point of information or a single idea or principle. The clip is shown to the students and then used as a focal point for a discussion. Shorter clips may be re-run.

47. **Film Preview.** Same as a videoclip preview, except a larger version. These longer films can be stopped at 15- to 20-minute intervals, questions asked, or a short discussion of key ideas conducted. Prior to the showing of the film or video, the instructor may want to focus attention of certain points and clarify any new vocabulary. These are often accompanied by a handout with questions for study in small groups after the showing.

48. **Exploration Exercise.** A technical form or artifact is explored and is presented as a handout rather than an integral part of a study guide.

49. **Group Work Exercise.** A whole class of students is given a problem or situation to solve in a 10- to 20-minute period of time. All directions and rules are printed in a handout, on an overhead transparency, or written on the blackboard, and explained by the instructor.

50. **Rank/Report.** Given a series of current items/issues, students, working in small groups, rank the importance of items or issues and report the results with a justification from each group.

51. **Did You Notice?** This is a follow-up technique to draw attention to significant points of a videoclip just viewed.

52. **Quasi-Dramatization.** The instructor speaks with authority, empathy, intensity, and high enthusiasm and engages the students in conversation.

53. **Adversarial Lecture.** Two speakers discuss their different points of view on a "hot" topic. The instructor gives a lecturette with comments on each side. Students question both the speakers and instructor as to why he or she made certain comments.

54. **Student Lecturette.** These are given on a preselected topic by a student with an accompanying handout with fill-ins. The student asks questions and uses a brief exercise.

55. **Surveys.** This is a poll of student opinions or values during a class. Responses are tallied immediately after the survey and discussion of the results follow. The edges of 3" x 5" cards can be colored with magic markers with each colored edge designating a response. For example, a red edge means agree very much; a green edge means agree; a blue edge means agree somewhat; a yellow edge means disagree.

56. **Paraphrases.** Tell the class in your own words what the instructor or another student just said. This technique can be used several times throughout a class. The instructor stops and poses the question to the class. The students are given two or three minutes to write their responses. Students then question each other and clarify their responses. The final results are shared with the class.

57. **Consequences.** Tell me what you think the consequences will be if this is not done or mastered. This technique usually relates to the learning performance objectives for a class. The students speculate as to the need for mastery and discuss what would happen if they did not master the objective.

58. **Choices.** Given data on an event and several choices, student are asked to discuss the choices, select one choice or provide an alternative choice, and identify the consequences of the selected choice with justification.

59. **Out-to-Lunch.** Two people lunch at a table together while teaching. The students pose questions during this presentation. This can get quite humorous as the discussion heats up.

60. **In the Fishbowl.** One student volunteers (or is selected) to study an issue as a preclass activity because of background, experience, or special interest. This student sits in the middle of a circle of six to eight other students who grill the "expert" for 15 to 20 minutes while the rest of the class observes. Other students are then invited to ask questions of the "expert." The instructor or another selected student summarizes.

61. **Successive Strategies.** Different instructional strategies are presented sequentially, such as discussions about an event followed by a short film or videoclip(s), followed by a role play, game or progress quiz.

62. **Debriefing.** All students discuss impressions and key happenings after a field trip or significant event. One or two students then summarize and generalize the conversation and report to the whole class.

63. **Equipment Demonstration.** The instructor disassembles and re-assembles equipment. Students should have a sketch of the equipment with key parts/segments left blank for fill-ins. New vocabulary should be defined. After the demonstration a student volunteer is asked to go through the procedure with the instructor providing significant cues.

64. **Handouts.** These are special documents, reports, pictures, etc. that are given to students for discussion. Each item is preceded by key questions to direct the students' attention. These questions are answered by students before class and then discussed during class.

65. **Check Lists.** A special handout in which each item is checked off as discussed by the instructor and or students.

66. **Reinforcing Fill-Ins.** The student fills in a word or phrase to a question. The instructor then writes the correct fill-in. The student modifies his/her response if necessary.

67. **Learning Contract.** A formal written agreement between the instructor and student to complete a mutually agreed upon task or skill. The instructor can provide a predesigned learning contract or the students can develop their own. This includes the learning performance objective(s); learning resources; completion time allowed; and evidence of mastery.

68. **Structured Notes**. A detailed verbal outline of a presentation with key words/phrases left out. The latter are filled in by the student as the lecture progresses.

69. **Interactive Study Guide.** Highly organized sets of student notes, graphics, pictures, graphs, charts, and other activities used in conjunction with a lecture. Key notes, which require fill-ins, phrases or other visual materials are printed in logical, numbered segments called displays.

70. **Word Pictures.** These are combinations of key words and phrases and geometric shapes to show relationships among ideas. They are used during a lecture to graphically convey ideas and concepts. Word pictures require the student to fill in words or phrases.

71. **Labeling a Diagram.** Each student is given an unlabeled diagram or picture. The student copies the labels as they are filled in by the instructor during the presentation.

72. **Lecture Outline.** A general outline of a lecture. Main ideas and sub-ideas are listed in a very general format. This requires a great deal of detailed note-taking.

73. **Ice Breakers.** Techniques that are used at the beginning of a class to reduce stress, introduce people, focus attention on the learning objectives, or make an important point. They can be in the form of a joke, story, use of an artifact, demonstration, newspaper headline, or videoclip.

74. **Challenge Problems.** Working alone or in a small group, students work out given problems which the instructor challenges them to do within a specified time. The instructor then discusses the correct answers. One half of the class time is left for the students to challenge the instructor with problems that they have previously constructed. The instructor thinks aloud as the problem is solved.

75. **Study Group Contract.** A group of students agree in a written contract to meet at set times after class and assist each other to master specified areas of competence. Usually, there is a group grade.

76. **Question Outline.** A series of questions, which are given in writing to the students, provide an outline to follow during the presentation by the instructor or student. After several questions, the students form pairs and check the comprehensiveness of their answers. Time is provided for clarification.

77. **Interactive Questioning Strategies.** Questions will be asked of the students are planned by the instructor prior to the class. Each question is written out, related to a learning performancem objective, and classified as recall, comprehension, application, or problem solving. The students are given the questions prior to class without the classifications. The students have previously

been taught how to classify questions. Upon being asked a question, the student repeats it, classifies its intent and, in case the student cannot answer it, explains what should be known at each intellectual level for a correct answer to. Other students help within the learning sequence.

78. **Student-Generated Questions.** The instructor explains to the students how to ask questions at different learning levels. Each of the four learning levels (recall, comprehension, application, and critical thinking) are explained and examples are provided. Every time a student asks a question, he or she explains the intellectual level.

79. **Quality Circles.** Quality circles consist of from 8 to 12 students meeting periodically with the instructor to discuss the progress of the course and points of confusion that need further clarification and additional examples. The instructor acts as facilitator. This increases contact with students and involves them more in the progress of the course. Quality circles provide continuous feedback for course improvement. The instructor uses brainstorming techniques and attempts to arrive at some type of consensus with the group. Students appreciate the opportunity to participate in class decisions that affect them. Quality circles would take place prior to a class with students making recommendations to an instructor during the beginning of a class.

80. **Psychodrama.** A structured role play in which the students take on the role of a person in an event or incident. Given clear goals and directions, students prepare with background readings and are then assigned a role. The students are provided with a script of a general scenario.

81. **Tinker Toys.** Small groups of students are provided with sets of tinker toys and told to develop a product with two moving parts, title it, describe its functions, and write and assemble a user's manual. After constructing the machines, the small group must make an oral presentation explaining why the product should be built.

82. **Learning Packages (Modules).** These are self-contained, self-paced, and self-directing packages of teaching-learning materials containing all print and non-print materials in a variety of formats. The student(s), studying alone or in small groups, work through a series of learning activities that lead to achievement of the learning performance objectives. Learning packages can be used as pre- or postclass preparation for an audio or video conference.

83. **Alter Ego.** Students take a stand on a predetermined issue selected by the class. Two students with different points of view are paired. One stands behind the other, who is seated, and argues for the opposite points of view of the seated student. After the presentations, the class discusses each position and then votes on one preferred position with the simple majority winning.

84. **The O/P Panel (Optimistic/ Pessimistic)**. A whole panel of five to eight students argues for 15 minutes on the optimistic side of an issue and then the same panel argues for 15 minutes on the pessimistic side or worst case scenario of the same issue. The whole class discusses the issue for 10 minutes, forms an opinion, and individual students are then polled by the instructor.

85. **Crossfire**. A closely moderated, heated, and argumentative discussion on a pre-determined controversial issue. The topic is given to four or five student panelists prior to the class so they can prepare background material. Students ask questions. At the end of the exercise students are polled and the results are given to the panel for their summary comments.

86. **Lecture Delay and Summary**. Students are not allowed to take any notes during the first 10 to 15 minutes of a lecture. The instructor requires undivided attention and will allow student questions after 10 to 15 minutes. The students are asked to summarize key points, draw diagrams, and write down as much detail as appropriate. The students are given five to 10 minutes, after which time they are asked to swap notes and check for accuracy and comprehensiveness.

87. **Active Review**. After the instructor summarizes the lecture, students are asked to review the structure within the total framework of the class. Students quietly read through their notes for two to three minutes and identify any points of confusion. They clarify any points of confusion by asking questions of each other and the instructor.

88. **Pyramiding (Snowball Groups)**. Given a problem, students first work alone, then in pairs and finally in foursomes (maximum), during which time they compare, refine, and revise their conclusions and recommendations. This technique was originally developed at the Open University in London.

89. **Instant Questionnaire**. A questionnaire is not designed to measure learning directly but rather to solicit values and opinions. Five or six short questions are presented on an overhead transparency. Students select one to five possible responses. Group response is solicited.

90. **Three, Two, Points**. The students are asked to summarize and then discuss the two or three most important points of a lecture. The instructor writes down what he or she thinks were the three most important points and then asks how many of the students also chose these points. This is done prior to sharing the learning performance objctives with the students.

91. **Learning Cell**. Students are divided into pairs and are given a specific assignment, or choose one from a variety of available assignments. The assignment (not longer than 15 minutes) is read during the class period. Each student prepares a series of questions derived from the reading assignment.

Students take turns asking each other questions, which are collected and reviewed after class by the instructor.

92. **The Quiet Question.** During the last five minutes of class the instructor hands out a half-sheet of paper that says:
    "A question I still have about (topic of lecture) but have been afraid to ask is…"
    Responses to these questions are addressed during the first five to 15 minutes of the next class.

93. **Concentric Circles.** This procedure is used with large groups of students. A small group of five or six students form within a larger group and conduct a discussion. The outer circle listens and takes notes. At a given point, the two circles reverse roles with the outer circle conducting the discussion and the inner circle listening.

94. **Controlled Discussion.** This is used after a lecture usually with large groups. Students ask questions and comment, but under the direct control of the instructor for a prescribed period of time.

95. **Step-by-Step Discussion.** A carefully prepared set of handout notes with a sequence of questions laid out dealing with the topic of the lecture. This forms the framework of the discussion. A time limit is set by the instructor.

96. **Free Group Discussion.** The topic and direction of the discussion are under the direction of the student groups. The instructor observes and comments.

97. **Audience Engagement.** The audience is engaged either physically: stand up; put your right hand up if…; put both hands up if…; hold the card up...; wave your hankerchief if... ; hold the spoon, fork, or knife up if... .

98. **Show Me Your Colors.** Each student is provided with a 5" x 8" index card. Each edge is colored with a highlight pen or felt-tip marker pen. One edge red, green, blue, or orange, or some other color. Ask a multiple choice question, and then ask for a color such as red. True or false would require two colors. Ask for an opinion—two colors or more. A rainbow effect means confusion. All requested colors showing means understanding. A very inexpensive responder device.

99. **The Question Box.** Students are encouraged to write their questions down about any topic covered in the class and deposit them in a central location such as a shoe box brought to class by the instructor. At a certain time one or more classes is dedicated to answering these questions. For large classes, the instructor could pre-print half page carbon copy pages. The student would write the question(s) and submit it any place on campus at designated spots. The instructor of record or teaching assistant would write a response on the second half of the sheet and return it to the student within 24 hours. The original is

returned to the student and the carbon copy is retained by the instructor for future reference when reviewing the course. These are called "Quick Notes."

100. **Lecture Reaction Panel.** This consists of three to five students chosen by the instructor. The students sit at an angle facing both the instructor and students. They listen carefully, ask questions, and then are given ten minutes to prepare a summary of the most important points of the lecture. Questions are then solicited from the class at large.

101. **Question Challenge.** The class is given a reading assignment either from the text or other outside reading. Each student is asked to write two questions from the reading that require responses above factual information. During the next class, each student asks their questions of the class. The instructor moderates. The class is asked if they are satisfied with the answers to the questions.

102. **What Would You Do?** Students work in pairs. Each group is provided with a camcorder for the purpose of making a two- to four-minute trigger video. Each pair identifies a problem or opportunity in their discipline and creates a video scenario. The problem or opportunity is presented without a conclusion. The rest of the class, working in groups of four, views the trigger video and is told to turn the tape recorder off. They identify the problem or opportunity, identify alternative courses of action and the probable consequences of each action, and make a recommendation. They turn the videotape recorder back on and view how a professional in their field handled the problem.

103. **Group Collage.** Using magazine cutouts, the students create a visual representation of an idea. This can be done in groups of three or four as a homework assignment. The topic is selected or assigned to the students. Each group is asked to explain their montage.

104. **Role Reversal.** Like a general role play except that the roles are reversed. You play me and I will play you. It will help the participants gain an understanding of the other person's viewpoint and values. It helps students to see how they are perceived by others.

105. **Mirroring.** A role play with the added dimension of participants being able to walk up to one of the characters and interpret what they really mean when they say something else.

106. **Videotape Feedback.** Any of the above techniques can be videotaped by another student.

107. **Round-Table Discussion.** One group of four to six students sits at a round table situated in front of the class. After selecting a topic or given a topic, each student selects a different viewpoint. The rest of the class listens in as the panel discusses the topic for a specified period of time. The panel is allowed to use a

flipchart or blackboard. The class is then allowed to ask questions of the whole panel. The instructor acts as moderator.

108. **Structured Discussion.** Class discussion focused around specific learning objectives that are either posted on a flipchart or blackboard, or handed out to each student. Different groups can address different objectives or the whole group can focus on one objective. Students work within a defined time period.

109. **Cartoons With the Captions Removed.** Cartoons dealing with the topic under discussion are periodically put on the overhead projector with the captions removed. The students are asked to make up a caption.

110. **One Minute Feedback.** During the last few minutes of class, students are asked to respond to one of the following types of questions, which are reviewed after class by the instructor:
    a. What was the most confusing point that I made in class today?
    b. What were the two most important points that you learned today?
    c. What did you like best about today's class?

These techniques have been provided to stimulate your own imagination about the many possibilities for involving your students in their own learning. Adapt them to your classroom needs.

BIBLIOGRAPHY

Armistead, Colm. (1984). How useful are case studies. <u>Training and Development Journal</u>, 75-77.

Arwady, Joseph, & Gayeski, Diane M. (1989). <u>Using video: Interactive and linear designs</u>. Englewood Cliffs, NJ: Educational Technology Publications.

Berquist, William H., Phillips, Steven R., & Quehl, Gary H. (Eds.). (1975). <u>A handbook for faculty development</u>. Washington, DC: The Council for the Advancement of Small Colleges.

Black, Ronald A. Psychodrama in classroom teaching. <u>College and University Teaching</u>, 26(2), 118-120.

Bruce, Corrine. (1985). Breaking the ice. <u>Training and Development Journal</u>, 26-28.

Christensen, C. Roland. (1981). <u>Teaching and the case method</u>. Boston: Harvard Business School.

Cyrs, Thomas E. (1977). Designing learning packages. In <u>Handbook for the design of instruction in pharmacy education</u>. Baltimore: American Association of Colleges of Pharmacy.

____. (1977). <u>Handbook for the design of instruction in pharmacy education</u>. Baltimore: American Association of Colleges of Pharmacy.

____. (1977). Improving lecture presentation formats through student interaction. In <u>Handbook for the design of instruction in pharmacy education</u>. Baltimore: American Association of Colleges of Pharmacy.

____. (1976). How to design learning modules. <u>The Journal of Practical Nursing</u>.

Cyrs, Thomas E., & Smith, Frank A. (1990). <u>Teleclass teaching: A resource guide</u> (2nd ed.). Las Cruces, NM: Center for Educational Development, New Mexico State University.

Davis, Larry Nolan, & McCallon, Earl. (1976). <u>Planning, conducting, and evaluating workshops</u>. Austin, TX: Learning Concepts.

Duncombe, Sydney, & Heikkmen, Michael H. (1983). Role playing for different view points. <u>College Teaching</u>, 36(1), 3-5.

Esbensen, Thorwald. (1978). <u>Student contracts</u>. Englewood Cliffs, NJ: Educational Technology Publications.

Fisch, A.L. (1970). The trigger film technique. <u>Improving College and University Teaching</u>, 286-289.

Frederick, Peter J. (1989). Involving students more actively in the classroom. In A.F. Lucas, <u>The department chairperson's role in enhancing college teaching</u>. San Francisco: Jossey-Bass Publishers.

____. (1986). The lively lecture–Eight variations. <u>College Today</u>, 34(2), 43-50.

Gibbs, Graham. (1987). Improving student learning during lectures. <u>Medieval Teacher</u>, 9(1), 11-20.

Gibbs, G., Habeshaw, S., & Habeshaw, T. (1987). <u>53 interesting things to do in your lectures</u>. Bristol, England: Technical and Educational Services.

General Physics Courseware. (1983). <u>Fundamentals of classroom instruction</u>. Columbia, MD: G.P. Courseware.

Grossman, Stephen R. (1984). Brainstorming updated. <u>Training and Development Journal</u>, 84-87.

Ideas for the classroom. (1989). <u>The Chronicle of Higher Education</u>, 19.

Johnson, Dale A. (1989). Training by television. <u>Training and Development Journal</u>, 65-68.

Jonassen, David H. (1985). Interactive lesson designs: A taxonomy. <u>Educational Technology</u>, 7-16.

Knowles, Malcolm S. (1986). <u>Using learning contracts</u>. San Francisco: Jossey-Bass Publishers.

Kogut, Leonard S. Quality circles: A Japanese management technique for the classroom. <u>Improving College and University Teaching</u>, <u>32</u>(3), 123-127.

Massoumain, Rijan. (1988). Successful teaching via two-way interactive video. <u>Tech Trends</u>, 16-19.

Odiorne, George S. (1970). The case study and its variations. <u>Training by objectives</u>. London: The MacMillan Co.

Osterman, Dean M. <u>Five alternatives to lecturing in higher education</u>. Information Futures.

Phoenix, Charlotte Y. Get them involved! <u>College Teaching</u>, <u>35</u>(1), 13-15.

Pichette, Michel. (1987). Some conditions for the development of interactive telelearning. <u>Media in Education and Development</u>, <u>20</u>(3), 100-103.

Pigors, Paul. (1976). Case method. In Robert Craig (Ed.), <u>Training and development handbook</u>. San Francisco: McGraw-Hill Book Co.

Porter, Kathryn W. (1990). Tuning in to TV training. <u>Training and Development Journal</u>, 73-77.

Richards, Tudor. (1974). <u>Problem solving through creative analysis</u>. NY: John Wiley and Sons.

Rickert, Shirley R. <u>You don't need ice of you're not skating: The effective use of icebreakers</u>. Paper presented at the 1989 ISETA Conference, Ft. Collins, CO.

Romaine, Larry. (1981). Quality circles that enhance productivity. <u>Community and Junior College Journal</u>, <u>52</u>(3), 30-31.

Segall, Ascher J., et al. (1975). <u>Systematic course design for the health professions</u>. NY: John Wiley and Sons.

Simpson, Raymond J., & Galbo, Joseph J. (1986). Interaction and learning. Theorizing on the art of teaching. <u>Interchange</u>, <u>17</u>(4), 37-51.

Thiagarajan, Sivasailam. (1989). Interactive lectures: Seven more strategies. <u>Performance and Instruction</u>, 35-36.

____. (1988). Beyond brainstorming. <u>Training and Development Journal</u>, 57-60.

Webster, William E. Student-developed case studies. <u>College Teaching</u>, <u>36</u>(1), 25-27.

Weston, Cynthia Cranton. (1986). Selecting instructional strategies. <u>Journal of Higher Education</u>, <u>57</u>(3), 259-288.

Chapter 13

Alternatives to the Traditional Lecture

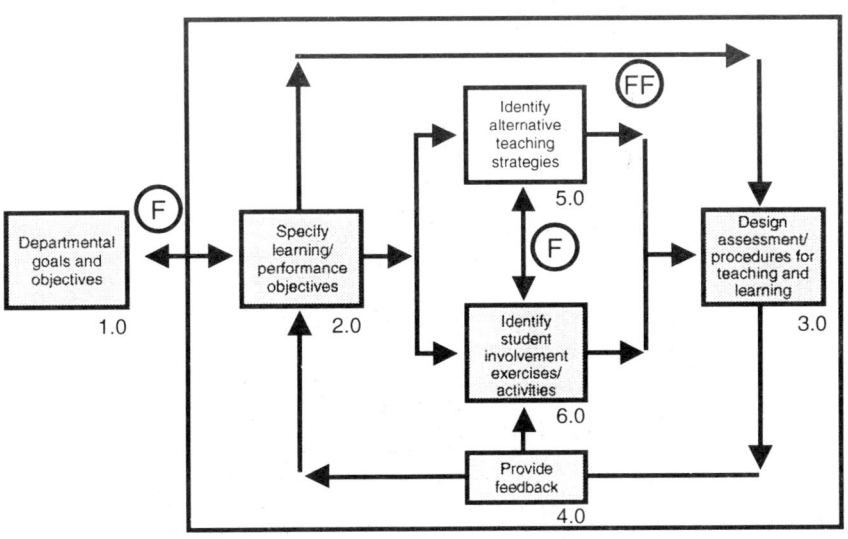

ALTERNATIVES TO THE LECTURE

LEARNING PERFORMANCE OBJECTIVE
Describe the feasibility and desirability of using either of these three alternatives to the lecture in your classes: cooperative, contract, and problem-based learning. (Level 2).

KEY IDEAS
1. Three major alternatives to the traditional lecture are cooperative learning, contract learning, and problem-based learning.
2. These alternatives will require a different approach to planning and organizing a course.

NEW VOCABULARY
- cooperative learning
- contract learning
- problem-based learning

There are three major alternatives to the traditional lecture that are noteworthy: (1) cooperative learning; (2) the learning contract; and (3) problem-based learning. All can fit into the time frame traditionally allocated for the lecture.

COOPERATIVE LEARNING

Students may work either cooperatively or competitively in our colleges. However, the system of grading favors competition rather than cooperation. Norm-referenced learning using a five-part letter grading system is most reflective of the way we encourage students to compete for grades. The focus of the bell curve is to balance the grades between pass and fail. Theoretically only 5% of the students in a class should get an "A." This establishes a negative interaction among students because if one student should be awarded an "A" it reduces the possibility of another student getting an "A." Students are forced to compete for the theoretical 5% of the class that should earn an "A." This is the "me" approach to learning, which is in direct opposition to one of the major priorities of business and industry–the need for cooperation, mutual support, and problem-solving in team projects, which, in turn, creates the need for an interdependent "we" approach to teaching and learning.

Cooperative learning has been practiced for many decades and provides a viable alternative to the traditional instructor-centered lecture. Cooperative learning is best exemplified in the active learning movement, which has been discussed in detail in this book. Cooperative learning is a structured and systematic approach to small-group problem solving that incorporates the use of heterogeneous teams of students. It maintains individual accountability while promoting positive and supportive interdependence. One of the goals of cooperative learning is to enhance development of individual social skills, such as decision making, and effective communication within a small group. Astin (1992) has reported that "… the peer group emerges as [having] the greatest single effect on the educational process." Cooperative learning capitalizes on the power of the peer group working together in a structured environment to solve an academic or social problem.

When students work cooperatively toward a mutually shared goal, for whatever reason, they are seeking outcomes that will benefit themselves as well as the group. This attitude fosters and reinforces the idea that "nobody is smarter than all of us." Johnson, Johnson, and Smith (1991) define cooperative learning as "… the instructional use of small groups so that students work together to maximize their own and each other's learning." These researchers go on to point out that for a lesson to be cooperative, five basic elements must be present: positive interdependence, face-to-face promotive interaction, individual accountability, social skills, and group processing. The social skills must be taught formally, just as are the cognitive skills.

These key elements and characteristics of cooperative learning have been further described in the November 1992 issue of The National Teaching and Learning Forum. Cooperative learning opportunities must include the following five elements:

1. Positive interdependence. Students involved in cooperative learning activities must see the need for mutual cooperation if the project is to succeed.
2. Face-to-face promotive interaction. Students must teach each other with the consultative support of the instructor. They share what they know with each other.
3. Individual accountability. Each student is totally accountable for their own actions and the actions of the group. Anyone within the group should be able to answer any part of the problem under consideration.
4. Interpersonal and small-group skills. These skills include leadership, decision-making, trust-building, communication, and conflict-management. As part of the cooperative learning process, they are taught formally.
5. Group processing. This involves a reflective process of looking at how well the group functioned to achieve the goals of the project.

Most efforts at cooperative learning do not replace the more traditional lecture teaching strategies. Cooperative learning activities are interspersed within the traditional classroom format for short periods of time and shift responsibility from the instructor to the student to work through structured exercises and activities.

REFERENCES AND BIBLIOGRAPHY

Astin, Alexander. (1992). What matters in college? In James Rhem (Ed.). The National Teaching and Learning Forum, 2(1).

Bonwell, Charles C., & Eison, James A. (1991). Active learning: Creating excitement in the classroom. ASHE-ERIC Higher Education Report No. 1. Washington, DC: The George Washington University, School of Education and Human Development.

Cooper, James, & Others. (1990). Cooperative learning and college instruction. Long Beach, CA: The California State University Foundation.

Johnson, David W., Johnson, Roger T., & Smith, Karl A. (1991). Cooperative learning: Increasing college faculty instructional productivity. ASHE-ERIC Higher Education Report No. 4. Washington, DC: The George Washington University, School of Education and Human Development.

Kagan, Spencer. (1985). Cooperative learning resources for teachers. Laguna Niguel, CA: Resources for Teachers.

Millis, Barbara J. (1992). An introduction to cooperative learning. Seminar presented at the Annual Meeting of the Professional and Organizational Development, FL.

____. (1991). Fulfilling the promise of the "seven principles" through cooperative learning: An action agenda for the university classroom. Journal on Excellence in College Teaching, 2, 139-144.

____. (1990). Helping faculty build learning communities through cooperative groups. In To improve the academy: Resources for students, faculty, and institutional development. Stillwater, OK: New Forums Press.

The National Teaching and Learning Forum (1992). Elements of Cooperative Learning, 2(1), 3.

CONTRACT LEARNING

A learning contract is a formal written agreement between the instructor and an individual student or group of students to complete a designated amount of work or master a particular skill within a specified amount of time at a predetermined level of proficiency. Knowles (1987) defines a learning contract as "… a plan for acquiring specified knowledge, understanding, skills, attitudes, or values by a learner." Hoover (1981) notes that the ultimate goal of a contract is to "… develop individuals who not only know how to direct their own learning but who develop initiative and major responsibility for learning as well."

All learning contracts have common elements: a purpose, which explains why the contract is important; learning performance objectives, which specify what the student is to learn and what skills are to be performed; learning activities, exercises, and resources, which describe how the student is to achieve the learning performance objectives; evidence of achievement, which describes how the student and instructor will know when the student has mastered the learning performance objectives; and verification of learning, which describes how the evidence provided by the student can be validated.

There are a number of ways that a contract can be designed and assigned. The instructor can specify the learning performance objectives, select the resources, and specify the evidence of achievement. These predesigned contracts can be given to a student or the student could select from an array of predesigned learning contracts. The instructor could specify the learning performance objectives and then negotiate a variety of resources with the student or allow the student to identify the most appropriate resources, which are then reviewed and approved by the instructor. The instructor could assign the evidence of achievement or negotiate it with the student. The students could design their own learning contracts and have them approved by the instructor.

Once the learning contract is approved, the student works independently or with small groups of students. A well-designed contract will have a series of self-correcting progress quizzes that allow students to judge their own progress toward mastering the learning performance objectives.

This alternative to the structured lecture presentation allows the student to become self-directing and self-pacing as well as self-correcting. The technique requires that the students are highly motivated and accept full responsibility for their own learning. Knowles (1987) has observed that the learning contract is one of the most effective techniques to use when adults are involved.

Self-directing learning contracts may include such possible activities as:

- reading chapters in a text
- attending a formal training session
- practicing with a particular instrument
- constructing a specialized bibliography
- attending a movie for review
- attending a play
- attending a special lecture series
- completing a self-assigned project
- constructing a questionnaire
- designing handouts
- producing a product
- developing a needs assessment
- conducting a workshop
- giving a presentation
- performing at a recital
- listening to a television program
- producing a videotape
- summarizing readings
- consulting experts
- self-assessment
- writing a special grant
- taking a course
- writing a paper
- developing a photo presentation
- designing a teaching portfolio
- participating in a poster session
- developing a marketing strategy
- participating in an apprenticeship
- participating in community activities
- documenting procedures
- developing an annotated bibliography
- forming a study group
- attending meetings
- documenting the progress of something
- identifying professional competencies
- designing a rating scale
- reviewing the literature on a special topic
- reviewing reports
- conducting on-site visitations
- participating in a clinical internship
- presenting a paper
- participating in a teleconference
- traveling to a foreign country
- keeping a personal diary
- establishing a professional network

Producing evidence that the student has satisfactorily achieved the learning performance objectives requires that some type of product must be developed. These products could consist of such things as:

- a videotape of a presentation
- a written case study
- a live poster session
- a microteaching videotape
- a lesson outline
- a teaching portfolio
- a painting or sculpture
- a manual
- a workshop

Given the product agreed upon by the student and instructor, this evidence must be validated. The validation could use people and criteria such as:

- an agreed upon set of criteria against which a presentation would be critiqued
- agency peers
- verbal feedback
- rating scale
- questionnaire

- interviews
- test score
- peer review
- skill performance
- course grade
- evaluation of a videotape section
- quality of product or presentation
- observational criteria
- consultant
- supervisor
- pre- or post-test score
- student portfolio score

The learning contract is a powerful tool for learning and embodies all of the principles of cooperative learning. A sample learning contract for the subject of adult learning is provided on the next page.

REFERENCES AND BIBLIOGRAPHY

Auakiian, D.P. (1974). Writing a learning contract. In D.W. Vermilye (Ed.), Lifelong learners: A new clientele for higher education. San Francisco: Jossey-Bass Publishers.

Barlow, R.M. (1974). An experiment with learning contracts. Journal of Higher Education, 75, 441-450.

Caffarella, R.S. (1983). Fostering self-directed learning in post-secondary education: The use of learning contracts. Lifelong Learning, 7(3), 7-26.

Cross, R.P. (1979). The missing link: Connecting adult learners to learning resources. Princeton, NJ: College Board Publications.

Esbensen, Thorwald. (1978). Student contracts. Englewood Cliffs, NJ: Educational Technology Press.

Hoover, Kenneth H. (1981). A sourcebook of student activities. Boston: Allyn and Bacon.

Knowles, Malcolm S. (March, 1987). Enhanced HRD with contract learning. Training and Development Journal, 62-63.

____. (1986). Using learning contracts. San Francisco: Jossey-Bass.

Lindquist, J. (1975). Strategies for contract learning. In D.W.Vermilye (Ed.), Learner-Centered Reform. San Francisco: Jossey-Bass Publishers.

Newcomb, L.H., & Warsbrod, R.J. The effect of contract grading on student performance. (ERIC Documentation Reproduction Service No ED 093 967)

PROBLEM-BASED LEARNING

Problem-based learning provides a viable alternative to the teacher-centered and subject-centered classroom so often found in colleges today. Although originally developed for the health professions to introduce students to real-life problems the first day of class, it also has strong implications for the non-health related programs in all disciplines. Brandon (1992) describes the elements of a typical seminar session in his course entitled, HLS 481: Interdisciplinary Seminar:

> This class is unlike your traditional instructor-centered and subject-based class. Instead, it is student-centered and utilizes a "problem-stimulated learning" approach. In this class a problem will be presented at the beginning of each session. The desire is for your group to generate

Learning Contract - Title: The Adult Learner

What Learning Objective(s)	Working with two other students, write a collaborative paper & poster that: 1. Describe the differences between the adult learner & traditional students & areas of possible tension between them. 2. Explain the different teaching/learning strategies for use with adult students. There will be a shared grade. Completion date: 4 weeks.	
How Learning Activities and Strategies	1. View the videotape/Interactive Study Guide: Cyrs, Thomas (1991), Adapting College Instruction for the Adult Student: The Need for Participation. 2. View the videotape: "The Adult Learner." 3. Read: "What is Active Learning," & "The Modified Lecture" in Bonwell, Charles C. & Elson, James A. (1991) Active Learning: Creating Excitement in the Classroom. 4. Read: "The Emergence of a Theory of Adult Learning: Andragogy." in Knowles, Malcolm (1978), The Adult Learner: A Neglected Species. 5. Read: Merriam, Sharon B. & Caffarella, Rosemary S. Learning in Adulthood. San Francisco: Jossey-Bass Publishers, 1991. 6. Read: Cross, Patricia K. (1981) Adults as Learners. San Franciso: Jossey-Bass Publishers. 7. Read: Fiske, Marjorie & Chiviboga, David A. (1990) Change & Continuity in Adult Life. San Franciso: Jossey-Bass Publishers. 8. Read: Knowles, Malcolm S. (1986). Using Learning Contracts. San Francisco: Jossey-Bass Publishers. 9. Produce edited videotape: Interview of 10 adult students & identify sources of stress/conflict in the classroom with non-adult students. You will have to design an interview schedule. 10. Conduct a literature search in ERIC, Psychlit, & Agricola on the Adult Learner. 11. The instructor will be available for personal consultation. Please call for an appointment.	Date
Evidence of Achievement or Product	1. Completed paper. 2. Edited interviews with 10 adult students. 3. Interview schedule.	
Verification of Learning	*Quality of the interview schedule using the criteria provided by the instructor. *The final shared paper must be free of grammatical & spelling errors & typed in APA format. It must cover all areas agreed to with the instructor. *The edited videotape must not exceed 10 minutes & deal with major issues only. *The paster session must meet the criterai explained in Teaching Tip: How To Conduct a Poster Session & peer review by fellow students using the criteria in the Teaching Tip.	

Instructor: _____   Student: _____

Date: _____

Center for Educational Development

unanswered questions through interaction with the problem, which will guide subsequent learning. Problem-based learning has been defined as "learning that results from the process of working toward the understanding or resolution of a problem," p. 3, Tips for Tutors, UNM-SOM, Primary Care Curriculum.

The elements of a typical session will include:
  A. Problem identification
     1. Generation of hypotheses
     2. Mechanisms and causes in relation to hypotheses
     3. Identification of learning issues
  B. Evaluation
     1. Self-evaluation
     2. Group-evaluation

The essential characteristic of any problem-based program is a curriculum organized around specific real-world problems rather than around independent disciplines. The total curriculum is integrated and interrelated rather than presented as separate disciplines. Knowledge recall of factual data is minimized so that higher level problem-solving skills can be emphasized. According to Bruhn (1992), problem-based learning has two major objectives: (1) To acquire an integrated body of knowledge related to a given problem, and (2) to develop and apply problem-solving skills. In order to accomplish these objectives, students direct their own learning based on work-related problems identified by the instructor. This competency-based program requires that knowledge, skills, and attitudes are interrelated. This type of program is relevant in situations in which knowledge and skills must adapt immediately as both knowledge and skills change at an exponential rate.

The organizing principle of problem-based learning is to place students into study groups, give them a problem, and ask them to solve the problem in terms of the physical, social, ethical, and environmental implications, and to understand how these are interrelated. Walters and Matthews (1989) define a problem as

> A set of circumstances in a particular setting which is new to the student, where the use of pattern recognition alone is insufficient, but where specific items of knowledge and understanding have to be applied in a logical analytical process in order to identify the factors involved and their interaction.

The problems provided by the instructors are highly structured and include the whole range of intellectual skills from recall of factual knowledge to application and critical thinking. Only part of the needed information is provided to the students. This can be conflicting, confusing, and contradictory. The job of the student is to propose hypotheses and review all possible alternatives, make inferences, request additional information, and logically deduce the best hypothesis supported by the data. An example of such a problem can be found in the course HLS 481, taught by Brandon (1992).

SAMPLE PROBLEM

SETTING (Initial information provided): A 30-year-old Hispanic male presents himself to the Public Health Office with symptoms of indigestion (what he calls Empacho), bloating, and constipation. He has recently moved here and has a green card that enables him to work in the fields.

Questions:
1. What are this person's problems? Prioritize your list.
2. Choose one problem. Can you think of possible hypotheses that might account for this?
3. Based on your hypothesis and mechanism, what further information do you want to know?

ADDITIONAL INFORMATION PROVIDED:

Mr. Gilberto H. moved here from Chihuahua, Mexico approximately three months ago. He came with his two older sons, ages 15 and 17. His wife stayed in Chihuahua with their three youngest children, ages 10, 7, and 18 months. He and his two sons live in an apartment with a cousin in San Miguel. He owns a 1959 Chevy pickup in average running condition.

His symptoms began two months ago and have increased over the last two weeks. He now complains of indigestion, bloating, and constipation daily. His diet, when he does eat, is normal. He also has nausea and occasional vomiting, but no diarrhea. This is the worst he has ever felt. He went to the curandera approximately two weeks ago. She treated him with yerba buena and it did not help.

He is under a lot of stress because he is worried about his wife, who does not have any resources, and his three children, who are still in Chihuahua. He works as an onion topper, and is currently waiting for the onion harvest to begin. The recent hail storm has damaged the crop, and harvesting is set back two weeks. His sons are healthy and plan to work with him in the fields. He is worried because they have found some friends who drink heavily and he has noted alcohol on their breath early in the morning.

He has a green card and wants to remain a Mexican citizen. They are currently helping with a landscaping job to pay for food to eat. They have no savings.

Other pertinent history: His father died of Empacho at age 52. The rest of his family is healthy. His seven brothers and sisters all live in Mexico.

There are a number of different formats used for problem-based learning that can be applied in different educational settings: (1) Students can be assigned to small groups with a faculty member serving as tutor; (2) Students may meet in small groups without an assigned instructor to solve a problem. An instructor can be called upon as an expert in some area; (3) Case method teaching can be utilized in which a larger group of students is engaged in a discussion of a problem previously analyzed by another group of students; (4) Case-based lectures can be used. The class begins with a case provided by the instructor. Comments by students are solicited and discussion follows; (5) Students can engage in independent study using a variety of learning resources including computer-assisted instruction, books and articles, audiovisual resources, and so forth.

Problem-based learning is a viable alternative to lecture-based class but will require rethinking your philosophy of teaching. A review the literature and discussion with faculty who use this approach should be completed before a decision to jump into problem-based learning is made.

REFERENCES AND BIBLIOGRAPHY

Barrows, H.S., & Tamblyn, R.M. (1980). Problem-based learning: An approach to medical education. NY: Springer.

Brandon, Jeff. (1993). HLS481: Interdisciplinary seminar. (personal communication, 1993). Las Cruces, NM: Department of Health Science, College of Human and Community Services, New Mexico State University.

Bruhn, John G. (1992, Summer). Problem-based learning: An approach toward reforming allied health education. Journal of Allied Health, 161-173.

Schmidt, H.G. (1983). Problem-based learning: Rationale and description. Medical Education, 17, 11-16.

Walton, H.J., & Matthews, M.B. (1989). Essentials of problem-based learning. Medical Education, 23, 542-558.

Wilkerson, LuAnn, & Feletti, Grahame. (1989). Problem-based learning: One approach to increasing student participation. In A.F. Lucas (Ed.), The department chairperson's role in enhancing college teaching: No. 37. New directions for teaching and learning. San Francisco: Jossey-Bass Publishers.

VARIATIONS ON THE LECTURE

Other resources that describe variations within a lecture or alternatives to it include:

Bentley, Donna Anderson. (1986). More ammunition for the notetaking feud. Improving College and University Teaching, 29(2), 85-87.

Bligh, D. (1972). What's the use of lectures? England: Penguin.

Bonwell, Charles C., & Eison, James A. (1989). Active learning: Creating excitement in the classroom. ASHE-ERIC Higher Education Report No. 1. Washington, DC: The George Washington University, School of Education and Human Development.

Brooks, David W. (1987, October). Alternatives to traditional lecturing. Journal of Chemical Education, 61(10), 858-859.

Cowan, John. (1984, December). The responsive lecture: A means of supplementing resource-based instruction. Educational Technology, 24, 18-21.

Gibbs, Graham, & Jenkins, Alan. (1984). Break up your lectures: or Christaller sliced up. Journal of Geography Education, 8(1), 27-39.

Kelly, Brenda Wright, & Holmes, Janis. (1979, April). The guided lecture procedure. Journal of Reading, 602-604.

Osterman, Dean N. (1979). <u>Five alternatives to lecture in higher education: An analysis</u>. Pullman, WA: Information Futures. (These include: Audio-Tutorial; Computer-based Education; Guided Design; Learning Packages; Personalized System of Instruction.)

_____. (1980). <u>A new teaching approach: The feedback lecture</u>. (ERIC Documentation Services ED 190 121)

Ruhl, Kathy L., Hughes, Charles A., & Schloss, Patrick J. (1987). Using the pause procedure to enhance lecture recall. <u>Teacher Education and Special Education</u>, <u>10</u>(1), 14-18.

Section II

Activities and events during class

Chapter 14
  The Art and Craft of Constructing an Exciting Lecture

Chapter 15
  Lecture Presentation Skills

Chapter 16
  Creating a Stimulating Classroom Environment

Chapter 17
  Classroom Questioning Strategies Above Recall

Chapter 18
  Alternative Student Handout Formats

Chapter 14

The Art and Craft of Constructing an Exciting Lecture

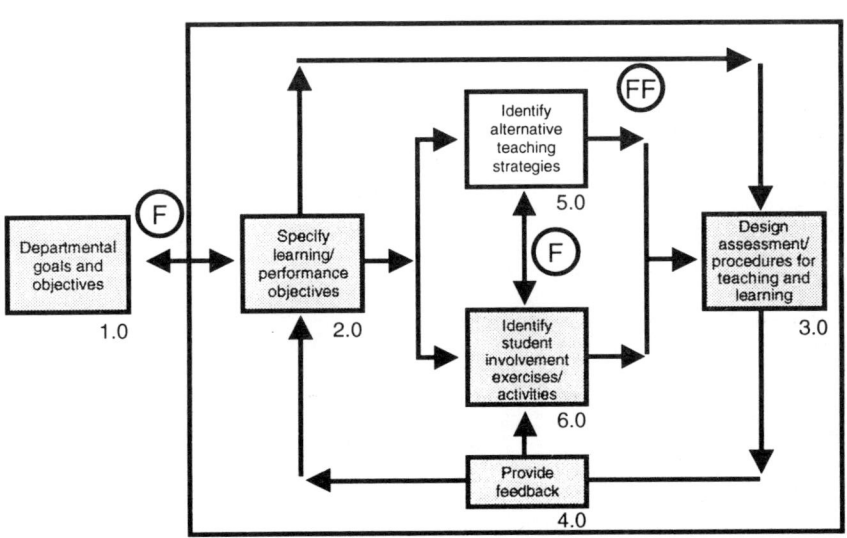

"Excited teachers excite students."

THE ART AND CRAFT OF CONSTRUCTING A DYNAMIC LECTURE

LEARNING PERFORMANCE OBJECTIVE
Develop a 50-minute lecture using at least five of the components described in this chapter. (Level 4).

KEY IDEAS
1. The lecture as currently used, will continue for at least 25 more years. It needs to be more effective, involving, and exciting. These are acquired skills.
2. The research indicates that the traditional lecture is effective for motivation and information transfer. It is ineffective for critical thinking and problem-solving skills.
3. The most appropriate lecture format is: review key points of previous lectures; preview the learning performance objectives of the lecture; present and involve; and summarize the key points.
4. There are over 20 potential lecture components that will improve it.
5. Key lecture points should be reinforced with visual and verbal analogies for storytelling techniques.
6. Instructors use a variety of intellectual patterns to organize lectures.

NEW VOCABULARY
- lecture
- word picture
- imaging
- storytelling
- expressiveness
- key points
- fill-ins
- pacing
- silence
- attention span
- clarity
- enthusiasm
- explanations
- visual and verbal analogy
- definition
- handout
- transitions
- problem centered lecture
- sequential lecture
- comparative lecture
- thesis lecture
- freehand lecture
- formal oral essay lecture
- provocative lecture
- lecture demonstration
- set induction
- ice breaker
- examples
- grabbers and stabbers
- organizational patterns

The lecture is the most widely used, while at the same time the most highly criticized, method of instruction in post-secondary education. It is designed to cover a body of information in a defined period of time—usually 50 to 75 minutes. Unfortunately, the lecture as a presentation skill provides too much emphasis on verbal explanation from the instructor to the student without adequate visual reinforcement. On the other hand, a well-developed lecture can provide a conceptual framework that builds bridges and makes connections between the students' prior knowledge and experience and their current knowledge and experience through analogies, examples, stories and demonstrations. The lecture can motivate, clarify, review, link, and expand content.

Cooper (1985) defines a lecture as "... essentially, informative speaking..." of which the major purpose is to "... secure clear understanding of the concepts presented." If the purpose of the lecture is primarily to transmit information (much of which could be provided in a textbook), then the function of the student is to take notes fast and accurately–almost like a stenographer.

The word "lecture" comes from the Latin "lecto," a noun related to the verb "legere," meaning to read. During the Middle Ages books were copied by hand, usually in monasteries, and were very scarce because of the time needed to copy them accurately by hand. Many were works of art. Teachers had to disseminate knowledge orally using these scarce books as the primary resource. When books became more available after the Gutenberg revolution, you would think that the oral tradition would have given way to more reading in the classroom. Certainly after the discovery of xerography you would think that the lecture would almost disappear. The time-honored lecture endures now as popularly as it did in the Middle Ages. It will probably continue for at least another 25 years or until the current generation of college instructors retire. They will be replaced by the Nintendo generation whose use of technology is an integral part of their lives rather than adjunct to it, as in our current generation of instructors.

Brown (1978) describes the lecture as

> ... a teaching period occupied wholly or mainly with continuous exposition by a lecturer. Students attending it may be given some opportunity for questions or a discussion, but in the main they have nothing to do except listen and take notes.

Boulton and Russell (1983) examined the active and passive roles of the instructor and student in the traditional classroom and note how sharply they contrast. In a lecture the instructor generally adopts the active role while the student has no choice but to accept the passive role. Given this reality, it isn't unreasonable to conclude that the best way to learn is to teach. The teacher's active role of organizing and presenting a lecture makes the traditional lecture method a very effective method of learning–for the instructor.

THE LECTURE PREFERRED

The learner has been described as one of the most ineffective instructional strategies. Regardless of the criticism, there are a number of instances when the lecture is preferred. Inspiration and motivation are obvious preferences. When few qualified instructors and quality instructional materials are available in certain disciplines and there is inadequate time for development, the lecture is an obvious choice. When there is conflict and confusion in available data, expert advice in the form of a lecture would be welcomed. When resources are scattered and generally unavailable and time is critical, the lecture may be the only option. When specialized information is hard to obtain and in constant flux, the lecture might be preferable (Sweeney and Reigeluh, 1974; Waggoner, 1984).

ADVANTAGES OF THE LECTURE
The lecture format is inexpensive and efficient. One instructor can provide a lecture for hundreds or even thousands of students. If the lecturer is well-prepared and develops the lecture carefully, many students can benefit. How many lecturers possess these qualities? A lecture is flexible since the subject matter can be adjusted easily to meet changing information if oral delivery is used.

If efficiency is required, for whatever reason, the lecture method takes less time to cover subject matter than other instructional strategies such as discussion skills and case methods. This is especially true if the major objective is to transmit information when hard to obtain data is synthesized easily, effectively, and efficiently in a lecture format. Well-planned questions embedded in a lecture allow students to explore their value systems and establish their own priorities.

DISADVANTAGES OF THE LECTURE
The lecture is used primarily as an information transfer system and minimizes student interaction. The flow of information is generally unidirectional with the instructor doing most of the talking. The effectiveness of the lecture is dependent on the listening and note-taking skills of the students, who have to guess what is nice-to-know and what is need-to-know, unless the instructor provides adequate cuing. Hartley and Cameren (1967) have noted that "... student notes taken during lectures are demonstrably poor records of even the factual content of lectures, containing an average of about a fifth of the 'information' units and only a tenth of the 'content.'" This is not surprising since most faculty have little, if any, training in the development of an effective lecture. Most faculty model those lecturers they perceived to be effective when they were students.

During most lectures the student is generally passive and has no control of the flow and direction of the information and ideas. The lecturer often assumes that the student possesses the skills necessary to master the content presented. Few, if any, instructors provide the students with a statement of the learning performance objectives that they are expected to master during the lecture.

Lecturers notoriously cover too much material in one lecture and overload students with information. Cooper (1985) states that "most students can handle five to nine 'bits' of information comfortably. Thus, only a few main points should be covered in a single lecture." Too often instructors cover 20 to 25 key points in a lecture that results in cognitive overlaod for the students.

WHAT DOES THE RESEARCH SAY ABOUT THE LECTURE?
The research has consistently berated the lecture format as currently practiced in colleges and universities. However, it is hypothesized throughout this text that the lecture will continue as the major delivery format in higher education. It is the purpose of these chapters to suggest ways that the lecture can be systematically improved and delivered and viable and practical alternatives used in lieu of it.

The research on lecturing falls into two main categories:
1. lecture effectiveness and,
2. the lecture format as compared to other instructional strategies.

There is almost no research on specific methods to train lecturers to either develop or deliver a quality lecture.

Lecture effectiveness examines student notetaking skills. It is concerned with what is effective student notetaking and what the lecturer can do to increase the effectiveness of student notetaking. It does not cover the techniques that the lecturer uses to develop an effective lecture. One of the most useful findings in the research on student notetaking was found by Collingwood and Hughes (1978) " Students achieved better when given some form of lecture notes rather that relying on their own notes."

Some other major highlights of the research on lecturing includes:
   a. "... the lecture is possibly reserved for those objectives at the lower end of Bloom's Taxonomy of cognitive objectives." (University of London, Teaching Methods Unit, 1978).
   b. "... students when listening to a discourse within their range of understanding and taking the customary notes, are rarely able to recall no more than 10% of the essential information of the lecture at the conclusion and only 50% of that or 20% a week later." (McLeish, 1968).
   c. "Available research consistently concludes that lectures are one of the least effective methods of conveying information ... though lectures sometimes produce better immediate recall than reading. Tests of recall several hours or days later indicate that a single lecture does not produce more learning of information that a single reading of the same material." (Lowman, 1985; Bowman, 1979).
   d. "Research on what can be remembered following classes indicates that most college students can absorb only three or four points in a 50-minute period and four to five in a 75-minute class, regardless of the subject being taught." (Lowman, 1985).

TYPES OF LECTURES

As instructors begin to develop professional teaching skills, they should be aware that there are a variety of different types of lecture formats. Brown (1974, 1978) describes the more common types.

Classical lecture–Also known as the expository lecture, is divided into broad
> sections, subsections, and sub-subsections. The main themes are clearly identified and readily comprehended. This is the most common form of the lecture and, if well-constructed, the easiest for students to take notes. As the thesis is developed by the instructor, the beginning and end of each section is identified through the use of cues and transition statements. The major pitfall of this category of lecture is that it could be nothing more than a boring litany of related and unrelated facts. The use of examples, applications, analogies and metaphors, and illustrations are needed to keep the lecture interesting and moving. Handouts will assist students with the connections between sections and with notetaking. Hoover (1980) refers to this as a formal lecture that is designed to provide a synthesis of information and solve problems for the learner through demonstration of problem-solving skills. There is minimal student interaction or opportunities for questioning.

Problem-centered lecture—This is most useful when you want to explore alternative points of view and their solutions as well as the relationships among them. When used, a brief and clear statement of the problem is needed. Each problem or point of view requires clear statements of available evidence for and against it and acceptable solutions. The most common errors contained in this form of lecture are unclear and excessively long statements of the problem, confused evidence for and against each side, impulsive cross-referencing among different problems, and the failure to summarize each alternative. Well designed handouts would help to minimize these problems.

Sequential lecture—A series of linked statements that lead to a conclusion characterizes this format. It is very important to highlight each main point in the sequence. This category of lecture is most commonly used in math-based subjects and is considered the most difficult to make meaningful and interesting.

Comparative lecture—Comparison of two or more types of processes, themes, works, theories, ideas, or systems best describes this type of lecture. This "compare and contrast" approach is intellectually demanding for both the instructor and especially the students when there is a heavy demand on short-term memory. It is easy to confuse the student with too much data and push them into "information overload." Handouts would help the student to follow the comparison.

Thesis lecture—This begins with an assertion or stated thesis and proceeds to justify it by bringing together a wide range of evidence and arguments that may be presented in major sections or in problem form.

Freehand lecture—These are spontaneous presentations given by experts in their field. They depend on the oral and verbal acuity of the instructor.

Formal oral essay—A highly polished and carefully constructed presentation, this type of lecture is usually READ with emphasis and conviction. The data presented supports a conclusion _already_ reached by the instructor. Although uncommon because of the time needed for development, it can be intellectually stimulating and motivational.

Provocative lecture—Intended to stimulate student thinking about a topic, it is designed to challenge and question basic assumptions held by the student.

Lecture demonstration—This combines the use of artifacts, props, equipment, and experiments to illustrate a topic during and following the lecture. It is imperative that students see unobtrusively all relevant details.

Lecture recitation—Developed to involve students by asking preplanned questions and soliciting responses, students are also asked to read prepared material aloud.

<u>Lecturette</u>—Students are actively involved in activities and exercises following a formal or informal 10 to 20-minute presentation.

LECTURE FORMAT

Regardless of the type of lecture, all lectures have four main components that answer different questions:

- REVIEW- "Do you remember?"
- PREVIEW- "This is where we are going today and how we are going to get there."
- PRESENTATION- "Here is my message to you."
- SUMMARY- "This is where we have been."

The *review* (Do you remember?) component encompasses any problems that the students had with previous homework assignments as well as points of confusion in the previous lecture. It presents students with an opportunity for clarification and answers to any pressing questions. It usually does not exceed three or four minutes.

The *preview* (This is where we are going today and how we are going to get there.) section provides a broad overview for the current lecture through the use of key questions to be addressed as well as the learning performance objectives that the students are expected to achieve. This overview shows the structure of the upcoming presentation and presents new vocabulary. This takes only one or two minutes.

The *presentation* (Here is my message to you.) section introduces all new concepts and ideas sequentially from simplest to most difficult. The instructor should "grab" the attention of the students when the lesson is begun (Now hear this!). Create some anticipation and make the students receptive through the use of personal anecdotes, or a good story as to why the lesson performance objectives are important. The use of some type of handout from a general outline to the use of an interactive study guide will assist the students to visualize the lecture structure and take notes more precisely and completely. The presentation should include a maximum of three or four points for a 50-minute lecture and five or six main points for a 75-minute lecture (Cooper, 1985).

This presentation section should be designed to involve students actively in their learning through the use of activities, exercises, and preplanned questions. Provide as much feedback as possible to as many students as possible when the opportunity presents itself.

The *summary* (This is where we have been.) section provides a review of the lecture questions or learning performance objectives. This section can provide a brief review of the next lecture topic and how the sequence of lectures are linked together.

LECTURE COMPONENTS

A well-constructed lecture can incorporate many of the following techniques singularly or in combination. Each of these lecture components will be explained and discussed throughout this text.

1. Set induction or ice breakers,
2. Examples (for instance) and non-examples (don't confuse this... with that...),
3. Analogies and metaphors–verbal and visual,

4. Preplanned questions involving higher order skills,
5. Well constructed, clear and unambiguous definitions,
6. Illustrations and word pictures,
7. Repetition of key points,
8. Transitions and cues to important ideas,
9. Handouts,
10. Imaging,
11. Stories and anecdotes to make and clarify points,
12. Humor,
13. Special figures of speech,
14. Expressiveness,
15. Visualization,
16. Limited key points,
17. Appropriate vocabulary,
18. Focused attention through fill-ins,
19. Relevant and meaningful content,
20. Varied pacing,
21. Student involvement,
22. Enthusiastic presentations,
23. Specific learning performance objectives,
24. Clear explanations,
25. Stimulus variation to hold attention,
26. Use of reinforcers.

PURPOSES OF THE LECTURE

A well developed lecture with many illustrations and examples can be a delightful experience for both instructor and student. Good lectures take preplanning and practice and are usually appreciated by the students.

Before constructing a lecture determine the exact purpose(s) that the lecture is intended to achieve. Does the instructor intend to:

summarize important points about ideas or techniques,
clarify confusing and complex material found in texts and other readings,
persuade students to a particular point of view,
stimulate students to the possibilities of new and innovative ideas and procedures,
provoke students to do something,
humanize through attitude and values exploration,
personalize through the use of personal anecdotes and experiences,
synthesize hard to find research results and trends,
evaluate a position by providing a specific set of external criteria,
compare and contrast different research results on the same topic,
critique a composition or new piece of art,
create a new product or technique or procedure and demonstrate it to students.

In summary, we have explored the four major components of every lecture as review, preview, present, and summarize. A variety of possible techniques that could be used in a lecture has been listed and a variety of different purposes for a lecture have been identified.

During the remainder of this chapter we will review many of the techniques that can be used to assist in the design of a quality lecture.

PACING

How fast a lecture is presented by an instructor can influence student note-taking and comprehension. According to Greene (1928) most students are capable of taking notes at only 20 words per minute, yet lecture presentation rates vary from 45 to 240 words per minute. Ladas (1980) put a ceiling of 135 words per minute speaking rate as too fast for most students to record notes accurately.

One technique available to the lecturer is to vary the pacing by changing sentence patterns to prevent boredom and to hold attention. Other techniques that can aid in varying the pace include:
- The use forceful and colorful topic sentences,
- Cues as to what is important through words, gesticulations, and intonation,
- Simplification of complicated and lengthy sentences,
- Use of different figures of speech,
- Use of a variety of examples and non-examples,
- Use of attention getters such as poems, newspaper articles, dramatic effect, video clips from current classic films, and visuals,
- Use of silence to force a response,
- Speaking rapidly when presenting familiar material and slowly when introducing new concepts.

THE USE OF SILENCE

The use of silence during a lecture can have a dramatic effect for a variety of reasons. Bailey (1984) has categorized seven types of situations in which the instructor can use silence effectively during a lecture:

1. <u>Pause-time silence</u> occurs any place during a lecture when the instructor is having a dialogue with a student. During the dialogue and after a statement has been made, the use of silence will allow the student to reflect on what has been said.
2. <u>Discipline or control silence</u> is designed to control the unacceptable behavior of a student by not responding. When you are attempting to get the attention of a class after there has been a lot of talking or laughing, stand before the group and ask for attention. Stand and look around the group without comment. When you have the class attention say "thank you" and proceed.
3. <u>Silent demonstrations</u> consist of teaching without verbalization when showing something is more important than verbal explanation.
4. <u>Transitional silence</u> is used when you want to move from one teaching concept to another. It signals the end of one point and the beginning of another.
5. <u>Humorous silence</u> is used to provoke laughter. This will take practice and the right timing. Watch master comedians. They use just the right amount of time—in seconds at times. Bob Hope is one of the masters of this technique.

6. <u>Confusion or disorganizational silence</u> results when students can't figure out what is going on. This usually results when the instructor has not planned properly. It can be very embarrassing.
7. <u>Wait-time silence</u> is the period of time that lapses after an instructor asks a question. The purpose is to let the student think about the question before answering. Wait at least three seconds or longer (Rowe, 1980). Smiling while waiting is an important reinforcer.

ATTENTION SPAN OF STUDENTS

How often have students attended a lecture in which the lecturer went on and on and on without ever pausing to ask a question or solicit a comment? This can be boring and irritating. Students have a maximum attention span of <u>20 minutes</u> during a lecture, after which time there is a marked decline in attention followed by a peak just after the lecture ends (Johnstone and Percival, 1976; Lloyd, 1968; Maddix and Hoole, 1975).

Gibbs and Jenkins (1989) note that "After about twenty minutes their (students') performance bottoms out and remains at a low level until the end when it briefly rises again. These low levels of attention and arousal are mirrored by markedly less notetaking by students during the middle sections of a lecture–dropping to as low as 5% efficiency according to Hartley and Cameron (1967)–and by much poorer subsequent recall of information after the first 20 minutes."

NUMBER OF POINTS TO BE COVERED

Presenting a student with too many points at once during a lecture is like the use of telephones during a disaster. Everyone tries to use them at once. The system cannot handle them and immediately goes into overload. It either shuts down or only lets a few calls trickle through. When an instructor tries to present 20 to 25 points during a lecture period of 50 minutes, the students go into a mental overload. They either learn nothing, or, at best, learn only a few points.

How much can a student remember from a lecture? Research has indicated that during a 50-minute lecture, the instructor should cover a maximum of three to four (3-4) points, regardless of the subject area taught. Students can absorb and comprehend four to five points in a 75-minute lecture (Eble, 1976; McKeachie, 1978; Cooper, 1985). Cooper (1985) is more conservative when speaking of teachers as public speakers. She states that "... only a few main points should be covered in a single lecture."

ENTHUSIASTIC LECTURERS

A dynamic lecture is like a dynamic speech. When asked what the most important parts of a speech were, Demosthenes would reply, action, action, action. By action he meant change, variety, and verbal and non-verbal activity. He also meant enthusiasm.

Enthusiasm is energy and energy attracts. Enthusiasm when lecturing results in believability. It means that we care about and value what we teach for ourselves as well as for our learners. This commitment is expressed in instruction with appropriate degrees of emotion, passion, animation, and energy (Wlodkowski, 1985). How many instructors and colleagues fit this description? These instructors are like magnets–students are drawn to them. They love and value teaching, and it shows. Enthusiasm and activity during a lecture can generate a great deal of interest in a subject (Rosenshine, 1971).

Collins (1976) has identified eight indicators of high instructor enthusiasm: namely:
1. Rapid, uplifting, and varied vocal delivery,
2. Dancing, wide-open eyes,
3. Frequent, demonstrative questions,
4. Varied, emotive facial expressions,
5. Selection of varied words,
6. Ready, animated acceptance of ideas and feelings,
7. Exuberant overall energy level,
8. Believability.

The research indicates that enthusiasm is related to increases in learner motivation and achievement (Rosenshine,1971; Cruickshank, 1980; Coats and Smidchens, 1966; Isaacson, McKeachie and Milholland, 1963; Weaver, 1982). Weaver and Cotrell explain (1987):

Enthusiasm is the most convincing orator. It is an infallible law of nature. The simplest person, fired with enthusiasm, is more persuasive than the most eloquent person without it. ... Lecturers need a certain amount of aggressiveness, boldness, and forcefulness. They can do this by:
1. Demonstrating an active commitment to the topic by showing what they have done, how they are involved, and what their plans are for future involvement.
2. Demonstrating an emotional commitment such as complete ego involvement. Instructors can let students know that they believe in what they are doing, that your information, knowledge, and idea can make a difference—by being a believer ... .

Weimer (1987) in her book, <u>Teaching Large Classes Well</u>, suggests that "It is passion that creates the intense, driving, transcending feeling that can raise lecturing to a special place of greatness." This "passion" can excite and motivate students to a high level of learning after they leave an electrifying class.

The passion displayed by an instructor is the result of their love and belief in their subject and their willingness to express it as they feel and live it. This is an acquired skill that requires training and feedback.

CLARITY OF PRESENTATION
Clear teaching is viewed as a state in which a teacher who is in command of the subject matter to be taught is able to do that which is required to successfully communicate with the students. Following the lecture, most learners are able to understand the material presented (Hines, Cruickshank and Kennedy, 1985; Lawson-Smith, 1978). Research reveals that instructional clarity is consistently and positively associated with learning (Gephart, Strother and Puckett, 1981; Gephart, 1981).

Clarity is directly related to the way that we present materials and the way it has a positive impact on students. When instructors present material clearly, they must approach and organize the subject matter as if it was unfamiliar to them. Emphasis and focus must be placed on key ideas, important assumptions, early observations, general principles, and critical insights in a subject (Loman, 1985).

Two criteria that Wlodkowski (1985) proposes as guidelines to help us establish and develop instructional clarity are:

1. Instruction is understood and followed by most of our students.
   a. The vocabulary and descriptions are familiar to the learners.
   b. All new concepts are explicitly defined.
   c. The instructor uses examples and analogies that are familiar to the student.
   d. The need-to-know and nice-to-know are distinguished clearly.
   e. The lecture organization is logical and orderly and the connections and relationships are obvious among of all parts.
2. The learners are provided with a way to comprehend what has been taught if it was not clear in the initial presentation.
   a. Students are provided an instructional clarity checklist to provide feedback to the instructor.
   b. Each lecture is videotaped for review after class.

USE OF DEFINITIONS

A definition is used to explain a word or phrase in order to let the student understand exactly what the instructor means by it. It is a statement that explains the relation that one class of things bears to the next larger class. There is a basic pattern to all definitions: X is a component of class Y which has certain distinguishing characteristics explained by Z. For example Lincoln (1982) states that we can give a definition by :

- comparison or analogy: " ... is like ..."
- synonym: a word or a phrase that means approximately the same thing as the word defined.
- function: what an object or person does
- analysis: naming the class of the person or thing it denotes and then giving one or more distinctive features. For example, a plover is a bird (class) that lives on the shore (feature).
- description: listing the attributes of the thing defined by partitioning it into its constituent parts.
- environment: describing the environment in which it is found.
- example: a "for instance" in which the idea is applied in every day experience.
- negative statement: telling what it is not.
- etymology: the study of the roots of words that identifies where it came from.

According to Trimmer and Summers (1984) definitions may be classified as three types: short, stipulative, and extended. The short definition explains a word by providing a brief identification of its meaning similar to that provided by a dictionary. This is usually a conventional use or the way ordinary, non-specialized people would use it.

The stipulative definition identifies the particular meaning of the author's use of a particular passage or word such as "love," "power," or "security." The stipulative

definition has been referred to as a sentence definition by Pickett and Laster (1975). A three-step method is proposed for writing this common type of definition.
- First, the term or species is stated. This is simply the word to be defined.
- Secondly, the class or genus is specified. This is the group or category of similar items in which the term can be placed, i.e., a chair is a "piece of furniture."
- Third, the distinguishing characteristics are described. These are the essential qualities that set the term apart from all other terms in the same class. The "chair" is a piece of furniture. It is made of natural bamboo and bound together with thin leather.

The sentence or stipulative definition covers only one meaning of a word and may actually be longer than just one sentence.

The extended definition can include both the short and stipulative varieties but goes beyond both. This could begin with a dictionary definition but modifies and illustrates it to provide the writer's view of the subject. An extended definition goes beyond just stating the essence, or primary characteristic, of a term. This is a definition in depth and detail and may contain such information as synonyms; origin of the term or item; data concerning its discovery and development; description of how it functions; explanation of its uses; instructions for operating or using it; examples and illustrations; comparisons and contrasts; different styles, sizes, methods, and data concerning its manufacture and sale.

The extended definition thus uses examples and non-examples and possibly a compare and contrast strategy to further define and clarify the term. Another procedure used when extending a definition is to describe the concept by dividing it into its parts (analysis) or demonstrating where it fits into a larger scheme (cause/effect). This type of definition is very prescriptive and often based on recommendations of a number of cited authorities (Pickett and Laster, 1975). These researchers have also provided us with a number of general principles for giving a definition:
1. Know when to define a term–student background and context of the term.
2. Know to what extent to define a term depending upon its complexity.
3. The sentence, stipulative or short definition consists of three parts–the term, the class, and the distinguishing characteristics.
4. An extended definition gives information beyond stating the origin and use of the term.
5. A crucial factor in giving a definition is understanding the essence of the term being defined.

Some other useful advice provided by Brusaw, Alred, and Oliv (1987), explains that definitions should normally be stated positively and should focus on what the term is rather than what it is not. They also suggest that we should avoid the phrases "is when" and "is where"–they fail to include the category. For example, "A contract is when two or more people agree to something," or, "A day-care center is where working parents can leave their preschool children during the day."

MAKING CONNECTIONS AMONG IDEAS

Good teachers build bridges to make connections between the students' prior knowledge and what they want students to learn in their current classes through sets of examples and non-examples, stories, demonstrations, analogies, and metaphors. Making linkages or connections among concepts and subtopics within and among lectures is a critical element in clarifying a lecture. We can make these connections formally and with good planning.

There are both <u>outward</u> connections and <u>inner</u> connections. Outward connections link previous lectures together and with future lectures. Individual lecture topics are also linked to the total course as described in the course syllabus. Since the instructors have options and strong positions about the subject matter presented, they should link their subject matter in terms of their personal and professional position and biases. Instructors should link their subject matter topics to the students by speaking at their level and connecting to their personal experiences using appropriate examples and illustrations. Instructors should make inner connections by making the structure of the lecture clear through the use of learning performance objectives or the big questions addressed during the lecture. Several other suggestions will help:

- Use cues or verbal markers to emphasize key points.
- Review and summarize each intermediate or supportive learning performance objective.
- Cross-reference with earlier points made in previous lectures.
- Use redundancy by repeating earlier points with newly introduced points.
- Re-use earlier examples.
- Draw it all together in your lecture summary.
- Use handouts and note the connections in writing.
- Use graphic organizers and word pictures to show visual connections.

EFFECTIVE EXPLANATIONS

Thyne (1963) has defined explaining simply as giving understanding to someone else. Gage (1971) elaborates by stating that explaining is the skill of "engendering comprehension" either orally, visually, verbally, or extemporaneously of some process, concept or generalization.

The ability to explain something with a high degree of clarity involves the abilities of the instructor and student. A good explanation makes clear and quick connections between the known and unknown. The instructor making an explanation must consider the knowledge and experiences of the student.

There are three types of explanations that address the questions of what, how, and why. Interpretative (what) explanations specify the central meaning of a term or statement or they clarify an issue, i.e., "What is a novel?" or, "What is death?" The second type of explanation is descriptive and answers the question "How?" This type describes processes, structures, and procedures, for example, "How do you make taffy?" or "How do you construct a lecture?" The last type of explanation is labeled reason-giving and addresses the question "Why?" This involves principles and generalizations, motives, obligations, values, and includes causes. For example, "Why am I studying effective lecturing," or "Why am I studying what constitutes a good explanation?" A good explanation could contain one or more of these types.

There are seven steps in preparing and designing effective explanations according to Brown (1978):

1. Decide exactly what you want to explain; why you want to explain it; and how to explain it. Determine what you think the student will find interesting about the topic and what they should know about the topic. Form simple questions.
2. Find the hidden variables in the explanation. Underline key words in all questions and describe the relationships among them. If the relationships are not obvious, or even hidden, point them out.
3. State the key points. Each section of a lecture should have a key point that the instructor wants to make. Elaborate each key point and use examples, illustrations, analogies, and metaphors. Begin with a definition, interpretation, or concrete example and build your explanation.
4. Design the keys. Write the problem to be addressed in question form and then write a question for each key point. One technique expresses the key principles as a simple pithy statement. Use minimal technical terms (define each if you use them) and avoid long complex sentences. Cue the student that you are about to make a key point: "Put simply ...," " Put briefly..." " The important point is...," " The next point is... ." After you provide a brief and unambiguous example or illustration, provide any major qualifications or elaborations. Identify any exceptions, snags, difficulties, or problems.
5. Summarize the key points made and come to a conclusion.
6. Design your lead-in or orientation. The instructor can use ice-breakers or grabbers such as a provocative question, a story or a humorous situation. This is designed to capture the interest of the student. For example:
   "Have you ever thought about what would happen if... ?
   "Let me tell you a story... ."
   "What do you think this object is ... ?"
7. Write out your design in narrative format and in outline form (Brown, 1978).

Good explanations use linking statements to show the relationships among statements, principles, events, and objects, and report either cause/effect or comparison and contrast (Rosenshine and Hiller, 1968). Gage (1972), in his reported research, has shown that the use of statements that link parts of explanations and use direct speech, metaphors, or analogies, contribute to the effectiveness of an explanation.

USE OF ANALOGY
Analogy is a relationship of similarity between two things, a likeness in some function, effect or circumstance. It provides an interpretative bridge between the familiar and the unfamiliar. Analogical thinking occurs when a person draws a conclusion about an unknown factor on the basis of its resemblance to a factor that is familiar or known (Good, 1981). Relationships in analogy problems include such things as association, purpose, cause and effect, part to whole, part to part, action to object, object to action, synonym, antonym, place, degree, characteristic, sequence, grammatical and numerical (King and Glynn, 1986).

Analogies stimulate thought and suggest solutions to a problem. If two things show similarity in some way, we then can compare them point by point and assume that if two or more things agree with each other in some ways, they will probably agree in others. This is demonstrated in the way the legal profession uses precedent, i.e., what was upheld as true in case A should be accepted as true in case B, which closely resembles case A.

An analogical approach to explaining something helps in classifying, categorizing, and fitting pieces and bits of knowledge into an overall scheme of things. It helps us to see the forest as well as the trees. A map is a graphic analogy that shows the locational relationship between two points on the map using the same relationship that exists between the two actual places they represent (Andrews, 1981).

There are three components to an analogy:

1. The **topic** is the material to be taught that is unfamiliar to the student such as a concept, theory, principle, procedure, or problem to be solved. For example, the eye is the topic in the eye/camera analogy and the atom is the topic in the atom/solar system analogy. The topic is that which is to be learned by the student.
2. The **analog** is the subject that is already familiar to the student that we call upon to facilitate the learning of a topic. There is usually only one analog per analogy. For example, the camera is the analog in the eye/camera analogy and the solar system is the analog in the atom/solar system analogy. A concept may function as a topic in one analogy and as an analog in another.
3. The **analogous attributes** are those similar attributes or descriptions shared by both the topic and the analog. These attributes could be physical, structural, or functional if they act in a similar way. There could also be consequential similarities if a similar or same underlying cause creates similar effects. In order for a statement to be considered an analogy, there must be at least one analogous attribute.

Analogies have a concretizing function in that they render undesirable attributes to the abstract topic (atom) and make it perceptible by comparing it with concrete, imaginable analogs (i.e., the solar system).

Analogies can be useful and interesting during a lecture especially if the information is difficult or abstract and not easily understood—outside the immediate learning experience of your students.

When developing an analogy use the term ... "is like... ," "is similar to... ," "may be compared to... ," or "shares similar functions as... ." Instructors must decide if they want to use a verbal or visual format or a verbal/visual format. The use of artifacts is especially useful and can be humorous at times. An analogy should be introduced early in the instructional sequence and repeated several times. It has been shown that the use of concrete analogies lead to improved student performance (Simons, 1984).

Hunt (1982) notes that "In a sense, all learning proceeds from analogy. ... Some cognitive scientists suggest that reasoning by analogy is the foundation of all general intelligence." He goes on to suggest that "Analogy is a powerful teaching tool with a long and respected heritage. ... There is probably no better way to make an abstract concept come alive and become accessible to students than to use a well-drawn analogy." Roundtree (1990) suggests that "Analogy can be a potent means of clarifying a new idea. That is, we can point out all the ways in which the new idea is similar to one that learners are already familiar with."

There are many ideas for the use of analogy. An instructor could have students clip newspaper articles, identify videoclip segments from existing commercial full length videos, or magazine articles to illustrate ideas and concepts and make connections with them. Another technique is to have students identify and summarize difficult passages from texts or other readings in their own words and then provide illustrations from their own personal experiences.

Some examples of analogies include:
1. Teaching is much like fishing, it depends on the type of lure that you use and the type of instructional strategy selected. Sometimes they bite and sometimes they don't. Change the lure and you increase the chance of catching the fish. Sometimes they learn and sometimes they don't. Change your instructional strategy and you will increase the probability of learning taking place.
2. A mind is like a parachute. It can only work when it is open.
3. A database will hold and organize information for you just as an office file does. Your information is stored in electronic files like the folders in your office file cabinet.
4. A body's ability to contain stress is much like a barrel that overflows when the water reaches the top. We all have rain barrels to contain our stress-related symptoms. When they reach the point of overflowing, we may have serious illness (Silberman, 1990).

EXPRESSIVE LECTURES

Expressiveness is defined by four constituents, namely, the physical movements associated with teaching behavior, voice inflection, eye contact, and the use of humor (Perry and Abrami and Leventhal, 1979). Perry explains that "When students are asked to describe an ideal teacher, or to specify characteristics important for good teaching, expressiveness is frequently mentioned directly or indirectly, by means of such terms as enthusiasm, rapport, charisma, and dynamic personality." Other terms associated with the concept of expressiveness include such things as friendliness, personality style, warmth, intelligence, pragmatic and dynamic characteristics.

The research has shown that expressiveness directly affects student achievement positively (McDonald, 1982).

EFFECTIVE LITERARY DEVICES TO IMPROVE YOUR DELIVERY

The lecturer can create dramatic effects in a lecture delivery through the use of different speech devices in order to reinforce, give force to what is said, and to spark the listeners' attention. This can be created through the use of dramatic devices in speech, parts of speech, and varied pacing.

Triad

One dramatic speech technique is the use of the *triad*–a grouping of words, phrases, clauses, or sentences into *threes*. Some examples of triads include:

"Never in the field of human conflict was so much owed by so many to so few."
                                    Winston Churchill

"... we cannot dedicate—we cannot consecrate—we cannot hallow—this ground."
                                    Abraham Lincoln

"For thine is the kingdom, the power, and the glory."
                                    Lord's Prayer

"Friends, Romans, countrymen; lend me your ears."
                                    William Shakespeare

"Hit hard, hit fast, hit often."
                                    Admiral William Halsey

"Teaching in a teleclasroom:
How do you look?
How do you sound?
How do you move?"
                                    The author

"When you teach in a teleclassroom: practice and practice and then practice some more."
                                    The author

Some of the other more important figures of speech that can add spice, capture attention, and aid retention include:

Acronym—is a mnemonic device to help students to recall the names or parts of something and the order that they have to be remembered. A good acronym helps to spell something that has a meaning. Once you have identified the steps or concepts to be remembered, see if they spell anything or can be given a meaning. An acronym is not an analogy. The latter helps us to explain the parts of something rather than just remember them.

Allegory—an extended analogy that uses the fable or analogy. It often begins with, "In the beginning... ," or "Once upon a time... ."

Alliteration—the deliberate use of the same letter or sound at the beginning of a word or sentence to jog the memory.

"Peter piper picked a peck... ."

"His pride was lashed, his ambitions were smashed, his hopes were dashed."

Hyperbole—emphasis is shown through exaggeration or overstatement.

"I warned you a thousand times not to do that."

"I have told you a million times ... ."

Oxymoron—is an intentionally contradictory or incongruous statement used for effect.

"That is about as clear as mud."

"Bob is effectively ineffective."

Personification—nonhuman objects are given human qualities.

"The machine chattered incessantly."

Litotes—a positive idea is obtained by substituting the opposite idea with a negative.

"She's no spring chicken."

"Not bad, huh?" (Pretty good, yes?)

USE OF ICEBREAKERS TO START A COURSE OR LECTURE

An icebreaker is a technique designed to get a class started on a new topic. It is meant to "warm up" a group of students; to promote a getting acquainted process in situations in which group learning will take place. The major objective is to put students or participants of a class or workshop at ease. The first class can influence the direction of the entire course.

Most icebreakers include some type of interaction between two or three students on a limited basis. The icebreaker will also assist in the building of team spirit. University Associates (1989) and Applied Skills Press (1983) describe a wide variety of structured experiences that can be used for effective icebreakers. Some of the icebreakers described by the latter group include:

Uncle Fred's Suitcase—This exercise challenges the students to remember the items they have packed into an imaginary suitcase. This icebreaker is effective any time during the course.

Duo Interviews—This exercise asks the students, working in pairs, to prepare and then present introductions of each other to the entire group. This is most effective at the beginning of a course.

Identification—Students share some important personal information that is revealed by what they carry in their purses, wallets, or billfolds.

Philosophy of teaching—The students are asked to write sentences about their philosophies of teaching and to respond nonverbally to other group members' statements of philosophy.

<u>Press release</u>–Students become acquainted as they work in pairs to create press releases for one another.

Brue (1985) classifies icebreakers according to the kind of information they provide and the way information is revealed. The "Personality Report" asks students to volunteer specific information about themselves. It allows students to voice concerns and fears about the course. The "Personality Clue" icebreaker indirectly elicits information about individuals in groups. By describing favorite childhood toys, students reveal certain aspects of their personalities as they talk briefly about their favorite toys and why they chose them as favorite. The "Attitude Report" asks students to describe their attitudes towards the topic at hand. The "Attitude Clue" icebreaker indirectly demonstrates group feelings toward a subject.
The same author recommends several cautions that should be observed in selecting a particular icebreaker.
- Don't get cute. The icebreaker must serve a specific purpose and directly relate to the learning goals. If not, don't use it.
- Never use icebreakers that could embarrass the students. The objective of this type of exercise is to create a climate of trust.
- Don't let the icebreaker drag on. Once the point is made and the objective achieved, move on to the next part of the lesson.

The use of icebreakers can be very useful in loosening up a new group. Choose them carefully and cautiously.

Some excellent sources of icebreakers are:
Forbes-Greene, S. (1983). <u>The encyclopedia of icebreakers.</u> San Diego, CA: University Press.
Newstrom, J., & Scannell, E.E. (1980). <u>Games trainers play</u>. NY: McGraw-Hill.
Pfeiffer, J.W., & Jones, J.E. (Eds.). (1983). <u>Structured experience kit.</u> San Diego, CA: University Associates.

GRABBERS AND STABBERS–BEGINNING YOUR CLASS
A good way to start a class either in lieu of an icebreaker or combined with an icebreaker is through the use of set induction or attention-getters to capture the attention of your students and make a point dramatically. These are called grabbers and stabbers. Stoneall (1991) suggests that "The mind grabber helps participants to make the transition from work, home, or whatever activity with which they were involved before the training session (or class) began." Grabbers and stabbers must directly relate to the topic and learning objectives. Some suggestions include such things as:
1. Newspaper article–"How many of you read the article on the front page of last evenings newspaper entitled... .?" (Hold up the headline). "If you didn't you will after this lecture." Summarize the article and raise questions or provide comments.
2. "Teaching on television is a lot like eating peanuts... ." This use of analogies both verbally and visually establishes a good opening.

3. "The learning objective of today's lecture is... . I can't express too strongly how important it is! What do you think the consequences would be if you did not master this skill? Let me hear from you."
4. "Up to this point we have studied x-y-z. Today's lesson will help you to pull it all together and allow you to see the forest as well as the individual trees. Let me show you how this happened in a little story that proved embarrassing, and now that I think of it, pretty funny."
5. Recite a poem related to the learning performance objectives.
6. Use an artifact. Walk into class with a fishing rod, lures (hookless), wading boots and a fishing hat. Cast the lure into the students several times and reel it in–use silence. After a moment ask the students what you are doing. Make your point, "Fishing is a lot like teaching. It depends on the kind and size of lures that you use. Different lures for different fish. Use different instructional strategies for different students."
7. Put a controversial statement, comment, or conclusion on the blackboard, read it, and ask for comments.
8. Begin your class with a short videoclip and ask why it is significant or what it means in terms of teaching.

CREATING GOOD EXAMPLES

Whenever a new idea, concept, principle, or procedure is introduced, it should be clearly defined and then followed with several relevant examples. An example is the use of current knowledge to explain and amplify unknown ideas. *Exemplum docet*–the example teaches. The example provides a mental model of what we are trying to explain. This may be the hardest part of teaching. Creating clear and relevant examples takes time and experience. Examples can be given as analogies or metaphors. They help the students to bridge the comprehension gap between memory and application when designing a learning sequence (memory–**comprehension**–application). Examples assist in the development of a strong comprehension base that allows the student to make generalizations. Single examples are usually inadequate. The instructor should use a minimum or two, and preferably more examples (Roundtree, 1990).

When we use an example we are saying "For instance ... ." Good lecturers also use non-examples for contrast. When we are using non-examples we are saying, "Don't confuse this with ... that." This technique will assist the student to clarify ideas by contrast (Roundtree, 1990). The use of adequate examples may be the biggest singular problem in teaching. Too often the instructor assumes student comprehension of basic concepts and expects the immediate ability to apply the concept to new and unfamiliar information.

Examples must be accurate and appropriate for the type of knowledge they represent. For example, if instructors are dealing with facts, they must state the proposition to be illustrated; for concepts, state the definition of the category; for principles, state the definition of the relationship among independent and dependent variables; for skills, state the steps of the process of the characteristics of the resultant product.

Elements of the examples should be analogous to the elements in the definition.

Examples are used to motivate, explain, practice, and test. Different types of examples include the "best example," which is an epitome of its type. Motivational examples emphasize the positive or negative consequences of knowing an idea. Expository examples complete, elaborate, and label instances that provide the substance for an explanation. Interrogatory examples are unlabeled illustrations that are used as a problem to be solved.

Examples must be crystal clear in their meaning. Yelon and Massa (1972) explain that students are more likely to understand and remember statements and images that make up an example if they are:

- **Concrete**–Words, images or actions that portray an example should vividly refer to something observable and relevant.
    1. Use words that refer to some sensory mode such as vision, taste, smell, sound, or feeling.
    2. Use incidents, stories, and cases.
- **Brief**–Eliminate all but essential elements–get to the point.
- **Include familiar vocabulary**.
- **Displayed so that familiar characteristics are apparent**–Key elements should stand out by highlighting, annotating, and pointing out salient characteristics.
- **Clearly show how the attributes (variables) relate to their corresponding parts.**
- **Attributes in the definition**–Show either verbally or visually how the parts of the example fit the point.
- **Presented in an appropriate medium.**–The example should be presented in the same medium or be as close as possible to the medium that a student will confront it in the real world.
- **Present a clear example of what is illustrated**–Make a precise transition from the example and back to the point.

Examples should be interesting and related to the experiences and aspirations of the students. They should have novel aspects and should be realistic and credible. Novelty means a twist of humor, a joke, a cartoon, or some funny experience. Credible and realistic means that the person giving the example should have some type of personal connection with it.

Examples should range from easy to difficult and should represent varied situations and circumstances to cover the range of experiences that could be encountered.

WRAPPING YOUR LECTURE POINTS IN A STORY

Good stories enhance lectures because they are entertaining and have a specific message. The art of storytelling will greatly enhance the instructor's ability to capture and hold the attention of the students. As soon as the instructor says, "Let me tell you a little story that happened to me ... ;" "Listen to me ...; "The truth is ... ;" " This really happened ... ;" " I'm telling you ... ;" " Let me tell you what happened to me that will reinforce why today's learning objectives are so important...," he or she has the immediate attention of the student audience. McConnell in his article entitled, "Confessions of a Textbook Writer," describes the impact of stories.

If you want to capture the imaginations of young people, you have to tell them stories! Forget the facts, and copy down the anecdote. ... Students remember and use facts only when these dull bits of data are placed within a memorable and interesting context.

Everyone loves a good story, particularly if it is personal to the storyteller. A story has to be built into the body of the lecture and should be told as if the instructor, a friend, or a family member were there. The instructor should tell it in his or her own language–personalize it–make it a personal experience, even if the storyline has to be stretched a little bit. Dale Carnegie (1962) reminds us that if you begin a talk with phrases that answer who, how, when, what, and why, you will be using one of the oldest communication devices in the world to get attention–the story.

Each story should be directly related to the learning performance objectives. They should be brief and interesting. Wrap the most important points in a story or short anecdote. Instructors can begin a lecture or summarize a lecture with a relevant story. An interesting technique is to tell half of the story at the beginning of a lecture and the second half as a summary.

Techniques of storytelling that will require practice include such things as timing (watch Bob Hope and the comics on TV); silence and pause–a fraction of a second will make a difference; pitch–loud and soft (even a whisper); body movement–gesticulation at the right moment; and personal belief and enthusiasm about what is said.

Stories are everywhere, but instructors must know each point that they want to make or reinforce. One technique that is very helpful is to identify the three or four major points that are to be made in each lecture. Write these down on a 5" x 8" file card. Write each point out as a narrative topic sentence(s). Begin immediately to look for stories and anecdotes to wrap the point in. The instructor should think of events in his or her life or in the lives of family members that could be used. The instructor should have a crisp and clear message to make. Know the point that the story will reinforce or illuminate. Think through the details of the story as a series of sequential scenes. Personalize the characters and give them names. If appropriate, describe some of their physical and/or personality characteristics–briefly. Write out the important points of the story in some detail, but not too much. Double or triple space so that more details can be added later. Practice telling the story before a mirror and to individual friends. Modify the details as feedback is received. Practice pacing and timing. After telling the story, ask the audience if they know the point that it was intended to make. If they missed the point of the story, tell them and then adjust the details as necessary.

Some of the sources of stories and humor include such areas as:
- Biographies of famous people
- Quotations
- Quips
- Comics
- Lyrics
- Limericks
- Parables rephrased
- Late night comedy shows

- Human interest stories in the daily newspaper
- Analogies
- *Time Magazine* and other magazines
- Mark Twain
- Will Rogers
- *Readers Digest*
- Bits and Pieces
- *Book of Quotations*
- Ethnic blessings
- Dinner speakers

As instructors become more aware of storytelling techniques, they will find an infinite variety of sources for good stories. Always carry a notebook to capture the moment.

A good technique for storytelling is to–plan it–try it–revise it–try it again–revise it again. Some of your stories will bomb. Don't panic. Try to figure out why and try it again. The more a story is used, the more polished the delivery will become.

LECTURE ORGANIZATIONAL PATTERNS

When faculty develop a lecture they follow organizational patterns similar to those they would use to write a textbook. Although a lecture could be built around only one pattern at a time, instructors frequently use multiple patterns within a lecture. Patterns include: descriptions, information transmission, definitions, cause/effect relationships, compare/contrast of ideas, sequential ordering, time sequence, procedures, problem solutions, symbols to depict ideas, organization, questioning, hierarchy of ideas, summary remarks, learning performance objectives to preview a presentation, verbal and visual analogies and metaphors, housekeeping activities, and references for outside class reading.

Each organizational pattern will be reviewed briefly and citations noted when appropriate.

1. **Descriptions** delineate the attributes and characteristics of a concept, key idea, principle, or rule by providing details. The clarifying list of attributes is not presented in any order of priority or importance.
2. **Information** consists of the basic facts and figures of a communication. They are presented in either random or systematic order. The relationships or connections among the pieces of information are indicated if relevant.
3. **Definition** includes the attributes of a concept, principle, rule, or procedure that indicate the possibilities and limitations of the term defined. Each definition that is introduced to the student for the first time should include several examples ("for instance... ") and non-examples ("don't confuse this... that... .").
4. **Cause/Effect** patterns present an event and its causes or antecedents. It links reasons with results. Interactivity between at least two ideas, events, or things in which one takes an action and another thing results from the action is also described. For example, we would reason that because it snowed heavily, the flowers would die from the excessive cold. If-then relationships are commonly used.

5. **Compare/Contrast** patterns point out the similarities and differences between two or more concepts, events, things, or ideas.
6. **Sequential ordering** depicts a progression of connected events in the order in which they occur or are related. This is not a time sequence, but leads to an outcome or product.
7. **Time sequence** –is a list of steps and the time allocated for each. The chronological order of two or more events, objects, or ideas is considered in the presence of the passage of time, frequently shown in tables similar to sequential ordering.
8. **Procedure** shows HOW to do something and the order of the steps to do it. This can be sequential or non-sequential. Included in this pattern are corrections to exercises and activities as well as complex lab procedures.
9. **Problem solution** presents the student with a real or contrived problem. The student, working alone or as part of a small group, identifies the facts as presented, identifies alternative courses of action, identifies constraints and probable consequences of each alternative, and makes a recommendation. The problem can be presented in the form of a written or visual scenario.
10. **Symbols** can be used in lieu of words and phrases and usually have a self-evident meaning to the user within a discipline. Symbols are used extensively in many disciplines such as mathematics, music, and chemistry as well as other disciplines. In addition to discipline-specific symbols, there are a number of symbols such as flags and stop signs that are universally understood within a given population.
11. **Organization patterns** show the intricate relationships among the parts of an academic or administrative entity. These relationships can be flat, sequential, or hierarchical.
12. **Questioning** patterns include all preplanned questions to be used within a presentation that are linked to a specific learning performance objective. On a higher level than simple recall of facts, they are usually prepared in a sequence from lowest to the highest level of learning.
13. **Hierarchy** shows the top-down or bottom-up relationship among concepts, ideas, rules, principles, and procedures. The effect can be cumulative. Hierarchies "... place lecture topics in sequences according to their importance, familiarity, or complexity in ascending and descending order.
14. **Summary** is used at the completion of a segment of a lecture related to a specific learning performance objective, as well as at the completion of the presentation. The summary reviews all major ideas and objectives covered in the teaching period.
15. **Learning objectives** describe in operational language exactly what is expected of the student at the completion of the lecture. The learning performance objectives are specified at the beginning of a lesson and serve as advance organizers of what is to come and possibly the order in which it will come. Learning performance objectives provide the overall structure on which the lecture presentation has been designed.
16. **Analogy and metaphor** shows the relationship between the known and the unfamiliar. The use of analogy is especially useful if the new ideas are

difficult and abstract—if they are outside the immediate learning experience of the student. Analogies use terms such as "is like." or "... "is similar to... ."
17. **Housekeeping** is an administrative activity that occurs within the lecture, usually at the beginning or end of the class. This includes such things as messages, procedural clarifications, introductions, and clarifying questions.
18. **References** are supplemental material beyond the real-time class. References can include such things as additional chapter readings in other texts, articles, and visitations.

Summary

The lecture can be a dynamic and exciting presentation technique if it is limited to 3-4 key points and is interspread with questions and student activities. A variety of different types of lecture formats were reviewed. Twenty-six lecture techniques were explained along with a description of 18 lecture organizational patterns.

The lecture, thoughtfully developed and properly presented, is still a powerful instructional strategy that will dominate higher education for at least 25 years because of its tradition and familiarity. Instructional technology will ultimately erode the presentation and cost effectiveness of the lecture as the use of lecture procedures are incorporated within the new technologies.

BIBLIOGRAPHY

Andrews, Alice C. (1982, September/October). The analogy theme in geography. Journal of Geography, 194-197.

Bligh, D.A. (1972). What's the use of the lecture? Harmondsworth, Middlesex, England: Penguin Books.

Bowman, J.S. (1979). Lecture-discussing format revisited. Improving College and University Teaching, 27, 25-27.

Brown, D.W. (1968). There's madness in our method. The ERIC Clearinghouse, 42, 341-344.

Brown, G.A., Bakhthrim, M., & Yongman, M.B. (1984). Toward a typology of lecturing styles. British Journal of Educational Psychology, 54, 93-100.

Brown, George. (1978). Lecturing and explaining. NY: Methuen.

Brue, Corrine. (1985, June). Breaking the ice. Training and Development Journal, 26-28.

Brusaw, Charles T., Alread, Gerald J., & Oliv, Walter E. (1987). Handbook of technical writing. NY: St. Martins Press.

Carnegie, Dale. (1979). Speak more effectively. NY: Dale Carnegie & Associates, Inc.

Coats, W.D., & Smidchens, V. (1966). Audience recall as a function of speaker dynamism. Journal of Educational Psychology, 57, 189-191.

Collingwood, Vaughn, & Hughes, David. (1978). Effects of three types of university lecture notes on student achievement. Journal of Educational Psychology, 155-180.

Collins, M.L. (1976). The effects of training for enthusiasm. The enthusiasm displayed by preservice elementary teachers. Published Doctoral Dissertation, Syracuse University.

Cooper, Pamela. (1985). Teachers as public speakers: Training teachers to lecture. Indianapolis, IN: Presentation at Central States Speech Association Convention. (ERIC Document Reproduction Service No. ED 258 302)

Cruickshank, D.R., et al. (1980). Teaching is tough. Englewood Cliffs, NJ: Prentice Hall.

Davis, James R. (1976). Teaching strategies for the college classroom. CO: Westview Press.

Davis, Robert J. (1965). Secrets of master teachers. Improving College and University Teaching, 13, 150-161.

Eble, Kenneth E. (1976). The craft of teaching: A guide to mastering the professor's art. San Francisco: Jossey-Bass.

Evans, Warren E., & Guymen, Ronald E. (1978). Clarity of explanation: A powerful indicator of teacher effectiveness. Paper presented at the Annual meeting of The American Educational Research Association.

Gagne, N.L. (1971). The microcriterion of effectiveness in explaining. In Westbury, Ian, Bellack, & Arona. Research into classroom processes. NY: Teachers College Press.

Gephart, W., Strother, D., & Ducketts, W. (Eds.). (1981). Instructional clarity. Practical Applications of Research, 3(3), 1-4.

Gibbs, Graham, & Jenkins, Alan. (1989). Break up your lectures or christaller sliced up. *Journal of Geography in Higher Education*, 8(1), 27-39.

Good, C.V. (Ed.). (1981). *Dictionary of education*. NY: Harper and Row.

Greene, E.B. (1928). Lecture as reading. *Genetic Psychology*, 4, 457-460.

Guide to effective teaching. (1978). NY: Change Magazine Press.

Hartley, J., & Cameren, D. (1967). Some observations on the efficiency of lecturing. *Educational Review*, 20, 30-37.

Hartley, J., & Marshall, S. (1974). On notes and notetaking. *University Quarterly*, 28, 225-235.

Hines, Constance V., Cruickshank, Donald R., & Kennedy, John J. (1985, Spring). Teacher clarity and its relationship to student achievement and satisfaction. *American Educational Research Journal*, 22(1), 87-99.

Hoover, Kenneth H. (1980). *College teaching today: A handbook for postsecondary instruction*. Boston: Allyn and Bacon, Inc.

Isaacson, R.L., McKeachie, W.J., & Milholland, J.E. (1963). Correlation of teacher personality variables and student ratings. *Journal of Educational Psychology*, 54, 110-117.

Johnstone, A.H., & Percival, F. (1976). Attention breaks in lectures. *Education in Chemistry*, 13(44), 49-50.

King, Debra Ann, & Glynn, Shawn M. (1986). *Teaching students to solve analogy problems: Increasing their skills in reasoning and making inference*. Atlanta, GA: Paper presented at the Annual Meeting of the Georgia Educational Research Association and Georgia School Test Coordinators. (ERIC Document Reproduction Service No. ED 284 194)

Kozma, Robert B., Bella, Lawrence W., & Williams, George W. (1978). *Instructional techniques in higher education*. NJ: Educational Technology Publications, Inc.

Ladas, H.S. (1980). Notetaking on lectures: An information processing approach. *Educational Psychologist*, 15, 43-53.

Lawson-Smith, Cecioly. (1978). *The lecture—a vital component of university life: A guide to assist faculty*. Montreal, CA: McGill University. (ERIC Document Reproduction Service No. ED 202 256)

Lincoln, John E. (1982). *Writing: A college handbook*. NY: W.W. Norton & Company.

Lloyd, D.H. (October, 1968). A concept of improvement of learning response in the taught lesson. *Visual Education*, 44, 23-25.

Maddox, H., & Hoole, E. (1975). Performance crement in the lecture. *Educational Research*, 28(44), 17-30.

McConnell, James V. (1978, February). Confessions of a textbook writer. *American Psychologist*, 159-169.

McKeachie, W.J. (1978). *Teaching tips: A guidebook for the beginning teacher,* (7th edition). Lexington, MA: Heath Publishing Company.

McLeish, J. (1976). The lecture method. In N.L. Gage (Ed.), *The psychology of teaching methods*. Chicago: University of Chicago Press.

Miller, M. (1978). Changing medical education in Western Europe. *Medical Education*, 12(2).

Milton, Ohmer, & Associates. *On college teaching*. CA: Jossey-Bass Publishers.

Perry, R.P., Abrami, P.C., & Leventhal, Barry. (1979). Educational seduction: The effect of instructor expressiveness and lecture content on student ratings of development. *Journal of Educational Psychology*, 71, 107-116.

Pickett, Nell Ann, & Laster, Ann A. (1975). Technical English: Writing, reading and speaking. San Francisco: Canfield Press.

Rich, John M. (1988, January). The structure of the lecture. Performance and Instruction, 31-34.

Rickert, Shirley R. (1989). You don't need ice if you're not skating: The effective use of icebreakers. Paper presented at the 1989 ISETA Conference, Ft. Collins, CO.

Rosenshine, B., & Furst, N. (1971). Research on teacher performance in criteria. In B.O. Smith (Ed.) Research in Teacher Education: A symposium. Englewood Cliffs, NJ: Prentice-Hall.

Rosenshine, B. (1971). Teaching behaviors and student achievement. London: National Foundation for Educational Research in England and Wales.

Rosenshine, B., & Hiller, D. (1968). Explorations of the teacher's effectiveness in explaining. Stanford, CA: Stanford University. (ERIC Document Reproduction Service No. ED 028 147)

Rowe, M.B. (1980). Wait-time rewards as instructional variables, their influence on language, logic and fate control. Journal of Research in Science Teaching, 17(5), 469-475.

Simms, P.R.J. (1976). Instructing with analogies. Journal of Educational Psychology, 16(3), 513-527.

Stoneall, Linda. (1991). How to write training materials. San Diego: Pfeiffer & Company.

Stuart, J., & Rutherford, R.J.D. (1978). Medical concentration during lectures. The Lancet, 514-516.

Sweeney, J.J., & Reigeluh, C.M. (1974, August). The lecture and instructional design: A contradiction in terms. Educational Technology, 7-10.

Thyne, J.M. (1963). The psychology of learning and techniques of teaching. London, England: University of London Press.

Trimmer, Joseph F., & Summers, Nancy I. (1984). Writing with a purpose. Boston: Houghton-Mifflin Co.

Weaver, R.L. (1982). Positive qualities of the large group lecturer. Focus on Learning, 8, 10-13.

Weaver, R.L., & Cotrell, H.W. (1986). Using interactive images in the lecture hall. Educational Horizons, 64, 180-185.

Wlodkowski, Raymond J. (1985). Enhancing adult motivation to learn. San Francisco: Jossey-Bass Publishers.

University Associates, Inc. (1989). Annual, developing human resources. San Diego, CA.

Yelon, Stephen, & Massa, Michael. (1990). Heuristics for creating examples. In Rose Ann Neff & Maryellen Weimer, Teaching college. Madison, WI: Magmd Publishing, Inc. 89-93.

Zeitoon, Hassan Hussein. (1983). Teaching scientific analogies: A proposed model. (ERIC Document Reproduction Service No. ED 230 423)

Chapter 15

Lecture Presentation Skills

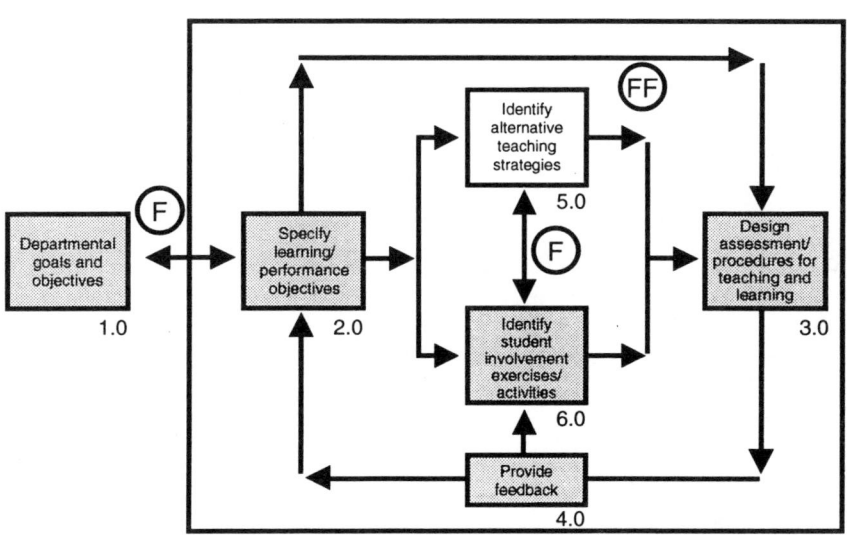

"Wrap your key points in a story."

LECTURE PRESENTATION SKILLS

LEARNING PERFORMANCE OBJECTIVE
Given a well-prepared lecture or lecturette, deliver it to a class using effective oral and non-verbal communication techniques such as personal qualities, delivery, and organization as outlined throughout this chapter and summarized on the "Lecture Assessment Criteria."

KEY IDEAS
1. The majority of instructors are very anxious and nervous speaking in front of their classes.
2. Presentation skills involves an integration of how you look, sound, and move.
3. A lecture laboratory can assist instructors develop effective presentation skills through immediate video feedback, self-assessment, re-tape, and re-critique.
4. By identifying positive attributes, and playing down negative attributes, instructors can gain a positive self-image.

NEW VOCABULARY
- oral communication
- lecture laboratory
- pace
- voice volume
- nervousness
- mind blowers
- gut wrenchers
- cotton mouths
- non-verbal communication
- body communication
- voice pitch
- articulation
- movers and shakers
- drippers
- garblers

Anxiety in public speaking
John Burroughs is an Assistant Professor of English in Arts and Sciences. This is his first year of teaching. He has two undergraduate classes of 25 and 50 students and a graduate seminar. Every time he goes to his larger classes to teach he gets butterflies in his stomach. His voice crackles, his knees shake, his mouth dries out, and he is a nervous wreck. He knows he lacks poise and self-confidence, yet he knows that he knows his class material well. He is petrified to stand before his class and speak to his students. He has complete stage fright. He is not alone.

   That part of teaching which causes the greatest anxiety for college instructors is public speaking, as exemplified in the lecture–especially to large groups of students. The successes of many college instructors depends on their ability to communicate orally in front of a class. This skill distinguishes teaching from research.

   Researchers generate new and important knowledge, which requires skills in the application of the scientific method. These same researchers when they teach require a different set of skills–the ability to communicate complex principles and concepts to students with a high degree of clarity so that they can understand and apply them in new and unencountered situations. This is the most essential skill that college instructors use. Yet they have little, if any, formal training in presentation skills. These are the skills that they will use most frequently in the classroom. It is assumed incorrectly that when instructors have mastered a subject area, they have the intuitive ability to communicate their knowledge to less informed students.

It is the purpose of this chapter to review basic verbal and non-verbal communication skills that are used in a traditional lecture and provide a series of exercises that will assist the instructor to develop them.

Presentation skills

Presentation skills involve an integration of how you look, sound, and move. This is accomplished by the use of feedback through self-assessment and peer review. On the following page is Exhibit 1, "Oral Presentation Skills: A Personal Inventory." Please read and complete this exercise before continuing. Having completed this exercise, the instructor will now have some perceptions of their own speaking ability. Look on the positive side. Everyone has some very positive aspects. The objective is to identify them and build on them. As weaknesses are identified they can be noted for improvement. This is best accomplished through video feedback in a lecture laboratory such as the one presented in Exhibit 2. A lecture laboratory consists of two video cameras, a TV monitor, a videotape recorder, and a switching device that allows the instructor to move easily between the camera focused on him or her, and a camera that will allow recording of anything under it. This ideal situation will allow instructors to videotape themselves for a one to three-minute period of time, and then to view themselves immediately on camera. Speak about anything that comes to mind. As instructors view themselves, they should note what they like and what they would like to improve upon. Very short segments of videotaping are preferable to longer segments since the same initial observations will be made. As instructors view themselves they should keep in mind that they can't change their physical appearance immediately. They will project what they see.

The personal critique

After the instructor has made several videotapes, a little more formal presentation should be prepared for practice. Some suggestions for a brief two- to three-minute presentation are listed below. Select an idea from the list, or choose one of your own, and outline some thoughts on paper. Videotape yourself. Always look at the camera and smile as much as possible. Play this videotape back and once again note your positive points. Select a second topic and repeat this process. Improvement will be noticed each time.

- A joke,
- A personal story,
- A war story,
- My most memorable teacher,
- A leader who has impressed me,
- The most influential person in my life,
- The thing that I value most,
- The funniest thing that ever happened to me,
- The best vacation I ever had,
- Thank you, America,
- My flag,

Exhibit 1
Oral Presentation Skills
A Personal Inventory

Have you ever known an instructor who...

_____ 1. Captured your attention and kept it throughout a lecture?
_____ 2. Was so enthusiastic about his/her topic that it turned you on?
_____ 3. Used body language effectly to make a point?
_____ 4. Appeared to be totally at ease when speaking?
_____ 5. Was so insecure when lecturing that it detracted from the lecture?
_____ 6. Never varied the presentation tone?
_____ 7. Mumbled so many words that you had a hard time understanding what was said?
_____ 8. Never moved from the lectern?
_____ 9. Used personal vignettes so effectively that it captured your imagination?
_____ 10. Used humor at the right moment to reinforce key points?

Exercise: When you completed the above Personal Inventory, you had someone in mind. On the left side of this sheet list what each person did or said to make you think of them. On the right hand side, use the same descriptors to rate yourself.

Descriptor   How would you rate yourself?

1. _____   1. _____
2. _____   2. _____
3. _____   3. _____
4. _____   4. _____
5. _____   5. _____
6. _____   6. _____
7. _____   7. _____
8. _____   8. _____
9. _____   9. _____
10. _____   10. _____

What would you like to change about your oral presentation skills?

Exhibit 2

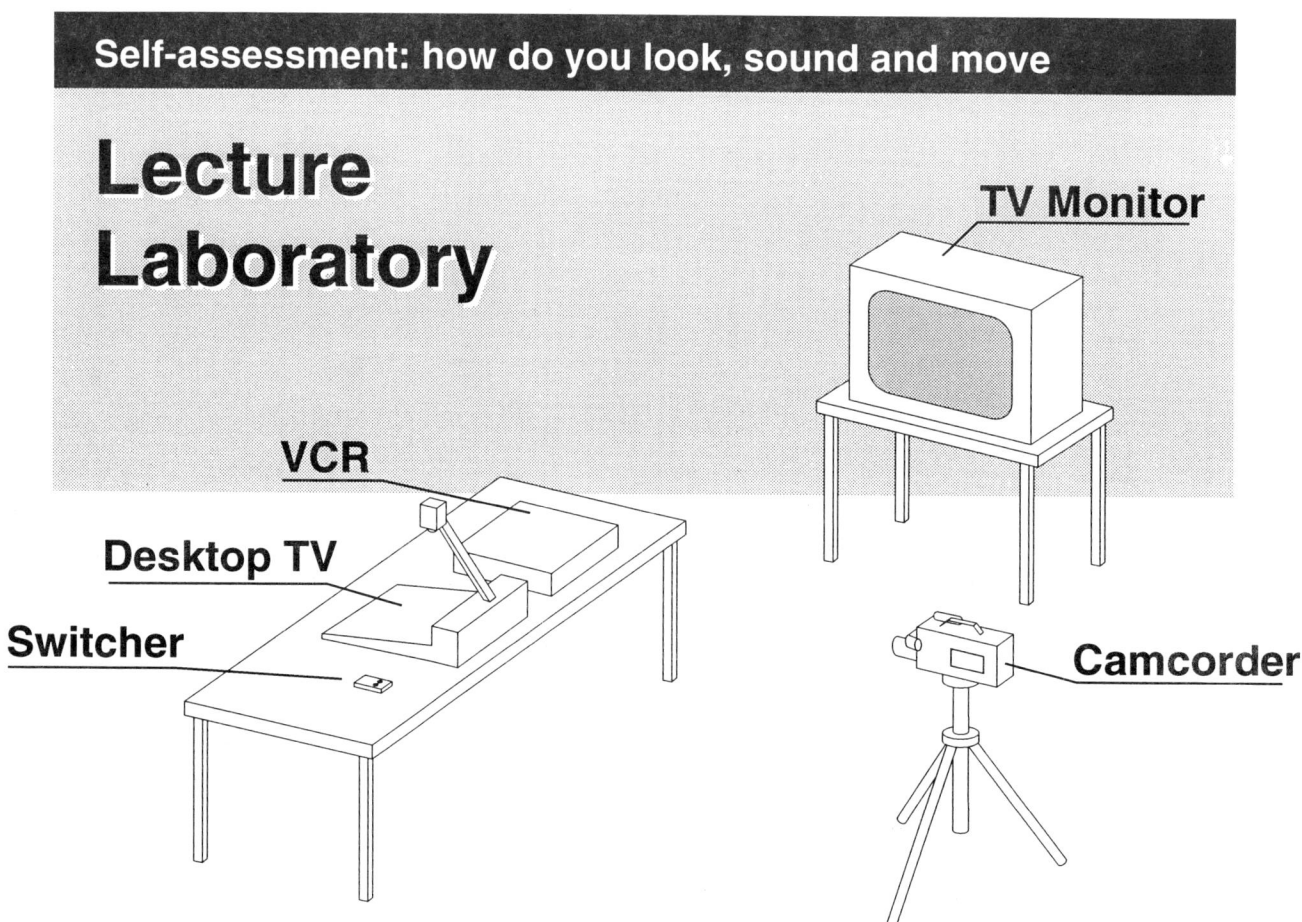

- How to make a ...,
- My favorite... is... .

After you have made and reviewed several videotapes, turn to Exhibit 3, "Winning Ways: The 30-Second Critique," on the following page. Read this exercise carefully and note the emphasis on your positive features. Look for your most interesting and positive qualities as you speak. Several copies of this page would be helpful since you should ask several colleagues and family members to view your presentation and then check off your positive qualities. A re-taping of the story would be helpful, using the data you have received.

Non-verbal communication
Turn to Exhibit 4, "Body Communication." Read the instructions carefully. Videotape as many of these gestures as possible. Non-verbal communication may be more important than oral communication to make certain points. Non-verbal communication can complement or contradict oral communication in a classroom.

Speech personality
All speech has a distinctive personality that is made up of a number of integrated components: pitch, volume, tempo and pacing, vitality and enthusiasm, voice quality and articulation (Hyde, 1979).

Pitch is the high and low frequency of a voice. It conveys meaning to normal conversation. Interest can be stimulated which helps students to pay attention. A lower pitch is preferred. A voice pitch can be lowered with practice.

Volume is the ability to project the voice. An instructor can maintain interest in a class and emphasize key points by varying the volume of the voice. Lowering the volume to a whisper at times also can emphasize important points. This can be used as a dramatic effect. The whispered points may have to be repeated for clarification.

Pacing is important when introducing new concepts. The instructor should use a slower pace when introducing newer concepts, and a faster pace when reviewing material already covered in previous classes. If well-coordinated handouts are used, a faster pace can be used. If handouts are not used and the students are required to copy a large amount of notes, a slower pace is recommended. Pacing should be varied to maintain student interest. Students, especially adults, cannot listen with attention for more than 15-20 minutes without varying the presentation pace.

Enthusiasm and vitality can direct attention, place proper emphasis, and excite students. If the instructor loves to teach and loves what they teach, the enthusiasm can brighten the classroom and motivate students.

Voice quality
Vocal cords vibrate to produce sounds, which are controlled by teeth, lips, tongue, and nasal passages. Hyde (1979) has suggested two nonsensical paragraphs that can be used to help evaluate the quality of the voice and how well an instructor articulates. Record these two passages on audio or videotape and then listen to them. Assess the quality of your articulation and ask some family members and colleagues to also assess it. These exercises have been typed in capital letters in 14-point print to assist you in the readings.

Exhibit 3

Winning Ways: The 30-Second Critique

Who are you? How do you feel about your image as an instructor?

We all exaggerate our inadequacies: too tall, too short, too fat, too thin, too dark, too light, too quiet, too loud; and underrate our strengths.

What do you *like* about yourself? You can't change what you have. Take advantage of your good points. *Everyone* has some. One way is to think positively about your best attributes. Do you know what they are? Think positively. Everyone has personal characteristics that make them special and distinguish them from everyone else. Forget those negatives because *everyone* else has them.

The secret of *self-esteem* is to know who you are and what those things are that make *you special*. The key is to identify your special features. Build on your plusses and forget your negatives. How do you want others to see you? One technique is to videotape yourself for short periods of time (two to three minutes), review your videotape alone and then with colleagues. The first technique is called "The Real You." Look for those things that you *like* in the videotape.

A number of volunteers will be asked to give a two-minute presentation on a topic. The instructor will play back a 30-second random sample and identify those positive personal attributes that you can build on in your TV teaching.

Features to look for:

    ___ 1. Eyes: sparkle, movement, dancing
    ___ 2. Dimples: location and prominence
    ___ 3. Fingers: shape, length, movement
    ___ 4. Hair: neat, disarray, long, short, color
    ___ 5. Nose
    ___ 6. Cheeks: defined
    ___ 7. Neck: long, slender, short, undefined
    ___ 8. Body language: natural movement, artificial
    ___ 9. Frown: relationship to eyes and eyebrows
    ___ 10. Upper teeth: partial or full
    ___ 11. Mustache
    ___ 12. Waist-up profile: left and right
    ___ 13. Laugh
    ___ 14. Whites of eyes show when open wide
    ___ 15. Eyebrows: movement, prominence
    ___ 16. Goatee
    ___ 17. Ears: movement, wiggle
    ___ 18. Forehead: frown
    ___ 19. Shoulders: movement
    ___ 20. Smile: mouth open or closed
    ___ 21. Lips: shape, prominence
    ___ 22. Voice: tone and inflection
    ___ 23. Hands: movement, rings
    ___ 24. Lower teeth show
    ___ 25. Beard: black, salt-and-pepper
    ___ 26. Finger nails: shape
    ___ 27. Chuckle: soft/loud
    ___ 28. Arms: movement
    ___ 29. Chin: shape, prominence
    ___ 30. Pacing: fast, slow, timing

The things that I like most about myself...

Once you have identified those features that you like, practice them in front of a camcorder or mirror. Then select several features that you would like to improve upon and practice those. Use a camcorder and ask several people to review your tape.

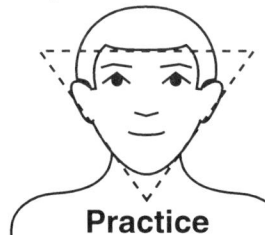
Practice

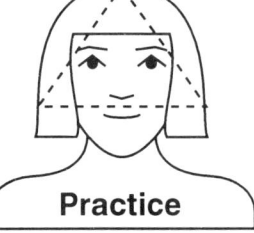
Practice

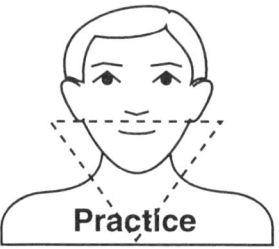
Practice

Visual triangles that combine features.

BODY COMMUNICATION

Non-verbal communication can be accomplished with almost any part of the body. When you are going to use body parts to communicate in a classroom, practice in front of a mirror to get the effect that you desire. Also consider the impact that certain movements or gestures could have on different cultures. On the left hand side of this form is a description of body movements. On the right hand side list what you think is the intended communication. Videotape yourself completing each gesture. Play the tape back after you complete two or three gestures. Combine several gestures and look at the different effects you can create.

DESCRIPTION	INTENDED COMMUNICATION
1. Winking one eye	
2. Closing both eyes	
3. Rapidly winking both eyes	
4. Opening both eyes widely	
5. Turning head from side to side	
6. Nodding head back and forth	
7. Jerking head to one side	
8. Shrugging shoulders	
9. Rapid circular motion of hand toward body	
10. Holding arm straight out with palm out	
11. Holding arm straight out with hand straight up	
12. Pointing index finger at source	
13. Gesturing with index finger toward body	
14. Puckering mouth	
15. Leaning whole body toward a person	
16. Walking toward a student	
17. Smiling	
18. Laughing	
19. Turning back toward a person	
20. Waving arms	
21. Staring at a student	
22. Silence for 10 seconds	
23. Pause	
24. Touching a shoulder	
25. Wink and smile	
26. Frown	
27. Hi, Mom!	

This list of non-verbal communications is by no means exhaustive. It is only a sampler. As you watch television, note the non-verbal communication devices practiced by seasoned actors and actresses.

THE BATTLE OF ATTERBURY

THE BIG BATTLE WAS ON! CANNONS THUNDERED AND MARCHING GUNS CHATTERED. THE TROOPS, WEARY AFTER MONTHS OF CONSTANT STRUGGLE, FOUND THEMSELVES REJUVENATED BY A VISION OF TRIUMPH. ATTERBURY, THE JUNCTION OF THREE MAIN ROADS, WAS ON THE HORIZON. USING WHATEVER ANNOYING TRICKS HE COULD, JACQUES DEATHRIDGE, THE FORMER MILLIONAIRE PLAYBOY, WAS MUCH IN CHARGE AS HE EYED THE OIL CAPITAL OF THE FEUDAL REPUBLIC. FEW MEN WOULD SAY THAT THE BEIGE BERETS HAD NOT CASHED IN ON JACQUES' FLASH OF GENIUS. THEN THE RATHER UNCOMMON ENGLISH FELLOW, A ZANY HALF-WIT TO MANY WHO NOW WOULD WRITHE IN AGONY, LOOKED PUZZLED FOR A MOMENT; THE MOB ON TOP OF MANHASSET HILL WAS FRANTICALLY THROWING HIM A SIGNAL. HE SNATCHED THE MESSAGE FROM THE COURIER. "MY GRACIOUS," HE MUTTERED. "ATTERBURY IS OUR OWN CAPITAL!" ELATED, NONETHELESS, HE INVITED HIS AWED BAND TO PLAY IN HIS HONOR. AFTER A SOLO ON THE DRUMS, JACQUES SPOKE TO THE MULTITUDE: "REJOICE,

MY FELLOW CITIZENS! ALL IS NOT BAD! AT LEAST OUR TROOPS HAVE WON ONE VICTORY!"

WILLIAM AND HIS FRIENDS

THIS IS THE STORY OF A LITTLE BOY NAMED WILLIAM. HE LIVED IN A SMALL TOWN CALLED MARSHVILLE. FRIENDS HE HAD GALORE, IF ONE MAY JUDGE BY THE VAST NUMBERS OF CHILDREN WHO VISITED HIS ABODE. EVERY DAY AFTER SCHOOL THROUGH THE PATHWAY LEADING TO HIS HOUSE, THE LITTLE BOYS AND GIRLS TRUDGED ALONG, SINGING AS THOUGH IN CHURCH. OUT INTO THE YARD THEY CAME, A VISION OF JUVENILE HAPPINESS. BUT, JOYOUS THOUGH THEY WERE, THEY SERVED ONLY TO WORK LITTLE WILLIAM UP INTO A LATHER. FOR, ALTHOUGH HE ASSUAGED HIS PAIN WITH COMIC BOOKS AND THE DRINKING OF MILK, WILLIAM ABHORRED THE DAILY ROUTINE. EVEN ZERO, HIS DOG, WAS AGHAST AT THE DAILY APPEARANCE OF THE RUNNING, SINGING, SHUFFLING, OPEN-MOUTHED FELLOWS AND GIRLS. BEAUTIFUL THOUGH THE SIGHT MAY HAVE BEEN, WILLIAM FELT THAT THEY USED THE AVENUE LEADING TO HIS ABODE AS AN AWESOME ITEM OF LUSH MALFEASANCE. THEIR OILY VOICES

ONLY ADDED FUEL TO THE FIRE, FOR WILLIAM HATED MUSIC.

"OOOO," HE WOULD SAY, " THEY MEW LIKE CATS, BAA LIKE SHEEP, AND MOO LIKE A COW. MY NERVES ARE RAW." THEN BACK INTO HIS MENAGE THE LITTLE GIGOLO WOULD SCAMPER, FAST ACTION EARNESTLY BEING HIS DESIRE.

NERVOUSNESS

All instructors experience some degree of nervousness when they teach, especially to larger classes. Powers (1992) suggests that we need to control and manage nervousness so as not to detract from the presentation and adversely affect the learning process. Nervousness is natural and will keep an instructor awake and alert as well as on his or her toes. Nervousness manifests itself in a number of different ways, the most common of which include such things as:

- **Movers and shakers.** These instructors can't sit still and can't stop physically shaking. They pace furiously. Pointers on an overhead projector or on a flip-chart should be avoided since the shaking will be magnified. These instructors should brace themselves against something in the classroom for support such as a chair, wall, or desk.

- **Mind blowers.** While teaching, these instructors forget their own names. They use extensive and obtrusive notes. When they forget where they are in the presentation, they should say, "I just blew my mind," pause, collect their thoughts, and continue.

- **Drippers.** These instructors sweat profusely and it runs off of their nose. They have a handkerchief in hand constantly, wiping forehead and sweaty palms.

- **Gut wrenchers.** These instructors are on the verge of getting sick in front of the class. Their stomachs are in knots and they need antacids and Pepto Bismal constantly while they are speaking.

- **Garblers.** Students often cannot understand what they are saying because they are speaking too fast and not enunciating their words.

- **Cotton mouths.** These teachers are easy to identify. Their mouths dry out and their tongues stick to the tops of their mouths. They constantly drink water or some other beverage and eat hard candy.

If an instructor experiences periods of or constant nervousness, they should seek assistance from colleagues, a speech department, a teaching assistance unit, or a media department that has videotaping equipment available and staff to help them with feedback. With assistance and training coupled with feedback, presentation skills can be improved dramatically.

To assist instructors with lecture presentations, Exhibit 5, "Lecture Assessment Criteria," has been provided. This can be used for the full lecture or lecturette. It includes sections on "Personal Qualities," "Delivery," and "Organization." This type of evaluation should be used at least twice during a class. Combined with the "One Minute Feedback," the instructor has available several powerful tools to help him or her to improve their presentation skills. Consider having classes videotaped for self-assessment purposes.

Exhibit 5

Lecture Assessment Criteria

4=Very Well done
3=Well Done
2=Fairly Well done
1=Needs Improvement

	4	3	2	1

1. <u>Personal Qualities</u>

   a. Appearance _____
   b. Poise _____
   c. Personality _____
   d. Enthusiasm _____

2. <u>Delivery</u>

   a. Posture _____
   b. Body Language/Movement _____
   c. Eye Contact _____
   d. Involves Students _____
   e. Humor _____
   f. Rapport with Students _____
   g. Pacing _____
   h. Enunciation _____
   i. Appropriate Vocabulary _____

3. <u>Organization</u>

   a. Previews Lecture in Introduction _____
   b. Use of Attention Getters _____
   c. Logical Development _____
   d. Focused Attention on Important Points _____
   e. Defines and Clarifies Terms _____
   f. Grammar _____
   g. Adequate Use of Examples _____
   h. Prepared Questions _____
   i. Use of Analogies/Metaphors _____
   j. Summarizes _____
   k. Timing _____
   l. Appropriate Handouts _____
   m. Uses Other Media _____

BIBLIOGRAPHY

Carnegie, Dale. (1979). <u>Speak more effectively</u>. NY: Dale Carnegie and Associates, Inc.

Hyde, Stuart W. (1979). <u>Television and radio announcing</u>. NY: Houghton-Mifflin Co.

Klopf, Donald E., & Cambra, Ronald E. (1983). <u>Speaking skills for prospective teachers</u>. Englewood, CO: Morton Publishing Co.

Powers, Bob. (1992). <u>Instructor excellence</u>. San Francisco: Jossey-Bass, Publishers, 87-90.

Chapter 16

Creating a Stimulating Classroom Environment

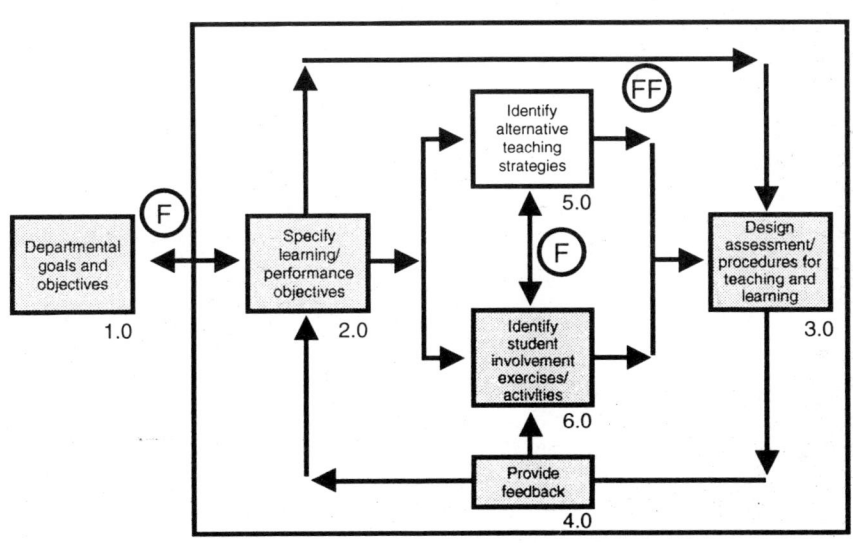

"The magic of teaching."

CREATING A CLASSROOM ENVIRONMENT THAT STIMULATES LEARNING

LEARNING PERFORMANCE OBJECTIVE
Explore a kitchen, workshop, or garage and select several artifacts that you could use to illustrate a teaching point either through example or visual analogy. (Level 3).

KEY IDEAS
1. A stimulating classroom environment will excite students.
2. An instructor can use transient (projected) stimuli and persistent (non-projective) stimuli to present key ideas.
3. Instructors can see by looking. There are many sources of ideas to use in teaching including: toy stores; supermarkets; hardware stores, etc.

NEW VOCABULARY
- persistent and transient stimulus
- build up
- dramatic incident
- hangup
- flip chart

Bill Stewart is a student at New Mexico State University. He is in his freshman year and hopes to major in history. During his second semester of world history he walked into class. He was stunned. Two tripods with cartoons from the Bolshevik revolution greeted him at the classroom door. A large picture of Lenin was hung in front of the room. Significant quotes were hung on the classroom walls along with three major American newspapers. On the blackboard the instructor had written three questions highlighted in colored chalk. Russian music from the days of the revolution was playing in the background. Street scenes were showing on the campus cable television and class had not yet begun! The instructor arrived wearing a uniform dating from the Russian revolution. He stood at attention in front of the class, opened a parchment, and read the public edicts of the day. He stunned the class by reading the names of six class members that were to be executed without trial for counter-revolutionary activities immediately. Bill said he would never forget that class. He could recall most of the points that the instructor made to answer those three question written in colored chalk on the blackboard–ten years later.

    Did you, as a college student, ever walk into a classroom where the physical environment grabbed your attention; stimulated your imagination with ideas hung on the walls, cartoons, quotes, poster boards, music? If you were so lucky, your immediate response was probably, "WOW!" Why would you respond in such a way? The environment got you in the mood for some heavy learning. It caught your attention and got your mind working right away. Ideas were planted and your attention was focused. You probably got the feeling that this instructor had really planned the lesson and had spent a lot of time thinking about what was to be taught and might have even gotten excited about the material. Even better, the instructor had transferred this excitement to you. You were responding even before the class began. If you have had this experience, you were one of the lucky students. It rarely happens in a college classroom, but it can with a little thought and preparation.

There are two techniques for maintaining student attention during a typical class period: involve them in a variety of activities that stimulate their interest, and make presentations (lecturettes) electrifying by varying the types of instructional materials used. Most faculty lectures are presented without instructional materials or at best with overuse of the overhead projector, chalkboard, or 35mm slides. Presentation techniques are too often boring.

There are many quick and inexpensive techniques that can keep your presentation "moving." You can use a variety of the techniques that Bill's instructor used to get your students in the mood for the class and to stimulate them the class begins.

Every class period (50 to 75 minutes) is based on key points that the instructor wants to make–three or four for a 50-minute lecture; five or six for a 75-minute lecture. Some points are more complex than others and will require more time, practice, and preparation. Sometimes important ideas need to be kept in front of the student throughout the class period.

One technique is to break a class period into short time slots to cover each point. After it is determined if in-class student activities will be used, the instructor will have time to prepare brief, 10- to 20-minute lecturettes to either introduce, clarify, or summarize the key points made. It may be that the instructor wants to use a lecture format for the entire period. If it is decided to use the latter, keep in mind that the maximum attention span without a change of pace is 15 to 20 minutes.

When the instructor presents in either a lecturette (10 to 20 minutes) or full lecture pattern (50 minutes of uninterrupted presentation), there are two kinds of stimulus materials that can be used. Transient stimuli are presented and then immediately removed. These are represented by 35mm slides, overhead transparencies, blackboard, films, or videotape. Persistent stimuli are ever present in front of the student. These include textbook pictures and graphics, material left on the blackboard, posters, newsprint hang-ups, tripod posters, etc. Varying a presentation with both transient and persistent stimulus materials will hold the interest of students for longer periods of time.

Determine the most important key points that are to be kept in front of students during the entire class period. Analyze the material for ideas that need to be built up on the blackboard or flipchart and then left up during the whole period.

EXAMPLES OF PERSISTENT STIMULUS VARIATION TECHNIQUES

1. **Two Overhead Projectors.** One overhead projector is used for the regular presentation-transient stimulus. The second overhead is used to keep key ideas and phrases in front of the students for longer periods of time–persistent stimulus. The transparency is left on for a long period of time and changed only when a new key point is made.
2. **Newsprint Hangups**. Print word pictures with key points and single words or phrases by hand. Multi-colored pens can show emphasis. If there is more than one newsprint sheet, number each one for reference. The individual newsprint sheets are taped to a wall or blackboard. These can be laminated for longer wear. You can write over the lamination with temporary, water-soluble pens.
3. **Posterboard Hang-ups (30' x 40').** For more permanent displays involving diagrams, graphics, graphs, etc., poster board is preferred. The use of multi-

colored pens can provide emphasis. In lieu of hand printing, you can use a variety of lettering techniques (including your computer). The poster board can be laminated for long-lasting use. Once laminated, you can write on them with non-permanent colored pens.

4. **Vellum Hang-ups.**. Vellum paper is more expensive and permanent than newsprint. The vellum can be plotted on an engineering drafting machine. In addition to words and phrases in large print, the computer can be used to generate complex diagrams and graphs. Laminating can preserve the vellum indefinitely. Non-permanent colored pens can be used to write on these hang-ups.

5. **Computer Graphics.** These can be used for large type on a limited size paper–up to 11" x 17", depending on the printer used. Although smaller than the newsprint and poster board, they are quick and inexpensive to prepare. Care must be taken not to make these smaller hang-ups too busy. They can be laminated and mounted on either cardboard or foamcore for extended use.

6. **Tripod Displays.** Inexpensive tripods are available in either wood or metal. Several tripods can be used to display poster boards, large black-and-white or color mounted pictures or photographs, signs, or graphs which contain key points.

7. **Flipchart.** For readability, these are best used in groups of less than 30 students. Flipcharts can be used alone or in pairs in lieu of the blackboard or overhead projector and in most instances can be just as effective. They can be predesigned or generated as the instructor teaches. If the instructor wants to use them as persistent stimulus, individual pages can be torn off and taped to the wall.

8. **Puppets.** The use of hand-held puppets allows the instructor to speak through a third party for contrast, humor, analogy, or metaphor. They are relatively inexpensive and quite durable if properly cared for. This instructor uses a hand-held parrot. As the parrot is manipulated, the question is asked individually of a number of students, "Does the parrot represent teaching?" Is teaching like parroting? Do we want the students to give back to us the exact words that we utter? What does the research tell us about the kinds of questions asked in the traditional college classroom? What does the research tell us about the kinds of intellectual skills required of our students in our tests? Isn't that parroting?

   How could elephants or donkeys be used? How could an instructor use a puppet on each hand to role play an important principle, idea, or concept?

9. **Artifacts.** There is a wide range of artifacts that can be used creatively in teaching to make a dramatic and meaningful point. The only limitation is the instructor's daring and imagination and a slight willingness to take some intellectual risks. The creative use of verbal and visual analogy and metaphor provide exciting opportunities. Several examples of possible analogies might include: the structure of a subject is like an umbrella; teaching is just like fishing; using performance objectives is like target shooting; and constructing a good teaching/learning sequence is like playing with children's building blocks. Think visually. Pick up an object in a kitchen and ask how it might relate to a subject area. Visit a toy store and look at the different toys. How could they relate intellectually to a discipline?

Donald Roush, Executive Vice President Emeritus, uses an umbrella to demonstrate the structure of a discipline by comparing each rib to each component of the discipline of teaching and showing that a single rib does not make an umbrella. It is all of the ribs and all of the components of a discipline working as a unified whole that distinguishes an umbrella as an umbrella and a discipline as a discipline.

Toy dart guns and cardboard targets can be used to make a point about the use of learning performance objectives. The target is turned around so that the blank side is showing. A student is handed the rubber dart gun and asked to hit the bull's-eye. When the student states that there is no bull's-eye to hit, the instructor draws the parallel to learning performance objectives by stating that if you don't know where the bull's-eye (or learning performance objective) is, how can you be expected to hit it or even know if you have come close. The target is then turned around and the student tries to hit the bull's-eye with the toy target gun. If students know what to hit–if they know what the learning performance objective is–they might stand a chance of success or at least know how much off-target they were. The analogy is, "Writing performance objectives in terms of learning outcomes is just like going target shooting."

Constructing a teaching/learning sequence is just like playing with building blocks. A student is given a series of 2" x 2" x 2" blocks each marked with a K for knowledge, C for understanding, A for application, or a CT for critical thinking. The blocks are stacked from lowest to highest: 6 Ks, 5 Cs, 4 As, and 3 CTs to form a pyramid. During the fun of stacking, the instructor explains each of the levels in this modified taxonomy. A student is then asked to remove one of the C blocks. When removed the whole pyramid falls apart drawing a lot of laughs. The analogy? When instructors constructs a teaching/learning sequence they must include all of the building blocks. If any part is left out the entire structure will fall apart.

10. **Build-ups.** Using any kind of heavy cardboard or poster board cut in uniform sizes (3" x 9" x 12"). instructors can hand print or print from your computer and mount to the poster board, key ideas in a sequence, word pictures, or conceptual outlines. Place a 1- to 2-inch strip of velcro on the back of each card. Cut 1- to 2-inch pieces of velcro and stick on a wall, blackboard, newsprint, or poster board. Stick each idea on the piece of velcro as the sequence, list, or model is built up. Magnetic boards can also be used if available. The use of flannel boards, although a bit more expensive and difficult to make, can also be used with this procedure. Different colored paper can make your presentation more attractive.

An instructor can build an idea on a blackboard and draw the linkage lines with white or colored chalk. By moving the cards around the instructor can show new and different relationships among the ideas. To be effective this must be planned in advance and practiced.

11. **Laminated Cards.** A number of students are handed 5" x 8" laminated cards, each with an idea, concept, or question printed on it. They are asked what the concept or idea has to do with the topic under discussion. If the student is unable to respond or comment he/she is asked to hand the card to anyone else

in the room for a response. When the question is answered, the student sticks it to the blackboard or flipchart or simply hands it back to the instructor.
12. **Grab Bags.** Small bags are filled with artifacts of some type. The students are given a concept and asked how the artifact in the grab bag could be used to teach the concept.
13. **Potpouri.** Some other possibilities that you might consider are tools, games, costumes, lapel buttons with silly or serious statements, signs, posters, candy, popcorn.

Individually and in combination, these ideas can enliven and inject energy into your class and in some instances will be talked about for some time.

TRANSIENT STIMULUS IDEAS
1. **Videoclips.** An excellent technique to reinforce points in a class is the use of short videoclips taken from TV shows or videotapes. For example, this instructor uses short videoclips as follows:
   a. Grading procedures: 90 seconds from the movie, "Flatliners," in which the lab instructor states unequivocally that there will be four As, three Bs, three Cs, and two Fs given. The students were in competition with each other.
   b. Teaching styles: Short clips from the movies, "Paper Chase," "Good Bye, Mr. Chips," "Dead Poets Society," and "The Eiger Sanction."
   c. Presentation Skills: Several sections from the videotapes, "The Speaker Has No Clothes," and "Be Prepared to Speak."
   d. First day in class: Two-minute videoclips from "Dead Poets Society" and "Paper Chase."
   e. Asking questions: Short videoclip from "Paper Chase."
2. **Dramatic Incident.** A journalism professor began his class. A woman ran into the classroom, threw a set of keys at the instructor, and screamed that she was divorcing him. She exited in anger. The instructor turned to the class with a shocked look on his face, sat down, put his head in his lap, and sat immobile at his desk for several minutes. The class was horrified and embarrassed. The instructor finally rose slowly from his desk looked at the class and said, "Well, what do you think?" He stood and said nothing for a seemingly long time. He then told the class that the incident was fabricated and asked them to write a newspaper story about what they had just observed. He went on to make the point that they should be observant about everything that happened around them and that it was their responsibility to be observant at all times.
Once you isolate exactly what you are looking for it will be easier to locate. As the great Yogi Bera used to say, "It's amazin' what you can see by lookin'."
3. **Card Tricks.** "Tell me when to stop at any place in the deck of cards and I will tell you with 100% accuracy what the card is." This is repeated three or four times amid the comments, "How was that done?" This is simple and effective and fun to do. The analogy? I can predict with a high degree of accuracy the intellectual level of your classroom questions and test items. Why is this so? What does the research tell us about the intellectual level of classroom questions and test items?

4. **Contrasting 35mm slides**. The use of two slide projectors and two side-by-side screens allows the instructor to compare and contrast visual images to make a point. This is a powerful technique that requires considerable planning and coordination.
5. **Flowers**. An artificial bouquet or a real flower is handed to a student with a note attached. The student opens the note to find a question, directions to do something, or a comment that he/she is asked to make.
6. **Balloons**. Balloons are stuffed with a tightly folded question, concept, idea, or directions to do something. The student must break the balloon to retrieve the note. This is a good attention getter and can lighten things up quickly.
7. **Envelopes**. A sealed envelope with the name of the student is prepared with a note containing a question, comment, or directions to do something such as print on a flipchart or blackboard. A larger manila envelope could contain a 3" x 9" velcro card that the student would have to add to a model or list.

Chapter 17
Classroom Questioning Strategies Above Recall

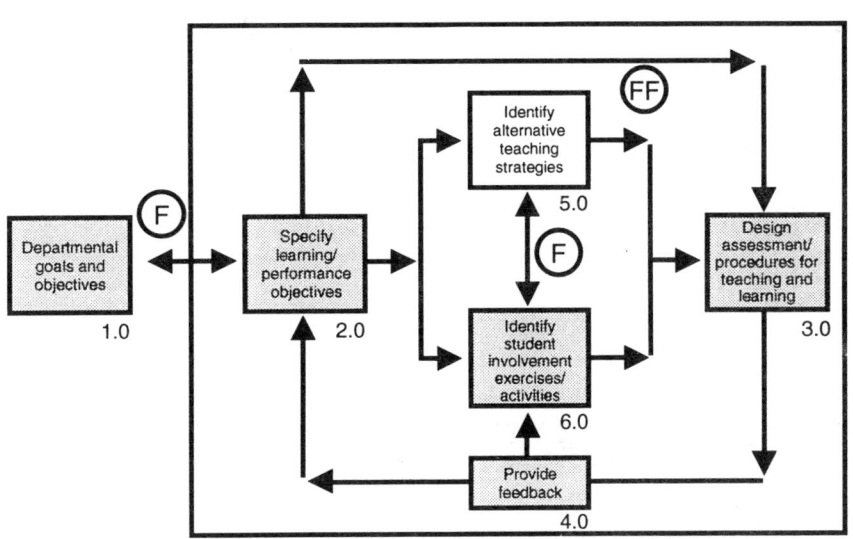

General Questioning Strategies

LEARNING PERFORMANCE OBJECTIVE
Select several learning performance objectives at the application or critical thinking levels and construct several examples of classroom questions at the same level. Show these examples to several colleagues and see if they agree with the intended questioning level.

KEY IDEAS
1. Classroom questions, well thought out in advance of class, will require students to use ideas rather than just remember them.
2. The cognitive level of questions should be derived from the learning performance objectives.
3. The use of probing questions will assist students to develop critical thinking skills.
4. College classroom questions deal primarily with recall and comprehension rather than application and critical thinking.

NEW VOCABULARY
- hierarchical
- rhetorical questions
- study questions
- procedural questions
- probing questions
- compliance questions
- trivial questions
- provocative questions
- linking questions
- clarifying questions

WHAT IS A QUESTION?
A question is the presentation of an intellectual exercise that calls for a student response covertly or overtly either orally or in writing. Brown (1975) describes a question as any statement that tests or creates knowledge in the learner.

USES OF QUESTIONS
Relevant classroom questions serve several important functions. They assist students to organize their thoughts and sequence their learning. Questions guide learning by emphasizing what is important and relevant. Discussion is stimulated around important points. Cues are provided as to how the student will be tested. If all of the questions emphasize recall of factual data, students will use this as a cue to study for a recall test. On the other hand, if many questions require students to use higher order intellectual processes, this will cue them to use study methods above recall. Factual questions emphasize a single correct answer. Other questions have many correct answers and require the student to make a preference. Some questions can have competing correct answers and require students to make a reasonable judgment that involves values and attitudes as well as logic. Questions such as choice of abortion; support for capital punishmant; and military support for Czechoslovakia fall into this category. Questions provide students the opportunity to integrate and synthesize their prior learning experiences with their current learning opportunities. Appropriately phrased questions can provide an opportunity for students to explain and express their

values and attitudes. When appropriate, questions can be used as a control device for troublesome students.

Stodolsky (1981) has identified five instructional purposes of questions in recitation lessons:
1. Review,
2. Introduce new material,
3. Check answers to homework,
4. Check answers to practice problems,
5. Check understanding of materials and ideas.

GOOD CLASSROOM QUESTIONS

Questions that are well thought out in advance of the class will require students to use ideas rather than just remember them. Classroom questions deal with two distinct aspects of learning: different levels of thinking and the complexity of the subject matter that the thinking process must deal with. For example, each of the following questions requires a different level of thinking, progressing from remembering and understanding through application.
1. Recall or remembering: "What are the key parts of a multiple-choice and a true-false question?"
2. Understanding: "Compare and contrast the advantages of a multiple-choice question over a true-false question."
3. Application: "Does the following multiple-choice item meet the criteria of an acceptable test item?"

Good questions are characterized by a number of qualities. They are prepared and thought out in advance, yet appear to be spontaneous. The intellectual intent of the question is known in advance of asking it. The question is concisely worded and easily understood. The student must think about the response to the question before answering it. These questions must be related directly to the learning performance objectives. More than a few quick words are required to answer the question. An open, rather than a closed response, is required of these questions. They use when, where, who, and how words.

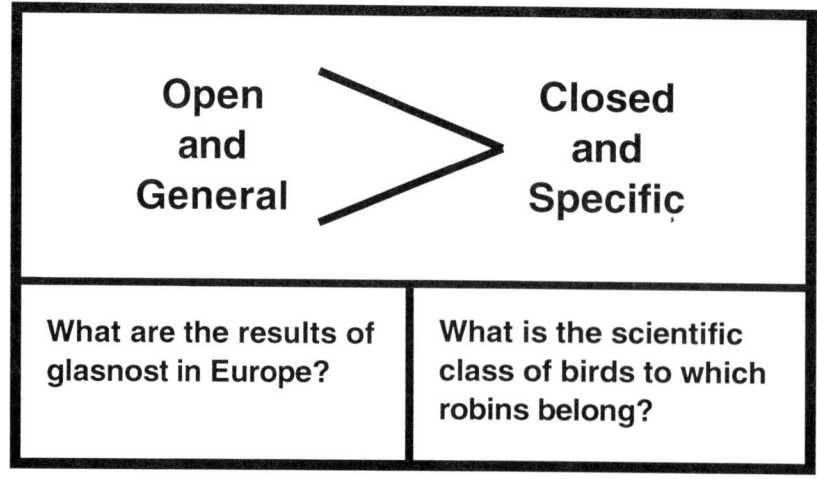

DESCRIPTIONS OF QUESTIONING TECHNIQUES
At the expense of providing "labels" for different kinds of questioning techniques, these descriptions provide for a broad categorization and in some cases may overlap:

Compliance Questions
Someone in authority asks a student to comply with rules or regulations previously established and agreed upon. For example:
"Will you please stop talking?"
"Will you please stop smoking?"

Rhetorical Questions
These are questions for which no answer is expected. The question is asked for effect only. For example:
"Is the Pope Catholic?"
"Do birds fly?"
"Do fish swim?"

Trivia Questions
These are designed to elicit bits of related and unrelated information relevant to the class learning performance objectives. These are similar to the questions found in the game of "Trivial Pursuit."

Study Questions
Study questions are used to accompany homework assignments and special projects or to focus attention on significant events while watching films, or videotapes. These questions are designed to assist the student to discover relationships among ideas.

Provocative Questions
Provocative questions are frequently phrased in overstatement or understatement or express an extreme value or attitude and are designed to capture the student's attention and possibly elicit an immediate emotional response. A provocative question must be related to a learning performance objective.

Procedural Questions
Procedural questions ask if certain procedures have been followed. For example,
"Have you finished the book yet?"
"Do the blueprints comply with local regulations?"

Linking Questions
This strategy can be employed when the instructor is trying to gather facts from a student. The response from one question provides the stimulus to the next question. The instructor continually branches until he or she feels that the pool of data from the student has been exhausted. The instructor is unsure of any conclusions or cause and effect relationships. This is for the purpose of general data gathering. There are no hypothesis proposed, although they could lead to the formulation of a hypothesis.

Probing Questions

These are intermediate questions that require a student to expand on and develop a minimally adequate response by making it clearer, more accurate, more specific, or more original. The instructor leads the student to the original question by capitalizing on existing knowledge and understanding. This type of question is used when the instructor believes in the possibility of the student reaching a conclusion and continually probes backward asking the key question, "Why?" At each step the student is asked to substantiate statements with factual information and support rationale. The use of "why" forces the student to go beyond shallow surface responses and think above the recall and comprehension levels.

Probing questions use prompting and clarifying techniques. When prompting is used, the instructor asks a series of recall questions to substantiate what the student already knows about the original question because it is reasoned that the student has the ability or already knows the answer. The use of prompts guides the student through the critical thinking process. The instructor must take care not to interpret or rephrase the student's response.

Probing questions usually require intellectual skills at the application (rule using) or critical thinking (rule selection) level and are used to assist the student to integrate and focus prior experiences and learning on the questions presented. The following suggestions for asking probing questions are "templates" around which instructors can build their own approach:

- What do you mean by that...
- Would you phrase that another way...
- How could you demonstrate that...
- Please give me an example of...
- Have you ever experienced that...
- Compare and contrast this...with this...
- If this condition existed...what would you predict as the probable outcome...
- That was a good response. Now add this condition...
- What do you think caused that...
- Can you think of an opposing argument for that response...
- What criteria did you use to make that judgment...
- What are two alternative recommendations that you could make...
- Which of the following conditions would have to be altered for this to happen...
- Give me a reasonable argument for...
- What is the relationship between...
- Why did this appear to cause...that...
- Here is a probable situation. What actions would you take and why would you take them?
- How would this apply today given the same circumstances...
- Do you feel that these data allow us to arrive at this conclusion...
- If you had to rank these ideas in order of...
- Given the line of reasoning just presented, why do you think some students in the group might object?
- To what extent, if any...
- Given the different points of view just presented, how can we reconcile...

When a student has difficulty answering an initial question, the instructor can use intermediate probing. This provides cues and hints and asks for clarification and is always building on existing knowledge.

Values Questions

Probing questions, in addition to exploring the cognitive skills of students, can also create an opportunity to allow them to explore their values and attitudes. Value questions employ strategies that allow a student to explore what their values are and what might have influenced their values position. These questions should encourage students to express, to explore, and to modify their own values and attitudes. When instructors use this probing technique they must guard against making judgments about the relative worth of the expressed values and attitudes no matter how much these values and attitudes contradict their own values and attitudes. An environment must be created that will help students explore their values and document why they have developed these particular values and attitudes. Some possible approaches to questioning include:

- Would you choose this over... Why...
- Would you be willing to express that in a public forum...
- Would you give your time to see that happen...
- If you had extra money, would you give some of it to support that issue...
- What actions have you taken lately to support that position...
- We all have to make choices in life. Given these data what choice would you make and why...
- What have you done about that...
- What would you be willing to do to see that happen...
- Did you do that or take that position out of love of and respect for...or out of fear of retribution...
- Which other possibilities have you explored...
- I don't agree with your position on that, but I respect your right to hold it. I arrived at my conclusions as a result of.... How have you arrived at your position...
- Are you aware of the consequences of that action...
- Who or what group do you think most influenced that attitude...
- If someone gave you a check for $10,000 to solve that problem, how would you spend the money?
- What application do you think this will have 10 years from now? What would you like to see happen...

These descriptions are provided as broad guidelines covering different techniques that can be used to question students within the classroom setting or in a testing situation.

Clarifying Questions

Clarifying questions are used when the answer is correct but too narrow. The student is requested to continually improve and expand the answer without any hints. The instructor asks the student:

- To explain
- Tell why
- Restate that another way
- Are there any other reasons?
- What else could you add?

In addition to prompting and clarifying techniques, there are several others suggested by Svessmuth (1978):
- Justifying: The student is asked to justify a response with "Why?" or "Why that?"
- Refocusing: This is used when the student has missed the point of the question and is used to bring him/her back on track.
- Expanding: Use silence or non-verbal communication to ask for more or ask other students to amplify on the response.
- Redirecting: A technique used to get other students involved. As soon as a student has completed a response, another student is asked to expand and/or comment.

Hierarchical Questions
Hierarchical questions provide a sequence that leads the student from seemingly unrelated responses to the application of a skill. The student's responses proceed from recall through understanding of relationships to using the rule, procedure, or data in unfamiliar situations.

DEVELOPING A POOL OF QUESTIONS FOR CLASSROOM USE AND TESTING
Having a pool of questions developed around the key subject matter topics at various levels of intellectual and attitudinal skills can be an invaluable source of teaching material. After class, write down as many student questions as can be recalled. Note how often each question was asked in different classes if more than one section of the same class was taught. Incorporate these questions in the next class and provide multiple examples. Encourage students to visit before or after class with questions. Note and use these questions. Toward the end of class, ask each student to write the two questions that they felt were most important. Using the hierarchical classification scheme provided in this chapter, write the same question at different intellectual levels.

At the beginning of the class, ask the students to pose the two or three most important questions that need to be answered during the class. Ask colleagues for copies of their tests and exams and share yours with them. Ask one (or several) colleagues to attend your class and write down questions that they feel are important.

Write to colleagues at other universities for copies of their tests and exams on the premise that you will share yours as the basis of establishing a "question pool." Show them how you have rated the questions hierarchically. The pool of questions that you can generate from these procedures will also assist you in formulating your student learning objectives.

GENERATING YOUR CLASSROOM QUESTIONS
The final guide for either the generation of classroom questions or selections from a pool of questions should be the student learning performance objectives.

Student learning performance objectives define exactly what it is that you want the students to recall as important information and what it is that you want them TO DO with the information.

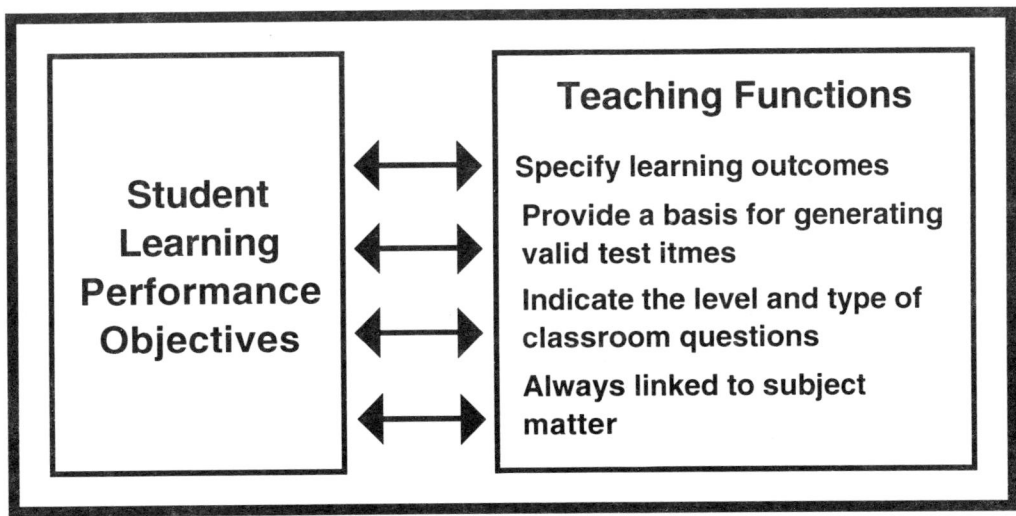

Note that all linking arrows are two-way. In other words, not only do the student learning performance objectives provide the basis for the four teaching functions, they can also be derived from the four teaching functions.

Student learning performance objectives should be defined before teaching takes place and should be provided to the students so that they know what is expected of them. These objectives, defined in terms of learning rather than teaching, must be explicit and action oriented and provide a basis for sequencing the instruction.

If the instructor is unsure of the student learning performance objectives, review tests and exams. If a test or exam item requires a higher level learning skill (higher than memory or simple comprehension), then it is a specific example within a class of performance. It is possible to derive many specific test situations from a well-stated student learning performance objective. For example:
- Analytical skills are not taught in a vacuum.
- Analytical skills are linked to specific subject matter and to specific situations.
- A single test item represents one of many possible specific test situations.

A TECHNIQUE TO DERIVE STUDENT LEARNING PERFORMANCE OBJECTIVES
As a course is developed particular attention should be given to the kind of thought processes that students are to develop in addition to the particular body of information that they are to remember. Questioning strategies will help to guide and stimulate higher thought processes. If part of this chapter on questioning strategies was treated as a lecture and the specific performance objectives were not known, then the instructor could use the following procedures:

A. Before the lesson identify the major points to make during the class. The major points of the lesson that would be derived from this chapter would include:

Point 1: Different kinds of classroom questions require different levels of intellectual responses.
Point 2: Classroom questions should be derived from and lead to achievement of the student learning performance objectives.
Point 3: There are effective ways to frame classroom questions.
Point 4: There is a direct relationship between the student learning performance objectives, classroom questioning strategies, and test/exam items.

B. Once the major points have been identified, then it is determined what it is that the students are TO DO with the major points. How should the students "perform?" In other words, what are the student learning performance objective that relate to each major point?

Point 1. Different kinds of classroom questions require different levels of intellectual responses

<u>Student Performance Objectives:</u>
  a. Describe the four major hierarchical levels of classroom questions and how they differ from each other.
  b. Given a variety of sample classroom questions, identify the intended intellectual response using the classification levels described in class.
  c. Construct three examples of classroom questions in your discipline at each of the four classification levels.

Point 2. Classroom questions should be derived from and lead to achievement of the student learning performance objectives.

<u>Student Performance Objectives:</u>
  a. Given a student learning performance objective, classify it within one of the four skill levels and construct at least two classroom questions that match the same level.
  b. Construct a student performance objective at one of the upper two classification levels and design a sequential questioning strategy that should logically lead the student to mastery of the objective.

Point 3. There are effective ways to frame classroom questions.

Point 4. There is a direct relationship between the student performance objective, classroom questioning strategies, and test/exam items.

<u>Student Performance Objectives:</u>
  a. Describe the relationship between student learning performance objectives, classroom questioning strategies, and text/exam items.
  b. Construct one example at either of the two higher levels of a student learning performance objective, two or three classroom questions, and at least two test items. Explain why the questions and test items are valid.

LINKING CLASSROOM QUESTIONS TO STUDENT PERFORMANCE OBJECTIVES AND TEST ITEMS

The proposed four-level classification scheme has been reviewed. The relationships between classroom questions, student learning performance objectives, and test items should be more meaningful. Look at the following model:

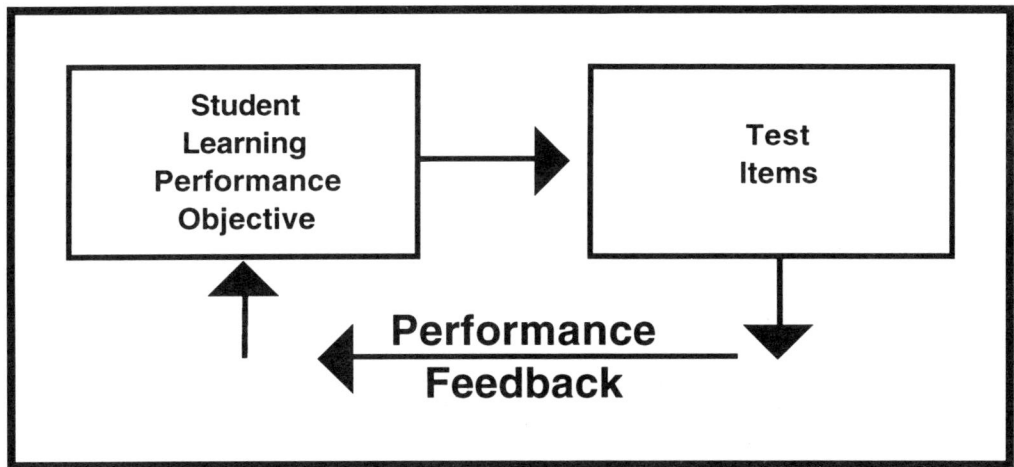

Test items must assess, in some way, the student learning performance objectives if they are to be valid. If a student learning performance objective calls for critical thinking behavior, then the test item must require critical thinking behavior.

The purpose of student assessment, either through observable performance, product development, or traditional paper and pencil tests, is to provide data to the instructor indicating to what degree the learning performance objectives have been mastered. There must be a direct link between the intended student performance and measure of that performance. If this condition does not exist then the measure of the performance is invalid. For example, if the student learning performance objective called for an understanding skill and the test item called for application skill, the test situation would be an invalid measure of the objective. The test item should have been at the understanding level. Now add classroom questioning strategies to the instructional model.

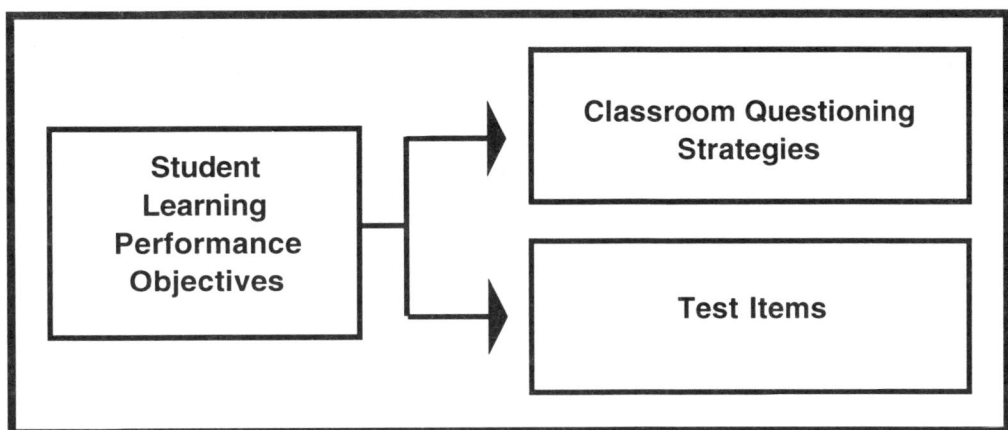

There must be a direct linkage between what the student was intended to learn as expressed in the student learning performance objectives and how that learning was tested. This link is referred to as teaching strategies, either live or mediated.

Regardless of the teaching strategy used, it is the use of questions that guide the student learning. These classroom questions must lead the student to the same intellectual level as expressed in the objectives and measured in the test items. If the objective calls for critical thinking behavior then the classroom questions must be sequenced in such a way as to allow the student to achieve at this level on the tests and most importantly provide for adequate practice.

The student learning performance objective was classified at critical thinking—the highest level of learning. The teaching strategy was sequenced starting at the memory and understanding levels to assure that the student understood all of the basic concepts through application of the rules or procedures and finally to problem solving. The development of the test items followed the same logic. If the student did not perform at the expected levels as indicated on the tests, a logical system exists to analyze our teaching strategies. If there are serious consequences to non-achievement then there is no choice but to revise the teaching strategy.

A QUESTIONING STRATEGY AT THE APPLICATION LEVEL

An example of a technique that can be used at the application, or rule using, level of learning provides a method for sequencing classroom questions. The example used is taken from a graduate lecture given by the author and exemplifies deductive rather than inductive teaching.

An Outline of the Questioning Strategy

At the memory and understanding levels:
1. Here is a rule, law, principle or definition...
2. Here is a definition of each concept...
   (There may be five, six, or more different concepts)
3. This is an example of concept 1...
4. This is another example of concept 1...
5. This is a non-example of concept 1...
6. This is an example of concept 2...
   (This process of providing examples and non-examples of each relevant concept is repeated for the entire rule or principle if the instructor feels it is appropriate)
7. This is an example of how the rule applies...
8. This is a non-example of the application of the rule...

As we move to the application level, the student is asked to apply the knowledge to unfamiliar situations:
9. Is this an example of the application of the rule...
10. Please give me an example of the application of the rule...

This questioning strategy can also be used in reverse as an inductive approach to teaching. The student is presented with numerous examples and non-examples or rules, principles, or data and asked to identify the rule or principle.

An example of the application of this questioning strategy

Definition: Performance Objective (abbreviated)
> A **student** learning **performance objective** states in **precise language** what it is that the student is expected to do as a result of the **learning experience**.

Major Concepts (in bold in the definition)

Concept 1. **Student**. The actor or any person performing. The emphasis is on the student rather than the instructor.
Example
  a. The student will...
  b. The physician will...
  c. The pilot will...
Non-Example
  a. The teacher will...
  b. The instructor will...
(The non-example emphasizes what the teacher or instructor will do rather than what the student will do.)

Concept 2. **Performance Objective**. A behavior, learning outcome, expectation, or end result. It describes what the actor or performer will do.
Example
  a. The student will describe the experiment.
  b. The physician will calculate the dosage.
  c. The pilot will estimate the time of arrival.
Non-Example
  a. The student will view a film.
  b. The physician will discuss the dosage with his colleagues.
  c. The pilot will read the instruments.
(Viewing, discussing, and reading are learning activities that the students engage in as a means to achieve a learning performance objective. They are not ends or outcomes.)

Concept 3. **Precise Language**. Language that is specific enough that it is capable of measurement or observation.
Example
  a. ...describe...
  b. ...calculate...
  c. ...estimate...
Non-Example
  a. The student will understand the experiment.
  b. The physician will comprehend how to calculate the dosage.
  c. The pilot will appreciate the procedure for estimating the time of arrival.
(This is vague language open to multiple interpretations without further clarification.)

Concept 4. **Learning Experience**: An activity that describes how the student will achieve the learning performance objective. This involves any teaching strategy employed, whether live or mediated.
Example
   a. After reading the lab guide and viewing the demonstration, the student will describe the experiment.
   b. Given the pattern profile and current vital signs, the physician will calculate the dosage.
   c. After participating in the flight simulator and given all pertinent data, the pilot will estimate time of arrival.

Non-Example
   a. The student will describe the experiment accurately.
   b. The physician will calculate the dosage within 1 milligram of the recommended dosage.
   c. The pilot will estimate the time of arrival within two minutes of the actual arrival.

(These are not learning activities that describe how they will achieve the learning performance objective. The additional descriptions are standards of performance that indicate when the student has performed satisfactorily.)

MAJOR SEQUENCING ERROR

The most critical problem in teaching and questioning sequences is an inadequate comprehension of the concepts, rules, and principles on the part of the student. The teaching sequence often jumps from an information recall level to an application level without insuring that the student has an adequate understanding. The latter is accomplished with the use of examples and non-examples, which help the student to learn discrimination skills. After an example is provided, the student is shown opposites and told "don't confuse this with... ." When the instructor feels that the student understands the concept, the student is given an example and is asked, "Is this an example of...?" If the student is able to classify correctly, he or she is working at the application level.

A non-example is not a poor example. It is an opposite of or contradiction of the rule. This technique is used to provide contrast to reinforce the students understanding of the concepts involved. Some instructors feel that the use of examples and non-examples for each concept is too time consuming. Instead they move from the rule, law, principle, or definition directly to examples and non-examples of the whole rule. If the students have difficulty constructing examples they then back up to the more difficult concepts based on the notion that if the students don't fully understand the individual concepts within a rule, etc., they will not be able to apply the total rule.

Derivation of examples and non-examples is a cumulative process over many years of teaching.

ASKING QUESTIONS AT DIFFERENT INTELLECTUAL LEVELS

Example 1

STATEMENT: You watched the news last evening on Channel 7. One of the events was the capture and execution of a Vietcong soldier in civilian clothes by the Chief of Police in Saigon, whose name was Van Thang.

Level 1 Recall Knowledge
What was the name of the Chief of Police?

Level 2 Understanding
Describe everything that was reported about the capture of the Vietcong soldier from any source.

Level 3 Application
According to international law, was the execution of the Vietcong soldier by the Chief of Police a valid execution? Document your position.

Level 4.1 Critical Thinking-Analysis
The news in Boston showed a five second clip of the execution. The Chief of Police put the gun to the soldier's temple and pulled the trigger. You saw the head dip slightly away. Why was the film edited this way?

Level 4.2 Critical Thinking-Synthesis
If you were the news editor at this time, what dialogue would you construct for what impact?

Level 4.3 Critical Thinking-Evaluation
Could different camera angles have created a different effect? How could this have been done?

Example 2

The Dynamics of Interviewing.

Level 1 Recall Knowledge
What are the six (6) components of an interview?

Level 2 Understanding
When do the psychological barriers to good communication bias the interactions? Explain these reasons and their relationships to physiological barriers.

Level 3 Application
Did the interviewer follow established procedures for interviewing in each of these video clips?

Level 4.1 Critical Thinking-Analysis
Was there evidence of bias on the part of the interviewer during this session? Identify each instance of bias and explain how the interviewer could have prevented the bias.

Level 4.2 Critical Thinking Synthesis
How would you design a role playing scene to train interviewers? Design a brief scene for role playing that demonstrates good questioning techniques.

Level 4.3 Critical Thinking-Evaluation
Read the example of the medical interview dealing with cardiac symptoms and neurotic manifestations. How would you rate this interview based on the "Interviewing Rating Scale?" Justify your final conclusions.

FRAMING STUDENT QUESTIONS WITH POSITIVE FEEDBACK

Set the stage and ask questions early in your classes. Begin first with a few probing or open questions, possibly written on the blackboard or on a handout. Demonstrate at the beginning of class that responses to closed questions with fixed answers are inadequate. Tell the students that these types of answers are not expected now but they will be expected in the next three or four classes.

Use simple wording that is clear and concise. Start with questions at the recall or understanding level–questions that many students can answer correctly. Praise the correct answer and provide positive feedback and encouragement both verbally and non-verbally with a nod, smile, touch, or approach. Never use verbal or non-verbal put-downs. Some suggestions on how to provide positive feedback could include:

- We agree on that answer.   Correct answer.
- Great! Let's continue...   True...logical response.
- Valid answer.   Right on!   Exactly!
- Precisely.   Fine.   Please proceed...   You did well...
- Good try...   Just right.   Keep up the good work!
- Appropriate answer.   Right again...   Positively...keep going!
- Congratulations!   Good response.
- That was a good connection you made...

Ask only one question at a time. The student should have a reasonable chance of making a correct response since it should be within his/her knowledge and experience. If the instructor uses technical language or new vocabulary, assurances should be made that the student is familiar with the individual concepts. Plan questions ahead and be aware of the type of cognitive process that the question is intended to elicit.

After a question is asked, the instructor should wait for the answer. Crappo (1988) notes that "The first rule of thumb is simple: After you ask the question, shut up!" Barnes (1988) observes that "The silence seems long, awkward, and uncomfortable, but endure it. Wait patiently, smile, relax, and look as though you believe with all your heart that someone will help you out." The silence of the instructor can stimulate a student response.

If a student appears to be inattentive, ask a question of the student by name but answer the question so as not to humiliate the student who will get the hint immediately.

Don't glare, smirk, or frown at an incorrect response regardless of how far out it may seem to be. Rephrase the question at a lower level. Any type of embarrassment can devastate a student's self-confidence and self-esteem. Don't let any one student dominate the class. Solicit answers by name from non-participative students. If the instructor is not receiving questions from the class, call on a student by name and ask if he/she or any other student would like to respond. Student's thought processes are stimulated by instructor questions.

Students learn as they are questioned and tested. If the instructor uses a preponderance of recall questions, students will memorize. On the other hand, if the instructor probes with questions, students will learn critical thinking skills. Dillon (1988) recommends, "Ask a higher-level question, get a higher-level answer."

ANSWERING STUDENT QUESTIONS

If a student asks a question and the instructor does not understand it, ask the student to restate it. If the instructor still don't understand it, ask other students for help.

If an instructor does not know the answer, he or she should always be honest. Admit it, but say the answer will be provided in the next class. Solicit help from other students to help find the answer.

If questions are received that are irrelevant to the present class, the instructor should tell the student that the topic will be addressed at a future time or that he or she will be available after class. It is helpful to repeat or paraphrase a question asked in class for clarity and so that other students can hear it.

Most classroom questions used by college instructors emphasize acquisition and recall of factual information. Fact questions require the student to remember previously presented information from lectures and readings. Higher cognitive questions require students to use and apply the information in critical thinking exercises in which information is manipulated to create and support responses.

In order to prevent overemphasis on recall questions, instructors need to develop classroom questions systematically, strategically, sequentially, and in writing in order for their students to develop critical and reflective thinking skills. A lawyer would never approach a courtroom when defending or prosecuting a friendly or hostile, naive, or expert witness, unless the type, kind, and sequence of questions to be asked had been carefully thought through and written out. Lawyers have learned specific principles and techniques of questioning (Woodbury,1984). This is essential since they must question witnesses who may not want to provide answers, a somewhat similar situation to questioning college students (Kestler, 1982).

Brophy and Good (1986) conclude that, "...the form of a teacher question signals the student as to the expected level of response, thus controlling the student's thought or response pattern." Taba (1966) described questioning as "the single most influential teaching act." There is a growing body of evidence that demonstrates that appropriate questions, when properly asked, contribute to a significant improvement in student learning (Redfield and Rousseau, 1984; Brophy and Good, 1986). If this is so, then why do we continue to identify poor quality questions in college classrooms–questions that do not go above the information recall level? Stevens (1912) noted, "I believe that the remedy for many of the present evils of instruction lies in the improvement of our methods of questions." Little has changed over the past 80 years.

In a study of 40 college classrooms at different universities, Barnes (1983) found that only 3.65% of class time was devoted to questioning by faculty and those questions were dominated by requests for factual information. Almost 63% of all questions asked required only memory. The conclusion of Barnes was that professors ask few questions that require students to "think." Similar findings were noted by Boyer (1987) and Hamblen (1984).

Lange (February 1982) observes, "One of the prime findings from all the research on questioning is that teachers usually ask literal questions, ones that ask merely for simple facts." Gall (1976) has observed, "Research spanning more than half a century indicated that teachers questions have emphasized facts... even though educators generally agree that teachers should emphasize the students' skill in critical thinking rather than in learning and recalling facts."

Gall (November 1984) reported in a meta-analysis of research on classroom questions, that 60% emphasized recall, 20% procedural, and 20% mixed emphasis at the analysis, synthesis, and evaluation levels. Kloss (1988) concluded, "Recent research to determine whether teachers ask higher level questions shows the answer repeatedly to be an unqualified no."

Carner (1963) notes, "... the research shows overwhelmingly that teachers use memory questions in over 70% of their teaching time."

While examining the overall levels of intellectual discourse in college classrooms, Fischer and Grant (1983) found,

> Professors used a limited number of cognitive levels ... . Regardless of characteristics in the college environment, they had a direct style of teaching, did most of the talking, and most frequently applied the lowest cognitive skill, knowledge, to their subject matter. Influenced by this teaching style, college students employed a limited range of cognitive skills in their classroom discourse. ... (Professors) convey information and interpret it for students, but they do not analyze, synthesize, or evaluate it.

Other studies have indicated a range of 60%-80% of instructor questions require only the lowest levels of cognitive thinking–knowledge (Gall, 1970; Galloway and Mickelson, 1973).

Summary

The research that has reviewed the quality of classroom questions in public school and college classrooms has persistently found a preponderance of low-level recall questions that reinforce passive classrooms. In order to overcome this problem, instructors should write out their questions before a class and identify the intended cognitive level that will be required in the student response. The selection of classroom questions cannot be left to chance. Good questions clarify, expand, probe, and stimulate learning. Instructor questions are the means used to communicate the key elements of the subject matter. Factual questions limit and direct the type of learning and limit or eliminate critical thinking. Wilen (1986) observed, "The persistence of the view of teaching as imparting knowledge and learning as recalling and repeating information is the reason for the narrow choice of questions used in instruction." Students learn as they are tested and questioned during class because these provide strong cues as to what the instructor thinks is important. Appropriate questions provide practice before the test.

CHAPTER SUMMARY

Asking appropriate classroom questions requires thought and planning and has a direct relationship to the student learning performance objectives and student assessment procedures. The complaint is often heard, "The instructor teaches one thing and tests another." Without adequate preplanning this can easily happen. If there are no student learning performance objectives, then there is no logic for the derivation and sequence of classroom questions and development of valid test items.

This chapter has provided a rationale and model for the derivation of classroom questions at a variety of intellectual skill levels as well as specific techniques and procedures for overall questioning strategies in the classroom. It has been shown that effective questions:

- Can probe student values and attitudes as well as their cognitive skills. They can also encourage students to document their point of view so that they move away from opinion only.
- Stimulate discussion between student and instructor and among students.
- Keep students alert and better prepared because of the type of questions they expect.
- Review and emphasize by focusing attention on important points of the class.
- Help the instructor to sequence a lecture based on the four-level classification scheme described in this chapter.
- Assist the instructor to diagnose the level of student understanding as described in this chapter.
- Should be derived from student learning performance objectives and developed before the class.
- Should progress from lower skills (memory and understanding) through the higher levels of learning (application and critical thinking).
- Should provide appropriate practice for the learning performance objectives.
- Should preview the type of assessment procedure that is intended to be used.

Well-prepared questions are the basis for interactive classroom teaching. Without well thought out classroom questions, a lesson becomes a monologue that fails to capture the essence of good teaching.

BIBLIOGRAPHY

Adams, T.H. (1964). <u>The development of a method for analysis of questions asked by teachers in classroom discourse.</u> Unpublished doctoral dissertation, Rutgers University.

Anderson, J., & Graham, A. (1980). A problem in medical education: There is an information overload. <u>Medical Education,</u> 14, 4-7.

Barnes, Carol P. (1983). <u>Questioning in the college classroom. Studies of college teaching.</u> Carolyn L. Ellner & Carol P. Barnes (Eds.). Lexington, MA: Lexington Books, 61-81.

Bloom, Benjamin S. (Ed.). (1956). <u>Taxonomy of educational objectives, handbook 1: Cognitive domain.</u> NY: David McKay Co., Inc.

Boyer, Ernest L. (1987). <u>College: The undergraduate experience in America.</u> NY: Harper and Rowe.

Brophy, G. & Good, T. (1986). <u>Teacher behavior and student behavior. Handbook of research on teaching,</u> (3rd ed.). M. Wittrock (Ed.). NY: Macmillan.

Brown, M.N., & Keeley, S.M. (1981). <u>Asking the right questions.</u> Englewood Cliffs, NJ: Prentice-Hall, Inc.

Brown, George. (1975). <u>Microteaching.</u> London: Methuen and Co., LTD., (Unit VI: Questioning and Answering).

Carner, R.L. (1963). Levels of questioning. <u>Education,</u> 83, 546-550.

Clegg, A.A., Farley, G.T., & Curran, R.J. (1967). <u>Training teachers to analyze the cognitive level of classroom questioning.</u> Research Report No.1, Applied Research Training Program, University of Massachusetts.

Clegg, A.A. Jr. (1971). Classroom questions. In Lee C. Deighton (Ed.), <u>The Encyclopedia of Education,</u> 2. NY: Macmillan.

Cox, Richard, & Unks, Nancy. (1967). <u>A selected and annotated bibliography of studies concerning the taxonomy of educational objectives: Cognitive domain.</u> PA: University of Pittsburgh Press, Working Paper 13.

Crapo, Raymond F. (1988). Questioning: The epitome of the art. <u>Training and Development Journal,</u> 46-49.

Cyrs, Thomas E. (Ed.). (1978). <u>Handbook for the design of instruction in pharmacy education.</u> MD: American Association of Colleges of Pharmacy.

___. (Ed.). (1974). <u>Improving instruction in environmental science.</u> Boston: New England Consortium on Environmental Protection (EPA Contract No. 68-02-0314).

Cyrs, Thomas E., & Kent, Alvin. (1978). <u>Assessing student performance: Improving your testing ability.</u> Minneapolis: Educational Development Associates.

Dahlberg, E.J. (1969). <u>An analysis of the relationships between the cognitive level of teacher questions and selected variables.</u> Unpublished doctoral dissertation, University of Oregon.

Davis, O.L., & Morse, K.R. (1970). <u>The questioning strategies observation system.</u> Report Series No. 35, The Research and Development Center for Teacher Education, The University of Texas at Austin.

Davis, O.L., Morse, K.R., Rogers, V.M., & Tinsley, D.C. (1969). Studying the cognitive emphasis of teachers' classroom questions. <u>Educational Leadership</u> 26, 711-719.

Dillon, J.T. (1988). Questioning in education. In Michael Meyers (Ed.), Questions and Questioning. NY: Walter de Gruyter.

___. (1982). The multidisciplinary study of questioning. Journal of Educational Psychology, 74, 147-165.

Farley, G.T. (1968). Increasing the cognitive level of classroom questions: An application of Bloom's taxonomy of educational objectives. Unpublished doctoral dissertation, University of Massachusetts.

Gall, M. (1992). The use of questions in teaching reading. Eric Documentation Reproduction Services ED 067 650.

___. (1984, November). Synthesis of research on teacher's questioning. Educational Leadership, 42(3), 40-47.

___. (1970). The use of questions in teaching. Educational Research, 40(5), 707-721.

Galloway, C.G. & Mickelson, N.I. (1973). Improving teachers' questions. Elementary School Journal, 74(3), 145-148.

General Physics Corporation. (1983a). Principles of instructional design. Columbia, MD: General Physics Corporation.

___. (1983b). Fundamentals of classroom instruction. MD: General Physics Corporation.

Givens, Cheryl, & Grant, Grace E. (1983). Intellectual levels in college classrooms. In Ellner Barnes, Studies of college teaching. Lexington, MA: Lexington Books and D.C.Heath and Co.

Hamblen, Karen A. (April 1984). The application of questioning strategy research to art criticism instruction. Paper presented at the annual meeting of the American Educational Research Association, New Orleans, LA.

Hennings, Dorothy F. (1975). Mastering classroom communication. CA: Goodyear Publishing Company.

Hoover, Kenneth H. (1980). College teaching today: A handbook for postsecondary instruction. Boston: Allyn and Bacon, Inc.

Hunkins, Francis P. (1972). Questioning strategies and techniques. Boston: Allyn and Bacon, Inc.

___. (1970). Analysis and evaluation questions: Their effects upon critical thinking. Educational Leadership (Research Supplement).

___. (1969). The effects of analysis and evaluation questions on various levels of achievement. Journal of Experimental Evaluation, 38, 45-58.

___. (1976). Involving students in questioning. Boston: Allyn and Bacon, Inc.

Hunter, Madeline. (1976). Improved instruction. El Segundo, CA: Tip Publications.

Hyman, Ronald T. Questioning in the college classroom: Idea paper no. 7. Manhattan, KS: Kansas State University Center for Faculty Evaluation and Development.

___. (1979). Strategic questioning. NJ: Prentice-Hall, Inc.

___. (1977). Questioning in the classroom. (ERIC Document Reproduction Service ED 138 551)

Kerry, T. (1984). Classroom task analysis. British Journal of In-Service Education, 10, 23-25.

Kestler, J.L. (1982). Questioning techniques and tactics. Colorado Springs, CO: Shepard-McGraw-Hill.

Kloss, R. J. (1988). Toward asking the right questions. The Clearing House, 61(3), 245-248.

Ladd, G.T. (1969). <u>Determining the level of inquiry in teachers' questions</u>. Unpublished doctoral dissertation, Indiana University.

Laird, Dugan. (1978). <u>Approaches to training and development</u>. Reading, MA: Addison-Wesley Publishing Company.

Lange, Bob. (1982, February). ERIC/RCS Report: Questioning technique <u>Language Arts</u>, <u>59</u>(2), 180-185.

McKeachie, Wilbert J. (1969). <u>Teaching tips: A guidebook for the beginning teacher</u>. Lexington, MA: D.C. Heath Co.

McMaster, Robert K. (1973). Socratic method: More than it seems. <u>Contemporary Education</u>, 150-151.

Ostendorf, Virginia A. (1989). <u>Teaching through interactive television</u>. Littleton, CO: Virginia A. Ostendorf, Inc.

Payne, S.L. (1951). <u>The art of asking questions</u>. Princeton, NJ: Princeton University Press.

Redford, Doris L., & Rousseau, Elaine Waldman. (1981, Summer). A meta-analysis of experimental research on teacher questioning behavior. <u>Review of Educational Research</u>, <u>51</u>(2), 237-245.

Rickards, J.P., & DiVesta, F.J. (1974). Type and frequency of questions in processing textual material. <u>Journal of Educational Psychology</u>, <u>66</u>, 354-362.

Rosinger, Lawrence. (1968). The class' answer as a teaching device. <u>English Journal</u>, 1032-1035.

Russell, I. Jan, Hendricson, William D., & Herbert, Robert J. (1984, November). Effects of lecture information density on medical student achievement. <u>Journal of Medical Education</u>, <u>59</u>, 881-889.

Sanders, Norris M. (1966). <u>Classroom questions: What kinds?</u> NY: Harper and Row.

Smith, Barry J., & Delahaye, Brian L. (1983). <u>How to be an effective trainer</u>. NY: Wiley Professional Development Programs.

Stevens R. (1912). <u>The question as a measure of efficiency in instruction</u>. NY: Teachers College, Columbia University.

___. (1912). The question as a measure of efficiency in instruction: A critical study of classroom practice. <u>Teachers College Contributions to Education</u>. NY: Columbia University Press.

Stodolsky, S.S., Ferguson, T.L., & Wimpellberg, K. The recitation persists, but what does it look like? <u>Journal of Curriculum Studies</u>, <u>13</u>, 121-130.

Sund, Robert, & Carin, Arthur. (1978). <u>Creative questioning and listening techniques.</u>

Svessmuth, Patricia. (1978). <u>Ideas for training managers and supervisors</u>. CA: University Associates, Inc. (Section 18–How to Use Questions Effectively).

Svessmuth, Patricia, & Stengels, Marit. (1978). Questions, answers, and Socrates. In Patricia Svessmuth, <u>Ideas for training managers and supervisors</u>. CA: University Associates, Inc.

Taba, Hilda (1962). <u>Curriculum development–Theory and practice</u>. NY: Harcourt, Brace and World, Inc.

Wilen, W., & Clegg, A. (1986). Effective questions and questioning: A research review. <u>Theory and Research in Social Education</u>, <u>14</u>, 153-161.

Woodbury, H. (1984). The strategic use of questions in court. <u>Semiotica</u>, <u>48</u>, 197-228.

Chapter 18

Alternative Student Handout Formats

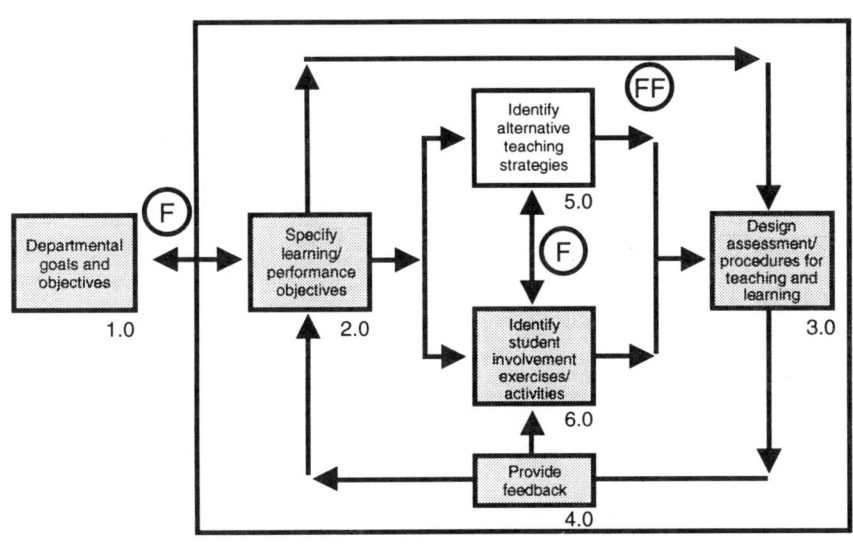

"How much note-copying?"

ALTERNATIVE STUDENT HANDOUT FORMATS

LEARNING PERFORMANCE OBJECTIVE
Select several different types of handouts. Design them and use them in a class you are now teaching. Evaluate their effectiveness. (Level 4).

KEY IDEAS
1. Handouts reduce student note-copying and provide a structured overview of a lesson.
2. Handouts focus student attention to the most important key ideas.
3. There are 17 different handout formats.

NEW VOCABULARY
- handout
- structured notes
- split-page
- topic outline
- skeleton notes

Used literally, the term "handout" refers to any type of written information distributed to students as an adjunct to their classes. It refers to written material designed to facilitate learning in a course of instruction, a lecture, or small-group class (Brown and Tomlinson, 1980). They are designed to aid the student to see the structure of the course and to provide a framework for notetaking. (Hartley and Marshall, 1974). Handouts can be used for private study before or after a class or used during a class.

When developing a course, the instructor must decide if he or she will write key notes on the blackboard, overhead projector, or use prepared overhead transparencies. The instructor will also have to decide if students will copy these notes as they are written or use a prepared handout in lieu of verbatim copying. If a handout is used, the instructor will then have to decide how much information to provide and how much the student will have to copy.

This chapter explains 17 different student handout formats that can be used during a presentation. How much copying the student will have to do is evident in each format.

Use of Handouts
Depending on the type of handout used, the amount of advanced planning will vary. A general topical outline or use of full copies of overhead transparencies will require minimal planning while the use of an interactive study guide with word pictures will require a great deal of preparation. The use of some type of handout will allow the instructor more time to model application and problem-solving skills and utilize more examples. Serendipity is not precluded when using a handout. The instructor can always elaborate when there is a "teachable moment."

Students can use handouts for review after a lesson as well as at exam time. Information transfer is enhanced with the use of fill-ins that direct the students' attention to significant key concepts and phrases. It is possible to use handouts to manage student time by directing them verbally and in writing to complete a variety of in-class and after-class learning activities and practice opportunities. The use of handouts can make it clear to the students what material is considered most important. (Hartley and Marshall, 1974).

The use of any handout improves note-taking skills. Research has clearly indicated that students are generally incomplete notetakers, "...recording a relatively small percentage of critical lecture ideas" (Kiewra, 1987), ranging from 11% (Hartley and Marshall, 1974) to 62% (Locke, 1977). Few students have ever been taught or advised about notetaking and review (Palmatier and Bennett, 1974; Carrier, 1983).

Students with different abilities and levels of prior knowledge may require different notetaking strategies. Detailed lecture notes could be supplied for everyone with the expectation that students who benefit from taking their own notes will continue to do so (Carrier, 1983).

What Does the Research Tell Us About the Use of Handouts?

Howe and Godfrey (1977) in their research on student notetaking found that students who receive handouts do better in tests than those who do not and that the use of handouts were particularly useful to poor note takers.

Bentley (1989) found that "...immediate recall and delayed retention of lecture material were enhanced by either taking notes or looking at an outline while listening to a lecture. Suprisingly, results were just as good for looking at an outline as they were for notetaking."

A number of researchers have reported that students who received lecture outlines scored significantly better than students who received either a complete transcript or a full set of instructor notes. (Northcroft and Jernstedt, 1975; Freyberg, 1956; Fisher and Harris, 1973; Fisher and Harris, 1974; Annis and Davis, 1977).

It has also been reported that structured worksheets can improve recall of key points of a lecture presentation in both a live and videotaped format (Green et al, 1986).

Findings indicate that students who listen to a lecture and review the instructor's notes generally achieve more than do students who take and review their own notes. (Fisher and Harris, 1973; Kierwa, 1985a, 1985b). This has implications for the use of the interactive study guide since it is generally a replication of the instructor's graphic notes.

That notetaking is a prevalent student behavior from entry to exit in a lecture is well known. Brown and Davis (1981) have noted

> In a typical lecture class, a large amount of student time is devoted to the recording, reorganizing and reviewing of lecture notes.... Whatever the instructor can do to improve the quality of the listening environment including the use of clear and explicit lecture organization, highlighting techniques to explain critical information, as well as special accommodations for some students, should lead to more productive use of student time.

The use of handouts certainly meets these criteria. In the absence of handouts, the students will have to look for cues (often absent) and for important ideas, most of which will be missed. Review the 17 handout formats presented in this chapter. Note the different levels of completeness and detail. Each format has its own special use.

DECISION CRITERIA FOR HANDOUT FORMAT SELECTION

There area number of decisions that an instructor will have to make about the use of student handouts:

- How much of the notes presented by the instructor will the students have to copy verbatum?
- Will the student have to decide what is important and what is unimportant as the instructor lectures?
- To what degree does the instructor want to focus student attention on key points?
- Will the instructor use graphics and/or word pictures to show the structure of a presentation?
- Does the instructor want the students to have an accurate set of notes for later review?
- How much time is the instructor willing to spend preparing quality student handouts?

The following 17 handout formats are presented for review. For further information, please refer to the bibliography.

1. Full copy of an overhead transparency.
2. Reduced overhead transparencies–two to four per page.
3. General topical outline.
4. General topical outline with a two- to three-paragraph summary.
5. Detailed topical outline with or without a summary.
6. Notespace with commentary.
7. One or two word pictures with commentary.
8. Structured notes.
9. Structured worksheet.
10. Skeleton notes.
11. Split page notes.
12. Labeled diagram.
13. Lecture question outline.
14. Interactive study guide.
15. Full lecture script.
16. Article with discussion questions.
17. Instructor notes.

Presentation Format 1
Full Copy of an Overhead Transparency Master or Other Graphic

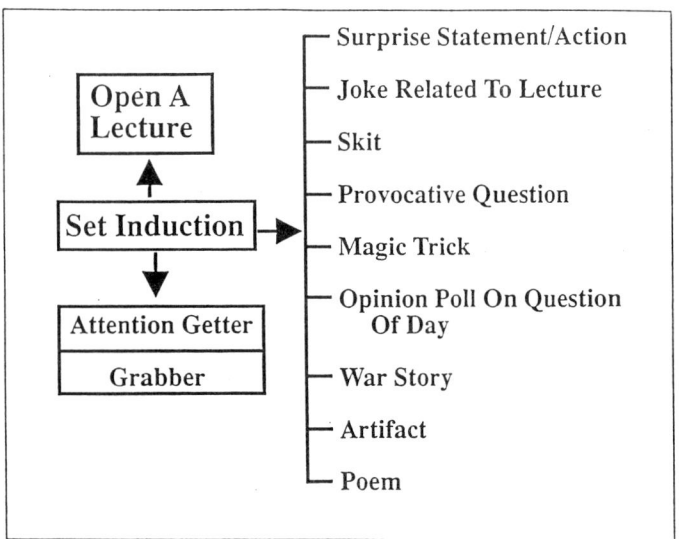

Description
This is the quickest and easiest presentation outline to use. The (TV) overheads or other graphic are copied in black/white and collated in the order that they are presented. These could be fill-ins if key words and phrases have been omitted in the original and which will be written in by the instructor. This format can be effective if a limited number of (TV) overheads are used. It will be cumbersome and expensive if a large number of individual (TV) overheads are used with large numbers of students.
Source: Cyrs, Thomas E. Course entitled "EDUC 501: Essential Skills for College Teaching." New Mexico: New Mexico State University, 1991.

Presentation Format 2
Reduced (TV) Overheads

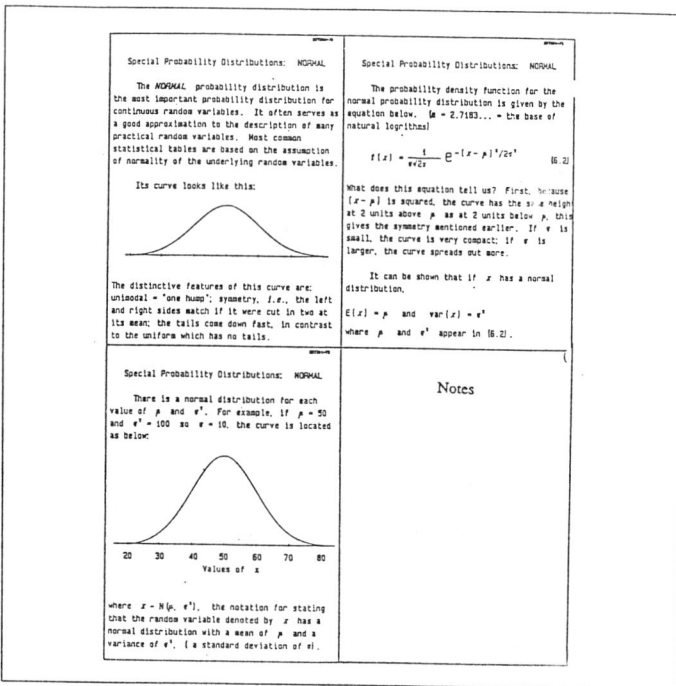

Description
Three or four full-sized (TV) overheads are photo-reduced and reproduced on a single page with or without fill-ins. This instructor restricted each (Tele)lecture to three (3) (TV) overheads. Space is provided for additional note-taking.
Source: Urquhart, M. Scott. Course entitled "EST 251: Statistical Applications for Business, 1990.

Presentation Format 3
General Topic Outline

Preparing Your Telelecture
General Lecture Outline

A. Four Main Components of a Telelecture

B. Review
  1. Problems with previously assigned homework
  2. Key points of previous lecture
  3. Answer student questions

C. Preview
  1. Performance Objectives, Big Questions
  2. New Vocabulary

D. Presentation
  1. Use lecture outline or Presentation Outline

Description
The general topic outline is an easy and quick type to prepare. Adequate space is left between topics and sub-topics for student notes. This type of outline provides a broad structure and sequence of topical presentation and emphasizes very broad topics only. Details will have to be written by students as they listen and process information. As the lecture progresses s/he usually references the student as the when the lecturer is. For example, the lecturer might say, "Let's move on to point B.2 entitled key points of previous lecture."
Source: Cyrs, Thomas E. Course entitled "EDUC 501: Essential Skills for College Teaching." New Mexico: New Mexico State University, 1991.

Presentation Format 4
General Lecture Outline and (Tele)lecture Summary

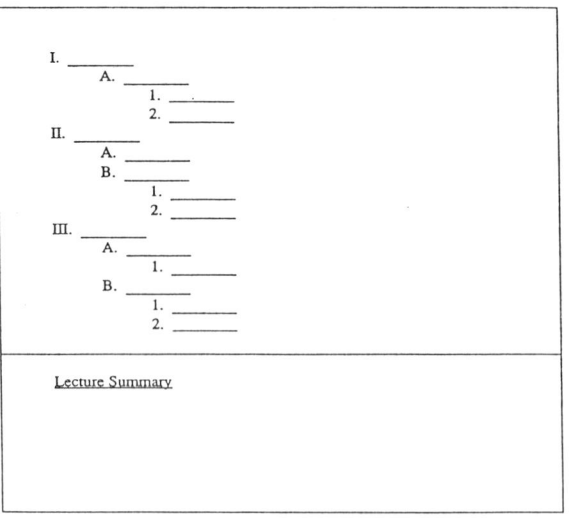

Description
The instructor provides a full general outline (1-3 pages) of the (tele)lecture and then provides a 2-3 paragraph summary.
Source: Freyberg, P.S. "The Effectiveness of Notetaking." in *Education for Teaching*, (1956) Volume 39, pp. 17-24.

Presentation Format 5
Detailed Topical Outline With Commentary

```
I. Four main components
   A. Review
      1. Problems
      2. Key points
         a. As related to learning objectives
      3. Questions
   B. Preview
      1. Big questions
         a. Level of skill
      2. Vocabulary
         a. Review of old vocabulary
         b. New vocabulary in the lecture
   C. Presentation
      1. Formats
         a. Review 14 different formats
      2. Visualization
         a. Clip art
         b. Electronic art
      3. Examples
      4. Humor
         a. Self-directed
         b. Spontaneity
   D. Summarize
      1. Review
         a. Learning objectives
         b. Key questions
      2. Preview
         a. Learning objectives next lesson
      3. Closure
         a. Wrap it in a story
   E. Telelecture critique
Commentary
```

Description
This presentation format provides greater level of detail and structure than the general outline. It can be carried to any level of detail that the instructor feels appropriate. The bottom 1/4 or 1/3 of the page is left for commentary or questions that the instructor did not cover in class. This commentary is pre-planned and provides additional examples or information supplementary to the (tele)lecture.
Source: Cyrs, Thomas E. Course entitled "EDUC 501: Essential Skills for College Teaching." New Mexico: New Mexico State University, 1991.

Presentation Format 6
Notespace With Commentary

```
                    Lecture Topic
                 Learning Objectives




Commentary
Objectives and tests: Remember - Test items must be a valid measure of the
   intended learning outcome as specified in the objectives. Test items must be
   at the same level as the learning objectives.*
      Verbs that require a response above recall:
         describe         compare
         create           produce
         analyze          design
         summarize        identify
         diagnose         evaluate
         infer
*Remember: Levels of learning from lowest to highest: Recall, understanding,
   application (rule using), problem-solving (rule selection).
```

Description
The instructor does not provide any type of (tele) lecture outline. A "commentary" or "problems" space is provided at the bottom 1/3 of the page for supplementary information that was planned not to be covered during the lecture. Additional problems could also be provided for practice.
Some instructors use the "commentary" space to express their personal opinions about a topic.
Source: Cyrs, Thomas E. Course entitled "EDUC 501: Essential Skills for College Teaching." New Mexico: New Mexico State University, 1991.

Presentation Format 7
Word Picture With Commentary

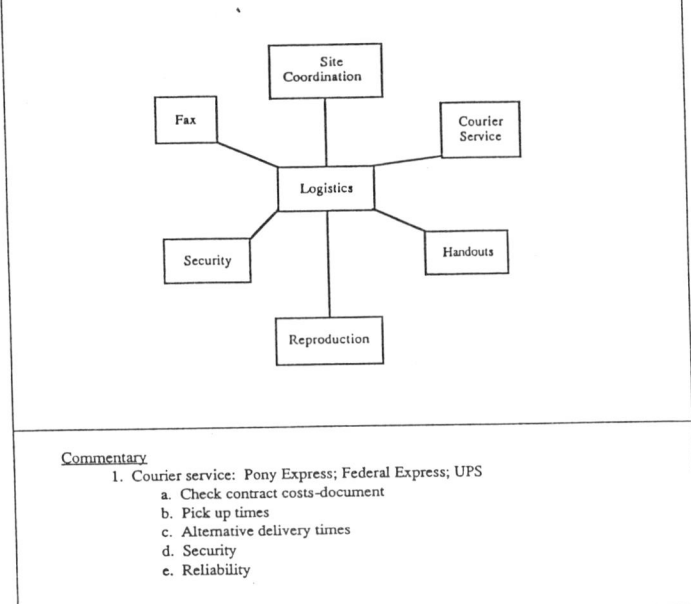

Commentary
1. Courier service: Pony Express; Federal Express; UPS
   a. Check contract costs-document
   b. Pick up times
   c. Alternative delivery times
   d. Security
   e. Reliability

Description
The instructor may use 1-3 Word Pictures per lecture. S/he may emphasize some concepts more than others. The commentary space allows for deliberately planned ancillary information.
Source: Cyrs, Thomas E. Course entitled "EDUC 501: Essential Skills for College Teaching." New Mexico: New Mexico State University, 1991.

Presentation Format 8
Structured Notes

Description
Major portions of the (tele)lecture are outlined verbally with key word and phrases left out. The student's attention is focused on these keywords and phrases and they are required to write them in. This format uses very detailed outlines. The lecture is broken down into "exhibits" or "displays" which are logical segments of instruction which progress systematically to achieve the learning objectives. The exhibit or display can be used to direct the student to complete activities and exercises before and after class.
Source: Carruthers, Gary. Course entitled "Beyond Production Functions into the Wonderful World of Microeconomics. Workbook." New Mexico: New Mexico State University, 1980. (See also: Smith and Tompkins, 1988.)

BIBLIOGRAPHY

Annis, L., & Davis, J.K. (1977). The effect of preferred method of study, various study techniques and cognitive style on recall recognition. Paper presented at the annual meeting of the American Educational Research Association, NY.

Bentley, Donna Anderson. More ammunition for the note-taking feud: The spaced lecture. Improving College and University Teaching, 29(2), 85-87.

Bligh, D. (1972). What's the use of lectures. Harmondsworth: Penguin Books.

Brown, G.A., & Davis, J.M., (1981). Can explaining be learnt? Some lecturer's views. Higher Education, 10, 573-580.

Brown, George, & Tomlinson, David. (1980). How to improve handouts. Medical Teacher, 2(5), 215-220.

Carrier, Carol A. (1983). Notetaking research. Journal of Instructional Development, 6(3), 819-827.

Carter, J.F., & Van Matre, N.H. (1975). Note taking versus note having. Journal of Educational Psychology, 67, 900-904.

Christian, David, & McShane, Anne. (1988). Providing study notes: Comparison of three types of notes for review. Journal of Educational Psychology. 80(4), 595-597.

Collingwood, Vaughan, & Hughes, David C. (1978). Effects of three types of university lecture notes on student achievement. Journal of Educational Psychology, 70(2), 175-179.

Cyrs, Thomas E., & Smith, Frank A. (1990). Teleclass teaching: A resource guide (2nd ed.). NM: Center for Educational Development, New Mexico State University.

Day, Ruth S. (1980). Teaching from notes: Some cognitive consequences. New Directions for Teaching and Learning, 2, 95-113.

DuBois, Nelson F. (1986). A review of the research on notetaking from lecture: Some new directions to investigate. (ERIC Document Reproduction Service No. ED 274 896)

Fisher, J.L., & Harris, M.B. (1974). Notetaking and recall. Journal of Educational Research, 67, 291-292.

Fisher, J.L., & Harris, M.B. (1973). Effect of notetaking and review on recall. Journal of Educational Psychology, 65, 321-325.

Freyberg, P.S. The effectiveness of notetaking. Education for Teaching, 39, 17-24.

Gary, Thomas S. (1975). Use of student notes and lecture summaries as study guides for recall. (ERIC Document Reproduction Service No. ED 147 687)

Gibbs, Graham, Habeshaw, Sue, & Habeshaw, Trevor. (1987). 53 interesting things to do in your lecture. Bristol, United Kingdom: Technical and Educational Services, Limited.

Green, Thomas G., et al. (1986). The effect of structured worksheets on student performance. Journal of Dental Education, 50(10), 616-617.

Hartley, J. (1976). Lecture handouts and student notetaking. Professional Learning and Educational Technology, 13(2), 58-64.

Hartley, J., & Marshall, S. (1974). On notes and notetaking. Universities Quarterly, 28, 25-35.

Hartley, James, & Davies, Ivor K. (1978). Note-taking: A critical review. Programmed Learning and Educational Technology, 15(3), 207-224.

Hartley, James, & Trueman, Mark. (1978). Note-taking in lectures: A longitudinal study. Bulletin of the British Psychological Society, 31, 37-39.

Hohn, Robert L., et al. Instructor Supplied Notes and Higher-Order Thinking. (ERIC Document Reproduction Service No. ED 316 472)

Howe, J.J.A., & Godfrey, J. (1977). Student notetaking as an aid to learning. Exeter, England: Exeter University Teaching Services Department.

Kiewra, K.A. (1987). Notetaking and review: The research and its implications. Instructional Science.

____. (1985). Learning from a lecture: An investigation of notetaking, review and attendance at a lecture. Human Learning, 4, 73-77.

____. (1985). Students' notetaking behaviors and the efficacy of providing the instructor's notes for review. Contemporary Educational Psychology, 10, 378-386.

Klemm, W.R. (1976). Efficiency of handout 'skeleton' notes in student learning. Improving College and University Teaching, 24(1), 10-12.

Locke, E.A. An empirical study of lecture note-taking of Emory college students. Journal of Educational Research, 77, 93-99.

MacManaway, L.A. (1968), Using lecture scripts. Universities Quarterly, 327-337.

McDonald, R.J., & Taylor, E.G. (1980). Student note-taking and lecture handouts in veterinary medical education. Journal of Veterinary Medical Education, 7(3), 157-161.

McDougall, I.R., McNicol, G.P., & Gray, H.W. The effect of timing on distribution 'handouts' on improvement of student performance. British Journal of Medical Education, 6, 155-157.

Northcraft, G.B., & Jernstedt, G.C. Comparison of four teaching methodologies for large lecture classes. Psychological Reports, 36, 599-606.

Palmatier, R.A., & Bennett, J.M. (1974). Notetaking habits of college students. Journal of Reading, 18(2), 15-18.

Powers, Sandra M., & Powers, William A. Instructor-prepared notes and achievement in introductory psychology. Journal of Experimental Education.

Smith, Patricia L., & Tompkins, Gail E. (1988). Structured notetaking: A new strategy for content area readers. Journal of Reading, 46-52.

Spires, Hillary A., & Stone, Diane P. (1989). The directed notetaking activity: A self-questioning approach. Journal of Reading, 36-39.

Taylor, D.W. (1972). Students sheets improve large-group instruction. Science Teacher, 39(4), 53-54.

Weaver, Richard L. II, & Cotrell, Howard W. (1985). Mental aerobics: The half-sheet response. Human Sciences Press.

Section III

Activities after class: Assessment

Chapter 19
Constructing Valid Tests to Match Your Learning Objectives

Chapter 20
Classroom Formative Feedback Techniques

Chapter 21
Self-Assessment of Your Teaching Effectiveness

Chapter 22
Creating a Professional Teaching Portfolio

Chapter 19

Constructing Valid Tests to Match Your Learning Objectives

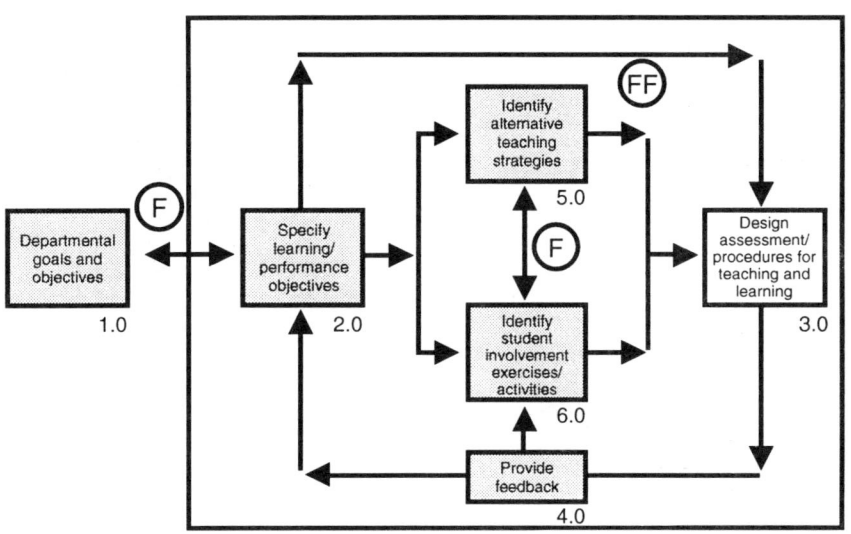

Special thanks to Alvin Kent, former Director of Media Services at Iowa State University, who originally co-authored the material in this chapter for another project.

"Students learn as they are tested."

Joint Statement on Rights and Freedoms of Students
on
Protection Against Improper Academic Evaluation
by
American Association of University Professors
U.S. National Student Association
Association of American Colleges
National Association of Student Personnel Administrators
National Association of Women Deans and Counselors

Students should have protection through orderly procedures against prejudiced or capricious academic evaluation. At the same time, they are responsible for maintaining standards of academic performance established for each course in which they are enrolled.

(Milton and Edgerly, 1976)

CONSTRUCTING VALID TESTS

LEARNING PERFORMANCE OBJECTIVES
Using the learning performance objectives from a section of your course, identify the most valid assessment procedures. Justify to the class why they were valid.

KEY IDEAS
1. All testing techniques, performance on paper and pencil, must be based on the same cognitive level as the learning performance objective and the same class of behavior to be demonstrated.
2. Criterion-referenced tests are absolute measures of performance rather than relative measures as demonstrated in norm-referenced.
3. Instruction can be qualitatively improved through testing.

NEW VOCABULARY
- valid tests and reliable tests
- criterion-referenced
- content validity
- predictive validity
- essay tests
- norm-referenced
- normal curve
- construct validity
- performance test

One of the most significant issues in education is test validity–did the test measure what it was intended to measure. A test, regardless of the type, is an instrument to systematically measure a sample of student performance. It is systematic in the way that it generates a sample of performance from a domain of performance, in methods of scoring, and in interpreting results. Performance includes skills, knowledge, and attitudes.

The selection of a test procedure must be based on the type of performance required of the student. The learning performance objectives that define specifically what the student is expected to do form the framework for the development of testing situations. The experiences that students have in the learning activities in which they engage must have a clear relationship to the objectives and tests. Furst (1958) showed this relationship graphically.

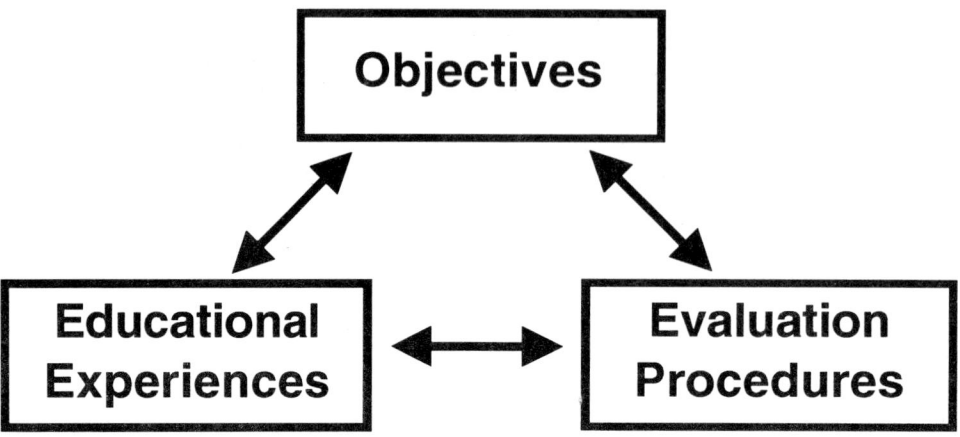

There are several purposes for classroom testing. Tests provide *summative data* for the instructor to show differences among student scores and indicate student performance against predetermined performance criteria. This can be shown as a grade or P/F. They provide *formative data* as feedback to the instructor for the purpose of improving instruction. Tests also provide *diagnostic data* for the student to indicate strengths and weaknesses in relation to mastering the learning objectives.

From the viewpoint of the student, testing serves several purposes. One is to provide feedback *during* a course to show where additional mastery is needed relative to the performance objectives. Another purpose is to motivate the student by demonstrating the degree to which the student has mastered the material.

NORM-REFERENCED TESTING

Test results can be reported as norm-referenced or as criterion-referenced.

Norm-referenced testing is the more common method. Based on the assumptions of classic parametric statistics, it uses a comparative approach in which one student's performance is compared to another in reporting data. It poses the question, "Did John do as well as Mary and Bob?" Student scores are reported at the 90th or some lower percentile compared to all other students. Norm-referenced tests are designed to maximize variance among student test scores. They promote the concept of average score distribution in which some students receive a high score, most a middle score, and a few a low score. In other words, this testing approach is designed to fail students or at least have a few score at a low level. It does not indicate what a student can, in fact, do. It only compares one student with others in the peer group. In this situation, test items are designed primarily to discriminate between high and low scores on any test. High achievement theoretically translates as "The pursuit of excellence." Low achievement indicates a lack of mastery or competence in a skill or knowledge base.

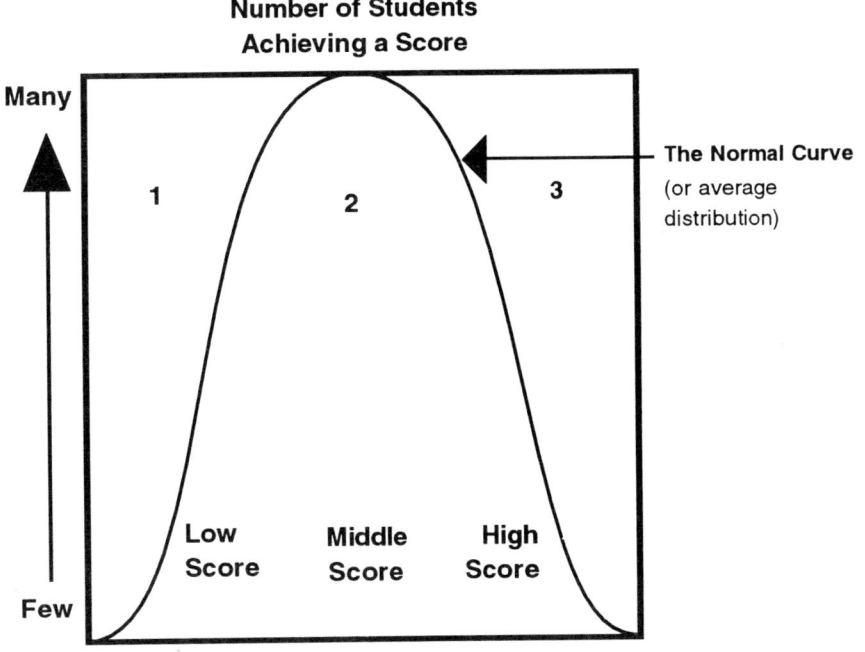

CRITERION-REFERENCED TESTING

Criterion-referenced testing is relatively new and is based on the assumption that mastery of certain performances is critical to the future success of the student. Mastery of certain skills may also have critical consequences for "safe" performance in such areas as the health professions and engineering. Criterion-referenced or mastery learning is based on the research of Carroll (1963) and Bloom (1968). Once a mastery level is determined, comparative data is useless. The most critical question posed in this approach is, *"To what degree did the student meet the required level of performance as specified in the learning performance objectives?"* This approach considers the standard of performance as the criterion against which to judge someone. Can a surgeon get a less than competent grade, a "B-," in open heart surgery or say that he or she did not learn that piece of anatomy? How would you like to fly in a plane in which the pilot got a "B" in takeoff and a "C" in landing? Would you like to cross a bridge when told that the bridge engineer received an average of "B-" in bridge-building?

Criterion-referenced tests are designed to *minimize* variance. Evaluation is based on how closely the student comes to achieving the performance objective.

The student's achievement is compared with his/her *own* progress. Test items are designed to discriminate between the student's ability or lack of ability to reach a designated level of performance. High achievement translates into virtually all students reaching a minimum level of performance.

In summary, the option for testing that is chosen will interact and reflect upon the approach to teaching. The major questions addressed in these two approaches to testing are very important. *Norm-referenced testing* asks, "What proportion of my class (or peers) learned more or less than me." *Criterion-referenced testing* asks, "How much of the specified performance has the student learned?"

TESTING AS A MEANS TO IMPROVE INSTRUCTION
Instruction can be qualitatively improved through testing. If the learning performance objectives have been stated specifically before instruction began and if they are shared with the students participating in the instruction, *test results will provide the following data:*
1. Did the test item measure the learning performance objective?
2. To what degree did the student meet the criterion level in the objective?
3. Was the instructional activity adequate to assist the student to meet the criterion level?
4. Were the sequences of the instruction adequate?
5. Did the instruction provide enough examples?

TEST VALIDITY AND RELIABILITY
When developing a test, the instructor must deal with two closely related problems. The knowledge and skills to measure must be identified. This is called validity, which is the extent to which a test measures what it is supposed to measure. The second problem deals with constructing the most dependable means to measure the performance. This is called reliability, which is the degree to which performance, as shown in the test score, remains consistent when the test is taken repeatedly. A test cannot be valid unless it is also reliable. However, the reverse is not necessarily true. Test validity is a function of reliability. Test reliability is not a function of validity. Test validity addresses the question, "Are the items in a test specific to the task(s) they are expected to measure?" Four types of validity can be checked in relation to this question and its answer:
1. *Content Validity.* Which tasks or objectives do the test items represent and how close is this representation?
2. *Concurrent Validity.* With what other present observations of the students' performance do the tests scores agree and to what degree do they agree?
3. *Predictive Validity.* What kinds of future performance can be predicted by the test scores and how accurate is this prediction?
4. *Construct Validity.* This is the most theoretical type of validity and asks what other psychological features account for some degree of the test or performance.

Validity is not something "in the test." It is a bridge between learning and the quality of performance the test is expected to demonstrate.

PLANNING YOUR TEST
Before writing the actual test items, the instructor must develop a "blue print" for assigning the number of items to adequately test achievement of the learning performance objectives and the mastery of the course content.

The following chart is based on Bloom's Taxonomy (Bloom, 1956) and proposes a model for developing a test blueprint. Such a blueprint is the tool an instructor should use to build *balance*, or appropriate representation of all learning tasks into the test. Assigning the number items under the objectives to be achieved for each unit of course content represents their relative weight or importance in evaluating a student's overall performance.

EXAMPLE OF A FINAL EXAM BLUEPRINT

Objective Course Content	Define or State Concepts and Principles	Recognize Correct or Incorrect Applications of Concepts and Principles	Apply Principles to Solve a Given Problem	Analyze a Problem and Solve It	TOTAL ITEMS
1. Meeting the patient's needs	1				1
2. The nature of illness	2	1			3
3. Mental health and mental illness	2	1	4	3	10
4. The patient in surgery	3	3	3	5	14
5. Emergency and first aid	1	3	3	4	11
6. The older adult and dying patient	2	2	5	2	11
7. The critically ill and dying patient	4	2	6	6	18
8. Maternal health care	2	2	6	4	14
9. Child health care	2	2	3	5	12
10. Legal aspects of nursing	1	1	2	2	6
TOTAL ITEMS	20	17	32	31	100

MATCHING TEST ITEMS TO LEARNING PERFORMANCE OBJECTIVES

Performance objectives describe student performance in measurable language that specifies *what* is to be done; *how* it is to be done; and *when* it is satisfactorily done. Student assessment procedures (criterion tests) should be designed to measure the performance described in the performance objectives (Cyrs, 1987). These *criterion tests* are developed to reflect the circumstances of assessment described in the performance objective and allow us to judge when the student has performed satisfactorily or competently. The type of test will depend on the type of behavior described in the learning performance objective.

A procedure for writing criterion test items from learning performance objectives consists of ten steps:
1. Read the performance objectives carefully and note the specific behavior that the student is required to exhibit. Is further clarification necessary?
2. Is this behavior primarily cognitive, attitudinal, or manual?
3. If cognitive, does it require only memorization or a higher level of intellectual skill?
4. Is the objective content specific or content general?
5. Does the action call for the student to select an appropriate answer from several provided, as in multiple-choice, or does the student have to recall and write out the answer, as in essay or fill-in?

6. If the student is asked to remember and write out the answer, will a few words suffice or will the student have to write several paragraphs or a complete essay?
7. Are adequate criteria specified to judge the successful performance of this behavior?
8. Will the expected performance require interaction with other students or instructors?
9. Will the assessment of this objective require performance or will paper and pencil methods suffice?
10. Have all alternative assessment methods that would validly measure this objective been identified?

EXAMPLES OF PERFORMANCE OBJECTIVES DERIVED FROM STATEMENTS OF SUBJECT MATTER

Given statements of subject matter, it is possible to specify learning performance objectives at different intellectual skill levels.

PERFORMANCE OBJECTIVE	Explain the role of hormones vital to body functions.
INTELLECTUAL LEVEL	Comprehension. The student paraphrases the information provided.
SUBJECT MATTER	Insulin has three basic effects on carbohydrate metabolism.

PERFORMANCE OBJECTIVE	Describe how to administer prescribed medications to patients under hospital care.
INTELLECTUAL LEVEL	Comprehension. The student paraphrases information.
SUBJECT MATTER	Insulin prepared in a suspension should be rolled gently between the palms of the hands to mix, since shaking will form bubbles and result in inaccurate doses of the medication.

PERFORMANCE OBJECTIVE	Given specific treatments in medical-surgical situations, predict possible consequences.
INTELLECTUAL LEVEL	Application. The student must apply previous knowledge to new and unfamiliar situations.
SUBJECT MATTER	In treatment of pneumonia, prolonged use of oxygen at high concentration may cause a fibrosis of lung tissue, impairing the ability to expand.

PERFORMANCE OBJECTIVE	Given a disease, identify the symptoms.
INTELLECTUAL LEVEL	Comprehension. The student recalls information and paraphrases it. If the objective was, "Given the symptoms, identify the disease," students would work at the critical analysis level, evaluating and deciding which procedures and information to apply.
SUBJECT MATTER	Symptoms of hyperthyroidism include nervousness, apprehension, and irritability. The patient seems to be in constant motion–turning, twisting–and excessively concerned about things. The patient will have a rapid pulse even when at rest. Although the patient may have an increased appetite, there will be progressive weight loss due to the abnormal activity.

TYPES OF TESTS

There are two major classes of tests, which include performance tests and paper and pencil tests.

PERFORMANCE TESTS
Performance tests require the student to perform an actual task under simulated or real world conditions. The test utilizes rating or observation scales and assessment center methodology.

PAPER AND PENCIL TESTS: Essay Tests
Paper and pencil tests are either essay or objective. An essay test is occasionally called a discussion type test. The student responds to a question using his/her own words to express conclusions and the reasons for reaching them. During an objective test a statement is presented or a question is posed. The student must either select the correct response from a number of plausible alternative answers that are provided, or supply an answer limited to one word or short phrases.

Many instructors prefer the essay test because of its apparent ease of preparation relative to a 50- to 75-item multiple-choice test.

There are a number of advantages to an essay test. Many faculty feel that they are easy to prepare and administer. Essays support the development of expressive writing skills for the student as they prepare their answers. The essay can test a very wide range of cognitive skills, such as critical thinking, as well as allow the student to express feelings and emotions.

Countering these apparent advantages, there are a number of significant disadvantages. This test is very unreliable and subject to scoring bias. It is tedious and difficult to score accurately and it will require more time to grade. Articulate students usually score higher because of their excellent writing skills.

If the purpose of the essay is recall of factual information, it is not efficient or desirable. It is best used for the expression of critical thinking skills.

If an instructor decides to use essay questions, there are a number of guidelines that will be of benefit.

SUGGESTED GUIDELINES FOR THE ESSAY TEST
1. Select questions to sample a broad range of cognitive and affective objectives and content.
2. Require that all opinions be supported with data.
3. Be sure that students have well-developed writing skills.
4. Guide the student toward the desired response rather than using very general, open-ended questions.
5. Suggest the number of points the question is given and the recommend amount of time that should be spent.
6. Develop a *criterion checklist* against which the instructor will evaluate the test question:
   a. Cite how the answer should be organized;
   b. Determine how many points for writing skill as well as completeness of the answer;
   c. Determine key elements that should be covered in the answer and the number of points assigned to each element;
   d. Determine if spelling and grammar are important and how many points will be assigned;

e. Require the student to answer each question rather than provide a choice of questions since this will lessen reliability.
7. Problem-oriented and simulation questions lend themselves to this type of test.
8. Tuckman (1975) suggests that an essay test have a center structure:
    a. Statement of the situation,
    b. Statement of the problem,
    c. Response instructions.

BASIC SCORING TECHNIQUES

Scoring the essay test is always a tedious task but can be made simple and more reliable if:
1. Use an answer key or criterion check list.
2. Score the answers *question by question,* rather than student by student in a single sitting.
3. Conceal the identity of the student whose answer is being scored.
4. Writing style should not be confused with content.
5. Ask a colleague to rate a sample of the answers using the answer key.
6. Provide useful and constructive feedback on the answer.

TWO SCORING METHODS FOR EACH ESSAY ITEM

A. COMPONENT SCORING
   1. Using the criterion check list, identify significant points on each student's essay based on your ideal answer. *Assign a positive value.*
   2. Using the same criterion check list, identify inaccuracies and irrelevant points. *Assign a positive value.*
   3. Analyze the overall organizational structure of the answer and identify the student's ability to integrate the most significant points. *Assign a positive value.*
   4. Construct written comments to each student concerning the assessment of his/her response. *Assign a positive or negative value.*
   5. Total the positive and negative values for each item. *Record student score.*

B. COMPARATIVE QUALITY SCORING
   1. Quickly read each student answer.
   2. Sort answers into piles representing high, middle, and low quality.
   3. Carefully review each set of answers in their respective piles.
   4. Using an answering key or criterion check list, shift deserving answers into a more appropriate pile.
   5. Score each pile from highest to lowest quality.

PAPER AND PENCIL: Multiple-Choice Tests

One of the most popular and frequently used forms of paper and pencil test formats is the multiple-choice form. Although it appears fairly easy to develop, this is very deceiving. Multiple-choice tests are difficult and time-consuming if they deal with intellectual skills above simple recall and comprehension. There are several advantages to a multiple-choice test. Students can be tested on a large sample of the course content in a relatively short period of time. They are quick and efficient to score by hand using an answer key but machine processing is usually available in the computer center. The test items can measure a wide range of intellectual skills from recall of factual data, understanding, application, and critical thinking. Guessing is reduced to one in five as opposed to a 50/50 chance in true/false items.

A disadvantage of multiple-choice tests is the difficulty of constructing them with good distractors. There is too often a great deal of ambiguity in the choice of the correct answer.

All multiple-choice items have three main parts. These include the stem (statement or question), which begins the multiple-choice item; the distractors (incorrect responses which usually number three); and the last part is the correct response.

GUIDELINES

If you choose to construct multiple-choice test items, there are a number of guidelines that will be beneficial to you. Grammatical form should be consistent in each of the distractors and the correct answer. Inconsistency could provide unnecessary cues to the students. The length of the responses must be consistent. Match each test item to the performance objective it is designed to evaluate in order to maintain validity. Write reasonable distractors that are within the comprehension of the students. Try to avoid unnecessary jargon unless it was covered during class. Avoid obvious clues in the stem which are repeated in the distractors. Use either four or five distractors and avoid the use of negative statements in the stem or response. Limit the use of the "keyed response" such as "all of the above" or "none of the above."

SAMPLES OF DIFFERENT TYPES OF MULTIPLE-CHOICE ITEMS

DESCRIPTIVE vs. LABEL RESPONSES
   The term distal means
   A. Nearest the origin of a structure
   B. Farthest from the origin of a structure
   C. Nearest the midline of a structure
   D. Farthest from the midline of a structure

   An increase in the overall size of a tissue or organ is
   A. Atrophy
   B. Extrophy
   C. Hypertrophy
   D. Dystrophy

NEGATIVE STEM
　　It is not a function of the cerebellum to
　　　A. Regulate body temperature
　　　B. Maintain body balance
　　　C. Coordinate working of muscles
　　　D. Aid in maintaining muscle tone

BEST ANSWER
　　A reflex is best described as
　　　A. The response one gets from tapping the kneecap
　　　B. A sign of meningeal irritation
　　　C. An involuntary muscular contraction in response to a stimulus
　　　D. A voluntary movement of the skeletal muscle

INTRODUCTORY SENTENCE
　　A patient is admitted for an exploratory laparotomy. The surgical preparation would include shaving
　　　A. From the nipple line to the perineum
　　　B. The perineal area
　　　C. From the umbilicus to the perineum
　　　D. From the scapular area to the perineum

REPETITIOUS
　　Which is the best definition of a vein?
　　　A. A blood vessel carrying blood going to the heart
　　　B. A blood vessel carrying blue blood
　　　C. A blood vessel caring impure blood
　　　D. A blood vessel carrying blood away from the heart

CASE STUDY APPROACH
　　Ms. Andrews, age 21, is admitted to the hospital with a history of general malaise, nausea, vomiting, and evidence of jaundice. The admitting diagnosis is infectious hepatitis.
　　Hepatitis is an inflammation of the
　　　A. Gall bladder
　　　B. Liver
　　　C. Small intestine
　　　D. Stomach

PAPER/PENCIL TESTS: True/False Items

The true/false test item is somewhat similar to a multiple-choice item. The true/false item is a two-choice test item.

　　The advantages of the true/false test item includes the ease of construction as well as the ease of scoring by hand, with an answer key, or by computer. This type of test item allows for the fastest student response and can cover a broad range of subject matter. True/false items can form the basis for a future pool of multiple-choice items.

An obvious disadvantage is the susceptibility to guessing with a 50% chance for a correct response. Unfortunately, the ease of preparation leads to an overabundance of low level recall items that are often very ambiguous. If used exclusively they will overly influence students to learn lower level skills.

Well-constructed true/false test items can measure knowledge at a variety of levels.

COGNITIVE LEVEL		SAMPLE TRUE/FALSE TEST ITEMS
FACT	(T)	Hodgkin's disease is characterized by an increase in the size of lymph nodes.
EXPLANATION	(F)	A paralyzed patient must be watched very carefully for evidence of pressure sores, since nourishment to the area is decreased.
COMPUTATION	(T)	In order to convert a Fahrenheit reading to a centigrade reading you would subtract 32 from the Fahrenheit reading and multiply the fraction by 5/9.
APPLICATION	(F)	In taking blood pressure, you must take the systolic reading at the point where the sound stops.
ANALYSIS	(T)	Signs of increased intercranial pressure are indicated by vomiting, elevated blood pressure, slowing of pulse, slowing of respirations, and unequal pupils.
JUDGMENT	(F)	It is better for the nurse to have children of her own if she expects to have an adequate understanding of the sick child.

THE ARGUMENT FOR TRUE/FALSE TESTS
The basis for educational achievement is the command of useful verbal knowledge. All verbal knowledge can be expressed in true or false verbal propositions or sentences. The extent of a person's command of a particular area of knowledge is indicated by his/her success in determining the truth or falseness of related propositions. Having command of knowledge means one can use it to make decisions, draw logical inferences, or solve problems. It is knowledge that is available for use. True/false tests reflect usable knowledge.

HOW TO PREPARE EFFECTIVE ITEMS

1. Locate sources presenting bits of special knowledge: paragraphs, written procedures, etc.

Paragraph:
"One of the effects of digitalis is to make the heart beat slower. Therefore, the nurse must always check the pulse and if the rate is below 60, should withhold the medication until she notifies the physician."

2. Derive a proposition on which to base test items.

Proposition:
Digitalis must not be administered by the nurse to the patient if the pulse rate is below 60.

3. Restate the original idea in different words: the true and false versions are written in pairs. The false item is a contradiction that is worded to sound plausible.

Items:
(T) In giving digitalis the nurse must always take and record the pulse.
(F) In giving digitalis the nurse must always take and record the blood pressure.

4. Interpret the basic idea in terms of another one similar to the original.

More items:
(T) A patient is given digitalis to slow the heart rate.
(F) A patient is given digitalis to increase the heart rate.

OR

5. Develop another way of looking at the basic idea: true and false version. If possible, create novel situations to exemplify the proposition.

More items:
(T) If a patient does not exhibit signs of bradycardia, the nurse will administer the prescribed amount of digitalis.
(F) The nurse will administer the prescribed amount of digitalis only when the patient exhibits signs of bradycardia.

CHARACTERISTICS OF GOOD TRUE/FALSE ITEM

Good true/false test items are based on an important idea rather than trivia. They test more understanding than rote memory. The correct answer is defensible and not ambiguous. The wrong answer would seem reasonable to someone who does not possess the appropriate knowledge. The test item is based on a single idea that is concise and clearly expressed.

CHECKPOINTS TO OBSERVE WHEN WRITING A TRUE/FALSE TEST ITEM
- Use more false statements (perhaps two false to one true).
- Minimize use of inadvertent clues that may be used by the test-wise student.
- Use phrases in false statements that give them the impression of truth.
- Write the content or statement in both true and false version.
- Avoid vague terms.
- Avoid qualified statements such as "often," "occasionally," "never," "may," or "generally."
- Make all items approximately the same length to avoid giving student cues that one type may be longer or shorter.
- Avoid tricky questions.
- True/false items are dependent on a variety of sentence forms.
- Testing at an appropriate level of achievement, in large part, is related to the sentence form.

The following chart may be used as a guide in selecting some of the key introductory words or phrases to be used in items testing various aspects of learning. Obviously, there are slight variations possible with words or phrases, as well as others appropriate to a particular aspect of learning. Since all objective items rely on command of knowledge that is essentially verbal, the chart is useful for other types of tests as well.

PERFORMANCE TASK	INTRODUCTORY WORDS OR PHRASES
RECALLING FACTS	Any declarative statement.
GENERALIZING	All… Most… Many…
COMPARING	The difference between… Both…
INFERRING	If… When…
RELATING	The larger… The higher… The lower… Making… is likely to… Increasing… tends to… How much… depends on…
EXPLAINING	The main reason… is to… The purpose of… is to…
EXEMPLIFYING	An example of…
ANALYZING	Observing… reveals that… Studying… indicates that…
PREDICTING	One could expect that…
APPLYING	To… one must… In order to… one must use… One method of… is to… One essential step… is to… The first step…
COMPUTING	Item includes numbers and requires computation or estimation.
EVALUATING	A good… It is better to… than… The best proportion… The maximum variability… The easiest method… is to… While easy to… it is not… It is difficult to… It is possible… It is reasonable…

PAPER AND PENCIL TESTS: Completion or Short Answer Items

The completion item requires the student to fill in a short answer with his/her own words. Described as a constructed response test, it is a derivative of the multiple-choice test item.

Stem: The parasympathetic nervous system is part of the_____
Answer: autonomic nervous system.

The stem can be presented as an incomplete sentence as in the above example or in the form of a question:
Stem: Which part of the brain controls body temperature?_____

EXAMPLES

CALLED FILL-IN OR SHORT ANSWER ITEMS
Stem: Blood pumped from the left ventricle flows through the _____.
Answer: aortic valve.

GIVEN THE STEM, PARTIAL STATEMENTS, QUESTIONS, OR TERMS
Stem: If a patient is unable to lift his hips to get onto the bed pan, what should the nurse do?
Answer: Roll the patient on his side, put the bed pan in place, and roll the patient back on it.

THE STUDENT SUPPLIES A TERM, PHRASE, NUMBER, OR OTHER SYMBOL
Stem: The peak effect of insulin is reached in _____ hours.

ANY COMBINATION OF STEM AND ANSWER.
The student in each case is required to recall the response that the instructor has predetermined as correct. These test items should always be preceded with specific directions:

EXAMPLE
On the blank following each of the questions, partial statements, or words, you are to write the word, short phrase, or number that seems most appropriate.

If the answer is too obviously cued in a multiple-choice (or selected response) test item, then a completion or short answer item may be preferred.
Compare the two previous examples of completion items with their multiple-choice versions below.

The parasympathetic nervous system is part of the
   A. central nervous system
   B. autonomic nervous system
   C. sympathetic nervous system
   D. all of the above

Body temperature is controlled by
   A. thalamus
   B. thyroid
   C. hypothalamus
   D. none of the above

ADVANTAGES
- Easy to write certain items.
- Student must recall the answer (more apparent than real)

DISADVANTAGES
- Limited to questions that can be answered with a word, phrase, or symbol.
- Scoring tends to be tedious and subjective.
- Difficult to write items requiring short, sometimes specific answers that test higher learning levels.

GUIDELINES
1. Allow sufficient space for the student response.
2. Keep all response blanks of equal length to avoid cuing.
3. A question format is often more desirable than a statement completion. The grammatical style of the latter could influence the choice of answer.

PAPER AND PENCIL TESTS: The Matching Item
Matching items can measure a range of behavior but are most commonly used to measure recall behavior. A matching test consists of a set of "stems" or "questions" on the left hand side to which a set of responses on the right hand side are matched by the student.

ADVANTAGES
- Fairly easy to prepare.
- Efficient in the respect that the same set of responses can be used with several similar "stems."

DISADVANTAGES
- Difficult to measure higher levels of learning.
- Usually too many tricky questions.

GUIDELINES FOR EFFECTIVE MATCHING ITEM CONSTRUCTION
1. Keep the style and content of the stem and response columns homogeneous. It is preferable to use short responses of even length to avoid unnecessary clues.
2. Limit the number of stems from six to ten. Additional matches introduce fatigue and confusion to the matching process.

EXAMPLES OF MATCHING TEST ITEMS
Match the developmental phase with the appropriate chronological period of a person's life:

1. Oedipal		a.	0-1 year
2. Maturity		b.	1-3 years
3. Oral		c.	3-6 years
4. Adolescence		d.	6-12 years
5. Latency		e.	12-21 years
6. Anal		f.	21 years
		g.	35 years

For each term in Column A (premises), select the statement in Column B (responses that best define the terms in Column A). Mark your answer on the appropriate line in Column A. There is only one correct definition for each term.

A	B
____ 1. Split-half reliability.	a. An estimate of the degree of correlation between alternate forms of a test.
____ 2. Coefficient of stability.	b. An estimate of the relationship between two measures of the same person.
____ 3. Coefficient of equivalence.	c. A measure of the internal consistency of test results.
____ 4. Concurrent validity.	d. An estimate of the correlation between the results of two different measures obtained at the same time.
____ 5. Predictive validity.	e. An estimate of the correlation between the results of some measure and the results of some criterion of measure obtained at a later date.

ANSWERS TO THE EXAMPLES ABOVE
1. c   2. g   3. a   4. d   5. e

In the following items you are to designate the time period during which a particular sign or symptom of pregnancy can best be used. For each item, place an "X" in the answer space.

A. 1-3 months
B. 4-6 months
C. 7-10 months

	A	B	C
17. Colostrum expressed	___	___	___
18. Male	___	___	___
19. Goodell's sign	___	___	___
20. Braxton Hicks contractions	___	___	___
21. Cervical mucus positive fern	___	___	___
22. Ballottement	___	___	___
23. Leaking colostrum	___	___	___

Directions: On the blank before the name of each disease place the letter that precedes the medication for which the disease is known to respond best.

Disease	Medication
____ 1. Parkinson'	a. atropine
____ 2. Addison'	b. levodope
____ 3. Multiple Sclerosis	c. corticoid preparation
	d. unknown

FINAL TESTING CONSIDERATIONS

Regardless of the type or form of test that you have chosen, each item should be based on a stated learning performance objective to improve the test validity. In

constructing a test the instructor should make every effort to reduce test error. Toward this end several guidelines are suggested:
1. Advise the students in advance which test format will be used.
2. Before the test inform the students which learning performance objectives and content areas will be covered.
3. Review the grading policy and value of each test as it relates to the final grade.
4. Arrange several of the easiest items at the beginning of the test to reduce anxiety.
5. Arrange all test items in random order.
6. Make test instructions specific and explicit.
7. If possible, have a colleague check the test items for ambiguity.

ALTERNATIVE STUDENT ASSESSMENT PROCEDURES

Paper and pencil testing has traditionally taken the forms of the test types just described. From the perspective of teaching faculty, these appear to be safest. However, there are a number of other student assessment techniques that deserve consideration.

Open Book Examinations • This type of assessment procedure allows the student to use any references available, including the textbook, class notes, and handouts. Rather than memorizing a lot of material, the instructor wants the students to apply skills by using formulas, tables, graphs, and so forth. The emphasis is on application of essential skills rather than memory and restatement of data. This technique tends to reduce student anxiety. The research indicates that there is no clear benefit in achievement of learning outcomes (Boniface 1985).

One variation of the open book test is to allow the student to use crib sheets or provide them with the essential formulas, tables, or graphs, without the benefit of the open book.

Some instructors combine the open book with the standard classroom test.

Take-Home Examinations • These allow the student to take the examination home to complete within a prescribed time period. The student is expected to synthesize a lot of background reading, use references, and produce a logical summary to the assignment. This type of exam is useful when there is a great deal of writing required on the part of the student. Using this format, the student can explore much broader implications of an issue, since more time is available for reflection and bridge-building of ideas. To be fair to all students, the instructor should specify the amount of time that should be spent on each answer and the number of pages expected. Grading on this type of examination must be based on specific criteria that are shared with the students before they take the examination. The take-home examination can be combined with the in-class test.

Oral Examinations • Usually used at the graduate level, they are rarely used for undergraduate testing. To be absolutely objective, there should be more than one instructor administering an oral exam. They are time-consuming to give and difficult to grade. The oral exam creates undue stress and anxiety on the part of the students, who must "think on their feet." Most students have not been trained on how to take an oral examination and are easily intimidated, since it is very difficult to bluff or guess. If this exam format is used with a number of students, the instructor should use a prepared list of questions that are asked of all the students. Students should be informed in advance of the test exactly what is expected and any time parameters under which they must respond.

Mastery Testing • This approach allows the student to repeat a different form of the test a number of times. It is widely used in the teaching strategy known as the Keller Plan or Personalized System of Instruction. A large bank of test items is required for the alternative tests, which must be equivalent in difficulty level. Most students are required to retake the test within three to five days of the original testing.

Collaborative Testing • A small group of students, usually three to five, consult with each other during the test. Although they question and teach each other, they must turn in individual answer sheets. This type of participatory testing still requires individual accountability on the part of each student. Questions must be formatted at the critical thinking or application level of thinking. Knowledge and simple comprehension questions are inappropriate since these have only one correct response.

Paired Testing • This is a form of collaborative testing using pairs of students.

Performance Testing • Students must not only know and understand a procedure, they must apply it in front of the instructor, who assesses the processes used by the students as well as the final product. The instructor must have available a set of prespecified performance criteria that matches the learning performance objectives. These are shared with and explained to the student prior to assessment time. The performance criteria are usually in the form of lists or rating scales. Lists require the instructor to determine a yes-no check as to the presence or absence of a skill. Rating scales, on the other hand, allow the instructor to specify the degree of accuracy on a continuous scale.

Journal • This is a cross between a student notebook and a writer's diary (Stanley 1991). The students record their reactions to reading assignments as well as class sessions. They identify ideas and connections among ideas that they have trouble understanding. They list questions they have and speculations about the material. The students are required to reflect on and think about the material they are studying. The journal can be kept outside of class or the instructor can provide the last five minutes of each class period for the students to make journal entries. Journals are collected periodically and returned with comments from the instructor.

The instructor needs to provide specific criteria that will be used to judge the journal entries.

Some instructors have provided evaluative criteria for students or had the students generate their own criteria for peer review. In some instances, the instructors have had the students grade their own journals.

Portfolio • A student portfolio is defined as "a purposeful collection of student work that tells the story of the student's efforts, progress, or achievement in a given area" (Arter and Spandel 1992). The portfolio, kept by the student, provides a sample of the student's work and progress toward the learning performance objectives. The portfolio provides a sample of the best work of the student. It can contain poetry, papers, artifacts, videos of performance in theatre or music, speeches, artwork, musical compositions, and so forth. The portfolio is collected at mid-term and again at the completion of the course for evaluation and comment by the instructor. Portfolios should always be returned to the student.

BIBLIOGRAPHY

Airsaian, Peter W. (1971). The role of evaluation in mastery learning. In James H. Block (Ed.), Mastery learning theory and practice. Holt, Rinehart and Winston.

Anastasi, Anne. (1982). Psychological testing (5th ed.). NY: Macmillan Publishing Co.

Anderson, S.B. (1987). The role of the teacher-made test in higher education. In D. Bray and M. Belcher (Eds.), Issues in student assessment. New Directions for Community Colleges, 59. San Francisco: Jossey-Bass Publishers.

Arter, J.A., & Spandel, V. (1992). Using portfolios of student work in instruction and assessment. Educational measurement: Issues and practices, 11(1), 36-44.

Becker, H.S., Geer, B., & Hughes, E.C. (1968). Making the grade: The academic side of college. NY: Wiley.

Bennett, R., Rock, D., & Wang, M. (1991). Equivalence of free-response and multiple-choice items. Journal of Educational Measurement, 28, 77-92.

Ben-Shakhar, G., & Sinai, Y. (1991). Gender differences in multiple-choice tests: The role of differential guessing tendencies. Journal of Educational Measurement, 28(1), 23-25..

Bergman, Jerry. (1981). Understanding educational measurement and evaluation. Boston: Houghton-Miffin Company.

Bloom, Benjamin S. (1968). Learning for mastery. Evaluation Comment. UCLA, CSEIP.

Bloom, Benjamin S. (Ed.). (1956). Taxonomy of educational objectives, handbook 1: Cognitive domain. NY: David McKay Company, Inc.

Bloom, Benjamin S., Hastings, T., & Madaus, G.F. (1971). Handbook on formative and summative evaluation of student learning. NY: McGraw Hill.

Boniface, D. (1985). Candidates' use of notes and textbooks during an open-book examination. Educational Research, 27, 201-209.

Brown, Frederick G. (1970). Principles of educational and psychological testing. IL: Dryden Press.

Buchanan, R.W., & Rogers, M. (1990). Innovative assessment in large classes, College Teaching, 38(2), 69-73.

Burke, R. (1969). Self-evaluations and peer ratings. Journal of Educational Research, 62, 444-448.

Carroll, John B. (1963). A model of school learning. Teachers College Record, 64, 723-733.

Carter, K. (1986). Test-wiseness for teachers and students. Educational Measurement Issues and Practice, 5, 20-23.

Cates, W.M. (1984). Retesting: A logical alternative in college instruction. Improving College and University Teaching, 32, 99-103.

Chase, C.I. (1979). Impact of achievement expectations and handwriting quality on scoring essay tests. Journal of Educational Measurement, 16, 39-42.

Copperud, Carol. (1979). The test design handbook. NJ: Educational Technology Publications.

Crooks, T.J. (1988). The impact of classroom evaluation practices on students. Review of Educational Research, 58, 438-481.

Cyrs, Thomas E., & Kent, Alvin. (1978). Assessing student performance: Improving your testing ability. Minneapolis: Educational Development Associates.

Daly, J.D., & Dickson-Markman, F. (1982). Contrast effects in evaluating essays. *Journal of Educational Measurement, 19*, 309-316.

Dodd, D.K., & Leal, L. (1988). Answer justification: Removing the trick from multi-choice questions. *Teaching of Psychology, 15*, 37-38.

Dure, B. (1990). Letter grading gets an F. *U: The National College Newspaper*, 12.

Ebel, R.L. (1975. Can teachers write good true-false test items? *Journal of Educational Measurement, 12*, 31-36.

____. (1972). *Essentials of educational measurement*. Englewood Cliffs, NJ: Prentice-Hall.

____. (1967). Measurement and the teacher. In J.T. Flynn & H. Garber, *Assessing behavior*. Reading, MA: Addison-Wesley

Educational Testing Service. (1973). *Making the classroom test*. Princeton: Educational Testing Service.

____. (1973). *Multiple choice questions*. Princeton: Educational Testing Service.

Emrick, J.A. (1971). An evaluation model for mastery testing. *Journal of Educational Measurement, 8*, 321-326.

Falchikov, N., & Boud, D. (1989). Student self-assessment in higher education: A meta-analysis. *Review of educational research, 59*, 395-430.

Findlayson, D.S. (1951). The reliability of marking of essays. *Journal of Educational Psychology, 21*, 126-134.

Flynn, J.T., & Garber, H. (Eds.). (1967). *Assessing behavior*. Reading, MA: Addison-Wesley.

Frisbie, D.A. (1974). Multiple-choice and true-false: A comparison of reliability and concurrent validity. *Journal of Educational Measurement, 10*, 297-304.

Furst, Edward J. (1958). *Constructing evaluation instruments*. NY: Longmans.

Glaser, G.R. (1963). Instructional technology and the measurement of learning outcomes. *American Psychologist, 18*, 519-521.

Gorow, F.F. (1966). *Better classroom testing*. San Francisco: Chandler.

Green, J.A. (1975). *Teacher-made tests* (2nd ed.). NY: Harper & Row.

Gronlund, N.E. (1977). *Constructing achievement tests*. Englewood Cliffs, NJ: Prentice-Hall.

____. (1973). *Preparing criterion-referenced tests for classroom instruction*. NY: Macmillan Publishing Co.

Grussing, Paul G. (1978). Preparing classroom tests. In Thomas E. Cyrs (Ed.), *Handbook for the design of instruction in pharmacy education*, (F1-F24). MD: American Association of Colleges of Pharmacy.

Hanna, G.S., & Cashin, W.E. (1988). *Improving college grading*. Idea Paper no. 19. Manhattan: Center for Faculty Evaluation and Development, Kansas State University.

Hendrickson, J.M., Brady, M.P., & Algozzine, B. (1987). Peer-mediated testing: The effects of an alternative testing procedure in higher education. *Educational and Psychological Research*, 91-101.

Kriewall, T.E. (1972). *Aspects and applications of criterion-referenced tests*. Downers Grove, IL: Institute for Educational Research. (ERIC Document Reproduction Service No. Ed 063 333)

Jacobs, Lucy Chester, & Chase, Clinton I. (1992). *Developing and using tests effectively*. San Francisco: Jossey-Bass Publishers.

Kryspin, W.J., & Feldhusen, J.F. (1974). Developing classroom tests. Minneapolis: Burgess Publishing Co.

Lindeman, R.H. (1967). Educational measurement. Glenview, IL: Scott, Foresman and Co.

Livingston S.A. (1970). The reliability of criterion-referenced measures. Report No. 73 Baltimore: The Center for the Study of Social Organization of Schools, Johns Hopkins University.

Mehrens, William A., & Lehmann, Irvin J. (1973). Measurement and evaluation in education and psychology. NY: Holt, Rinehart and Winston.

Meskauskas, John A. (1976). Evaluation models for criterion-referenced testing: Views regarding mastery and standard setting. Review of Educational Research, 46, 133-158.

Milton, O. (1982). Will that be on the final? Springfield, IL: Thomas.

Milton, Ohmer, & Edgerly, John W. (1976). The testing and grading of students. Change Magazine and Educational Change, 55.

Milton, O., Pollio, H.R., & Eison, J.A. (1986). Making sense of college grades: Why the grading system does not work and what can be done about it. San Francisco: Jossey-Bass Publishers.

Nedelsky, L. (1954). Absolute grading standards for objective tests. Educational and Psychological Measurement, 14, 3-19.

Osterling, S.J. (1989). Constructing test items. Boston: Kluwer Academic.

Sahadeo, D., & Davis, W.E. (1988). Review—Don't repeat. College Teaching, 36(3), 111-113.

Stanley, L.C. (1991). Writing-to-learn assignments: The journal and the microtheme. In L.C. Stanley & J. Ambron (Eds.), Writing across the curriculum in community colleges. New Directions for Community Colleges, no. 73. San Francisco: Jossey-Bass Publishers.

TenBrink, Terry D. (1974). Evaluation, a practical guide for teachers. NY: McGraw-Hill.

Tuckman, Bruce W. (1975). Measuring educational outcomes: Fundamentals of testing. NY: Harcourt Brace, Jovanovich, Inc., 104.

Wesman, A.G. (1971). Writing the test item. In R.C. Thorndike (Ed.), Educational measurement. Washington, DC: American Council on Education.

Chapter 20

Classroom Formative Feedback Techniques

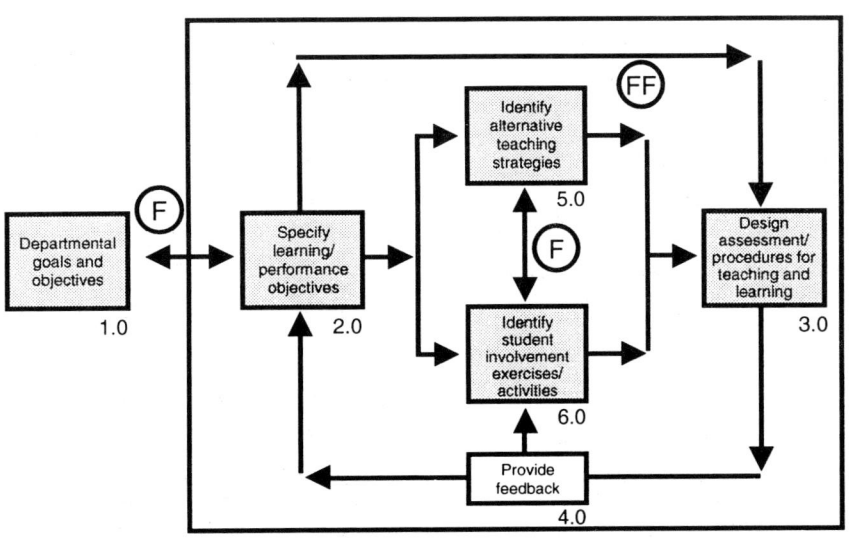

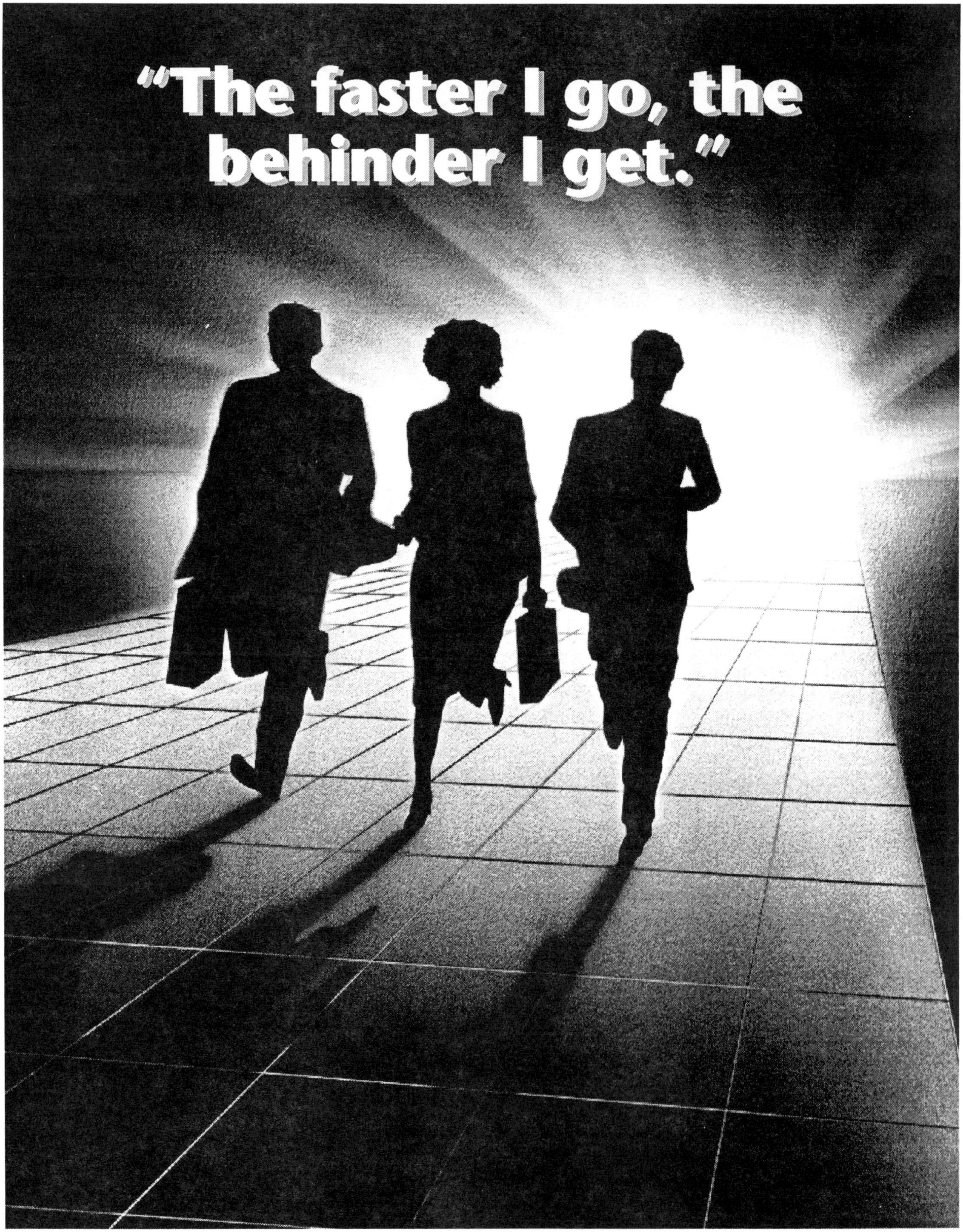
"The faster I go, the
behinder I get."

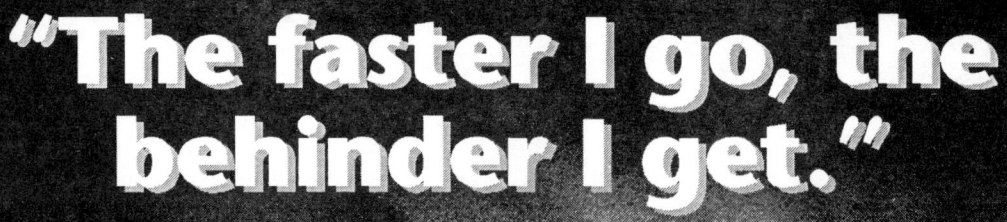

CLASSROOM FORMATIVE FEEDBACK TECHNIQUES

LEARNING PERFORMANCE OBJECTIVES
Develop a "one minute feedback" form and use it with a class. After review of the results, share them with the students and colleagues. (Level 4).

KEY POINTS
1. Intermediate checkups of teaching effectiveness provide formative feedback for teaching improvement.
2. The "one minute feedback" is a quick, easy, inexpensive, and effective feedback mechanism that can be used frequently during a course.

NEW VOCABULARY
- self-assessment
- one-minute feedback

Self-assessment is the basis of classroom formative feedback techniques. It provides information from students about the effectiveness of the instructor, the instructional strategies used, and the overall classroom environment. The students are asked to provide data to the instructor during the course anonymously, without fear or concern about retribution.

Angelo (1991) defines classroom formative feedback as "...small-scale assessments conducted continuously in college classrooms by discipline-based teachers to determine what students are learning in that class."

The primary purpose of formative feedback to both the student and instructor is to improve teaching and learning. The information is generated by the instructor and is controlled by the instructor, who does not have to share it with anyone unless desired.

Some classroom assessment techniques for students can take the form of ungraded self-tests. These self-corrected "quick quizzes" provide data to individual students to let them know how well they are progressing toward the learning performance objectives. Collectively, they indicate to the instructor how well the students are mastering the learning performance objectives and where some adjustments in instructional strategies are needed. These data provide insights for the instructor that would otherwise never be known. These procedures are used three or four times during a course (formative assessment) rather than at the conclusion of the course (summative assessment). These data will allow the instructor to reflect on what they are doing and the degree of effectiveness. Reflections on these data will allow for mid-course adjustments if necessary.

Self-assessment of teaching effectiveness can utilize questionnaires given to students during the class; interviews by the instructor, peers, or third parties invited for this purpose; and classroom videotaping. Students have responded positively and enthusiastically when asked by instructors for feedback on their teaching (Angelo, 1991). An excellent and imaginative source of self-assessment instruments and techniques has been provided by Cross and Angelo (1988) in their book entitled, "Classroom Assessment Techniques-A Handbook for Faculty" and in another book entitled, "How Am I Teaching? Forms and Activities for Acquiring Instructional Input," by Weimer, Parrett, and Kerns (1988). These two references provide a wide variety of suggestions that can be adapted easily for your course.

Classroom assessment is a preliminary step to classroom research conducted by college instructors. Cross and Angelo (1988) base their model of classroom research on five basic assumptions:

1. The quality of student learning has a direct relationship to the quality of classroom teaching.
2. Instructors must make their goals and objectives explicit in order to receive feedback on the extent to which the goals and objectives are being achieved.
3. Teaching can be most improved by research conducted by classroom instructors based on questions they formulate.
4. College instructors can be motivated, challenged, and renewed through their own classroom research.
5. College instructors need few research skills to conduct their own classroom research. The purpose of this research is "...not to discover the 'general laws' of learning but to find out what specific students are learning as a result of a given teacher's efforts."

These two excellent reference sources should be reviewed by instructors. Forms are provided in this book that will help to answer important and relevant teaching questions.

The three forms on the following two pages have been used by this author in graduate courses and professional development workshops to generate feedback from students and participants. The "One Minute Feedback" forms are given to the students three or four minutes before the end of class. They are unsigned and quick to use. A review by the instructor will indicate areas of success and possible confusion. They should be used several times during a course. The 3-2-1 form should be signed by the student and reviewed with the instructor.

The One Minute Feedback

Date:_____

The two most murky points I made today...

The One Minute Feedback

Date:_____

The most important point I learned today was...

3-2-1 SUMMARY

- 3 important things that I've learned:
  1.
  2.
  3.

- 2 ideas I will bring home and share:
  1.
  2.

- 1 action I will take immediately:
  1.

BIBLIOGRAPHY

Angelo, Thomas A., & Cross, Patricia K. (1993). <u>Classroom assessment techniques</u> (2nd ed.). San Francisco: Jossey-Bass Publishers.

Centra, J. (1973). Effectiveness of student feedback in modifying college instruction. <u>Journal of Educational Psychology, 65</u>(3), 395-401.

Cross, K.P. (1988). <u>Feedback in the classroom: Making assessment matter</u>. Washington, DC: American Association for Higher Education.

Cross, Patricia K., & Angelo, Thomas A. (1988). <u>Classroom assessment techniques.</u> Ann Arbor, MI: National Center for Research to Improve Postsecondary Teaching and Learning.

Mosteller, F. (1989). The muddiest point in the lecture as a feedback device, <u>On Teaching and Learning: The Journal of the Harvard-Danforth Center</u>, Cambridge, MA.

Weimer, Maryellen, Parrett, Joan, & Kerns, Mary-Margaret. (1988). <u>How am I teaching</u>? Madison, WI: Magna Publications, Inc.

Chapter 21
Self-Assessment of Your Teaching Effectiveness

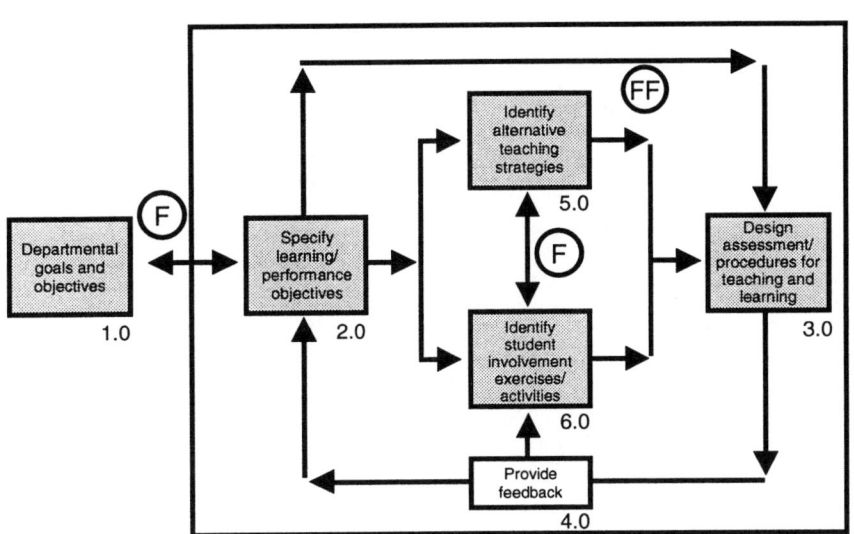

"You can be as good as you want to be."

SELF-ASSESSMENT

LEARNING PERFORMANCE OBJECTIVE
Complete the "self-assessment of teaching effectiveness." Identify areas of your teaching that you feel need improvement. Identify at least two sources of help on your campus.

KEY POINTS
1. The instrument, "Self-Assessment of Teaching Effectiveness," will assist instructors in developing their philosophy of teaching.
2. Combined with classroom feedback techniques, these data will contribute to the development of a teaching portfolio.

NEW VOCABULARY
- self-assessment
- evidence of effectiveness

An articulated and well-thought-out philosophy or approach to teaching directs the actions of instructors in the classroom and subsequently affects their students.

This Self-Assessment of Teaching Effectiveness can help instructors in developing statements and evidence about their philosophy of teaching and can also be used as a self-assessment tool of current teaching effectiveness and actions that they intend to fulfill in the future.

Some items deal with planning for teaching while others deal with classroom delivery skills and the social aspects of teaching. All professional dimensions of teaching (**bold type**) were identified by teaching faculty at New Mexico State University faculty in a 1980 study of competence in teaching.

The instructor should select those items that he or she feels relate to their philosophy of teaching and identify what type(s) of evidence they could provide relative to their effectiveness in this area. Instructors can also identify how they intend to improve on this teaching dimension. The Self-Assessment of Teaching Effectiveness can be incorporated as part of a professional teaching portfolio.

SELF-ASSESSMENT OF TEACHING EFFECTIVENESS

	EVIDENCE OF YOUR EFFECTIVENESS

1. How do you create a classroom climate that is conducive to learning?
  a. Enthusiastic about your subject
  b. Positive attitude toward teaching
  c. Motivate students
  d. Achieve a positive rapport with students
  e. Project a sense of confidence
  f. Other	

2. During interpersonal communications with your students how do you project a sense of respect for them?
  a. Listen attentively
  b. Do not interrupt
  c. Respond at the student's level
  d. Respond positively to students' questions
  e. Provide constructive feedback
  f. Respect cultural differences
  e. Other	

3. How do you demonstrate a commitment to teaching?
  a. Available to students beyond the posted office hours
  b. Well-organized courses
  c. Utilize a variety of teaching materials
  d. Create a positive dialogue with students
  e. Listen to students' concerns and respond appropriately
  f. Provide special help and tutorial sessions
  g. Actively promote student projects
  h. Other	

4. Do you practice a sense of professional ethics?
  a. Recognize student rights
  b. Give credit to students for original ideas
  c. Assess students on class-related activities only
  d. Distinguish between personal and professional judgment
  e. Other	

5. Do you attempt to project a constructive sense of humor?
  a. Use humorous examples to enhance presentations
  b. Use humor directed toward yourself rather than at students
  c. Remove any offensive cultural references
  d. Other	

	EVIDENCE OF YOUR EFFECTIVENESS

6. Do you make any attempt to determine the skill level of your students at the beginning of your class?
    a. Tell students the minimal skills that need to be mastered prior to your class
    b. Provide any special help sessions for those students who might need a review of these minimal skills
    c. Willing to adjust the expectations of your class if most of your students lacked a significant number of the minimal skills
    d. Other	

7. Do you participate in curriculum development activities within your department, college, NMSU?
    a. Contribute to developing new courses on new programs
    b. Participate on curriculum committees and volunteer to provide service beyond the regular meetings
    c. Attend faculty development seminars/workshops dealing with techniques of curriculum development
    d. Willing to make recommendations in writing for change in the current program
    e. Other	

8. Do you participate in identifying teaching material and resources?
    a. Recommend books for the library
    b. Recommend purchases of audiovisual material
    c. Other	

9. How comprehensively do you organize your courses?
    a. Provide your students with a detailed course outline
    b. Establish realistic goals and objectives
    c. Coordinate your course with lower and upper division courses
    d. Require your students to make reasonable purchases
    e. Test what you teach
    f. Coordinate your exam questions with your stated course objectives
    g. Provide adequate review for your students
    h. Revise your lectures frequently
    i. Other	

10. Do you demonstrate a variety of teaching approaches?
    a. Experiment with new teaching techniques
    b. Utilize audiovisual materials
    c. Pass out lecture outlines to your students
    d. Inform the students before the lecture what the expected learning outcomes are
    e. Other	

	EVIDENCE OF YOUR EFFECTIVENESS

11. Do you communicate the course content in such a way that your students can understand it?
    a. Introduce new vocabulary at the beginning of your lecture
    b. Define all new terms and provide examples
    c. Attempt to relate new content to the experience level of the student
    d. Other	

12. Do you create a classroom environment that elicits and tolerates different viewpoints?
    a. Recognize opposing viewpoints
    b. Present your personal biases without imposing them
    c. Present contrasting data bases and observations to challenge intellectual curiosity
    d. Recognize different problem solving strategies
    e. Other	

13. Do you make an effective presentation of your subject?
    a. Select appropriate supplementary materials to aid the student in learning
    b. Provide adequate examples of major concepts or principles
    c. Use audiovisual materials that are easy to read
    d. Provide adequate and appropriate handouts
    e. Other	

14. Do you exhibit effective communication skills?
    a. Project voice so that all students can easily hear
    b. Use good voice intonation
    c. Enunciate clearly
    d. Speak in complete sentences
    e. Avoid distracting mannerisms
    f. Seek training in any of these skills
    g. Other	

15. Do you utilize effective classroom questioning techniques?
    a. Encourage student questions
    b. Respond positively to student questions
    c. Answer your own questions
    d. Allow adequate time for a student to respond
    e. Assist with follow-up of questions by providing additional information
    f. Relate key classroom questions to stated learning outcomes
    g. Questions progress from simple to complex
    h. Other	

	EVIDENCE OF YOUR EFFECTIVENESS
16. **Do you use effective classroom time management strategies?** a. Begin and end your class on time b. Prepare a detailed presentation plan c. Communicate expected readings and assignments d. Provide adequate time for questions and discussions. e. Other	
17. **Do you present instructions in a logical sequence?** a. Stay on the subject during a lecture or demonstration b. Provide the lecture objectives at the beginning of the lecture c. Summarize and synthesize content periodically d. Provide enough examples e. Assist the students to distinguish between critical/non-critical materials f. Other	
18. **Do you use student evaluation as a learning and motivational technique?** a. Relate all stated course objectives to tests and examinations b. Apply consistently fair and objective standards to test and exam items c. State clear grading procedures d. Announce the type and time of tests and exams in advance e. Minimize opportunities for cheating f. Provide prompt and constructive feedback on all tests and exams g. Other	
19. **Do you describe and adhere to specified grading procedures?** a. Explain your grading procedures in writing at the beginning of your course b. Provide all criteria that you use for grading, assigning grades, weighing assignments and/or labs and testing c. Make provisions for a student to challenge a grade e. Other	
20. **Are you willing to meet student needs in non-classroom settings?** a. Participate in student projects b. Extend teaching to informal student interaction c. Participate in (not just sponsor) student organizations d. Encourage and invite individual contact e. Invite students to your home f. Other	

	EVIDENCE OF YOUR EFFECTIVENESS

21. Do you use campus teaching support services?
    a. Recommend: library, counseling services, minority service, CED, Learning Assistance Center
    b. Other	

Chapter 22

Creating a Professional Teaching Portfolio

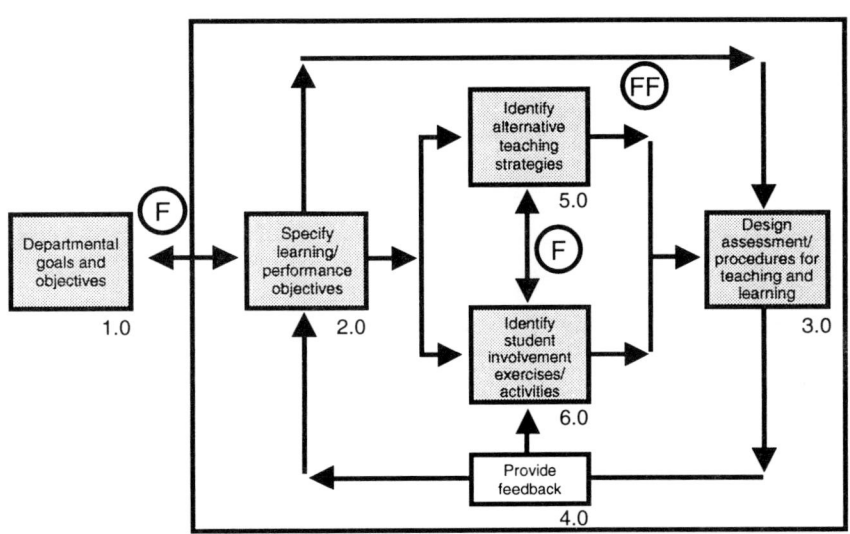

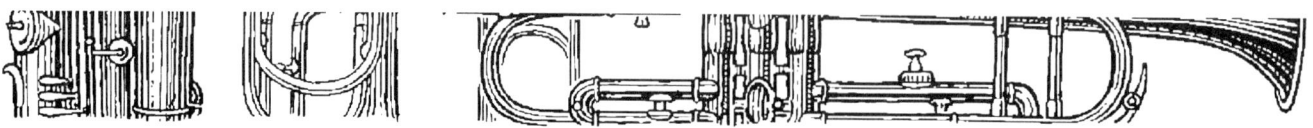

CREATING A PROFESSIONAL TEACHING PORTFOLIO

LEARNING PERFORMANCE OBJECTIVE
Construct a teaching portfolio that includes adequate evidence to demonstrate your competence in growth professionally as a teacher over a period of time.

KEY IDEAS
1. The teaching portfolio is a systematic process of documenting teaching competence and showing professional growth over time.
2. The portfolio is a technique of performance appraisal that is an effective motivator for change. The responsibility for its development rests primarily with the instructor who is preparing it.
3. The portfolio can be used for promotion and tenure; promotion only; special teaching awards; and teaching improvement.
4. A teaching portfolio is made up of artifacts: actual work samples; reproductions of instructional materials; attestations or reports from students and colleagues; and productions or specific evidence to document competence.
5. A major contribution of the portfolio is a section on reflections on teaching activities to show "why" instructors did certain things in the classroom. This demonstrates and documents professional growth over time.

NEW VOCABULARY
- teaching portfolio
- scholarship of discovery, integration, application, and teaching
- attestations
- outcomes assessment
- reflection
- teaching artifacts
- reproductions
- productions

Paul Defoe, an assistant professor in English, likes to teach. Over the past six years his teaching evaluations were average in his college and slightly above average in his department. Although he had no formal training in college teaching, he read widely about teaching methods, attended several preconference workshops on college teaching and attended four teaching seminars on his campus. He was not widely published, although he had submitted numerous articles.

Alice Pritchett is an assistant professor of engineering. During her six years of college teaching she published the minimal amount of articles required by her department for a positive tenure decision. Her reputation as an excellent teacher was well established. She kept a detailed and systematic record of her teaching activities that included such things as her past syllabi, student evaluations, peer reviews, reading lists, tests, exams, and handouts. Throughout the years, Professor Pritchett documented evidence of her growth as a teacher. She sought advise and training from the campus teaching improvement unit. In addition, she took a graduate course in college teaching and participated in several national teaching improvement seminars.

Both instructors were asked to provide specific evidence of their teaching effectiveness and demonstrate how they had improved as a teacher over the past six years. Which instructor do you think will have the best documentation? What is the most appropriate context to present it?

The process of assessing teaching must be initiated by and under the direct control of the instructor who will be assessed. One of the most promising techniques to accomplish this purpose is the professional teaching portfolio.

Assessment of teaching effectiveness has always been a sensitive issue in the Academy. It has been viewed somewhat negatively by faculty who see the potential punitive consequences rather than a positive effort to improve teaching. Traditionally, teaching assessment has been approached from a unidimensional perspective, providing a narrow view of the perception of "quality" teaching. Herman (1992) notes that, "Educational assessment is in a process of invention. Old models are being seriously questioned; new models are in development." She points out that the portfolio is one of the many examples in the later exploratory stages of development. Peter Seldin (1991), the initiator and founder of the concept of the portfolio, has noted that when he introduced the concept in 1989 there were between 10 and 15 universities exploring its use. In 1992, there are more than 400 institutions implementing some form of the teaching portfolio.

The concept of the professional teaching portfolio provides instructors with an opportunity to give a wide-spectrum look at what they consider to be "good teaching," putting the control of what is included in the portfolio where it should be–in the instructors' hands.

The teaching portfolio is a systematic process of documenting teaching competence and professional growth over time rather than the current helter-skelter descriptive approach so often employed by teaching faculty. It describes **what** you are doing in your teaching and **why** you are doing it as well as a reflection on **how well** you think you are doing it. Seldin (1991) defines the teaching portfolio as "... a factual description of a professor's major strengths and teaching achievements. It describes documents and materials which collectively suggest the scope and quality of a professor's teaching performance." In other words, it provides hard and direct evidence of "quality" teaching rather than loose descriptions. Wolf (1991) broadens this definition when he suggests that the portfolio "... also embodies an attitude that assessment is dynamic and that the richest portrayals of teacher (and student) performance are based on multiple sources of evidence collected over time in authentic settings." Edgerton, Hutchings, and Quinlan (1991) explain that "at the heart of the portfolio as we envision it are samples of teaching performance; not just what teachers say about their practice but artifacts and examples of what they actually do." King (1991) views the portfolio as "... collections of evidence which can be used to make inferences about knowledge, skills, and dispositions of teachers...." Collins (1990) suggests that the portfolio is evidence collected to "... allow a teacher to demonstrate their solution to teaching problems."

In the past the portfolio has been used to provide descriptions of what an instructor had done in the classroom primarily for the purposes of promotion and tenure. A group of researchers working at Stanford University on the Teacher Assessment Project (Shulman et al. 1988, 1990; Bird 1989; King 1989, 1990; Wolf 1990) suggested that, in addition to the descriptions of teaching events, instructors should also be trained and provided with opportunities to reflect on what they have done and to evaluate their perception of it over a period of time. Richert (1990) defines reflection "... as the time in the teaching process when teachers stop for a moment (or longer) to think about what has occurred to make sense of it in order to learn from their experiences in the classroom." This opens up new and exciting opportunities for instructors to talk about and document their teaching efforts–self-assessment with true meaning.

The portfolio is a technique of performance appraisal that is an effective motivator for change since the responsibility for the development of the portfolio rests primarily with the instructor who is preparing it. It is meant to help instructors accomplish their own goals more effectively. The portfolio system provides evidence of continuous faculty growth and teaching development over a long period of several years. It involves faculty more actively than any other process in their own evaluation and allows them to be in control of all events.

Most faculty and administrators would agree that the troika of teaching, research, and service has been given a lot of lip service over the years. Although talked about as equal and integrated, they are, in fact, separate and unequal when it comes to promotion and tenure. The major accepted form of scholarly activity is basic research–the true reward system in the Academy.

Boyer (1990) argues that the work of faculty might be thought of as having "... four separate, yet overlapping functions of scholarship. These are: the scholarship of discovery, the scholarship of integration, the scholarship of application, and the scholarship of teaching." He explains that the scholarship of discovery contributes to the essence of the intellectual climate of a university–what has traditionally been known as basic research. The scholarship of integration allows scholars to make links and connections among disciplines, fitting their specialized work into larger "intellectual patterns." These patterns are called interdisciplinary, interpretative, and integrative–the true synthesizing function of research. The scholarship of application asks how the knowledge taken from discovery and integration can be applied to contemporary social problems, how it can help people and institutions. This could fit nicely into the service function that is so important, yet given so little essential recognition of faculty service. Boyer notes that "To be considered scholarship, service activities must be tied directly to one's special field of knowledge and relate to, and flow directly out of, this professional activity." The service activity is held in high regard by faculty. Seventy-four percent of faculty feel that "colleges should be actively involved in solving social problems" (Astin, Korn, & Dey 1991). This observation of the service activity distinguishes it from "doing good" and provides another dimension of scholarship.

In the scholarship of teaching, Boyer (1990) argues that teaching is a

> ... dynamic endeavor involving all of the analogies, metaphors, and images that build bridges between the teacher's understanding and the student's learning. Pedagogical procedures must be carefully planned, continuously examined, and relate directly to the subject taught. ... Teaching, at its best, means not only transmitting knowledge, but transforming and extending it as well.

If teaching is to be considered a legitimate research activity and equal to what has been considered traditional research, it will have to be assessed with the same rigor as research but with different methods. Research techniques will include student assessment, self-assessment, and peer assessment. These can be effectively accomplished with the portfolio. Boyer concludes that, "When it comes to pulling all the evidence together, we are impressed with the portfolio idea–a procedure that encourages faculty to document their work in a variety of ways."

When asked in a national survey of faculty if their interests lie primarily in teaching or research, 72% responded very heavily in teaching or leaning toward teaching (Astin, Korn, and Dey, 1991). If these data are accurate, then why not accept and reward teaching on an equal footing with basic research? As the demand for quality teaching increases, influenced by the student-consumer movement, is it possible in the future that we will have two distinct and equally rewarded faculties, researchers and instructors? It is this conception of scholarship of teaching that is so important to faculty. The teaching portfolio should be seriously considered as a very important possibility for faculty to document and justify, quantitatively and qualitatively, what they prefer to do.

A major project designed to assist teachers in developing portfolios was reported by King (1991), "Those teachers who compiled portfolios of their work felt a greater confidence in themselves as teachers, increased clarity and organization in their work, and an increased ability to reflect on their practice as a result of their efforts." The idea of a teaching portfolio is supported by a number of presidents of academic institutions and associations, among whom are Derek C. Bok, past president of Harvard University; Ernest L. Boyer, President of the Carnegie Foundation for the Advancement of Teaching; and Lynne Cheney, Chairman of the National Endowment for the Humanities. Portfolios are currently in use at the University of Maryland, the University of Colorado at Boulder, Dalhousie University in Canada, the Department of Psychology at the University of Nebraska, the University of Pittsburgh, Gordon College in Massachusetts, Indiana University at Bloomington, Ball State University, Miami-Dade Community College, Syracuse University, the New Community College of Baltimore, Harvard University, Stanford University, and at least 400 other universities (Seldin 1991).

HOW TO USE THE PORTFOLIO
There are several uses for a teaching portfolio. It can be used for
- Promotion and tenure personnel decisions, or advancement in rank or salary within a discipline.
- Application for special teaching rewards as well as for teaching improvement.
- A professional résumé to provide a distinctive edge in a competitive field.

There is no one best way to create a teaching portfolio. As many procedures exist as there are faculty and institutions working on them. Edgerton (1991) notes that "… in much of the existing work in teaching portfolios, there is no particular conception of teaching, no education rationale, to suggest what should go into the portfolio."

Seldin (1991) suggests that there are five steps to creating a teaching portfolio.
1. Summarize your teaching responsibilities over the period of time covered in your portfolio. Also summarize either the departmental or your own criteria for teaching success.
   - List the number and types of courses you have taught and describe how your students were evaluated;

- State your assumptions about your teaching responsibilities and success criteria available.
2. Select criteria for effective teaching to include in the portfolio that reflect your teaching responsibilities.
3. Arrange the criteria in order. If the goal of the portfolio is teaching improvement, then the criteria could be attendance at preconference workshops or teaching improvement seminars.
4. Assemble support data. Collect everything that demonstrates what you have been doing and exactly what you accomplished in the areas of teaching, research, and service.
5. Incorporate the portfolio into your complete curriculum vitae.

Edgerten (1991) and Wolf (1991) explain that as you collect data to support your teaching efforts, you should go beyond the résumé-like portfolio, which simply lists and describes what you have done. Supplying artifacts (work samples such as syllabi, sample assignments, sample tests) alone is not enough. The artifacts need to be tied to reflection about what you have done, why you have done it, and the impact that the artifacts might have had. Without an explanation of why and how they were used, artifacts don't tell much about actual teaching. Artifacts plus reflection connect a product to a tangible instance of teaching competence which provides meaning within the context of a teaching classroom.

WHEN TO BEGIN DEVELOPING THE TEACHING PORTFOLIO

Start as soon as reasonable, even the first day of your first class. It is never too soon. Discuss with your department chairperson the criteria of successful teaching in your department and secure a copy in writing. If there are ambiguities, ask for clarification, preferably in writing. If you still feel that there are ambiguities, send a memo to your department chairperson stating what you perceive to be your teaching responsibilities and what you perceive to be the criteria of successful teaching. State in your memo that if there is any disagreement, you will be glad to meet as often as possible for the necessary clarifications. Ask for a copy of the department goals and objectives and explain how your course learning objectives support each one. Keep all documentation.

WHAT TO ASSEMBLE FOR THE TEACHING PORTFOLIO

A document is "...an instance or specimen that serves to show, point out, or provide evidence to prove something" (Collins 1991). Collections of documents called "entries" are used to provide this evidence in a portfolio. Each entry provides the evidence of the knowledge and skill of the instructor about a specific critical activity important to teaching, for example, the use of wait-time in questioning, the use of critical thinking questions, or the use of silence.

There are four classes of documents that are used within a portfolio:
(1) artifacts, (2) reproductions, (3) attestations, and (4) productions.

Artifacts are actual samples of the typical work of the instructor. Artifacts may include such things as lesson plans or notes about what worked or did not work in a lesson; samples of instructions for laboratory experiments; examples of different types of tests or other assessment instruments; samples of student work or papers; copies of course syllabi, an interactive study guide, or other types of handouts used.

Reproductions are examples of teaching that are transitory. These may include such things as overhead transparencies and hang-ups; photocopies of students notes; photographs of bulletin boards, flip charts, student displays, or poster sessions.

Videotapes. Another type of reproduction may include videotape of specific lessons taught. The tapes provide an example of teaching in one class. They have the highest fidelity to live teaching. The videotape should be accompanied by a written explanation of:
- The lesson learning performance objectives.
- Type(s) of instructional strategies used.
- Types of assessment procedures of the learning objectives.
- The probable learning outcomes.

The tapes should contain instructors' reflections about what they would do differently with another class, what they liked best about the lesson, and why they liked it, and possibly some comments from the students participating in the class.

Attestations are reports from other people. Attestations may include letters of commendation from colleagues or administrators and notes from students.

Productions include specific evidence prepared by instructors to document their knowledge, skills, and attitudes about the teaching/learning process. Journals would be an example of this. They include written reflections and introspections of what the instructor did or used and what the perceived result was. In lieu of the longer journals, written reflections about specific instructional strategies could be used. Productions may also include an explanation of a specific teaching model such as a performance-based, competency-based, or problem-based approach to teaching.

HOW MUCH DOCUMENTATION IS ENOUGH?
This is a value judgment that you, as an instructor, will have to make. When an artist, musician, or architect puts together a portfolio, they include samples of their best work only to impress the reviewer with their competence and creativity. So too with the college instructor. Include samples of your "best" work that show your command of teaching. Ken Wolf (1990) notes that "A portfolio does not need to be a comprehensive record of performance but a selective record of best work." Use documentation that demonstrates your professional growth over time–possibly over a performance period of one to six years. It is important to show how you have changed and grown in the area of teaching competence.

Portfolios usually consist of a summary of teaching effectiveness (six to ten pages) accompanied by addenda with as much specific evidence as the instructor feels is important. Seldin (1993) provides many samples of the summary portion of the teaching portfolio from numerous institutions and a variety of academic disciplines.

WHAT DATA TO USE IN THE TEACHING PORTFOLIO

Syllabi. Provide examples of syllabi from different courses over a period of several years. What does a syllabus mean to you? Is it a minimal document that provides bare-bones information for your students or do you consider your syllabus to be a binding contractual agreement between you and your students? How detailed are your syllabi? Are they different from or better organized than your colleagues'? How? Provide documentation (evidence) to make your point. Explain exactly what you mean. Avoid sweeping generalizations. Show how your syllabus has evolved and improved during the performance period that you are documenting. Provide a sample from your first year and from your last in the appendix. How have you used student feedback to change and refine the topics you have included as well as the assigned readings? How have you incorporated suggestions from your peers into the syllabus?

Textbook Selection. If you had to select your own textbook, describe the criteria for your choice. What is the source of your selection criteria? How were they applied? How did you arrive at your final conclusion? Did you review these criteria with your peers? How did you incorporate these suggestions into your final decision?

Grading Procedures. Describe your grading procedures. What is your rationale? Did you review the literature? Document it. Did you solicit advice from your senior faculty? Are your grading procedures different from your colleagues'? How? Do you feel that your grading procedures are innovative and unique? How? Do you incorporate learning performance objectives as a basis for your tests and grades? How do you relate laboratory work to classroom work? How many tests and exams do you give? Why? How have you arrived at this decision? Do you use such things as criterion checklists for essays, art, music, or other types of student-produced projects? Do you weight or "curve" your tests? How and why? Have you reviewed alternative grading procedures? Which ones? Have you explored the use of student portfolios?

Present Research Activities. Describe your current research activities in general. Provide detail in the appendix. Are you conducting any type of classroom research? If so, single this out from your other research. Have you produced any special research reports or monographs during this performance period? What is your funding record and amounts? Provide samples of your successful grantsmanship in the appendix, carefully labeled and easy accessed. Describe your philosophy of research and how it differs from (and is better than) your colleagues'.

Future Research Activities. What are the kinds of research activities that you may be involved in during the next five years? What are your priorities? Where does teaching research in the college classroom fit into your plans? Do you intend to apply for any type of grant for teaching research?

Professional Consultations. List all important consultations. How will they contribute to your research and teaching efforts within your department and college? Did these consultations provide positive publicity for the university? How much and what kind? Were your consultations local, regional, national, and/or international? Describe any type of publications, reports, or monographs that resulted from these efforts. Were you able to involve any of your students in this work? If so, how many and for how long? Include any letters of commendation or thanks from your clients that attest to your competence. Lastly, if not most importantly, will you be able to use this experience in your classroom teaching experience? If so, how?

Professional Travel. Describe any professional travel paid for by other clients that contributed to your university teaching, research, or service efforts. Was this travel national or international? Describe the funding source if it enhances your professional efforts: private foundation, other university, business or industry, military, other.

Professional Appointments. Describe any professional appointments to editorial boards, review committees, government groups, business or industry boards, health science groups, etc. Explain your specific role and contributions. How did these efforts benefit your department, college, and university? These appointments may also include such service organizations as Rotary International, Lions.

Service on College and University Committees. Describe each committee on which you served and your role on that committee, the mission of the committee, and the length of time that you served. Describe any products of the committee such as reports or publications.

Student-Related Activities. How involved have you been with students outside of regular class activities and with student organizations? These services often go unrecognized, yet they consume a great deal of time. This is not the time to be modest. Tell your story in as much detail as will benefit you. Your portfolio is the place to give yourself as much credit as possible for any type of student involvement. Have you sponsored any type of student organizations? What kind of time commitment have you made? How have you been involved in student recruitment activities and what type of special contributions have you made? Some instructors spend a lot of time counseling students after regular office hours on-campus and sometimes at home. Do you feel that your counseling skills have improved over time? How? On the average, how many times have you had drop-in conferences and how long do they last? Do you spend extra time with thesis advising? How much on the average?

Special Training. Describe any type of special training that you have received within the university or outside of the university that enhanced your research and teaching skills. This training could include preconference workshops or seminars, military training, attendance at institutes, participation in teleconferences, or formal courses taken with or without credit for teaching improvement.

Professional Services to Other Faculty. Some instructors spend a lot of time assisting graduate assistants and new faculty with their teaching efforts, course development, and syllabus design. At times they are asked to guest lecture, sit in on colleague's classes and make suggestions for teaching improvement. Document this in detail. Have you been asked to review research reports by your peers at your university or by colleagues at other universities? Have you been asked to review potential book manuscripts? How often? All of these little bits of information help to contribute to your professional growth and maturity.

Contribution to Your Academic Department. Have you been involved in such departmental activities as promotion and tenure committees, curriculum committees, special assignments, teaching evaluation committees, or administrative review committees?

Professional Associations. Active participation in regional, national, and international associations is highly regarded in some departments and colleges, while it may carry less weight in others. Have you held offices in any associations? How active have you been in the past and how active are you now? What offices have you held and for how long? Have you been active on any special committees? Have you conducted any special assignments for these groups and provided any type of report or publication? What has membership in these associations meant to you, your department, and college?

Community Services and Activities. These services and activities are highly value at some institutions. Are they valued at your institution? If so, include as much detail as you feel relevant. Have you headed any special type of charitable drive or campaign? Have you held office in a charitable, religious, or political organization? Have you been active or held office in a civic, social, or fraternal group? How has any of this activity contributed to your university? Most importantly, how has this involvement contributed to your classroom efforts? For example, this may have allowed you to make contacts for guest speakers in your classes and may have provided special resources or opportunities for student placement.

WHAT ARE POTENTIAL AREAS FOR REFLECTIVE STATEMENTS?

The purpose for reflection on your teaching activities is to show the "why" behind what you do in the classroom. Reflection can demonstrate professional growth in teaching over time. It can also demonstrate how you have used student and peer feedback to change and improve what you do. It shows that you care through introspection. Some potential areas for teaching reflection are:

- Use earlier and later developed course syllabi to demonstrate how you incorporated student course evaluation data and peer review to change your courses.
- Describe the criteria for selecting a textbook and the genesis of these criteria and if the textbook was changed on the basis of student evaluations.
- Explain the techniques used to design your lesson plans and how they evolved over time.
- Describe how you develop tests and how your process changed to incorporate more critical thinking skills.
- Explain your teaching model, the source of the model, and your efforts, both successful and unsuccessful, to match all components together.
- Describe a criterion checklist to evaluate your students and how it has evolved and changed with student feedback.
- Describe a new instructional strategy that you incorporated into your teaching and why it succeeded or failed.
- Explain your concern for gender bias in calling on students and how you addressed this in your classroom.
- Describe the grading system used in your course and the rationale behind it and any changes that you may have incorporated in your grading system as a result of student feedback.
- Keep a journal of your teaching during an entire class. Sit down for 20 to 30 minutes after each class and get your thoughts down on paper about what you liked or disliked.

WHAT ARE COMMON TOPICS USED IN EXISTING TEACHING PORTFOLIOS?
Seldin (1991) reported a number of samples of teaching portfolios. The following topics can be included in any portfolio:
- Statement of teaching responsibilities, philosophy, objectives, and instructional strategies.
- Syllabi, reading lists, assignments, tests, examinations, and handouts.
- Peer reviews and student evaluations.
- Videotape samples of actual instruction.
- Future teaching objectives.
- Unsolicited letters and statement from colleagues.
- Records of student performance on pre-tests and post-tests.
- Reviews of instructional materials and innovative strategies.
- Reflective statements on teaching improvement.
- Laboratory activities.
- Individual class objectives and activities.
- Examples of course enrichment.
- Teaching awards.
- Teaching-related committee work and activities.
- Writings supporting good teaching.

HOW DOES THE TEACHING PORTFOLIO RELATE TO OUTCOMES ASSESSMENT?
Assessment does not exist independently of teaching, since it is directly related to the teaching/learning objectives. If perceived by faculty as an *ex post facto* process independent of teaching, assessment will be construed as an administrative tool with possible punitive results. In contrast, outcomes assessment must be viewed by faculty as a developmental link to the improvement of classroom teaching, without any threat of retribution.

The purpose of any outcomes assessment effort is to find out what students are learning across the curriculum in each college, each department, and each course. This effort will allow the institution to document "what is" and to assist the faculty by providing directions as to "what should be" for desired student learning. These data will provide corrective feedback to all levels of the program to make necessary refinements. What types of refinements and how they are made will be determined through faculty consensus at the departmental and college level.

The primary purpose of outcomes assessment at any level (institutional or classroom) is and always should be to **improve** instruction and learning. This task can be viewed at both micro (lesson and course) and macro level (degree and college). Learning outcomes at the micro and macro levels should build hierarchically to the desired learning outcomes at the institutional level. For example, if critical thinking and interpersonal skills are an institutional priority, how and where are they supported and reinforced at the college, departmental, course, and class level?

Cross and Angelo (1988) note that

The quality of student learning is directly—although not exclusively—related to the quality of classroom teaching. Therefore, the first and most promising way to improve learning is to improve teaching. ... To improve their teaching, teachers need to make their goals and objectives explicit. They also need to receive specific, comprehensible feedback on the extent to which they are achieving those goals and objectives.

The use of goals and objectives (or "requirements" as described in the Total Quality Management (TQM) model) will compel instructors to define learning as the acquisition of knowledge, skills, and attitudes by students who actively apply this knowledge in such a way that it can be observed and assessed. This would include such things as critical thinking and problem solving, designing a product, creating an art piece or musical composition, writing a paper, proposing alternative solutions, and justifying the choice based on the probable consequences.

The specification of goals and objectives will require instructors to make explicit
- What they want their students to learn and do at the conclusion of each class and each course;
- How they want them to achieve the goals and objectives (the available resources);
- What criteria students must meet when the objectives have been achieved (the expected results).

This logic is consistent with the institutional outcomes assessment model and the TQM model at the micro level since it presents the desired and explicitly stated results or learning outcomes of programs. That will form the basis for all assessment. The feedback from assessment of the goals and objectives at the teaching/learning level provides the data loop into the total instructional support system and indicates what is needed for improvement. How this feedback loop would work is graphically illustrated with the Systems Approach to Teaching , or SAT, model (Cyrs 1970; Cyrs & Smith 1990).

Outcomes or objectives are stated in terms of desired learning and form the basis for the assessment process. They are consistent and validly reflect the goals and objectives of the external constituencies that influence them. These constituencies include the academic department responsible for the course, college, university, and societal context that fiscally supports the institution. The source of the learning objectives should support the societal needs and institutional priorities. Teaching and learning activities are selected on the basis of their ability to support and assist students in achieving the stated learning objectives. The latter can be stated at any level of specificity. It is the assessment criteria determined by faculty that will indicate when the learning objectives have been achieved to the level of satisfaction.This process is repeated at the class, course, major, department, college, and institutional levels.

The professional teaching portfolio is an integral part of this overall assessment process. It is the primary means of documenting and providing evidence of instructors' efforts as to how their classes and teaching contributed to the overall desired learning outcomes of the course, department, college, and institution.

BIBLIOGRAPHY

Arter, Judith A. (1992). Portfolios in practice: What is a portfolio? Paper presented at the Annual Meeting of the American Educational Research Association. (ERIC Document Reproduction Service NO. ED 346 156)

Astin, Alexander W., Korn, William S., & Dey, Eric L. (March, 1991). The American college teacher: National norms for the 1989-1990 HERI faculty survey. Los Angeles: Higher Education Research Institute, Graduate School of Education, University of California.

Barba, Marianne, Carrolton, Eleanor T., & Yeaw, M.J. (Spring/Summer, 1985). Portfolio assessment: An alternative strategy for placement of the RN student in a baccalaureate program. Innovative Higher Education, 121-122.

Berquist, William H., & Phillips, Steven R. (1977). Portfolio evaluation: A handbook for faculty development, 2, 56-64. Washington, DC: The Council for the Advancement of Small Colleges.

Berry, David, & Others. (1991.). The process and product of portfolio construction. Paper presented at the Annual Meeting of the American Educational Research Association. (ERIC Document Reproduction Service No. ED 332 995)

Biddle, James. (1992). Portfolio development in teacher education and educational leadership. Paper presented at the Annual Meeting of the American Association of Colleges for Teacher Education. (ERIC Document Reproduction Service No. ED 342 732)

Biddle, James R., & Lasley, Thomas J. (1991). Portfolios and the process of teacher education. Paper presented at the Annual Meeting of the American Educational Research Association. (ERIC Documentation Reproduction Service No. ED 334 165)

Bird, Tom, King, B., & September, R. (1988). BIO TAP handbook: Portfolio development for high school biology. Teacher's working document of the teacher assessment project. Stanford, CA: Stanford University.

Bird, Tom. (1990). Report on the rating procedures used to assess portfolios and assessment center exercises for high school biology teachers. Stanford, CA: Teachers Assessment Project.

____. (1990). The schoolteacher's portfolio: An essay on possibilities. In Jason Millman and Linda Darling (Eds.). The New Handbook on Teacher Education: Assessing Elementary and Secondary School Teachers (2nd ed.). Newbury Park, CA: Sage.

____. (1989). Report on rating procedures used to assess portfolios and standardized exercises for biology teachers (Technical Report B3). Stanford CA: Stanford University, Teacher Assessment Project.

Boyer, Ernest L. (1990). Scholarship reconsidered: Priorities of the professorate. Princeton, NJ: The Carnegies Foundation for the Advancement of Teaching.

Cheney, L.V. (1990). Tyrannical machines. Washington, DC: National Endowment for the Humanities.

Cole, Donna J. (1992). The developing professional: Process and product portfolios. Paper presented at the Annual Meeting of the American Association Colleges for Teacher Education. (ERIC Document Reproduction Service No. ED 342 731)

Cole, Donna J., & Others. (1991). Portfolio structure and student profiles: An analysis of education student portfolio reflectivity scores. Paper presented at the Annual Meeting of the American Educational Research Association, Chicago, IL. (ERIC Document Reproduction Service No. ED 335 307)

Collins, Angelo. (1991). Performance-based assessment of biology teachers: Promises and pitfalls. Paper presented at the Annual Meeting of the National Association for Research in Science Teaching. Lake Geneva, WI. (ERIC Document Reproduction Service No. ED 336 264)

____. (1991). Portfolios for biology teacher assessment. Journal of School Personnel in Education, 2, 147-167.

____. (1990). A teacher's portfolio: What is necessary and sufficient? A high school biology unit plan as an example. Based on a paper presented at the Annual Meeting of the American Educational Research Association, Boston, MA. (ERIC Document Reproduction Service No. ED 319 814)

____. (1990). Novices, experts, veterans, and masters: The role of content and pedagogical knowledge in evaluating teaching. Paper based on a presentation at the Annual Meeting of the American Educational Research Association, Boston, MA. (ERIC Document Reproduction Service No. ED 319 815)

____. (1990). Transforming the assessment of teachers: Notes on a theory of assessment for the 21st century. Paper presented at the Annual Meeting of the National Catholic Education Association, Toronto, Canada. (ERIC Document Reproduction Service No. ED 321 362)

Cross, Patricia K., & Angelo, Thomas A. (1988). Classroom assessment techniques–A handbook for faculty. MI: Board of Regents of the University of Michigan for the National Center for Research to Improve Postsecondary Teaching and Learning.

Cyrs, Thomas E. (1981). The professional portfolio. NM: The Center for Educational Development: New Mexico State University.

Cyrs, Thomas E., & Lowenthal, Rita. (1970). A model for curriculum design using a systems approach. Audiovisual Instruction, XV(1), 16-19.

Cyrs, Thomas E., & Smith, Frank A. (1990). Teleclass teaching: A resource guide (2nd ed.). Las Cruces, NM: Center for Educational Development, New Mexico State University.

Edgerton, Russell. (1991). The teaching portfolio as a display of best work. Washington, DC: AAHE National Conference on Higher Education.

Edgerton, Russell, Hutchings, Patricia, & Quinlan, Kathleen. (1991). The teaching portfolio: Capturing the scholarship in teaching. Washington, DC: American Association for Higher Education.

Fayne, Harriet R. (1991). Practicing what we preach: Key issues in faculty evaluation. Paper presented at the Annual Meeting of the American Association of Colleges for Teacher Education, Atlanta, GA. (ERIC Document Reproduction Service No. ED 330 266)

Ford, Michael P., & Ohlhausen, Marilyn M. (1991). Portfolio assessment in teacher education courses: Impact on students' beliefs, attitudes and habits. Paper presented at the Annual Meeting of the National Reading Conference. (ERIC Document Reproduction Service No. ED 343 088)

Forrest, Aubrey, & A Study Group on Portfolio Assessment. (1990). *Time will tell-Portfolio assisted assessment of general education.* Washington, DC: American Association of Higher Education.

Foster, S.F., Harrop, T., & Page, G.C. (1983). The teaching dossier: A system of performance evaluation with data and a case study from dental education in British Columbia. *Higher Education in Europe*, 8(2), 54-57.

Foster, M.J. (August, 1983). Portfolio analysis in the planning of higher education. *Higher Education*, 12(4), 389-397.

Furtwengler, Carol, & Others. (1986). *Multiple data sources in teacher evaluation.* Paper presented at The National Council on Measurement in Education. (ERIC Document Reproduction Service No. ED 274 677)

Gordon college professional development through growth plans: A summary report. (1988). Wenham, MA: Gordon College.

Hart, Kathleen A. (1989). *Faculty performance appraisal: A recommendation for growth and change. Accent on improving college teaching and learning.* Ann Arbor, MI: National Center for Research to Improve Postsecondary Teaching and Learning. (ERIC Document Reproduction Service No. ED 129 348)

Herman, Joan L. (1992). What research tells us about good assessment. *Educational Leadership*, 49(8), 74-78.

Hutchings, P.A. (1991). The teaching portfolio. *The Department Chair.* 2(1), 33-35.

Jarvis, Donald K. (1991). *Junior faculty development: A handbook*. New York, NY: The Modern Language Association of America.

King, Bruce. (Summer, 1991). Teachers' views on performance-based assessments. *Teacher Education Quarterly*, 109-119.

____. (1990). *Thinking about linking portfolios with assessment center exercises: Examples from the teacher assessment project*. Stanford, CA: Teacher Assessment Project, Stanford University.

____. (1989). *Report on the use of assessment center exercises to assess biology teachers* (Technical Report B2). Stanford: Stanford University, Teacher Assessment Project.

Lee, Elizabeth A. (1992). *Reflecting on teaching*. Paper presented at the Annual Meeting of the American Educational Research Association. (ERIC Document Reproduction Service No. ED 353 240)

Mathies, Bonnie, & Uphoff, James K. (1992). *The use of portfolio development in graduate programs*. Paper presented at the Annual Meeting of the American Association of Colleges for Teacher Education. (ERIC Document Reproduction Service NO. ED 343 855)

Mills, Barbara J. (1991). Putting the teaching portfolio in context. *To Improve the Academy*, 10, 215-232.

Nagel, Nancy G., & Engel, Joanne B. (1992). *Preservice teacher portfolios and professional licensure: A formative report*. Paper presented at the Annual Meeting of the American Educational Research Association. (ERIC Document Reproduction Service No. ED 343 902)

Nweke, Winifred C. (1991). *What type of evidence is provided through the portfolio assessment method?* Paper presented at the Annual Meeting of the Mid-South Educational Research Association. (ERIC Document Reproduction Service No. ED 340 719)

Ohlhausen, Marilyn M., & Ford, Michael P. (1990). Portfolio assessment in teacher education: A tale of two cities. Paper presented at the Annual Meeting of the National Reading Conference, Miami, FL. (ERIC Document Reproduction Service No. ED 329 917)

Pascal, C.E., & Wilburn, M.J. (1978). A mini-guide to preparing a teaching dossier. Ontario Universities Program for Instructional Development Newsletter. Ontario, Canada: Ontario Universities Program for Instructional Development Newsletter, 19(20).

Robbins, Mary E.; And Others. (1991). Transforming teaching and learning through collaboration. Paper presented at the Annual Meeting of the College Reading Association. (ERIC Document Reproduction Service No. 341 057)

Rolls, Dorothea M. (April, 1987). Documenting experiential learning: preparation of a portfolio for college credit. Lifelong Learning, 10(6), 19-21.

Richert, Anna E. (1990). Teaching teachers to reflect: A consideration of program structure. Journal of Curriculum Studies, 22(6), 509-27.

Sashkin, Marshall. (1981). Assessing performance appraisal. San Diego: University Associates.

Savitz, Fred R. (Fall, 1984). A prototype for portfolio development. Community Catalyst, XN(4), 13-16.

Scriven, Michael. (1988). Evaluating teachers as professionals. (ERIC Document Reproduction Service No. ED 300 882)

Seldin, Peter. (1993). Successful use of teaching portfolios. Boston, MA: Anker Publishing Co., Inc.

____. (1991). The teaching portfolio. Boston, MA: Anker Publishing Co, Inc.

Seldin, Peter, & Annis, L. (1990). The teaching portfolio. Journal of Staff, Program, and Organization Development, 8(4), 197-201.

Seldin, Peter, & Associates. (1990). How administrators can improve teaching. San Francisco: Jossey-Bass Publishers.

Shore, B.M., & Others. (1986). The teaching dossier: A guide to its preparation and use. Montreal, Canada: Canadian Association of University Teachers.

Shulman, Lee. (November, 1988). A union of insufficiencies: Strategies for teacher assessment in a period of educational reform. Educational Leadership, 36-41.

____. (1987). Knowledge and teaching: Foundations of a new reform. Harvard Educational Review, 57(1), 1-22.

____. (September, 1987). Assessment for teaching: An initiative for the profession. Phi Delta Kappan, 69(1), 39-44.

Stemmer, Paul, Brown, Bill, & Smith, Catherine. The employability skills portfolio. Educational Leadership, 46(6), 32-35.

Stewart, Valerie, & Stewart, Andrew. (1979). Practical performance appraisal. Westmead, England: Gower Press.

Swan, William S., with Margulies, Phillip. (1991). How to do a superior performance appraisal. NY: John Wiley and Sons.

Teacher Evaluation Study. Beginning Teacher Portfolio Study. (1986). Tampa, FL: University of Southern Florida, College of Education. (ERIC Document Reproduction Service No. ED 277 689)

Terry, Gwenith, & Eade, Gerden. E. (1983). The portfolio process: New roles for meeting challenges in professional development. Paper presented at the annual conference of the Association of Teacher Educators. Pensacola, FL. (ERIC Document Reproduction Service No. ED 229 342)

Terry, Gwenith, L., & Others. (1983). The portfolio process in professional development. Paper presented at the Annual Meeting of the American Association of Colleges for Teacher Education. (ERIC Document Reproduction Service No. ED 227 073)

Varus, Linda, & Collins, Angelo. (1990). Portfolio documentation and assessment center exercises: A marriage made for teacher assessment. Teacher Education Quarterly.

Watkins, Beverly T. (May, 1990). New technique tested to evaluate college teaching. Chronicle of Higher Education, 36(35), A15-17.

Weinberger, Helene, & Didham, Cheryl K. (1987). Helping prospective teachers sell themselves: The portfolio as a marketing strategy. Paper presented at the annual meeting of the Association of Teacher Educators. (ERIC Document Reproduction Service No. ED 278 678)

Williamson, Ronald E., & Osborne, Debra C. (1985). Instructional Planning and beginning teacher assessment: Taking the anxiety out of accountability. (ERIC Document Reproduction Service No. ED 286 856)

Wolf, Kenneth. (October, 1991). The schoolteacher's portfolio: Issues in design, implementation and evaluation. Phi Delta Kappan, 129-136.

____. (1991). Teaching portfolios: Synthesis of research and annotated bibliography. San Francisco, CA: Far West Laboratory for Educational Research and Development.

____. (1990). Evaluating teacher knowledge and skills in student assessment through teacher portfolios and assessment center exercises. (Technical Report L2). Stanford, CA: Stanford University, Teacher Assessment Project.

SUBJECT INDEX

A
Acronyms, 14-19
Action terms, 7-13, 8-12
Active
    classroom, 5-7
    learning, 11-4
    review, 12-14
Adaptation, 8-23
    (psychomotor), 8-24
Adult student, 10-3
Affective learning, 8-7, 8-19
Allegory, 14-19
Alliteration, 14-19
Alter ego, 12-13
Analogy, 14-16
    analogous attributes, 14-17
    topic, 14-17
Analysis, 8-7
Andragogy, 10-4
Application, 8-8, 8-14
Artifacts, 16-5
Assessment, self, 21-3
Assumption, 2-3
Attending (receiving), 8-20
Attention-getters, 14-21
Attention span, 14-11
Audience engagement, 12-15
Automatic performance (psychomotor), 8-27

B
Balloons, 16-8
Behavior, 7-5
    ultraspecific, 7-22
Behavioral analysis, 8-4
Behavioral objective, 7-4
Behavioral task, 7-13
Belief, 2-4
Bell curve, 13-3
Biographical sketch, 5-8
Body communication, 15-9
Brainstorm session, 12-4
Build-ups, 16-6
Buzz sessions, 12-4

C
Card tricks, 16-8
Cartoons with captions removed, 12-17
Case study, full 12-5
Challenge problems, 12-12
Character dialogue, 12-8
Characterization by a value, 8-20
Check lists, 12-11
Choices, 12-11
Circumstances of assessment, 7-14, 7-16
Clarify, of presentation 14-12
Clarifying, questions 17-6

Clinical experiences, 11-7
Cognitive
    skills, 8-4
    strategies, 8-15
Complex overt response, 8-27
    (psychomotor), 8-27
Comprehension, 8-8, 8-13
Concentric circles, 12-15
Concepts, 8-12
Connections, 14-15
    inward, 14-15
    outward, 14-15
Consequences, 12-10
Content
    analysis, 7-10, 8-4
    general, 7-5, 7-7, 7-14
Continuum of performance, 10-5, 11-7
Contrasting 35mm slides, 16-8
Cooperative learning, 11-8, 13-3
Cotton mouths, 15-13
Course
    blueprint, 5-4
    structure, 8-4
Creative behavior, 8-17
Criterion, checklist, 19-10
Critical
    incidents, 12-7
    thinking, 8-8, 8-16, 9-4
Crossfire, 12-14
Cue selection (psychomotor), 8-24

D
Debate, 12-8
Debriefing, 12-11
Definition, 14-13
    extended, 14-14
    short, 14-13, 14-14
    stipulative, 14-11
Definitions, use of, 14-13
Delivery system, physical, 11-7
Demonstration, 12-7
    with practice, 12-7
Demonstrations
    equipment, 12-11
    silent, 14-10
Diagram, labeling a, 12-12
Did you notice..., 12-10
Discovery learning, 8-15
Discussion
    controlled, 12-14
    free group, 12-15
    panel, 12-5
    round-table, 12-16
    step-by-step, 12-15
    structured, 12-16
DIVE, 10-5

Divergent thinking, 8-15
Dramatic incident, 16-7
Drippers, 15-12

E

Energy, 14-11
Entry level, 8-6
Envelopes, 16-8
Error, latitude for, 7-19
Essay
    basic scoring techniques, 19-10
    comparative quality scoring, 19-10
    component scoring, 19-10
Evaluation, 8-18
    course, 5-10
Evidence, 2-9
Examinations
    open book, 19-19
    oral, 19-19
    take home, 19-19
Example
    best, 14-22
    interrogatory, 14-22
    motivational, 14-22
Examples, 14-22
    creating food, 14-22
Exampling, 12-7
Exercise
    exploration, 12-10
    group work, 12-10
Expectations, 7-4
Expert consensus, 7-18
Explanation
    descriptive, 14-15
    hidden variables, 14-16
    interpretive, 14-15
    keys, 14-16
    linking statements, 14-16
    reason-giving, 14-15
Explanations, effective, 14-15
Extrapolation, 8-12

F

Feedback
    formative, 22-3
    one-minute, 22-4, 12-16
    techniques, 22-3
Feeling judgment, 4-4
Field trips, 12-8
Fill-ins, reinforcing, 12-11
Film preview, 12-9
Fishbowl, 12-11
Flipchart, 16-5
Flowers, 16-8
Formative test data, 22-3

G

Gablers, 5-13
Games, 12-6
Goals, 1-4
Goal specification, 5-3

Good teaching, 2-5
Grab bags, 16-7
Grabbers & stabbers, 14-21
Group collage, 12-16
Guest
    interview, 12-8
    speaker, 12-5
Guided response, 8-26
    (psychomotor), 8-26
Gut wrenchers, 15-12

H

Handout, 18-3
    article with discussion questions, 18-9
    detailed topical outline with commentary, 18-7
    general lecture outline & lecture, 18-6
    general topic outline, 18-6
    interactive study guide, 18-9
    labeled diagram, 18-8
    note space with commentary, 18-7
    question outline, 18-9
    skeleton notes, 18-8
    structured notes, 18-7
    structured worksheet, 18-8
    study guide, 18-9
    summary, 18-6
    overhead transparency, full copy, 18-6
    word picture with commentary, 18-7
Handouts, 5-8, 19-3, 12-11
Hangup, 16-4
Hierarchical structure, 8-5
Hyperbole, 14-20

I

Ice breakers, 12-12, 14-20
Ideas
    connections, 14-15
    connections among, 14-15
Imitation, 8-26
    (psychomotor), 8-26
In-basket, 12-9
Incomplete statements, 12-7
Indicator behaviors, 8-20
Inferrred capability, 7-12
Informed capability, 7-12
Instructional
    materials, 5-8
    media, 7-7
    objective, 7-4
    planning, 7-4
    strategies, alternative, 5-4, 5-7
    strategy, 11-6
Instructor notes, 18-5
Intents, 7-4
Interactive
    learning, 11-6
    study guide, 12-12
Intermediate performance objective, 8-6
Interpretation, 8-12
Interview, student, 12-4
Introversion, 4-4

Intuitive perception, 4-4
Involvement, student, 12-3

J
Job analysis, 7-10
Journal, student, 19-21
Judging, perception, 4-4

L
Laminated cards, 16-7
Learner analysis, 5-3
Learning
    activities, 7-7, 8-6
    cell, 12-14
    classification, quick reference guide, 8-10
    contract, 12-11, 13-3, 13-5
    domains, 8-7
    objectives, 7-4
    outcomes, class or range, 7-5
    package, 12-13
    sequence, 8-3, 8-4
    unit, 8-7
Learning performance objective, 5-3, 7-4
    abbreviated definition, 7-5
Learning performance objectives
    components, 7-12
    content and form, 7-12
    expanded definition, 7-5
    misconceptions about, 7-9
    prerequisites to writing, 7-10,
    rating, 8-8
    specifying, 7-9
    uses, 7-9
Lecture, 14-3
    adversarial, 12-10
    assessment criteria, 15-15
    charisma, 14-18
    classical, 14-6
    comparative, 14-7
    components, 14-8
    delay & summary, 12-13
    demonstration, 14-7
    expository, 14-6
    expressive, 14-18
    ormal essay, 14-7
    format, 14-8
    freehand, 14-7
    interactive, 12-4
    literary devices, 14-18
    laboratory, 15-6
    organizational patterns, 14-25
    outline, 12-12, 18-4
    presentation, 15-3
    presentation, group-paced, 8-4
    problem-centered, 14-7
    provocative, 14-7
    purposes, 14-9
    rapport, 14-18
    reaction panel, 12-15
    recitation, 14-7
    sequential, 14-7
    thesis, 14-7
    with listening team, 12-4
Lecturer, enthusiastic, 14-11
Lectures, purposes of, 14-9
Lecturette, 12-4
    flip-flop, 12-9
    student, 12-10
Lesson plan, 5-9
Literary devices, 14-18
Litotes, 14-20

M
Mastery
    absolute, 7-21
    variable, 7-21
Mastery learning, 7-21, 19-5
Mechanism, 8-26
    (psychomotor), 8-26
Memory, 8-8, 8-11
    aids, 8-11
Metacognition, 9-4
Metacognitive strategies, 8-16
Mind blowers, 15-12
Mini case study, student, 12-5
Mirroring, 12-16
Mnemonics, 8-11, 12-7
Modeling, 12-8
Movers & shakers, 15-12
Multiple-choice
    best answer, 19-12
    case study, 19-12
    introductory sentence, 19-12
    negative stem, 19-12
    repetitous, 19-12
Myth, 2-4

N
Nervousnesss, 15-13
Newsprint hangups, 16-4
Nonverbal communication, 15-7
Norm-referenced learning, 13-3
Normal curve, 19-4
Notetaking, 19-5
    skills, 18-4

O
Objective
    inferred, 7-11
    test item specific, 7-15
Observable behavior, 7-5
Office hours, 6-4
One-minute feedback, 22-3
Operational definition, 7-4
Optimistic/pessimistic panel, 12-13
Oral presentation, 15-4, 15-5
    a personal inventory, 15-5
    skills: a personal inventory, 15-5
Organization (of value), 2-2, 8-2
Organizational patterns, lecture, 14-25
Origination, 8-27
    (psychomotor), 8-27

Out-to-lunch, 12-10
Outcome measure, 2-7
Oxymorons, 14-20

P

Pacing, 14-9, 14-10
Pantomimes, 12-9
Paraphrase, 12-10
Pause-time, 14-10
Pedagogy, 10-3
Peer
    group 13-4
    review, 15-4
    teaching, 12-5
Perception, 8-24
Performance, 7-5
    appraisal, 22-5
    nonessential, 7-12
    principal, 7-12
    proficiency, 7-16, 7-18
    level, 7-18
    stability, 7-19
Performance objective, 7-4. 19-7
Performance objectives
    learning, derived from subject matter, 19-8
    teacher, 7-4
Performer, 7-13
Persistent
    stimuli, 16-3
    stimulus, 16-4
Personal
    critique, 15-4
    satisfaction (affective), 8-21
Personification, 14-20
Philosophy
    of life, 8-23
    of practice, 2-3
Pitch, 15-7
Planning, course, 5-3
Play, view, 12-8
Points in a class, number of, 14-11
Portfolio
    date to use, 22-9
    documentation, 22-8
    how to use, 22-6
    professional teaching, 22-3
    reflective statements, 22-11
    relate to outcomes assessment, 22-12
    student, 19-21
    topics used, 22-12
    what to assemble, 22-7
    when to begin, 22-7
Posterboard hangups, 16-5
Potpouri, 16-7
Practice activity, 12-6
Preplanning, 5-4
Prerequisite course skills, 5-6
Presentation
    clarity of, 14-12
    points, 14-11
Presentation skills, 15-4

Problem-based learning, 13-3
Problem-solving, 8-16
Proficiency in practice, current state, 7-20
Proficiency level, 7-20
    establishing, 7-20
Proficiency variables, 7-16
Programmed instruction, 12-7
Prompting, 17-6
Psychodrama, 12-13
Psychomotor, 8-7, 8-23
Public speaking, 15-3
Puppets, 16-5
Puzzles, 12-8
Pyramiding, 12-14

Q

Quality circles, 12-12
Quasi-dramatization, 12-10
Question, 17-3, 18-3
    box, 2-1
    outline, 12-12
    quiet, 12-14
Questioning
    strategies, student-generated, 12-8, 12-12
    strategy, interactive, 12-12
Questionnaire, instant, 12-14
Questions
    big, 7-9
    rhetorical, 18-5
    trivia, 18-5
    use of, 17-3, 18-3
Quiz, progress, 12-6
Quizzicals, 12-9

R

Rank report, 12-10
Reaction panel, 12-8
Readings, short discussion, 12-6
Recall, 8-11
Receiving, 8-20
Redundancy, 14-15
Referent situation, 7-21
Reliability, 19-6
Resolution of uncertainty (psychomotor), 8-27
Responding, 8-20
Retention, long term, 8-11
Role
    playing, 11-8, 12-6
    reversal, 12-10
Rule
    selection, 8-8
    using, 8-8

S

Safety requirements, 7-17
Scenario, written, 12-5
Scoring
    comparative quality, 19-10
    component, 19-10
Self-assessment, 20-3, 22-4
Self-esteem, 10-5, 15-8

Self-test, 10-5
Sensory
    stimulation (psychomotor), 8-24
    perception, 4-4
Set, 8-25
    (emotional), 8-25
    (mental), 8-25
    (physical), 8-25
Set induction, 14-21
Show me your colors, 12-15
Silence, 14-9
    confusion or disorganizational, 14-11
    discipline or control of, 14-10
    pause-time, 14-10
    transitional, 14-10
    use of, 14-10
    wait-time, 14-11
Simulation, 11-8, 12-6
Skits, 12-8
Small group problem solving, 13-3
Social skills, 13-4
Speech personality, 15-7
Story, 14-23
Storytelling, 14-23
Structure, 8-5
    flat horizontal, 8-5
    vertical or hierarchical, 8-5
Structured
    notes, 12-11
    worksheets, 18-5
Student
    audience, 5-7
    outcomes, 7-4
Study group contract, 12-12
Successive strategies, 12-11
Survey, 12-10
Syllabus course, 6-3
Symposium, 12-9
Synthesis, 8-8, 8-17
Systems approach, 1-5

T

Target audience, 6-4
Taxonomy, 8-8
Teaching
    method of, 7-7, 11-7
    philosophy, 5-7, 23-3
    performance objectives, 8-6
Teaching method
    experiential, 11-8
    individualized, 11-7
    instructor-centered, 11-6
    interactive, 11-8
Terminal performance objective, 7-4, 8-5
Test
    blueprint, 19-6
    completion or short answer, 19-15
    criterion-referenced, 19-5
    criterion, 5-3
    essay, 19-7
    essay, suggest guidelines, 19-9
    items specifity, 7-10
    matching, 19-17
    matching item, 19-17
    matching item, effective, 19-17
    multiple-choice guidelines, 19-11
    multiple-choice, 19-11
    multiple-choice, types, 19-11
    multiple-choice, 19-11
    norm-referenced, 19-4
    performance, 19-9
    planning your, 19-6
    scoring an essay, 19-10
    true-false, 19-13
    true/false, assessment for, 19-13
    true/false, characteristics of good, 12-14
    true-false argument for, 19-13
    true/false, how to prepare, 19-14
Testable objectives, 7-4
Testing
    collaborative, 19-21
    criterion-referenced, 19-5
    final considerations, 19-18
    mastery, 19-20
    norm-referenced, 19-4
    paired, 19-20
    performance, 19-20
Tests
    constructing valid, 19-3
    types of, 19-8
Theatrics, 12-7
Thinking judgment, 4-4
Three, two points, 12-14
Tinker toys, 12-13
Tradition, 7-20
Transient
    stimuli, 16-3
    stimulus, 16-4
Translation, 8-12
    (psychomotor), 8-25
Triad, 14-18
Trial & error, 8-26
    (psychomotor), 8-26
Trigger video, 9-7, 12-6
Tripod displays, 16-5
Tripods, 16-5

V

Validity, 19-6
    concurrent, 19-6
    construct, 19-6
    content, 19-6
    predictive, 19-6
Values clarification, 12-6
Valuing, 8-21
    criteria for, 8-22
Vellum hangups, 16-5
Videoclips, 12-9, 16-7
Videotape feedback, 12-16
Vignette, personal, 12-9
Voice quality, 15-7
Volume, speech, 15-7

Voluntary action, 8-21

W

Wait-time, 14-10
What would you do?, 12-15
Winning ways, 15-8
    the 30-second critique, 15-8
Word pictures, 12-11